Two Swordmasters & Two Women

Chiang Shiao-ho (江小鶴) & Bo Ah-ran (飽阿鸞)
Lee Mo-bai (李慕白) & Yu Ceo-lian (俞秀蓮)

Shiao Shen Yu 于孝慎

Copyright © 2021 by Shiao Shen Yu

All rights reserved. No part of this publication may be reproduced, distributed, or transmitted in any form or by any means, including photocopying, recording, or other electronic or mechanical methods, without the prior written permission of the publisher, except in the case brief quotations embodied in critical reviews and other noncommercial uses permitted by copyright law.

ISBN: 978-1-63945-092-3 (Paperback)
        978-1-63945-093-0 (Ebook)

The views expressed in this book are solely those of the author and do not necessarily reflect the views of the publisher, and the publisher hereby disclaims any responsibility for them.

Writers' Branding
1800-608-6550
www.writersbranding.com
orders@writersbranding.com

Contents

I: A Pledge under the Willow Tree
Chiang Shiao-ho (江小鶴) & Bo Ah-ran (飽阿鸞)

List of Characters 2
Prologue 4
1 5
2 10
3 23
4 33
5 44
6 65
7 78
8 94
9 100
10 112
11 119
12 137
13 147
14 157

II: A Living Widow
Lee Mo-bai (李慕白) & Yu Ceo-lian (俞秀蓮)

List of Characters 164
Prologue 165
1 166
2 178
3 192
4 204
5 216
6 230
7 245
8 256
9 268
10 281
11 294
12 307

*To My Mother
The source of my life
And the stories.*

**Special thanks to
Wen-Hshin Yang**

I

A Pledge under the Willow Tree
Chiang Shiao-ho (江小鶴) & Bo Ah-ran (飽阿鸞)

List of Characters

A Chinese name -- 2 or 3 words. No alphabet. One word, one sound.
1st word -- the Last name (surname). There are about 160 surnames in China. Thousands of Chinese with the same last name: Lee, Chang, Lung, Wong.
2nd and 3rd (sometimes only one) -- chosen randomly from all the Chinese words. One word would be the 'generation word.'
Master Bo's sons and students are sworn brothers. The **Zhi** generation.

Example **Lu** Zhi-chun (Uncle Lu in the story)
    Lu – Last name. **Zhi** – meaning courage. The '**generation** word.'
    Chun – meaning loyal.

Chiang Shiao-ho (江小鶴) his brother Chiang Shiao-leo (Little Loon)
Chiang Zhi-shen – Chiang Shiao-ho's (江小鶴) father
Lee Feng-jii – Chiang Shiao-ho's (江小鶴) sworn brother.

Bo Ah-ran (飽阿鸾)
Gi Kon-jii – Bo Ah-ran's (飽 阿 鸾) **husband** (in name only).
Master Bo – Bo Kung-Lung. An **eccentric** martial arts teacher.
    Bo Ah-ran's (飽阿鸾) grandfather.

Master Bo's two sons
Bo Zhi-un – Bo Ah-ran's (飽阿鸾) father.
Bo Zhi-lin – Bo Ah-ran's (飽阿鸾) uncle. He abused **Chiang Shiao-ho** (江小鶴)

Master Bo's students -- all of them are **Chiang Shiao-ho's** uncles.
Lung Zhi-chi He killed **Chiang Zhi-shen (Chiang Shiao-ho's** father)
Lung Zhi-tin Lung Zhi-chi's brother. Young **Chiang Shiao-ho** stabbed him.
Ma Zhi-min Uncle Ma He raised the orphan **Chiang Shiao-ho** for two years.
Lu Zhi-chun Uncle Lu He helped and sheltered the orphan **Chiang Shiao-ho.**
Feng (uncle Feng) / Lieu/ Chen

One-eyed-Yu Master Bo ordered him to cut out his left eye because he looked at a woman (not his wife).
Old Scholar-- No one knew his name. **Chiang Shiao-ho's teacher.**
The Mute----- No one knew his name. **Chiang Shiao-ho's classmate.**
Master Hsu-- Chiang Shiao-ho's first teacher.

Prologue

It was a cold night, and the only sound was the village dogs' barking. **Chiang Zhi-shen, (Chiang Shiao-ho's father),** ran to the south and hoped to cross the mountain to N. Szechwan and then Beijing. Twice he fell on the rocky path. Once, he almost fell into the rushing creek. He felt hopeless and preferred death; in another, he felt like turning back and fighting Master Bo and his students to death.

He kept going. With his muddy, bloody body and sword, anyone could have mistaken him for a bandit. So he dropped his sword and kept struggling ahead on his blistered feet. Sitting on a rock to rest and with excruciating pain, he took off his battered shoes, squeezed the blisters, and bandaged his feet with strips of his torn shirt. '*What terrible crime have I committed that makes me an inexcusable criminal? Do I deserve to be chased like a sheep by a pack of wolves? The law of the ruling Chin Dynasty has no death penalty for adultery. Will I live through this? Will I see my wife and sons again?*'

1

Chiang Zhi-shen, Chiang Shiao-ho's (江小鶴) **father,** hid in the hills and lived on wild berries for three days. A hunter shared some coarse food with him and told him the shortest mountain path to North Szechwan. He had taken a risk earlier and went home to get some silver and gulp down some cold rice. He had asked his wife for forgiveness and told her that he would go to Beijing. His two sons—twelve-year-old Shiao-ho and the baby—were sleeping when he caressed them with his cold fingers, and his tears dropped on their cheeks. He wondered whether he would stay alive to see them again. He did not know whether he had crippled the sadistic Bo Zhi-lin. He hoped that Master Bo and his sons wouldn't kill his family. *'Oh, what have I done? I should have considered the terrible consequence of my illicit, adulterous act, and...'* Suddenly he heard horses' hooves and then saw his pursuers. Two ferocious-looking men in their late thirties rode ahead of old Master Bo. They must be the Lung brothers, Master Bo's most capable students. *'Master Bo had sent for them to kill me.'* He desperately climbed up the rock, slipped, and fell on his back. One of them whipped him. Nearly blind with fear and anger, he shouted, "You are all murderers..." Lung Zhi-chi killed him before he could finish his accusation, before Master Bo could finish, "Wait! Don't kill him..."

Old Master Bo gazed at the dead man with pity. He said, "It's done; keep quiet about it."

In the evening, Master Bo went to Chiang's house and threw the silver found on Chiang Zhi-shen's body over the fence. The baby cried, and Master Bo felt sad and very old.

Chiang Shiao-ho (江小鶴) did not pay too much attention to his father's absence at first. He was used to his father traveling to some big city to work for days or half a month and coming back with nice toys for him and pretty clothes for his mom. But somehow, he knew his father's absence was different this time. His mother sobbed while she nursed his baby brother. He missed his father.

"Mom, when will Daddy come home?" Shiao-ho asked his mother.

"He went to Beijing, and he won't be back for at least a year or two. I told you already."

His mother, trying to suppress her tears, said rather harshly.

"But why are you crying so much? It cannot be true!"

He did not know why his tears rolled down his dirty cheeks. *'It's bad. Mom will not tell me, I will ask Uncle Ma. He should know.'* Uncle Ma married his mom's cousin and was also a student of Master Bo. His father told him that Master Bo's two sons and students were all sworn brothers. Each of his students keeps his surname and has the word "Zhi," meaning ambitious, as part of his first name.

The following day, Shiao-ho went to the training field. He proudly recalled that his Daddy moved quicker than most of Master Bo's students. At a break, he ran to Uncle Ma, held onto one of his legs, and asked, "Uncle Ma, where did my Daddy go? Mom won't tell me the truth. She only cries."

"Get out! You dirty, little bastard! How dare you come here!" Bo Zhi-lin, Master Bo's second son, yelled and then slapped Shiao-ho as if he were chasing away a dog.

Chiang Shiao-ho punched him in the stomach, and Bo Zhi-lin bent over in pain, "You dare attack me! I'll kill you!" However, he held his saber in check. He knew that his father and others were watching. Meanwhile, Shiao-ho jumped high and would have punched Bo Zhi-lin again if Uncle Ma had not held him back. Uncle Ma had a hard time restraining the boy.

"Stop! Shiao-ho!" Master Bo called thunderously, his face glowed deep red, and his long beard bristled. He looked murderous, but Shiao-ho was not going to show any fear. Instead, he pushed his chest forward, "I'm here to ask Uncle Ma about my father. Grandpa Bo, your son attacked me first."

Master Bo laughed, "Shiao-ho, brave boy! Your father has not been here lately. I miss him, too. Go! Go home and ask your mother."

"I'm not going. Mom will only cry; she won't tell me. I've come to ask Uncle Ma. Unless you, all of you, tell me the truth, I won't let you practice in peace."

Master Bo smiled, "Don't be naughty! Here are a few coppers. Go and buy yourself some candy and be a good boy."

Shiao-ho knocked the Old Bo's hand forcefully, and the coins scattered. "I don't want your money. Tell me where my father is? I'll leave."

Uncle Ma held Shiao-ho and said, "My good nephew, don't bother us. I'll take you home, and I will tell you." Uncle Ma sensed that Shiao-ho's life was in danger. He added, "Let's keep quiet. The officials are investigating Chiang's whereabouts already. We don't want the neighbors reporting us again." Master Bo understood readily. Ma dragged the belligerent boy away.

"The boy is a bad lot, just like his father," Bo Zhi-lin stated. "Why should we not beat him and kill him now?"

Master Bo whipped his son in the face and growled, "You're my son, and you are not like me at all. You are a shame."

"Grandpa! Please don't be angry!" Bo Ah-ran (飽阿鸾), his ten-year-old granddaughter, ran to him. Master Bo caressed the girl's long, black shiny ponytail with trembling hands. *Neither of my two sons will be very good at martial arts. If I die, my skills will be lost, and there will be nobody to protect my family against my enemies' revenge. I'd better teach this little girl all my skills in my remaining years.*' He asked Ma Zhi-min, a blacksmith, to forge a small, lightweight saber for Bo Ah-ran.

In the next few days, Shiao-ho led his group of mischievous village boys to harass Bo's students, especially Bo Zhi-lin. Bo Zhi-lin dared not go out of the gate anymore. One day a student showed up with a bleeding forehead, and another one came with a torn shirt. They claimed that Shiao-ho's gang had cornered them. Master Bo said furiously, "Terrible!" and Uncle Ma was afraid for Shiao-ho's life.

One day at dusk, Master Bo passed Chiang's place and walked toward the wheat field. He looked back and saw cooking smoke rising from every house and some boys heading homeward with the animals. It was getting dark. With his long graying beard waving in the breeze, old Master Bo looked this way and that way and stood like a hungry tiger awaiting his prey. Soon he saw Shiao-ho, holding a club, coming fast. Master Bo stopped the boy on the narrow pathway winding through the tall wheat field.

"Grandpa Bo, you dare fight me!" Shiao-ho swaggered to hide his fear, but his voice trembled. "Get out of my way!" With a low laugh, Master Bo unsheathed his sharp dagger and aimed it at the boy. His eyes blazed while the thought ran through him, *'If I kill you now, I won't have to worry about you killing me later.'* Somehow Master Bo missed; he was too slow, or the boy instinctively jumped back fast; he could not kill the boy. Immediately, the cunning Master Bo put the dagger flatly on his palm as if he wanted to show the boy his dagger. Shiao-ho did not realize that his life had been in danger and, because he wanted to have a real sword, he exclaimed, "A real dagger!"

"Shiao-ho, be a good boy, and I will give you this dagger." Master Bo said.

"Grandpa Bo, I promise that I will be good. Can I have it now?" Shiao-ho's genuine joy and innocence softened the old man.

Master Bo handed the dagger to Shiao-ho, "Do not harass my students. They are your uncles. You HEAR?"

"Thank you! Thank you! I promise that I will be good." Shiao-ho examined the dagger fondly.

Master Bo watched the boy for a while, torn between his fears of what the boy might do to him ten or twenty years later and his love of an innocent and courageous boy. He contemplated the opportunity, wanting to grab back the dagger and kill the boy. But he stopped himself. *'I'm over sixty. I don't want to be cruel anymore. It's bad enough that I had his father killed.'* He ruffled the boy's hair and said, "Shiao-ho, it's getting late. You'd better go home. Your Daddy has gone to Beijing. He will be away for a while."

"Grandpa Bo, I won't be a bother anymore. I don't think you're cruel."

The following day, no students came to Bo's training field with any unpleasant encounters with Shiao-ho. Master Bo taught them with high spirits, and he began to teach Bo Ah-ran.

At the end of the session, Master Bo called Ma, "Take these ten ounces of silver to Chiang's wife. Chiang Zhi-shen was my student for three years. He broke my rules, and I forced him away. I don't think he will be back soon. I am sorry for his wife and children, and I'll try to help them."

On his way to deliver the silver to Shiao-ho's mother, Ma thought, *'Why? Master Bo had the husband killed, and now he wants to help the widow and orphans. Lately, Shiao-ho has been making a lot of trouble, and Master Bo seems to tolerate him. What's going on? It's strange. Maybe Master Bo does have regrets.'*

Shiao-ho called, "Uncle Ma, see my shiny dagger. It's real and very, very sharp!" He brandished the seven-inch dagger.

"Be careful! Where did you get it? Don't cut yourself."

"Grandpa Bo gave me this dagger. Last night, he waited for me in the wheat field, showed me how shiny it was first, and then gave it to me. He didn't want me to bother the uncles anymore. He is not a cruel old man."

"He waited for you and gave you the dagger! Let me have a look at it!" Ma Zhi-min felt a chill all over. He took the dagger, rushed inside, and told Shiao-ho's mother, "Cousin, you and the boys must move to my home in town right now. Master Bo could not give Shiao-ho a dagger out of kindness. He…Never mind, pack some clothes, and I can come back for the rest." He tried very hard to keep the fear out of his voice.

"Uncle Ma, give me back my priceless dagger. Please!"

Ma handed the dagger back to Shiao-ho and said, "Keep it and learn how to use it well. In the future, you can use it to…"

Shiao-ho's mother sensed danger, "You think we must move, Cousin Ma?"

"You must move. Hurry up and pack. I'm going to borrow Brother Lu's mule for you to ride. I am taking you and the boys to my home in town."

Her teeth chattered, and she agreed, "Yes, yes, I'll pack."

"Shiao-ho, help your mom. Tell you what, I'll teach you how to fight and how to forge a dagger or a saber in my shop. If you learn the blacksmith trade, you can forge many swords, and you can earn a living." Ma said.

Shiao-ho jumped up and yelled, "Good! Let's move to town. I want to learn how to fight. I want to fight better than you, Daddy, and even Grandpa Bo."

Ma told Lu Zhi-chun his strong suspicion, "Master Bo wanted to kill Shiao-ho last night. He changed his mind at the last moment."

Lu Zhi-chun agreed, "If Master Bo wants to *'weed the roots,'* he must kill Shiao-ho now to assure he doesn't take revenge in the future. You and I, we have to protect Shiao-ho."

Ma said, "Master Bo is cruel and ruthless. Brother Lu, you better go to Master Bo's place to do some work for him. I am related to the Chiangs, and I do not want to get you in trouble. I better go."

Ma moved the Chiang family to live with him in town. He dared not tell his wife and Chiang's wife the depth of his fear. He sold Chiang's house. It did not bring too much. Chiang Zhi-shen had borrowed heavily against the house.

He behaved with extra care around Master Bo and Bo Zhi-lin. One day, Master Bo told him, "You are good to take care of the Chiangs. Here is some silver. Take it. I'll help you."

A month later, some villagers reported that they saw Chiang's remains lying in the creek up in the mountains. Chiang's wife knew for sure that her husband was dead. She remarried. Ma said, "I'm not merely a relative. I'm Chiang Zhi-shen's sworn brother. Cousin, I'd like to keep Shiao-ho with me. I would like to see Chiang's name and bloodline continue through Shiao-ho. You can take the baby with you; your new husband probably will adopt him."

2

Uncle Ma taught Chiang Shiao-ho martial arts and blacksmith skills for two years. Shiao-ho grew tall and strong. His father's tragic death and his mother's remarriage had made him bad-tempered. He learned to drink and frequently fought with the town roughnecks. Uncle Ma understood him and treated him with kindness, but his wife did not. She resented that the growing Shiao-ho ate too much. She was also jealous of the boy's good looks and the attention that her husband paid to the boy. So she wanted Shiao-ho to leave. The boy was not happy about staying either.

One day, Ma Zhi-min dragged himself home through the deep snow after his daily practice at Master Bo's. His wife complained, "Look at you! You have been practicing martial arts every day for seven years now. Are you skilled enough to be an armed escort and get rich? We would be better off if you had enough time to manage your shop."

Ma sighed, "You don't understand. I dare not stop going to Master Bo's. I have seen enough cruelty, and I honestly do not want to be a guard anymore. I must go there every day lest Master Bo get angry. If he is mad at me for any slight disobedience, we'll be in real danger. See what happened to the Chiangs!"

"Ah! Chiang Shiao-ho is just another mouth to feed. He's lazy. Why can't he go live with his mother? We hardly have enough food to feed our children," Ma's wife grumbled.

"Be patient, woman, you hear! It's I who kept him with us when your cousin remarried. I cannot throw a homeless boy out now. Shiao-ho is smart and strong; he forged some very nice pieces, and he sure earned his keep. Anyway, Shiao-ho will be sixteen years old in two years. Then he can go out and make a living for himself. Listen, I don't want to hear any more talk of this. Only two more years!"

"Uncle Ma, hurry! Your Shiao-ho hit Donkey Sam hard. Shiao-ho may kill him," a neighborhood youth shouted. Ma said on his way out, "Never mind. Donkey Sam deserves a good beating." He resented that the greedy Donkey Sam had arranged the adulterous meetings between Jade Flower and Shiao-ho's father.

Later, in Ma's shop, Shiao-ho knelt and said, "Uncle Ma, please tell me the truth. Who killed my father?"

"Sit, Shiao-ho. Your father violated certain rules set by Master Bo for his students. He verbally insulted the Bos and wounded Bo Zhi-lin and Chen. Later he was afraid he would get caught and left town. We heard that bandits killed him."

Shiao-ho sobbed, "It's not true. Donkey Sam called me names and said my father was a braggart and a coward. He also told me that the Lung brothers helped Master Bo hunt my father down and killed him. Besides, he said that it was you, Uncle Ma, who fetched the Lung brothers from Zie-Yin City for Master Bo. He ordered them to hunt down and killed my father. You must know the whole truth."

"Shiao-ho, I've tried to cover it up for two years, and even your mother does not know the whole truth," Uncle Ma told Shiao-ho the details.

"Shiao-ho, we really cannot blame Master Bo entirely. Your dad was to blame, too. Your father and the rest of us knew that old Bo is uncompromising when it comes to the *'death penalty for anyone who commits adultery.'* Master Bo killed his wife and her lover. He escaped from jail. That's why he hates anyone who commits adultery. Whenever he accepts a new student, he makes it very clear that he would kill anyone who defies this rule. Your father knew that; he violated the rules and insulted Master Bo. He was arrogant about his skills, and he thought Master Bo, old and slow, could not control him. Master Bo almost died of a stroke, and that's why he ordered me to fetch his accomplished students back home to enforce his rules. I dared not refuse to go, and besides, he could have sent someone else. I knew then that your father had no chance fighting against them."

"Uncle Ma, I'm grateful that you've taken care of me. Now I hate no one else but Master Bo, not only because he killed my father but also this." He showed Ma the dagger, "Master Bo gave me this dagger two years ago. I remember that night very well. It was dark, and there was nobody around in the wheat field. He looked vicious at first. I was afraid that he would beat me, but I didn't understand why he changed his mind and gave me the knife instead. I've been thinking about it again and again. Now I believe that Master Bo wanted to murder me."

"Lower your voice, Shiao-ho. That's why I insisted on moving you and your mother here the moment you told me about this dagger. I knew then that your family was in danger. I also taught you the martial arts for your protection." Ma continued, "For two years, Master Bo has known that you're living with me, and he has shown genuine concern once in a while. He often gave me some silver for your keep. I think that he genuinely regrets what had happened. I advise you to be forgiving. You'll have no chance of surviving if you want to go after him. Not only will you be killed, but my family will be in danger too. Think about it."

Shiao-ho gazed ahead for a long time. Then he kowtowed thrice. He thanked Uncle Ma for keeping his mother, his brother, and him alive.

"Come and eat!" Uncle Ma's wife called.

Uncle Ma patted Shiao-ho on the shoulder affectionately and said, "Let's go in and eat. Don't dwell upon the past any longer. Try to preserve your life, behave well, become a successful person and carry on your father's bloodline. That will be a better way of being a good son than dying a senseless death."

During the meal, Ma's wife complained about Shiao-ho's shortcomings again. Shiao-ho kept quiet and did not quarrel with her as usual.

It was still early, and the snowstorm worsened. Ma frowned, "It looks bad, and I still have to go to Master Bo's tomorrow." When he noticed Shiao-ho's melancholy, his heart went out to the poor boy.

"Shiao-ho, here are a few coppers. Buy yourself a drink. It's no use to brood over the past. We cannot do anything about it."

About six inches of snow had fallen, and it was still snowing. The only tavern in town remained open with a few noisy drinkers. Shiao-ho bought a drink and then wandered around town. His hand touched the sharp blade of the dagger in his pocket. Master Bo had intended to use it to kill him two years ago.

He decided that he would go to Bo's village to challenge Master Bo. '*I know I am only a boy, but I am strong and fast while he is old and slow. Maybe I can win.*' Pulling his worn padded jacket tighter around him, he thought, '*Anyway, if I kill him, with luck, and escape successfully, I will go far, far away and never come back. If I'm failed and die, folks around here will know that I've tried to avenge my father's murder, and it'll be an honorable death. I cannot stay here and depend on Uncle Ma any longer.*' He walked fast against the cold and snow and burst with bitter hatred when he passed by his old home. He knew the gate of Master Bo's must be closed at night, so he walked around and found a lower part of the earthen wall and jumped up. He could not reach the top at first. He jumped again, barely made it, and then he fell awkwardly inside the yard.

"Thief? Who dares come here?" Master Bo yelled.

"I come to kill you..." Shiao-ho charged at Master Bo with his dagger.

"You dare!" Master Bo raised one foot and kicked Shiao-ho in the stomach. "How dare you come to kill me! Boy, you would have been dead already if I didn't pity you. Ah! You are Shiao-ho!"

Shiao-ho managed to hold his dagger tightly, tried to get up and charge again.

Bo Ah-ran came, holding her saber, and shouted, "My uncle is away. I can protect my Grandpa!"

"Don't kill him!" Old Bo stopped his granddaughter and took the dagger away from Shiao-ho with bare hands. Shiao-ho charged ruthlessly at Master Bo again. He kicked the boy harder this time.

Shiao-ho cried, "I have to kill you. You killed my father!" Then he jumped up, like a trapped young tiger, and charged again. Master Bo grabbed Shiao-ho's two hands. He wanted to kill Shiao-ho at once, so he loosened one hand to pick up the dagger. Shiao-ho struggled and freed one of his hands. He reached up and grabbed Old Bo's beard.

"Donkey Sam told me that you murdered my father. I have to kill you even if I die!"

Master Bo hit Shiao-ho on the head with the back of the dagger. Shiao-ho passed out. Master Bo held the dagger, but somehow he did not have the heart to kill the boy. Instead, he pulled Shiao-ho up.

"Shiao-ho, I did not kill your daddy. I should have killed Donkey Sam, he was the instigator, and he was the one to blame."

Shiao-ho was dizzy, and he protested weakly, "Don't deny it. Everyone says that you are the killer."

Bo Ah-ran hit Shiao-ho hard on his back. Shiao-ho sobbed.

Master Bo's two daughters-in-law rushed out to see what the commotion was. Master Bo told them, "Nothing's wrong! Go back to bed!" He examined the dagger, gave it back to the boy, and said, "I gave you this dagger two years ago; I cannot believe that you want to use it to kill me now. It's too bad that you're so young and you don't know how to fight. You have to learn how to fight." Shiao-ho lowered his head in defeat.

Master Bo then ruffled Shiao-ho's hair kindly and said, "Good boy! You're the bravest boy I have ever met. Although you come to kill me tonight, I don't hate you. But I must tell you that I did not kill your father. On that day, I did not intend to kill your father, but ..." He stopped before he said the name, "I don't want to tell you this person's name. This person is very good at martial arts, and you're not his match. If you challenge him, he will kill you for sure. He is not softhearted."

Shiao-ho was convinced, and he thought, '*The Lung brothers are the killers, and I shouldn't have come here. I'd better leave.*' He stamped his feet and said apologetically, "Sorry! I should not have come here, and I won't bother you anymore. I am going."

"Ah-ran, open the gate!" Master Bo ordered. He thought, '*He is better than his father. He's brave, handsome, without his father's overbearing arrogance, and knows right from wrong. Maybe I can...*'

Bo Ah-ran called, "You! Stop right there!"

"What? Grandpa Bo let me go, and now you want to fight me? Let's fight."

"My Grandpa does not have the heart to hurt you. Every day my Grandpa burns incense and prays to Buddha. He could have killed anyone without a second thought before. He spares your life tonight, but I won't let you go free." She chopped at Shiao-ho fiercely.

Shiao-ho backed a few steps and shouted, "Stop! I'm not going to fight a girl. A good man never fights against a woman." But Bo Ah-ran came after Shiao-ho with her Kung Lung saber. Shiao-ho had no choice but to fence with her.

Shiao-ho managed to jump aside after ten passes. He said, "I don't want to hurt a girl! Do you dare fight me with fists? I don't want to wound you with my sharp dagger."

"Sure! Who's afraid?" Throwing her saber on the snowy ground, they started a fistfight. Shiao-ho was stronger and taller, but Bo Ah-ran was more skilled. Many times her fist hit his body, but Shiao-ho felt nothing at all.

He observed that Bo Ah-ran used the same styles that Uncle Ma had taught him, and he started to fight with growing confidence. A few minutes later, Shiao-ho hit Bo Ah-ran. She fell.

"Stop! You two young heroes! It's a good fight!" Master Bo called.

"Grandpa, he beat me," Bo Ah-ran cried.

"Hush! He is taller, but you are more skilled. Ah-ran, it's a fair fight!"

"Shiao-ho, did your Uncle Ma teach you what I have taught him? You fight with the Kung Lung styles."

"My father taught me two years ago." Remembering the importance of not getting Uncle Ma involved, Shiao-ho replied.

"It's a pity that your father died early. He had only been my student for three years, but he learned better than the others. He could have been an expert by now. Your father was an accomplished scholar, and he was not happy. He could not make up his mind between learning martial arts and passing the civil examination to become a magistrate, even a governor. Shiao-ho, it's late. The town gates must be closed for the night already. Stay here and go home tomorrow."

"Thanks. I will stay one night only." He added, "Tomorrow, I'm going somewhere far away. Uncle Ma does not know that I came here. He will be furious at me. I cannot go back to his house."

"Where are you going?"

"I must find a good teacher and learn the martial arts well so I can avenge my father's death."

"You are a child and a very naive one, too. Without a good recommendation, no one will readily accept you as a student. Besides, Master Lee, Master Hsu, and I are the leading masters of martial arts in this area. Why not stay right here; I'll teach you. Think about it." Master Bo and the children had a snack together.

Everyone was asleep; Master Bo was awake and thought, '*For forty years, I have wandered around China. I had never hesitated nor was afraid to fight; I killed quite a few. Why do I let a mere fourteen-year-old boy threaten me? I do not know what to do about him. If I spare his life now, he surely will be a threat later. It is better that I kill him now. But, I am very fond of him, he is so brave. I can't bear the thought of killing him.*' Master Bo stood outside the window of the room where Shiao-ho slept and listened. All he could hear was the sleeping boy's soft breathing. '*I worry too much. He is only a boy. I'll talk to him tomorrow and try to keep him here with me. I must keep him from going away to find a good teacher. With his physique, talent, and good teacher, Shiao-ho can be a real threat later. I'll teach him some skills and make him work for me. A couple of years from now, he will forget about revenge and will be just like a grandson to me.*'

The following day, when Master Bo was drinking a cup of tea, Shiao-ho told him, "Grandpa Bo, thank you very much! I'm going now."

"Where?"

"Last night, I was wrong to come here to kill you. I'm sorry that I offended you. Now I'm going to find a famous teacher and beg him to teach me. In two or three years, I'll be back to kill my father's murderers."

Master Bo felt a sudden chill again. He smiled, "You are too young to go away all by yourself. It is better that you stay with me. You do odd jobs for me, and I'll teach you all my skills. I'll point your enemy out for you and help you." He added emphatically, "You must know that you are only a boy, and you have no silver. You'll starve to death. Besides, the bandits may kill you. Don't say that I did not warn you!"

He knew that he had nowhere to go. Shiao-ho said, "I'll stay with you. But I don't want to be your student, and you'll have no control over me. I'm free to do anything, and I can leave any time." Master Bo sneered, "I would not accept you as my student even if you begged!" He took a sturdy steel poker and shaped it into a circle effortlessly with his hands. Holding it against his knee once, he broke the poker into two pieces.

"Did you see that, Shiao-ho? You can avenge your father's death successfully only if you can do this, too. Otherwise, you'll get yourself killed." he added gently, "Good boy, go out and shovel the snow now. We'll have breakfast soon."

Shiao-ho realized then that Master Bo indeed was highly skilled and had indeed spared his life last night. He thought, '*I will learn well. Besides, where can I go? I have no place to go. I'll stay here for a while. I may find out more about my father's death.*'

Uncle Ma came and saw him, "Here you are, Shiao-ho. We were so worried. Why are you here?" Ma whispered, "You cannot stay here…" Master Bo and Bo Ah-ran came out together.

Master Bo asked his students, "Do you remember this boy? He's Chiang Zhi-Chen's son, Chiang Shiao-ho. He was told that I killed his father." Master Bo looked fiercely at every student, particularly Lu Zhi-chun and Ma Zhi-min.

Ma said, "Teacher, Shiao-ho has stayed with me and helped me in my shop for two years. Last night he ran away, and I'm surprised to see him here."

"Ma Zhi-min, I did not say that you told him any lies." Master Bo continued, "I want you, all of you, to hear this. In the names of all the gods and ghosts, I swear that I did not kill his father, and I have a clear conscience. I'm very fond of Shiao-ho even though he tried to kill me last night. I'll keep him here with me, and I'll teach him. He is not one of you. He's not a student. I will treat him as my adopted grandson. *Ha! Ha*!" Master Bo closed his announcement with a hearty laugh. Everyone joined the laughter as if on cue. They congratulated Master Bo in unison. Ma also laughed and said the proper words of congratulation, but he was frightened.

The daily session began. Shiao-ho stood aside and watched. Master Bo did not tell him to join the practice. He carefully observed the forms and techniques of the other students and realized that everyone was far superior to him. Master Bo treated the others very severely but was extremely kind to Shiao-ho. Sometimes he ruffled the boy's hair fondly. Master Bo also did not object that Shiao-ho and Bo Ah-ran played together, even though Ah-ran's mother did not think it was proper. When it was nice outside, Master

Bo would take the children out for a walk in the evening after he lit incense and prayed before Buddha. Ma came to practice and did his share of chores every day. He looked at Shiao-ho often and was constantly waiting for a chance to have a private talk with the boy.

Bo Zhi-lin came home from Xian, and he dared not show his objection to his father's decision to adopt Shiao-ho as a grandson. He complained to his wife, "My father is surely not right in his mind. Instead of '*Weeding the Roots*' and killing Shiao-ho now as an assurance against the young boy's revenge in the future, Dad adopts him and keeps him here. That boy is a young wolf; he will be a killer soon."

"It's not your business. Your father wants to keep him. How can you object to his wish? Besides, Shiao-ho is only a boy. Your father gets his father killed, and now you want the boy dead, too. If the officials don't stop you, the gods and the ghosts will surely punish you later."

Bo Zhi-lin slapped his wife hard and said, "If everyone had a soft heart like you, we could do nothing." Bo Zhi-lin wanted to hit his pregnant wife again, but he restrained himself and walked out. Shiao-ho was feeding the horses, and he mercilessly took out his anger on the poor boy.

"You! Good for nothing! You give the horses too much feed. You want to stuff them to death?" He kicked the boy hard. Shiao-ho jumped up to strike back, Uncle Lu held him back.

It was spring and it got warmer. The newly sprouted leaves and grass, the rushing creeks, made the country fresh and alive. Shiao-ho was far from being happy. Every day Bo Zhi-lin would found ways to torture him. Chen was also mean to Shiao-ho. Now, with the novelty wearing off, Master Bo treated him with cool indifference, and he did not teach Shiao-ho martial arts as he had promised.

One day when Uncle Ma and Shiao-ho were cleaning the weapon-stands together, Ma whispered, "You can't stay here. It is a plot to keep you here and use you as a servant. Master Bo won't kill you as long as you're useful. But his son will not tolerate your existence. Do you know that the Lung brothers will be here for the Spring Memorial Festival? They or maybe one of them killed your father. If they know that you're Chiang Zhi-shen's son, they will kill you. You better leave. You can hide at my place for a few days. Somehow I'll borrow some silver for you to go to Szechwan, you'll be safe there. Lung brothers are afraid of Master Hsu." Shiao-ho did not follow Ma's advice. He seemed to have a scheme of his own, and he sharpened his dagger whenever he was out of the other's sight. In the afternoons when the students have left and the Bos were inside taking a nap, Shiao-ho took a horse out and rode secretly. Even though the horse repeatedly threw him off in the beginning, with perseverance, Shiao-ho rode very well.

One afternoon while he was riding, Shiao-ho heard Bo Ah-ran and other girls singing. His face suddenly lit up.

"Nice singing!" Shiao-ho clapped his hands.

Bo Ah-ran said, "Shiao-ho, you're riding again! If my uncle sees you riding, he'll beat you up again. Go! Go! He isn't taking a nap now. Grandpa has sent him out on an errand, and he may be back any minute. Go back quickly."

Shiao-ho laughed, "I want to hear you sing."

Another girl said, "Forget it. We will not sing for you."

Shiao-ho got off the horse, opened his arms wide, and laughed, "No! I won't let you pass if you don't sing."

Bo Ah-ran replied, "There's no way we'll sing for you," then she added softly, "Shiao-ho! You better listen to me and go back quickly. Why do you want to irritate my uncle? You know he will beat you up." She laughed suddenly, " Let's run! See whether he can catch us." All the girls laughed and ran. Shiao-ho started to chase them.

"Shiao-ho! Stop right there!" Bo Zhi-lin galloped up. The girls and Shiao-ho stood still. Bo Zhi-lin yelled at Shiao-ho, "Thief! Lazy Bones! You're riding again!" He hit Shiao-ho hard on the head and Shiao-ho saw stars. He wanted to challenge Bo Zhi-lin, but he realized that he, a boy and empty-handed, could not win. He sat down at the roadside and pulled at the grass and stared blindly at the ground. Bo Ah-ran sat down beside him.

"Shiao-ho, are you all right?"

Shiao-ho did not answer and she touched his shoulder, "Are you crying, Shiao-ho?" He wasn't crying before, but he started to cry now. His tears dripped onto the earth and Bo Ah-ran sobbed too.

After a while, Bo Ah-ran said, "You better get away from here. Sooner or later they will kill you." She wiped her tears with the back of her hands.

"I know. Uncle Ma and Uncle Lu told me to leave too. But I…have unfinished business here, and I don't want to leave yet."

"What business? Are you worried that you don't have silver?"

"I don't have silver, but…" Shiao-ho hesitated and then continued, "Silver is not the issue. I want to…" He grabbed her hand and said seriously, "You mustn't tell anyone that I want to leave. If they know, they will kill me for sure." Her face turned white and she promised, "I won't tell."

Bo Ah-ran practiced with the others in the morning and flew kites with her friends in the afternoon. Her father sent her a beautiful kite shaped like a butterfly. She liked it very much and she was very happy.

Shiao-ho's life became pure misery. Bo Zhi-lin ordered him to feed the pigs. At night, Shiao-ho was ordered to sleep in a little hut beside the pigpen. In a few days, Shiao-ho smelled and looked like a pig. However, after finding out that the Lung brothers would be here soon, he seemed to be in good spirits.

Ma and Lu were anxious for Shiao-ho to run away. Uncle Ma secretly gave Shiao-ho two ounces of silver and Uncle Lu gave him some, too. One day Uncle Lu gave Shiao-ho a few articles of clothing that were too small for his son. Shiao-ho accepted the silver and clothes but refused to leave. He carried the dagger with him day and night and it seemed that he was waiting for something to happen.

One afternoon, Shiao-ho herded the pigs along the creek. He let the pigs drink and feed nearby. He sat and daydreamed.

"Shiao-ho! Come and help!" Bo Ah-ran ran to him. "My kite is caught on the tall willow tree. I can't reach it; please come and get it down for me." Shiao-ho was always glad to see and to talk to Bo Ah-ran. He knew that whenever he saw her, he could temporarily forget his problems. It seemed to him that Bo Ah-ran had the power of comforting him. Sometimes he wondered if she was the only reason he stayed.

Shiao-ho shook his head and said, "No. It's not mine, and I don't care."

"Please, please. It's my favorite kite. I beg of you." She stomped her feet, pushed her lips out, and she was ready to cry.

"After I am gone, who will get the kite down for you?"

"After you leave, it will be too hot to fly a kite. You won't go away forever, will you? I will wait and fly a kite again when you are back." Shiao-ho thought, *'Will I and can I come back? I may be dead.'* There was a huge willow tree beside the creek, and the tallest branches had caught the kite. Bo Ah-ran wanted Shiao-ho to go up the tree and get her kite down, so she looked up at the tall boy and begged, "Please, please get the kite down for me."

Shiao-ho thought, *"If I can escape safely, when will I be back? By then, I'll be a big man, and she a grown woman. Maybe she'll be married before I'm back. If we meet again, she probably won't recognize me. How could she ever remember that I once had retrieved her kite from this willow tree?"*

"No, I can't get up this tree."

Bo Ah-ran grabbed his arm and begged, "I know you can do it. You can climb any tree." Shiao-ho said nothing for a while, and then he suddenly laughed, "Good. I'll get it if you promise me one thing."

"Anything you want."

"If I call you 'my wife,' will you answer me and call me 'my husband'?"

Bo Ah-ran blushed, but she wanted the kite bad; she bit her lower lips and nodded. She secretly did not mind calling Shiao-ho husband.

Shiao-ho climbed to the top branch quickly and freed the kite. Bo Ah-ran looked up with open hands on the ground and called, "Throw it down to me!" Shiao-ho did not throw the kite down. Instead, he held the kite in one hand and descended from the tree sure-footed, and he jumped to the ground from about ten feet high.

Holding the kite high in his hand, red-faced Shiao-ho said, "I'm going to call you my wife now." He called softly, "Bo Ah-ran, my little wife!"

Bo Ah-ran's face crimsoned. Looking around and making sure that there was no one about, she hesitated and murmured, "Yes, my husband." She took the kite and ran away.

The exhilarated Shiao-ho picked up the bamboo stick and started herding the pigs back. *'Great! I have a wife. Later, maybe ten years from now, I will be a skilled martial arts master or even a first-grade guard with a lot of silver. One day I'll dress up nicely, ride a good horse, come back here and marry her.'*

Two sweaty horses stood in Bo's stable. Shiao-ho heard someone call one of the riders Brother Lung; he knew that the moment came and the waiting was over. He was terrified and excited.

Shiao-ho closed the gates of the pigpens; he intended to join the others with his head high showing that he was not afraid. But he had a second thought, and he lowered his head and dropped his shoulders instead. He was not going to be conspicuous before he could take the measure of his enemies first.

When Shiao-ho walked into the big room where everyone was, Bo Zhi-lin grabbed him by the shoulder. Shiao-ho tensed up and thought that they were going to kill him. He prepared to draw his dagger out and fight them to the death. Uncle Lu walked up and put his hand on Shiao-ho's shoulder and said, "Shiao-ho, go and give the horses a good rub down!"

Bo Zhi-lin sneered, "Brother Lung. Do you know this dirty rascal? He is Chiang Zhi-shen's son. Remember how handsome his father was? Look at him; he is nothing but a dirty pig." The Lung brothers laughed. Bo Zhi-lin continued, "My father thought Shiao-ho a smart and brave boy earlier, but now he agrees with me that Shiao-ho is nothing but a coward and a simpleton." Lu Zhi-chun pushed Shiao-ho out of the room lest Shiao-ho would fight. But Shiao-ho said not a word. Uncle Lu did not like Shiao-ho's submissive attitude at all. *'Why did Shiao-ho take the insult? He must be up to something. I better stick around tonight.'* Master Bo sometimes asked Lu Zhi-chun to stay overnight, so it seemed quite natural that Uncle Lu would stay. The pigpen stood between the house and the stable. Shiao-ho deliberately left the exit unlocked, and he pretended that he was busy feeding the horses and cleaning the stable. He had to wait. He paced around, and the sun seemed to set extremely slowly. Uncle Ma came into the stable and said, "How come you are still here? Don't you know the danger? You are fourteen years old now, and you can work anywhere to stay alive. You know that the Lung brothers will be here for at least seven or eight days. Sooner or later, the Bos will tell them that you tried to kill Master Bo, and the Lung brothers will not let you live. Go! Go now. They are drinking." Shiao-ho said nothing.

Bo Ah-ran came and handed Shiao-ho a small package of steamed dumplings with meat filling, "They are delicious. I'll try to steal more for you." Shiao-ho hid the food. They were as warm as his tears.

Uncle Lu went to the kitchen to help out and noticed that Bo Ah-ran seemed to be very nervous. Her mother greeted Lu Zhi-chun, "I am glad that you will stay overnight. I will pack some of the dumplings for you to take home." She liked the steadfast Lu Zhi-Chun, and she hoped that later Bo Ah-ran and Lu's second son would get married.

On his way to the kitchen for his usual leftover, Shiao-ho met the drunken Master Bo. Who, with his extra bright eyes, looked at Shiao-ho fiercely. His look sent a chill down Shiao-ho's spine. *'Did he see through my plot?'*

After he ate, Shiao-ho whispered to the horse he used to ride when he saddled her. He then carefully packed his silver and the hot dumplings in a piece of cloth tied tightly across his back. He could hear his heavy heartbeats and the Lung brothers talking coarsely, almost sounded like quarreling. One of them shouted, "Damned that Hsu Min! He surely fights well with the sword. Luckily, there were two of us." Now Shiao-ho knew for sure that Master Hsu must be superior to the Lung brothers, and he hoped that he could be Master Hsu's student.

Shiao-ho took the horse out and rode fast toward the foothills. There he tied the horse to a big tree and walked back to the stable, and waited. When he heard the village night watchman sound the gong three times, he walked out of the stable, holding his dagger, stood in the dark, and waited. He could hear the Lung brothers' loud snoring, but Master Bo still coughed once in a while. It seemed to Shiao-ho that Master Bo had seen through his plot and deliberately coughed aloud to warn him. As the night call sounded the 4th time, Shiao-ho knew that he could not wait any longer. It would be dawn soon.

His heart pounding, Shiao-ho dashed to Lungs' sleeping room but could not push the door open. Holding the dagger between his teeth, Shiao-ho pushed the door with all his strength. As the door gave in, he fell into the room, but he quickly regained his footing, knifed someone, and dashed out of the room. Lu Zhi-chun lurked around the corner. He pretended to grab Shiao-ho, but he gave Shiao-ho a powerful kick, sending the boy rolling down the foothill fast. Everyone was out. Lu shouted, "The stable! He steals a horse."

Shiao-ho rode breathlessly toward the mountains, the same escape route his father used two years earlier. Hearing riders coming after him, Shiao-ho hit the horse with his fist, again and again, to urge it to run faster. A little while later, he heard no horses, and he thought he was safe. He started to relax a bit when he suddenly heard Uncle Lu, "I saw him running to the west!" Shiao-ho trembled.

The sounds of all other riders but one became faint. Shiao-ho wondered who was shadowing him. Uncle Lu whispered, "It's me. Shiao-ho! To the east and then south. You follow the creek and the narrow pass, and you will be out of the mountains. You will be safe in the north part of Szechwan Province. Take care." He handed Shiao-ho a package of dumplings.

3

Chiang Shiao-ho rode southward and now was in North Szechwan. He watered the horse at the creek and let the horse graze. He had a drink of water and washed the blood off his dagger and his arms. '*A lot of blood! I must have stabbed someone's abdomen! I might have killed one of my father's murderers, or at least I wounded him... Didn't they find my father's body at the bottom of this creek?*' He was not sure, but he knelt and kowtowed trice. "Daddy, I may have killed one of the murderers. If not, someday I'll be back to kill whoever murdered you so you can rest in peace." He didn't want to mention that his stepfather was mean and abusive. He thought about his mother, his baby brother, Bo Ah-ran, Uncle Ma, Uncle Lu and wondered when and how he would see them again. He was hungry and swallowed the dumplings and tears.

The carriages parked outside a restaurant each had an identical small white triangular flag with red trim and words. Shiao-ho could not understand the words, but he knew that they were not the ones of Master Bo's Kung Lung companies. The Kung Lung's flag was yellow with black trimmings and black words. He had seen Kung Lung's caravan passed by Uncle Ma's blacksmith booth. His father once explained the folks call Master Bo 'Bo Kung Lung.' Master Bo's superb martial arts skills are as mighty high as the 'Kung Lung' (dinosaur) mountain range. '*One day, I will defeat the Kung Lung School. But, how about Bo Ah-ran, isn't she a member of the Kung Lung school?*' He mounted the stairs like an adult.

"Hi! Boy! Are you looking for someone?" a waiter asked.

"I will have a drink and a meal. Serve me wine first! And see to it that my horse is fed." Shiao-ho pushed his chest out.

"Yes, Sir! Do you want a drink? Not water?" The waiter laughed.

"You think I'm too young? Tell you what! You see, I have silver here," he put his silver and the dagger on the table with a bang, "Serve me wine and a meal quickly, and feed my horse too."

"Yes, sir!" the waiter chuckled. Other guests laughed, too.

Shiao-ho gulped down the food and noticed that every other guest dressed neatly.

He looked at his torn jacket stained with pig poop, his dirty bare feet. *Where can I get some silver to buy some decent clothes? I only have enough to eat for a few days.* His dagger lying on the tabletop reminded him of Master Bo's savage expression before he gave him this very dagger. *He was going to kill me then.* Shiao-ho renewed his oath of revenge. He tensed up when he heard heavy steps coming upstairs and was ready to run when he saw Uncle Lu and Chen. Uncle Lu said, "Shiao-ho, I'm taking you back." Uncle Lu's eyes glared, signaling danger and compelling the boy to run. Shiao-ho darted between the tables when Chen tried to grab him. "Let's see which one of you dares to..." Shiao-ho shouted. Lung Zhi-chi came upstairs. Shiao-ho pushed the paper-paneled window open and jumped just as Lung Zhi-chi's heavy saber cracked the window frame. He landed on the back of a horse and cut the horse loose, held on for dear life when the horse bolted and ran through the frightened pedestrians. He thought that Lung Zhi-chi was in pursuit and gaining on him, Shiao-ho hit the horse rapidly. When he lost control, he jumped sideways off the running horse.

"Boy, are you all right? You were smart to jump off the horse and lucky to be alive. Is this your dagger?"

"Thank you, Sir. It's mine."

"This is a spirited horse. It is not easy to ride." Another man led the horse back to Shiao-ho. It was Lung Zhi-chi's big black horse, not the white one Shiao-ho had. He knew now that he had not killed Lung Zhi-chi. *Had I killed or only pierced someone else? Perhaps I killed his brother.* Besides an expensive-looking saddle, there was nothing else on the horse's back. He had lost his scanty silver in the restaurant. *No silver! How am I going to eat?* A wedding procession passed by with a troupe of musicians accompanying a red-curtained palanquin. The bearers and the musicians all looked at Shiao-ho and his torn clothes with contempt. Shiao-ho thought angrily, *Do you think that I'm too poor to marry a pretty girl? Never mind, I have Bo Ah-ran. She is waiting for me, and I'm going to have a grand wedding. You wait and see!*

Immediately he recalled another sad scenario. An old palanquin stopped at Uncle Ma's to carry his sobbing mother and his baby brother away to her new husband Ton's place and left him a bona fide orphan. Ton was a miser, and he was also abusive. Once, Shiao-ho's mother made him some new clothes. When Ton found out about it, he came to Uncle Ma's place and demanded them back. Shiao-ho wanted to fight him, but Uncle Ma held him back and said, "At least your mother and brother have a roof over them and food to eat. Not many men would marry a penniless widow with a child."

His tears mingled with the blood dripping from his nose. He passed a few village eateries, but he had no silver to stop and eat. *'I'm going to die of hunger in a few days, and that is that.'* He remembered the stories about the vagabonds who stole or earned a living with performances of boxing or swordsmanship on the roadside. *'Of course, I won't steal! But I can put on a show of boxing tomorrow at the market. Now I wish that I did not eat all the dumplings. But I was so hungry then.'*

He was afraid that he might be mistaken for a highwayman, so he stopped at an abandoned temple. *'Poor horse, be patient. I know you're hungry, me too. Tomorrow, I'll buy you some feed if I can.'* He tied the whining horse to a big tree, lay down on the cracked floor beside a shattered statue of Buddha, and slept. The horse's loud neighing woke Shiao-ho. He heard the sound of horse's hooves fading in the distance, *'Thief! Someone stole my horse.'* In the dark, he tripped and fell face down on a broken piece of brick. Somehow he got up and started to chase the horse thief on foot through the fog. He ran a while and heard the horse no more when he suddenly saw a person sprawled on the roadside. He was so scared, and he ran for his life. He stopped to catch his breath and realized that no one was chasing him. *'poor guy. He may be dead.'* The horse had thrown the thief and ran away, only the saddle left on the roadside. Chiang Shiao-ho walked away from the body at first, but he had an idea, and he turned back to the body and searched. Sure enough, he found a small fortune in the dead man's pocket. He also picked up the saddle.

"Best saddle for sale. Very Cheap! Best…" at the market he shouted.

Two soldiers seized and manacled Shiao-ho. "Why? I did nothing wrong! How dare you arrest me?" Shiao-ho kicked the soldiers to get free. "Buster, you kicked me." One soldier slapped Shiao-ho hard, and the older one said gently, "Boy, come with us to the court. We won't jail you if you're innocent." But the headstrong Shiao-ho, like a trapped young tiger, kicked and shouted all the way when they dragged him to the Magistrate's office. One soldier tried to calm him down, "Little brother, we're just doing our job. Someone reported that you are selling stolen goods. Please keep quiet and wait for the trial. Magistrate Fan is nice and just. He won't punish a young boy too harshly." But the indignant Shiao-ho continued to struggle and shout until he nearly lost his voice.

"Are you soldiers or robbers? Give me back my dagger and my silver!" Shiao-ho protested when they searched him and took away his dagger and a small amount of silver. "Little one, we'll give you back everything if you're innocent. Don't worry! Howling will do you no good." They locked Shiao-ho in a small dark room, paying no attention to the boy's cursing and begging. In the afternoon, four officers took him to court and pushed Shiao-ho to kneel in front of the Magistrate.

"Little one, what's your name?" With a Southern accent, the Magistrate asked gently.

"Chiang Shiao-ho. I'm innocent, and you better order them to give me back my stuff. Do you hear?"

"Ha! You're nasty. Why did you kill a man and steal his saddle and silver? The truth! Before I order you clubbed."

"Honorable Sir, I'm innocent. Last night a thief stole my horse and..."

"Stole your horse? How could you own a horse? I see you won't tell the truth without a beating. Club him twenty times!"

"Pardon me, and please pity me. I'm a runaway orphan. Master Bo killed my father and then..." Shiao-ho broke down.

"Hold him now and make inquiries! If he is telling the truth, I'll deal with that Master Bo," Magistrate Fan ordered.

They threw Shiao-ho into a cell with twenty-some other prisoners. They locked his feet but took the chain from his neck and untied his hands. The cell had one pail in the corner for the night soils, and the smell was unbearably repulsive. Shiao-ho threw up and then sat against the cold, damp wall and sobbed. One of his jail mates came to comfort him. During the night, Shiao-ho found that the shackles on his feet were for an adult, and they were loose on him. He secretly freed his feet and then put them back on and slept with the hope that he could escape in the morning. It was customary for the newest prisoners to empty the latrine bucket in the morning. With one hand carrying the odious pail, Shiao-ho was trying to loosen the cuffs on his feet. He slipped and fell. The night soils spilled all over the guard, who cursed and kicked Shiao-ho. Shiao-ho rolled away, freed his feet, and then ran. Twice he fell, but he picked himself up and ran even faster out of the courtyard and out of town. There was the sound of horses behind him; he thought that the soldiers were chasing him and ran even faster until he fainted. His last memory was of being lifted by powerful arms. A man held him on a running horse, and the stranger was not a soldier.

"You're a brave young rascal and cunning too. You acted like you have learned some martial arts. Who's your teacher?"

"Uncle Ma Zhi-min taught…" suddenly Shiao-ho was thrown off the horse. He regained his footing quickly and threw a rock at the stranger, who had doubled back.

"Why? You've saved me, and now you want to kill me? It doesn't make sense! Come down! Be a man and fight." Shiao-ho shouted.

The stranger dismounted and laughed, "Oh, young brother, I admire your guts. But I became angry as soon as I heard that your teacher's name has the word '*Zhi.*' There is not a good man among Master Bo's Kung Lung gang," he continued, "is Ma not a student of that mean Master Bo?"

"Yes. My father was Master Bo's student too. Master Bo and the Lung brothers killed my father. Uncle Ma helped me escape. Who are you, and why did you save me?"

"I heard about the murder. You are Chiang Zhi-shen's boy. Now the Bos want to catch you, alive or dead. I'm Wu Da, nicknamed Black Leopard. I have many friends. We rob the rich and help the poor. I admire your bravery and cunning and saved you."

"I won't be ungrateful. Someday I'll repay your kindness. Can you lend me some silver? I'm starved, and I need clothes and a weapon. The soldiers took my dagger and a bit of silver."

They stopped to eat. The used clothes they bought were too big and too long. Shiao-ho rolled up the sleeves and pant legs, tied the waist with straps torn from his old jacket. He also padded the shoes and tied them to his feet.

"You sure are resourceful, aren't you?" Black Leopard took him up the hill to the leader, a monk.

"Boy, Black Leopard said that you're brave and good at martial arts. We can use your help to do things that are difficult for us adults to do. But remember that we don't steal from or rob the poor or the old. Moreover, we never insult or hurt a woman," the monk told Chiang Shiao-ho. He did not want to be a bandit. '*Real heroes are not robbers. Master Hsu is a real hero, and he won't teach me if I'm a bandit.*' He would leave this group as soon as possible.

The soldiers must have pitied him for being so young. His wound from the twenty strikes was slight.

Two days later, the rowdy group left to rob a convoy. Shiao-ho stayed behind. The monks said, "I'd like to see your wound completely healed. Next time we will take you with us." Shiao-ho escaped the next day. He did not hesitate to help himself to a package of gold nuggets and silver. '*This is the loot anyway.*' He also took a saber. He escaped from the back slope. There was no path, and he got lost and fell. He lost one shoe, but he kept running on bleeding feet until dark and found an inn.

He asked the innkeeper, "Where can I find Master Hsu?"

"Master Hsu has a huge estate in Min-An County. It's about two hundred miles to the south from here. You can get there by boat quicker than by land." '*I don't know how to swim. I'd better go by land.*' Shiao-ho decided. He replaced his torn and unfit clothes and bought a horse, traveled uneventfully south to Min-An Town.

"How many students does Master Hsu have?" Shiao-ho asked around.

"None. Master Hsu does not accept any students. He set an impossible test for admission. He wants to hand his skills down to his sons. One is a bit older than you. Master Hsu is very arrogant. He does indeed have great skills, and he's number one around here." The long-winded clerk told him. '*Now, what should I do next? I need to find a good teacher to teach me.*'

Szechwan province is one of the wealthy provinces in China, and Shiao-ho found the folks there were all well-dressed and well-mannered. He started to learn to be polite. The hotel clerk advised him to talk to some professional security guards. Shiao-ho visited the biggest security company. He met two very friendly professional guards, and he told them his grievance. Nan, the older guard, said, "Master Bo and his gang, especially the notorious Lung brothers, indeed had a bad name here. No need to worry. The Lung brothers dared not come here anymore. Master Hsu punished them often. When the Lung brothers knew that Master Hsu and his son were away last months, they sneaked into Master Hsu's plantation and killed two servants. They bragged that they had killed two of Master Hsu's best students."

Lee, the other guard, said, "Master Hsu is conceited. He does indeed have great skills. He and old Master Lee are famous around here. But I'm not sure if he's Master Bo's match." He rambled on, "I do think you better seek the great Master Du '*Szechwan Dragon*' to teach you. Even if you can only learn twenty percent of his skill, I promise you that you'll meet no equals."

"Who is he, this *Szechwan Dragon*? Where can I find him?" Shiao-ho asked eagerly. Nan laughed, "He is only kidding. Master Du, the one called '*Szechwan Dragon*', was very famous twenty years ago. But, nobody knew why he'd suddenly gone from this area. Maybe he was dead. Nobody was his match even when he did not use the '*Tien Hsueh*' technique. He only applied this most effective killing skill when he wanted to defeat two to three hundred bandits quickly."

"What is '*Tien Hsueh*?"

'*Tien*' means to 'point at' and '*Hsueh*' means nerve cavity. It is one of the elite secret techniques of the militant Tao priests on Wu-Ton Mountain. Only two or three men used it so rarely that not many people know about it. According to what I have heard, one who knows how to use it can kill or cripple a man or make the man mute instantly by pointing his two fingers at one of the blood-flowing pressure points or a nerve cavity. Legend has it that only two masters in Szechwan Province knew how to do it. One *is Szechwan Dragon* Master Du in the north and another named *'Dragon Knight'* Master Gi in the west. Both of them were very famous twenty-some years ago, and both of them retired suddenly."

"Are they still alive?" the awed Shiao-ho asked.

"There is no information about Szechwan Dragon Du. Someone said his grandchildren are still in Szechwan. A few years ago, a traveler from Xian said that both Dragon Knight Gi and his son had passed away. His daughter-in-law and a grandson live in poverty." He then added, "Master Gi was first a student of the *Sho-Lin* school, of the warrior monks, but later he learned some more improved techniques, including *'Tien Hsueh'* and *Tai-Chi* swordsmanship from the *Wu-Ton* school."

"What is *Sho-Lin*? What is *Wu-Ton*? Are they the names of a mountain range like Kung Lung?" Shiao-ho asked.

"*Sho-Lin* is the name of a great Buddha temple. All the monks there knew how to fight well, and the martial arts techniques they have developed were called 'Sho-Lin' school. They emphasized physical strength. I heard that Master Bo's teacher was a master of the *'Sho-Lin'* school. They were usually big powerful men. On *'Wu-Ton'* mountain, the *Tao* priests had their temples everywhere. *Tao* priests developed the *'Wu-Ton'* school, emphasized the breathing and concentration methods called *'chi-kung'* (energy), and improved the *'Tien Hsueh'* technique. A sick and weak person can become a deadly fighter too. *Wu-Ton* masters preferred a lightweight, sharp two-edged sword. I believe Master Hsu is of the *Wu-Ton* school. I hope I did not bore you with my long-winded explanation."

Shiao-ho stood up and bowed. "Thank you so much. I hope you will teach me more. My father died, and I know nothing."

He asked again, "Does Master Hsu know the *'Tien Hsueh'* technique?"

"I don't think so. As I said earlier, Master Hsu is conceited. If he knows it, he won't hide it." Lee replied.

Shiao-ho felt hopeless. *'If all the great masters are dead, Master Hsu may not be Grandpa Bo's match. It will be almost impossible for me to avenge my father's death. Still, I better beg Master Hsu to teach me.'*

"Why did both famous 'Dragons' retire at the same time? Did they kill each other?" Shiao-ho asked again.

"No, they retired, or you can say that they withdrew themselves from the arena of the martial arts world. Master Gi, *'Dragon Knight,'* died a few years ago. One of the theories I heard was that another more skilled master defeated them and forbade them to bully anyone with their skills. They both were conceited with their superior skills until they met the best."

"Who is this supreme master?"

"No one knows. Someone said he's a short southerner, came from somewhere around Nanjing. That is all I know, Shiao-ho."

"Thank you both. I will tell Master Hsu my misfortune and hope that he will be sympathetic and be my teacher. Thank you both for taking the time to talk to me." Shiao-ho bowed to both of them.

One day someone told Shiao-ho that Master Hsu was back. Shiao-ho saddled his horse and rode toward Master Hsu's villa. He led his horse slowly and carefully, passing through the crowded streets. Three horsemen came from the north, and the first rider was a well-dressed, scholarly-looking man about forty, and his two followers seemed to be servants. '*He must be Master Hsu...*' Shiao-ho thought, '*It will be bad manners to trail them now. I'd better visit him tomorrow.*'

Shiao-ho went to Master Hsu's villa and requested an audience. When Master Hsu came out, Shiao-ho kowtowed and asked to be a student.

Master Hsu refused, "I don't want to have any students. Stand up, Boy." Shiao-ho kowtowed again and begged, "Please teach me the best martial arts. I must avenge my father's death. The Lung brothers killed my father. I wounded one of them. Lung Zhi-chi almost killed me. Please…"

"Boy, I don't believe you. There's no way you could have wounded one of the Lung brothers. Get out of here."

Shiao-ho cried, "I stabbed him when he was asleep. The Lung brothers killed my father. Master Bo almost killed me…" His words of grief and suffering gnashed out between sobs. Master Hsu was touched; he pulled the boy up, sat him on a bench, and ordered a servant to bring him a cup of tea.

Master Hsu said, "You truly want to be my student?"

"I swear. If I'm not honest, may the thunder strike me?"

"Lung brothers are my enemies, too. Chiang Shiao-ho, to be my student, you've got to be able to measure up to three requirements."

"I'll agree to a hundred!"

"I'm serious. First, you've got to have some martial art training."

"I do. Uncle Ma taught me the basics, and I can jump up on the roof from the ground, too."

"Good. Second, you must be able to endure hardship."

"Yes, I can. I am a homeless orphan, and I was hungry for days. Aunt Ma never let me have enough to eat..." He shed tears again.

"All right then. Third and the last! You have to have strength! Can you lift heavyweight?"

"Indeed I can! I helped Uncle Ma forge steel. I've strong arms."

"I want proof! Come with me, and I'll show you."

Master Hsu led Shiao-ho to the three six-foot-long steel rods in the corner of the yard. Pointing to the smallest one, with a diameter of about an inch, he said, "Four years ago, Steel Rod Monk came here with this and demanded a donation of a thousand ounces of silver if I failed to lift this rod and hold it over my head. I did, and he left without the silver."

"Three years ago, Steel Rod Monk came back with this," Master Hsu pointed at the mid-sized steel rod with a diameter of about three inches and demanded two thousand ounces of silver if I couldn't lift it. I lifted the rod, and he left empty-handed again." Hsu stood beside the biggest rod and continued, "Last year, Steel Rod Monk dragged this huge solid steel rod here and demanded four thousand ounces of silver. I tried twice and failed to lift it, so I had to give him the silver. I had to borrow the silver. He left with the silver and a smirk on his face." Shiao-ho looked in awe at the rusty rod with a bowl-like diameter, half-buried in the ground.

Master Hsu continued, "I swear that if anyone can lift the heaviest rod, I'll call him Teacher. I'll also call anyone my Brother if he can lift the mid-sized rod. To be my student, one will have to lift the smallest one, at least waist-high. It's been almost a year now, and no one has been able to lift the small rod. Shiao-ho! You're brave, and you have the determination to learn. I promise that I'll teach you all my skills without reservation the day you can lift it to your waist, but not one day sooner. Agreed? Take it or leave it."

The smallest rod and the medium rod were there side-by-side. The slender, medium height Master Hsu, lifted the mid-sized rod, moved it, and placed it beside the heaviest one. He said to the amazed Shiao-ho, "This is better. Not in your way."

Shiao-ho bent down, gripped the small one, and tried to lift it. Giving it all he had, he lifted it halfway to his knees and dropped it, and almost toppled over it. Gritting his teeth, Shiao-ho tried again and did even worse. Master Hsu said gently, "You can come here to practice every day. When you can do it, I'll teach you. Keep trying." Shiao-ho tried and failed again. He was hungry and tired. *'Of course, I can't do it today. I'm starving, and I'm tired. Tomorrow I can do it.'*

Early next morning, Shiao-ho went back and tried again. He managed to lift it a little higher. Master Hsu encouraged Chiang Shiao-ho, "You can't build the Great Wall in one day! Come and practice every day, and soon you'll call me Teacher."

Shiao-ho tried again and again until he was too tired to walk. Every morning, he would go to Master Hsu's place to practice. Moved by his determination, Hsu and his oldest son treated him with kindness, and the servants showed Shiao-ho sincere respect. One day, Shiao-ho almost lifted the rod waist-high, but he dropped it when he saw stars dancing. He felt lightheaded and had a sweet taste of blood in his mouth. He looked pale. A concerned servant asked, "Would you like some refreshments?"

"No. Thank you very much. My stomach hurts, but I'll be back tomorrow."

When Shiao-ho did not show up at his villa to practice for the next two days, Master Hsu, now fond of the boy, sent a servant to see the boy. Shiao-ho was very sick. Master Hsu moved Shiao-ho to his villa and called a doctor to treat him. He said, "Shiao-ho, don't worry. I'll look after you."

During his convalesce, Hsu Jan, Master Hsu's eighteen-year-old son, came to visit Shiao-ho once in a while. Between sobs and teeth-gritting, Shiao-ho told him: how did Master Bo exploited him as a servant and let his son abused him, how did Master Bo try to kill him one evening shortly after his father's death, and … Shiao-ho also told Hsu Jan about Bo Ah-ran, the kindness help he got from Uncle Ma and Uncle Lu… His sad story was touching and also a necessary relief for him. One day Master Hsu asked, "Shiao-ho, now you're well. Are you genuinely anxious to avenge your father's death?"

"Good. I am anxious to punish the Lung brothers. We're leaving today! We'll go to Zie-Yin City first to punish the Lung brothers, and then we'll go to Chengba, Master Bo's lair. You'll have your revenge; I will challenge them and even the score. If we win and come back safely, I'll teach you."

"Thank you. How many of us will be going?" Shiao-ho kowtowed.

"Only you and me, and my sword, I'll make Master Bo admit his defeat, lest I kill all his students."

Hsu Jan said, "Daddy, take me with you."

"No. You stay home! I need you here to protect the family."

"But… there are many students, and Lu Zhi-chun and the Lung brothers are very skilled. How can you fight all of them alone?"

Master Hsu said "I said that I, myself, am enough to stamp out the Kung Lung gangs. Say no more!"

4

Master Hsu wore a dark blue silk button-up shirt and a pair of matching drawstring ankle-length pants, and a wide yellow silk sash tied around his waist. He seemed relaxed on his white horse. His three-foot-long sword was tied along the horse's flank. Shiao-ho rode behind him. Master Hsu taught him to roll up his silver in a wide strip of cloth and then tied it crisscross over his shoulders, how to have his saber tugged in the fold on his back. "Shiao-ho, this way you'll have your hands free, and you won't lose your silver when you have to run. Don't put anything valuable in the saddlebag. You're a boy, and your enemy might take your horse." Shiao-ho almost cried because of Master Hsu's fatherly words.

Shiao-ho thought himself a good rider, but now he sweated and had a hard time keeping up. No matter how hard he tried to quicken his mount, Master Hsu's white horse was always a few paces ahead. When they stopped to eat at noon, Shiao-ho wanted to have a drink, but he didn't because his Teacher did not drink. Shiao-ho had never known anyone else, besides his granduncle, a magistrate, who talked and moved with such calm and authoritative manners the way Master Hsu did. He met his granduncle when his father took him to visit. Somehow he knew that Master Hsu was superior to his granduncle. Master Hsu was both a super martial arts master and a scholar. Shiao-ho admired Master Hsu very much, and he tried to emulate him. *'I'm so lucky to be his student, and I hope he will teach me how to read and write, too.'*

They came to a foothill with fewer pedestrians. At the entrance of the mountain path, Master Hsu stopped and handed Shiao-ho a small silver bell. "Shiao-ho, tie it to the neck of your horse." Master Hsu also had one. Their two bells jingled pleasantly together, echoing along the deserted mountain path.

Shiao-ho saw a group of rough-looking men, probably bandits, waiting for them; he tensed up and prepared to fight. But, none of the bandits had any weapons. Instead, one of them held a tray of refreshments.

The man said, "Greetings, Master Hsu. Please have some refreshments. You're most welcome to rest at our fort!"

"No, thanks!" said Master Hsu who rode on without stopping. The highwaymen stood back respectfully for them to pass. When they crossed the mountain, Master Hsu told Shiao-ho to take off the bell and said, "You'll put it on again when we have to cross another hill." Shiao-ho understood then that the bells were Master Hsu's signal for the bandits to know that he was passing. Riding behind Master Hsu, Shiao-ho looked at his god-like Teacher with awe and admiration.

One evening, Master Hsu led him to a villa. Mr. Yuan welcomed them.

Master Hsu said, "Chiang Shiao-ho is my student. Master Bo had his father killed. We're on our way to Chengba to confront him." Shiao-ho was so happy that Master Hsu acknowledged him as his student.

"We've heard about the killing, and I don't think we should judge Master Bo too harshly. Shiao-ho's father was in the wrong, too. Shiao-ho, your father was arrogant, and he provoked Master Bo's anger."

"Both Uncle Ma and Uncle Lu agreed with what you've said. They explained everything to me. But, Master Bo tried to kill me, too." Shiao-ho told them about the incident with the dagger. Master Hsu said, "Someone has to restrain this high-handed Master Bo. This time I want to settle the score once and for all. If I win, I'll forbid them to set foot in North Szechwan. If they win, I'll stay out of their way, never to enter their territory again."

"We'll accompany you. Master Bo has more than thirty students, and you will be outnumbered."

"No, thanks. Besides the Lung brothers, the rest of them are mediocre. Numbers do not mean too much. Judging by the Lung brothers' skills, I may not be able to defeat Master Bo. That's why I don't want you to get involved." Master Hsu said. Shiao-ho thought, *'If Master Hsu loses the fight, I'll be in real trouble. Can I come out of this alive?'*

Mr. Yuan's ten-year-old son came out to greet the visitors. When Master Hsu asked about the boy's martial art training, Master Yuan replied, "I started teaching him last year. He is skinny and weak, and he needs to learn more than boxing and sword fencing. In a year or so, I'm sending him to Master Kac to learn the *'Tien Hsueh'* (Attack vital points) technique." Shiao-ho thought, *'If Master Hsu loses the fight and I come out alive, I have to seek Master Kac to learn this marvelous 'Tien Hsueh'.'*

The following day, they crossed another mountain and were on the Kung Lung School's turf. Shiao-ho thought, *'We're close to my hometown now. I hope I can see my mother, my little brother, Uncle Ma, and Uncle Lu. I will see Bo Ah-ran soon. But what should I do? Will she talk to me if she knows that I'm coming with Master Hsu to wage war on her Grandpa?'*

Master Hsu did not take the bell off. He told Shiao-ho that he wanted everyone to know that he had come to this area. Outside Zie-Yin City, they met a convoy escorted by a Kung Lung Security Company. Instead of following the customary courtesy of travel, Master Hsu deliberately led Shiao-ho riding through the convoy. All the carriages stopped in confusion, and the guards looked angrily at them.

"It's very rude to ride through a convoy like that, but the Kung Lung guards recognize me, and they dare not protest," Master Hsu said. Somehow, Shiao-ho did not think that was the right thing to do. Later they met Mr. Yuan and nine robust armed servants. Yuan said they came to applaud Master Hsu, but Shiao-ho knew they were coming to assist Master Hsu.

"Teacher, have you traveled in this area before?" Shiao-ho asked. Master Hsu seemed to be familiar with the area.

"I had been here twice, seven years ago and three years ago," Master Hsu explained. "Behind his back, some of Master Bo's students, especially the Lung brothers, are downright wicked. Years ago, Kung Lung guards had a booming business in North Szechwan. They were conceited and behaved cruelly, and I chased them out of Szechwan again and again. I don't think that Master Bo knows his students' vice, and he must resent me. He is old now; otherwise, he would have challenged me already."

Master Hsu told Shiao-ho at the hotel, "It's only ten miles to Zie-Yin City. Keep your saber handy and be alert tonight. The Kung Lungs know that we are here and who knows what they might do during the night." Fear and excitement kept Shiao-ho awake. He thought he heard someone on the roof, or try to break in through the window many times throughout the night.

He was jumpy the following day. Master Hsu said kindly, "Shiao-ho, don't be afraid. The Lung brothers are nothing, but Master Bo is something else. He is old, but I dare not think it'll be easy to beat him."

They came to the Lung brothers' security company. Master Hsu rode through the gate. Lung Zhi-tin, whom Shiao-ho stabbed, was lounging on a cot with his stomach bandaged.

He shouted, "Ahe! Shiao-ho. You get Master Hsu here to help you!" He could not stand up. Shiao-ho wanted to stab him. "Stop! Shiao-ho, you're not going to beat an injured man!" Master Hsu called. Three armed men, Chen among them, came out.

"You, Rebel." Chen slashed at Shiao-ho and the other two fenced with Master Hsu. With his long, narrow, two-edged sword, Master Hsu disabled one quickly. Chiang Shiao-ho had a hard time defending himself against the experienced Chen. Master Hsu came to his rescue and pierced Chen's shoulder. "Hsu Min! Damn you. Come and fight me!" with a ferocious shout, Lung Zhi-chi joined the melee. Together with Kao, they held Master Hsu off for a short while, and then Kao was injured.

Lung Zhi-chi dashed out of the guard station with Master Hsu and Shiao-ho in hot pursuit. Yuan and his men conveniently blocked Lung Zhi-chi's escape. Shiao-ho was so happy that his father's killer did not have a chance to escape now. To his dismay, Uncle Lu jumped down from a galloping horse and immediately locked in a fight with Master Hsu. Lung Zhi-chi fled.

"Teacher, please stop! Uncle Lu is a good person." Shiao-ho shouted. Lu Zhi-chun successfully blocked Hsu's thrust with his heavy saber and pleaded, "Master Hsu, please stop. Let's talk over our differences."

"You know why I came. Lately, your Kung Lung gang has behaved rowdily in North Szechwan. I'm here to teach all of you a lesson."

"Let's solve our differences peacefully. Besides, Shiao-ho's father was insolent and deserved to be punished," Lu Zhi-chun said.

"I have my reasons to come here! The Lung brothers killed two of my servants. Then they bragged, saying they killed two of my best students. I don't have any students. I came here to even the score." He called, "Shiao-ho! Let's go to Bo's village to catch the coward Lung Zhi-chi."

Mr. Yuan told Shiao-ho, "Someone said that Master Bo killed your father. Not the Lung brothers." Shiao-ho sobbed.

Master Bo and his students waited for them at the gate. Bo Ah-ran, dressed in pretty pink silk, stood under a tree and waved her small saber at Shiao-ho furiously.

The stout Master Bo walked forward alone, "Master Hsu, Welcome! Your fame is far-reaching. Have you come here to help the renegade Shiao-ho avenge his father's killer? It is I who killed Chiang Zhi-shen. Please kill me alone if you can. Leave my students out of it."

"I'm here also on my account."

"I don't believe that I have offended you, Master Hsu."

"Not you. But you're blind to your students' atrocities in North Szechwan."

"Which one? I have always kept my students' behavior in check. Shiao-ho's father committed adultery, and I had him killed. Now, if you name the students who have offended you, I'll punish them myself and order them to give you a proper apology."

"The Lung brothers killed two of my servants while I was away. I demand justice. Lung Zhi-tin is indisposed. But I'll take the murderer Lung Zhi-chi back and we will hang him. "

"My students are my sons. I'll kill and punish them myself. But no one, not even *Szechwan Dragon* Du or *Dragon Knight* Gi will be allowed to hurt my students. You better leave Master Hsu!"

Master Hsu advanced a few steps but stopped when Master Bo said, "Wait! Hear me out first. Master Hsu, I know your skills are superior to my students. But I'm confident that I can beat you. If we could go back twenty years, I would never have allowed you to wound my students."

"Master Bo, let's talk no more! Let's fight!"

"Let me finish, Master Hsu! I'm old now, and my two sons are not good fighters. After I die, my sons and my students would be unable to defend themselves against my enemies. That's why I did not kill Shiao-ho."

"It's simple. Let me have Lung Zhi-chi, and I'll leave the others alone."

"You heard me wrong. I'm not afraid of you. I'll protect my students regardless of what will happen."

Master Bo brandished his saber once. Master Hsu blocked it, and he was surprised at Bo's strength. Master Bo continued, "Let's have a friendly duel and don't draw blood if it is possible. If you win, I'll kill myself, and you can kill my students at will. But, first, tell me what you'll do if I win."

Master Hsu bowed low and said formally, "I'll never come to this area, and your students will have a free run in North Szechwan. Agreed?"

"Agreed."

Two weapons clashed, and the fight began. Master Hsu thrust thrice in quick succession, and Master Bo successfully blocked them just as fast. They moved very fast. Sometimes their weapons clashed together, but they separated swiftly too. Shiao-ho and the others could not follow the fight fast enough to distinguish who's winning. Everyone watched with their mouths wide open and held their breath. Suddenly Master Hsu jumped out of the circle, and Master Bo, pale and gulping for air, stopped too. Then, to everyone's surprise, Master Hsu ran to his horse and galloped away without saying a word.

Startled and confused, Shiao-ho stood there dumbfounded. Mr. Yuan called, "Shiao-ho. On the horse, and let's go." He pushed Shiao-ho onto the horse and led them away. They followed Master Hsu and quickly rode southward along the curving mountain path, the same one where Shiao-ho's father was killed, and Shiao-ho had escaped. Finally, Master Hsu stopped when they reached North Szechwan.

"Why? Teacher, did you not want to hurt an old man?" Shiao-ho asked.

"Don't call me Teacher anymore. I'm not good enough to teach you. Come closer!" Master Hsu raised his right arm, and Shiao-ho could see the blood trickle through a cut and the bloodstains on the pants and boots.

"Master Bo wanted to protect his sons and students from revenge. He deliberately slashed me enough to hurt but not to kill. If he had not held back, I would have lost my right arm." Master Hsu continued with a sigh, "Even in his old age, he is better and stronger than I am. If he were young, more agile, and stronger, I would not have had a chance to hold him off more than ten passes." Shiao-ho's face was white as snow.

"Shiao-ho. I'll keep away from Master Bo's territory as long as I live. Even if I teach you all my skills, you wouldn't have a chance of beating the Kung Lung gang. Lu Zhi-chun is almost my match already. You have to learn more superior skills."

"But, Teacher, where can I find a better teacher than you. Please teach me." Shiao-ho knelt and begged.

"Go to Kaifeng and seek Master Kac to learn the '*Tien Hsueh*' technique. When I visited him seven years ago, we had a friendly meet. He pointed his fingers at my leg once; my leg went numb and immobile immediately. Of course, he cured me right away. If not, I might be a cripple by now. You go to him and tell him that I sent you, and he will accept you. You know I have to keep my word to leave the Kung Lung gang alone. Otherwise, I would have let my son take you there. Take care and good luck."

Mr. Yuan said, "Shiao-ho, you're too young to travel to Kaifeng alone. Come home with me. I'll take you and my son to Master Kac's next year. It's very dangerous for you now. Every Kung Lung member will hunt you down and kill you."

"No, thanks. I can't wait that long. I'll be careful. Thank you."

Shiao-ho stood there watching them ride away, and he felt very alone. *'I'm still close to home; I better see my mother, my young brother, and Uncle Ma. Who knows if I will be alive and back again? I know I have to cross Tu-Nan Mountain, and Dart Hu Li's bandits might kill me. Hu Li's throwing darts are deadly accurate. He wounded Bo Ah-ran's father before. Oh! Bo Ah-ran! Please don't hate me. I did what I have to do.'*

He waited until dark, and went to his mother's place. Ton, his mother's husband, would not let him in. "Go away! Your mother is my wife now, and I won't allow you to upset her. Every Kung Lung fighter is trying to catch you and kill you. I won't put my family in danger on your account." Shiao-ho walked back to his horse when a shadow came out from behind a tree. Shiao-ho raised his saber.

"Shiao-ho, it's me," Uncle Ma said hurriedly. "Here is a bit of food and silver. Lung Zhi-chi is in town looking for you. You better run. Let me show you another route out of town and hope they won't ambush you. Don't stop for anything until you're safely far away."

"Uncle Ma. You're my true father." Shiao-ho kowtowed.

The following day, he stopped at a small eatery close to the north entrance of the Tu-Nan Mountain pass. He shared the only table with an old scholar who was reading. Shiao-ho thought, '*I wish I could read and write. It's too bad my father died before he could teach me more. Uncle Ma is practically illiterate. If I could be Master Hsu's student, he may teach me. No one will teach me now. Ah! Master Kac may teach me if I am lucky enough to stay alive and reach him.*' He tried not to let his tears come.

With a Southern accent, the old scholar asked him, "Young boy, where are your folks? You can't be traveling alone on this dangerous mountain route?"

"I have a horse, and I know how to fight. Anyway, I have no family now. I'm not afraid of the bandits! If they dare rob me, I'll kill them." Shiao-ho forced himself to laugh aloud lest the stranger saw his tears, but his voice cracked, giving him away.

"Where are you going?"

"I'm going to Kaifeng."

"It's quite far. Do you have a relative there?"

"No one. I'm going to seek the famous martial arts Master Kac and beg him to teach me, so I can come back to avenge my father's death. Master Bo killed my father..." Shiao-ho broke down and sobbed as he told the Old Scholar about his sufferings. And then he said, "Grandpa, you're a learned man. You probably do not understand all of this fighting and killing stuff." Shiao-ho felt better after the talk.

"How old is this Master Bo?" the scholar asked.

"Oh! He is old. My father was his student, and I call him Grandpa Bo. He… killed my father because my father disobeyed him." Shiao-ho did not want to mention the name 'Kung Lung school'. He was afraid that the owner of the eatery might know some of the Kung Lung guards. '*I better not say anything more. Uncle Lu once told me that I should not tell strangers things.*'

They ate in silence. Shiao-ho thought, '*At least I have silver to buy food this time.*' He still had the silver and gold nuggets he took from the bandits.

He touched the pouch that he tied across his shoulders for assurance and finished his meal.

Shiao-ho asked, "Grandpa, we can ride in turn to cross the mountain."

"You go ahead. I'm not in a hurry. Take care," The old scholar picked up his book.

The owner told Shiao-ho, "Boy, you better wait here for a convoy and then go with them. It's not safe for a lone traveler, and you are so young." Shiao-ho figured that the only security company passing through here would be the Kung Lung guards. They were more dangerous to him than the bandits.

He replied, "Thank you. I don't think they will rob me, and I have nothing."

The mountain path gradually became steep and narrow, and Shiao-ho had a hard time reaching the first peak. When he stopped to rest, he saw another lone traveler standing under a tree on the next ridge. He pushed ahead to have a better look and found that the person was the same old scholar whom he had met at the eatery. When Shiao-ho bade him goodbye, he was still eating and reading.

Shiao-ho called, "Grandpa, is that you?" Catching his breath, "Oh! Grandpa, you must know how to fly. How did you get ahead of me on foot? I have a horse, and I started before you did."

"I know a shortcut," the old scholar smiled.

"No wonder. Am I on the right path?"

"Yes. After this peak, you'll have to pass two more before you are on a level road. There you will find a few houses. You can ask them for some water. You go ahead."

"Thanks." Shiao-ho let the horse gallop downhill. He looked back and saw the old scholar still standing there on the peak. *'He probably is composing a poem.'* He remembered that his father had said that scholars like to write poems about the scenery.

It was too steep to ride uphill, Shiao-ho had to lead his horse, and the going was slow. When he stopped to catch his breath, he suddenly saw that the old scholar was on his way down the next peak ahead. A chill went through him, and the hairs on his arms stood up, *'Oh! He must be a ghost or a mountain god. He is not human. What am I going to do? Hide? Where?'* He was scared, but he kept going and hoped that he would be out of the eerie mountain. Soon he was on the level road, and he felt better.

He heard the faint sound of shouting and weapons clashing ahead, and he quickly pulled his horse behind a rock and hid. Finally, he ventured out when it was quiet again. With his saber ready, Shiao-ho proceeded cautiously around a bend. What did he see almost scare him off his horse? About twenty men lay on the road and their weapons were broken. Shiao-ho thought they were all dead until one of them called, "Help! Young brother, go to the main camp and ask for help. We can't move...Ah! Who are you? You are not one of our men." None of them could move, and some of them moaned in pain.

"I'm a traveler. Are you all wounded? How come you're not bleeding?"

The man said, "Please be kind enough to go to our main camp to get us help."

"Who hurt you? There are so many of you."

"We're Hu Li's men. An old scholar disabled us with the *'Tien Hsueh'* technique. When we ganged upon him, he did not seem to move, but none of our weapons could touch him. He then pointed two fingers at us..."

Shiao-ho rode away fast, hoping that he could catch the old scholar. He knew that the Old Scholar must be a supreme master who had protected him. *'Who knows? He might be Master Kac. Doesn't Master Kac know 'Tien Hsueh'? Ah! He must have deliberately shown me his skills back at the peaks. I was too stupid to understand the hint. I should have realized that only a skilled master would dare travel alone. Wasn't he concerned that I was alone? I should have kowtowed to him right there and beg him to teach me. Now, where can I find him? Master Hsu is a scholar, too. Why did I think that he is an old scholar who knows nothing about martial arts? And why did he ask me how old Master Bo is? Does he know Master Bo? But he was nice to me.'*

It was dark, and Shiao-ho was tired and hungry when he rode out of the mountain pass. He wanted to find a place to eat first. But when he saw a convoy parked in front of the only inn, he quickly turned back toward the mountain. He did not want to take the chance of meeting any Kung Lung guards here. A man, probably a guard, saw him and called, "You! Don't turn back to the mountain; the bandits will surely come out at night."

Shiao-ho pretended that he did not hear him and kept going, but another guard stopped him and said, "If you want to die, it's your business. But I won't let you go, lest the bandits follow you here and rob us. Who knows if you're not a spy? Come with me to see my boss. You cannot fool us Kung Lung guards."

"Let go of my horse! I'll..." Shiao-ho whipped at the guard, wanting to escape desperately now.

A familiar voice, "What's going on? A thief? Chiang Shiao-ho! How dare you..." It was Bo Zhi-lin. Bo Zhi-lin did not know about Master Hsu's duel with his father yet. He was traveling with a Kung Lung Company on their way back to Xian.

Shiao-ho attacked Bo Zhi-lin ruthlessly. He knew that he had no chance of escaping, and he decided to fight to his death. At least he could wound or kill Bo Zhi-lin, who had tortured him so much. Bo Zhi-lin ran, "Brother Feng, help!"

A strong hand snatched Shiao-ho's saber away, and then a kick sent him rolling away like an egg. Bo Zhi-lin and the others attacked Shiao-ho with sabers and clubs. Shiao-ho fought back ferociously until he could not move anymore.

Feng ordered, "Don't kill him. Tie him up and send him back to Master Bo."

Bo Zhi-lin echoed elatedly, "Tie him up…" He kicked Shiao-ho again, and suddenly his back became numb. He tumbled down.

"Brother Bo, what's the matter?" the others asked.

"Don't push me! What? It's an old man."

An old scholar, out of nowhere, pushed them away and stood protectively beside Shiao-ho.

Feng asked, "You! Old man. What do you think you're doing? Go away! Do you hear? I'm not going to hurt an old man."

"I'm the boy's teacher. No one is allowed to harm him!" a crisp reply with a Southerner's accent.

Feng waved his saber menacingly, "Get out of my way right now! I'll…" and then, "Ache! Let go of my saber!"

No one could recall what had happened exactly. The old Scholar held Feng's heavy saber with two fingers, but the stout Feng could not pry it lose no matter how hard he tried. Next, the old Scholar seized the saber, threw it on the ground, and broke it into pieces with one foot.

There was silence. Everyone was too scared to move or talk when the old Scholar lifted Shiao-ho, carried the tall boy on the shoulder, and walked toward Shiao-ho's horse. Shiao-ho smiled through pain and tears. He had a super teacher now, his hardship was over, and everything would be all right.

"Wait. Please wait! Honorable uncle! Please tell us your name," the seasoned Feng Zhi-pan finally found his voice, "so we can tell our Teacher. We're Master Bo Kung Lung's students."

"No need to know my name. Just ask Bo Gen-fee to tell you whom he'd met thirty years ago at Tonby Mountain. He will know." The old scholar lifted Shiao-ho onto the horse's back and led the horse away.

"Ah! He knows Master Bo's real name! Who is he?" Feng Zhi-pan and all the Kung Lung guards whispered amongst themselves. They went to Bo's village with the now crippled Bo-Zhi-lin and the pieces of the broken saber.

Master Bo turned pale and almost fainted when he heard the old man said, "you should know whom you'd met thirty years ago at…"

"I sure deserved severe punishment for being cruel." Master Bo sighed, "Now all the gods and ghosts want to punish you, my sons and students, for my wickedness. How can I forget that scholar? Thirty years ago, I met him and received the only defeat and humiliation I have ever known. I was young and strong. I think he was a few years younger than me. But fighting him was like an egg fighting against a rock." He did not want to tell them that he was pulling a pair of gold earrings off a young woman's ears at that time. He continued, "Shiao-ho is brave and strong. If this scholar teaches him, Shiao-ho will be a super master soon. None of you will be alive when Shiao-ho comes back for revenge." He said again, "It's my entire fault. I should not have killed his father in the first place. I should not have let Shiao-ho live just because I'm old and have become soft and indecisive."

Ma Zhi-min said, "Teacher, please don't worry. I'll talk Shiao-ho out of it when he comes back."

Bo Ah-ran said, "Grandpa, I'll learn all your skills, and I will beat Chiang Shiao-ho. Oh! I hate him!"

Lung Zhi-chi said, "Teacher, please don't worry. When the renegade comes back, we'll ask all of our friends to come to our aid. Besides, starting today, we'll practice more to improve our skills. We're so many, and he is alone. We'll win!"

Master Bo thought a long time and said with determination, "Your skills are not very good because I have been holding back and not teach you some of my secret techniques. From now on I'll teach you all my skills. Then every one of you will be as good as I am. I don't believe that thirty-some Bo Kung Lung cannot beat one lone Chiang Shiao-ho."

5

Time flew by like one of Dart Hu Li's throwing darts. Ten years had passed since the old scholar took Shiao-ho away. Master Bo's beard had not a single black hair left at the age of seventy-six, and some of his students had grandchildren already. There had been many changes in the circle of guards and the field of martial arts. There was no news of Chiang Shiao-ho and his incredible teacher. Master Bo would ask these questions whenever one of his students returned home, or a friend came to visit him. Deep down in his heart, Master Bo knew that all his students put together couldn't stop Shiao-ho's revenge. He knew that Shiao-ho's teacher, the scholar, was truly superb. Some nights, when sleep evaded him, Master Bo shuddered with fear, recalling his complete defeat at the hand of that short scholar nearly forty years ago. Even at his best, Master Bo was as useless as an egg fighting against a rock in his confrontation with Shiao-ho's teacher.

"Any news of Chiang Shiao-ho? Are there any new outstanding young martial arts masters in your area?" Master Bo would ask these questions whenever any of his students returned home, or any friend came to visit him. Deep down in his heart, Master Bo knew that all his students put together couldn't stop Shiao-ho's revenge. He knew that Shiao-ho's teacher, the scholar, was truly superb. Some nights when sleep evaded him, Master Bo would shudder with fear when he recalled his complete defeat at the hand of that short scholar nearly forty years ago. Master Bo was as useless as an egg fighting against a rock in his confrontation with Shiao-ho's teacher, even at his best.

Bo Ah-ran's father taught many students, and his security station in Han-Chun City attracted good business. His second son, Bo Zhi-lin, had never fully recovered from the strange old Scholar's execution of '*Tien Hsueh*' on the back. He was disabled and could amble again after many years of doctoring.

Bo Ah-ran's mother had passed away years ago. Now, at twenty-two, Bo Ah-ran was average-looking, and her bound feet were not small enough to be considered admirable. She was Master Bo's only grandchild, and he spoiled her. Master Bo had taught her all his secret fighting techniques, so she was now superior to Lu Zhi-chun and the Lung brothers. Master Bo boasted often. "Master Hsu would not be able to last more than ten passes now in a duel with my Ah-ran." However, he never mentioned whether Bo Ah-ran could beat Chiang Shiao-ho. He often wondered, '*How advanced are Shiao-ho's skills now? Could my granddaughter at least defend herself if they were to meet and fight?*'

He smiled whenever Bo Ah-ran said, "I hope that damned Chiang Shiao-ho comes soon. The sooner he comes, the sooner I can beat him." Master Bo would think, '*It won't be that easy.*' and he would suddenly feel chilled all over.

Most girls would be married at the age of fifteen or sixteen, lest they become old maids. Because of her rather large feet and her mannish behavior, the ordinary country folks did not want Bo Ah-ran to marry their son. Many first-rate guards and martial arts masters came to Master Bo to ask for Bo Ah-ran's hand for their sons. Master Bo refused them all. Sometimes he would say, "My granddaughter does not want to get married yet." Indeed, Bo Ah-ran said again and again that she was not ready to be married. She seemed carefree, but she never forgot Chiang Shiao-ho and their secret pledge under the willow tree. Whenever she recalled that Shiao-ho had called her "my little wife" and she had answered "my husband," she blushed. She knew Shiao-ho well; his determination, his resourcefulness, his inscrutable endurance, and most of all, his wisdom to hold back his anger whenever he knew that any action of his would cause his imminent death. Many times, she had witnessed Shiao-ho submissively receive her uncle's severe beatings. Once, after her uncle kicked Shiao-ho rapidly, she helped the wobbly boy up and tried to stop the blood from flowing from his head. "It's bad," she had said. "Why did you not strike back? Maybe he will think twice before he kicks you again." Shiao-ho moaned, "I should not give him any excuse to kill me. Uncle Ma told me to endure everything and try to stay alive."

She knew in her heart that her Grandpa's fear of Shiao-ho was real, even though she often boasted that she could beat Shiao-ho. Even if Shiao-ho had just a mediocre teacher or no teacher at all, she knew that Shiao-ho would be difficult to fight if he ever came back. Now with his great teacher, Shiao-ho would be superb. With his strong physical condition and natural agility, Shiao-ho was a born fighter. She wanted to be prepared and kept busy every day with martial arts practice. She rarely missed training sessions. While everyone was sleeping, she would drill herself, jumping up and down from the roof and hopping from roof to roof. Every afternoon she rode, quite often, to that huge willow tree. There, under the branches, she often daydreamed about Shiao-ho. But she also hated Shiao-ho. She hated him for being a constant threat to her old Grandpa. She hated him for the impossible love between them, for causing her simultaneous longing for and fear of his return. Sometimes she chopped the huge tree trunk to relieve her frustration. The old tree suffered so many cuts that it began to die slowly.

She was secretly dreading Shiao-ho's impending revenge. Her grandfather's nefarious plot to use Shiao-ho as a servant and her uncle's relentless abuse would guarantee Shiao-ho's hatred for them. She often thought, '*If I'd been maltreated, I would not be forgiving either.*' She recalled how every time they had some delicacies to eat, she had to steal for Shiao-ho, who got only leftovers.

Bo Ah-ran despised her uncle Bo Zhi-lin. Her uncle even abused his wife. Her Aunt told her, "Your uncle is less than a bully. He's afraid of the strong, and he abuses anyone weaker than he is. He is so afraid of Chiang Shiao-ho. Sometimes he screams and then begs for Shiao-ho's forgiveness in his sleep. It's my misfortune to be his wife. I pity him."

She loved her Grandpa very much, and she was close to him. One day while they were having lunch, Master Bo looked at her and asked hesitantly, "Ah-ran, do you want to go out to see the world?"

"Where would I go?"

"Anywhere you want to go. You can travel through the mountain ranges to see the rushing rivers. You can see the real world that you would not have a chance to see if you stay home. You can also meet some martial arts masters and fighters from different schools."

"Sure, let's go. Grandpa, you have not traveled so long."

"No. I can't. I cannot leave home."

"Oh well! You can't or you won't? I don't want to be apart from you. So I'll not go."

"Ah-ran, you should not think that your skills are sufficient. They're far from excellent. You can't learn any special techniques if you stay home. I'd like you to go to your father's security station at Han-Chun City first, then Xian and Kaifeng. At Kaifeng, you'll seek Master Kac to teach you '*Tien Hsueh.*'"

"I don't want to learn '*Tien Hsueh.*' A true fighter would fight honestly with fists or weapons. I wouldn't call it an honorable victory if one wins with sly tricks."

"You have to learn this super skill. You have to know how to use '*Tien Hsueh*' to beat someone who might use it. Otherwise, someone could use '*Tien Hsueh*' to kill you instantly or slowly reduce you to a cripple like your uncle. Chiang Shiao-ho's teacher made your uncle a cripple with *'Tien Hsueh.'* Shiao-ho must have learned it now. I want you to go out for two reasons. First, you may hear something about Chiang Shiao-ho..."

"If I go out, I'll find out something about that renegade for sure. If I meet him, I'll kill him right away."

"If he is not hostile to us, or if his skills are mediocre, we won't kill him. Secondly, I think you should get married soon. Not one young man around here can match your skills. You'll have to go out to find someone suitable. I hear that there are some exceptionally skilled young warriors out there. One surely must be good enough for you to marry. I want you to promise me that you'll find a decent-looking young man who has skills superior to mine. As soon as you find one, promise me that you'll come back and let me make the proper arrangement. Although we are not of the gentry's class, we prefer propriety."

Bo Ah-ran blushed when Master Bo stressed again, "Promise me that you'll only take a note of his name and background first. I have to test him, and I want to make sure that he is skillful and honorable before you marry him. I want you to behave properly and maintain our good family name."

Bo Ah-ran was too shy to sound her opinion, but she did not protest either. She thought, *'If I leave home, I can start to look for Shiao-ho. If he still truly loves me, I will talk him out of the revenge business and have him marry me. We will be a happy family. If I stay home, I won't have a chance to talk to him alone when he comes back. Both of them, Grandpa and Shiao-ho, are strong-willed men. They would start the fight for life and death right away before I could say anything. I wish that I dared to tell Grandpa that I love Shiao-ho, but he is strongly against this kind of man and woman affair. He will be so angry if he knows, and he may kill me too.'*

Master Bo thought, *'It's true that one should not keep a marriageable woman at home. It's so true. My Ah-ran is thinking about marriage now.'*

They checked the calendar and consulted a fortune teller to choose a lucky date for Bo Ah-ran 's departure. She left with the fifty-year-old One-eyed Yu on a bright day in April. Master Bo had One-eyed Yu's left eye cut out because he had flirted with a woman while watching a roadside show. One-eyed Yu knew very well of Master Bo's eccentricity, and he was not thrilled at all to escort a spoiled Bo Ah-ran.

After they crossed the Bah Mountain, One-eyed Yu told Bo Ah-ran, "My good niece. We're away from home now, and we have a long way to go. I know that you have no trouble fighting anyone, and you will win, but I would advise caution and modesty. We'll be polite to everyone we meet. We don't want to show our weapons. We'll try to avoid a quarrel or a fight. We'll..."

Bo Ah-ran was impatient. "You don't have to tell me again. Grandpa has already told me many times."

"Master Bo has a lot of experience, and he wants us to have a safe journey. We have to be..."

Bo Ah-ran said, "Uncle Yu, will you stop lecturing me? Otherwise, I'll go by myself."

"My good niece. I just want us to be safe. That's all."

Her father did not like the idea of a young woman taking such a long trip. It was his father's idea; he could not send his daughter back home. He wanted to send some of his students to go with her, but he knew his willful and proud daughter would reject more company. He was worried that Bo Ah-ran and One-eyed Yu must pass the Tu-Nan Mountain, where Dart Hu Li wounded him ten years ago. He warned One-eyed Yu, "Brother Yu, don't tell Bo Ah-ran that Dart Hu Li and his gangs occupy the Tu-Nan Mountain lest she would provoke a fight. My father has spoiled her, and she is too proud of her skills for her good." Fortunately, Bo Ah-ran and One-eyed Yu crossed the mountain with many other travelers, and no bandits showed up. Next, they stopped at Lu Zhi-chun's new Kung Lung security station. Uncle Lu did not like Bo Ah-ran's itinerary either. He said, "It's dangerous to travel to the East, Bo Ah-ran. It's all right for you to go to Xian; Uncle Feng is there. His house is big, and his daughter-in-law is about your age. She will be good company for you. After Xian, you better go back home. There are a few young fighters out in the east. The most famous one is Gi Kon-jii, the grandson of the legendary *Dragon Knight*. This young man is about twenty and has great fighting skills. Even the famous Master Kac of Kaifeng was defeated when they had a friendly match. I heard that young Gi Kon-jii is on his way to the west. He said that he wants to have a duel with Master Lee and Master Hsu in Szechwan. He may even want to challenge Master Bo. If he meets you and finds out that you're Bo Kung Lung's granddaughter, he will surely want to fight you. You may win, or you may lose. Either way, Master Bo, at his age, would be forced to come out of his retirement."

One-eyed Yu said anxiously, "*Szechwan Dragon* and *Dragon Knight* were the two greatest masters thirty years ago. Master Bo told us again and again that we should not be conceited with our Kung Lung skills. Master Bo has repeatedly told us that anyone student of these two famous Dragons would easily defeat a hundred of us. Ah-ran, we better go home after Xian."

Uncle Lu said again, "There is something else I think that Master Bo should know. Customers from the East said that a young man with supreme swordsmanship is traveling northwest from the South. Someone speculated that he might be Chiang Shiao-ho. I assume that Shiao-ho must be a very skilled master now and will soon be on his way here to take his revenge on us."

Her eyes, so much like her Grandpa's, flashed anger. "Uncles, please don't worry. I'm going east to challenge that boastful grandson of *Dragon Knight*. As for the rebellious Chiang Shiao-ho, I'm going to find him and kill him." Bo Ah-ran raised her voice considerably. Her angry countenance and her brusque gestures made her look like a typical roughneck, not a docile young woman at all. Uncle Lu noticed One-eyed Yu's look of disapproval, and he signaled One-eyed Yu to say nothing more. Later he told One-eyed Yu, "It's no use to warn her anymore. She is spoiled, and she'll not listen to any advice.

Bo Ah-ran quietly saddled her horse at midnight and galloped along the well-used road to Xian. When she stopped for lunch, she drew curious attention to being a lone female rider carrying a weapon. She knew that there were only two more stops before Xian when she checked in at an inn for the night.

"Young lady, are you traveling to Xian all by yourself?" The inn attendant asked her. He noticed her two maiden-styled thick braids tied with red ribbons and knew that she was not married. Bo Ah-ran nodded.

She contemplated whether she should go to see Uncle Feng in Xian or not. She decided that she's not going to Uncle Feng's security station. *'I'd better go to Xian and find an inn to stay by myself. I'll do some sightseeing there and then go to the east. Further to the East, there won't be any Kung Lung security stations, and no one will advise me to go back home. I don't believe that young man Gi Kon-jii's skills are superior to mine. Chiang Shiao-ho's skills might be better. Maybe I will meet him there. I wonder whether we will recognize each other. Both of us are grownups now. He was tall, and now he must be even taller.'* Her eyes were moist. She also wondered if Shiao-ho's teacher found him a pretty wife already. *'If he is married, I don't want to see him, and I won't kill him, even if I could.'* She heard that the southern girls are petite and pretty with delicate features. Bo Ah-ran touched her large nose and looked down at her not-so-small feet, and sighed.

She came to a wide river with more than ten huge ferryboats crossing to and fro. "Excuse me. I want to go to Xian. Do I have to cross this river?" Bo Ah-ran asked someone standing beside a horse. "Yes. There is a boat ready to go now. You better hurry." The man sounded familiar. Bo Ah-ran recognized Uncle Lieu, who had left Chengba two years ago. Now he was a guard at Uncle Feng's security station at Xian. She tried to turn around, but it was too late.

Lieu was surprised to see her. "Ah-ran, who brought you here?"

She replied, "Uncle Lieu. It's my Grandpa's idea to let me come out to see the world. He ordered Uncle Yu to accompany me. At Han-Chun City, my father agreed with Grandpa's idea. But Uncle Lu insisted that I should go home soon. I don't want to go home, so I left Uncle Yu there. Grandpa suggested that I go to Kaifeng and Szechwan later."

Lieu was worried about Bo Ah-ran 's safety too. He watched her grow up to be an arrogant, conceited and willful young woman. So he did not argue with her but said agreeably instead, "Your Uncle Lu is just like your Grandpa. The older and the more skillful he is, the more cautious he becomes. With your excellent skills, you'll meet no equals anywhere. Let's go to Uncle Feng's first. I will ask Feng's permission to let me go with you. I want to see the world too." Bo Ah-ran said, "If I go to see Uncle Feng, will he stop me and send me home?"

Lieu laughed, "Who dares stop you? It's your Grandpa's idea and who dares not to obey. Uncle Lu is just too cautious."

The ferryboat docked. The passengers on board fought their way off, and more fought to get on. Uncle Lieu got them and their two horses on board. The flatboat was large enough to carry three carriages, five horses, and more than ten persons. A crew of five stood on the deck and sculled the slow-going boat.

"Uncle Lieu, Is it true that someone had met Chiang Shiao-ho?"

Instead of answering her, Lieu waved his hands slightly and tried to warn her not to talk about anything important in public. She did not understand the signal and said again, more or less to herself, "I'd like to challenge that famous grandson of the *Dragon Knight* after I beat Shiao-ho."

"My good niece, don't you enjoy the scenery and the boat ride? Do you see the flock of geese flying by?" Lieu tried to say something unimportant to make sure that Bo Ah-ran wouldn't say more. He noticed that everyone on the ferry was looking at her.

After the crossing, Lieu sighed, "My good niece, do you know anything about being cautious on the road? Who knows if that young man Gi Kon-jii wasn't on board with us?" Lieu looked around to make sure no one was following them.

Bo Ah-ran sneered, "So what! I hope that we would meet him. I will fight him right here. I left home to look for opponents to fight! You're as timid as Uncle Lu!"

Lieu tried to persuade her, "Ah-ran, be patient. We should find out the opponent's strength first and weigh our chances of winning before we fight. Also, we should enlist our friends' aid before the fight. Indeed you have great fighting skills, but you're a woman."

"If you don't stop talking nonsense, I will go to the East to fight that young man Gi Kon-jii and Chiang Shiao-ho alone."

Lieu said, "Chiang Shiao-ho is indeed our enemy. We could never forgive him for leading Master Hsu to fight us ten years ago. We have nothing against young Gi Kon-jii. If he does not provoke a fight with us first, we should leave him alone."

Bo Ah-ran looked around with wandering eyes. There were even some women on the street shopping. And there were tall, dark-complexioned men who wore white or black long robes with a lot of cloth wrapped around their heads. She even saw one tall man with yellow hair and skin as white as a dead fish's belly.

Lieu commented, "Xian is a big city; it had been the capital for many dynasties in the past, and it had many magnificent temples and palaces. There are many foreigners from other countries to the very west of us. They sure looked weird."

Feng Junior welcomed them warmly. He took Bo Ah-ran to the inner court to meet his mother and his wife. When Uncle Feng came in later, Bo Ah-ran stood up and said, "Uncle Feng! Greetings! You've grown a beard!"

Feng Zhi-pan smiled, "I'm an old man now, and you have grown tall. Master Bo and your father both agreed upon your journey to the east. We won't hold you back. Please stay with us for several days while I find someone familiar with the route to go with you."

"I don't need an escort. I've enough silver, and I've my Kung Lung saber to protect me."

Feng smiled, "Bravo! I heard that you want to challenge young Gi Kon-jii and Chiang Shiao-ho. I have no information about Chiang Shiao-ho's whereabouts. Gi Kon-jii is at Kaifeng. I've sent him an invitation. He will be here soon."

"Good! I'll wait. If I can beat him here, he will not dare go to Chengba to challenge Grandpa. Afterward, I'll go to the East to look for Chiang Shiao-ho. I hate him, and I'll kill him." She started to cry. Feng and his wife thought Bo Ah-ran was homesick, and they did their best to make her feel at home.

Lu Zhi-chun had arrived ahead of Bo Ah-ran and hid in another room. He complained that Master Bo was at fault for letting a young woman venture out alone. He told Feng, "I'm not worried about Chiang Shiao-ho at this moment since he might be dead. The pressing problem is Gi Kon-jii. He is *Dragon Knight's* grandson, and we are not his match. I followed Bo Ah-ran all the way here, and thank goodness there was no trouble on the road. Should we send someone to fetch her father? He can order his daughter home."

Feng Zhi-pan said, "I don't think so, Bo Ah-ran is very stubborn. I lied to her that I had invited young Gi Kon-jii to come so she would stay here and wait. My son and my daughter-in-law can take her around to do some sightseeing. She can visit many temples, and hopefully, she will not want to go to the East soon."

"It's better to get her father here. She has a bad temper, and who knows what trouble she will get if she stays. You know that she is not afraid of any one of us."

Feng laughed, "I don't think she is afraid of her father either. She is difficult, all right. I hope my docile and smart daughter-in-law can keep her interested in something domestic and keep her in."

Lu Zhi-chun said, "She won't stay in."

They were surprised that Bo Ah-ran did stay home a lot. She enjoyed the woman's company a lot. Her mother died when she was only fifteen. Besides a couple of old female servants, the only woman at home was her Aunt, who was older and was always sick. Now Bo Ah-ran enjoyed learning how to sew and how to cook. She daydreamed, '*If I can talk Shiao-ho out of revenge, then we will get married. I want to be a good wife.*" Her face got hot.

Every day she would ask, "When will that fellow Gi Kon-jii be here?"

"Soon."

On the ninth day, Feng Junior invited Bo Ah-ran to visit the famous pagoda sixteen miles south of Xian. He said, "Sister Bo, I'm taking my wife to the temple to burn incense and ask the deities there for blessings. Please come with us. We can visit the famous pagoda there. It was built during the Tong Dynasty almost a thousand years ago. In the temple, there were the bones of the first monk who went to India to bring back Buddhism. It's a place you must visit in Xian." Bo Ah-ran put on her favorite pink outfit. She insisted on riding her chestnut mare even though Feng Junior hired carriages for her, his wife, and a maid.

The seven-story tall pagoda stood at the center of a magnificent temple and had windows on each of its six sides. Bo Ah-ran walked around everywhere. She looked up and saw that people were looking down from the windows above. "Brother Feng, can we go up to the top floor of the pagoda?"

"Sure! Circular stairs are winding to the top level." He looked down at Bo Ah-ran 's feet first and continued, "Only you and I will go up. Your sister-in-law's feet are too small."

There were paintings, poems on the walls, and other displays on every level. Bo Ah-ran looked at them briefly as she climbed quickly. She could not read anyway. One Buddha statue sat in the center of the small area on the top level. A young scholar was writing a verse on the wall. Feng Junior did not know enough words to read the poem, but he recognized the signature: Lee Feng-jii from Beijing.

Bo Ah-ran noticed that the handsome young scholar's posture indicated good martial art training. The scholar finished the verse and picked up a sword with an iron handle and iron scabbard from a corner. He started to walk down. *'Ah! He must be a swordmaster and a pretty good one too,'* Bo Ah-ran thought, *'Look at his sword. Didn't Grandpa once warn me to beware of someone who carries a heavy sword like his? He said whoever has a plain-looking heavy sword must be very good at swordsmanship. I wonder how good he is.'*

She started to walk down, following the young scholar. Feng Junior called her, "Wait for me! What's the hurry?"

"Brother Feng, that young scholar knows martial arts very well. Did you see his sword? I want to know who he is."

He replied, "I don't think so. These bookworms always like to pretend that they are good at both the literary and the martial arts. To show off, they write verses everywhere and carry a sword. See his signature? Lee Feng-jii, I never heard of him. He is not famous." On their way back to town, they saw the scholar riding ahead. Bo Ah-ran believed that the young scholar must be one of the upstarts to challenge the Kung Lung School. She was determined to follow him.

Feng Junior was somehow jealous of the attention Bo Ah-ran paid to the young scholar. He said aloud, deliberately, "He simply wants to scare others with his sword!" When there was no response, Feng junior shouted in his usual bullying manners. "Hey, you! Stop! Who are you? What are you doing here?" When there was no reply, Feng Junior repeated it.

Lee Feng-jii turned around and shouted back, "None of your business."

"I want to know." Lee ignored him. Feng Junior quickened his pace, so the two horses almost touched each other. Reaching out his right hand, the stout Feng Junior intended to push the slender scholar off the horse. Instead, Lee Feng-jii pushed Feng Junior off his horse. Feng Junior unsheathed his Kung Lung saber and charged at Lee. Lee simply pierced Feng and rode away. Bo Ah-ran managed to get the injured Feng Junior back home.

Feng said, "We have to find him and fight him even if he has superior skills. He wounded my son. We have to fight him to even the score. We can't live with the shame. We must fight him to restore our reputation. Otherwise, who will ever buy our protection again?"

Lu Zhi-chun said, "Let us be patient and think of a perfect way to handle this. He indeed wounded my nephew, but the wound was only a surface wound. Lee Feng-jii could have cut off my nephew's arm, but he did not. We all know that only a superior fighter could hold back from inflicting serious injury and death. Master Bo told us to beware of two types of martial arts fighters we meet: monks or Tao priests and scholars. These two types would most likely have some special skills. The martial arts they have learned, the internal training that emphasized on *Chi-kong* (energy) are different from the external school we have learned from, and it is not easy to defend ourselves against them."

They found out where Lee was staying. Feng ignored Lu Zhi-chun's advice, led twenty-some armed guards to the inn where Lee Feng-jii stayed. Lu Zhi-chun disapproved of this course of action and stayed behind. He wondered, *'How can Feng Zhi-pan, Miu, and Pan be so gullible? They wanted to win by sheer numbers. The Lung brothers and these earlier students of Master Bo's are all bullies.'*

Feng warned everyone, "We will have a better chance of winning if we can surprise him." Lee was reading. Feng broke into the room through the paper window panels, chopped at Lee, and shouted, "You wounded my son today. My name is Feng Zhi-pan." Lee Feng-jii blocked Feng's saber, jumped out of the room, and fought the Kung Lung group. He shouted, "Your son is rude. He provoked the fight. Ah! Twenty to one! Shame on you!" In a short while, six members of the Kung Lung gang were wounded. From the roof, Lee shouted down, "I don't want to wound more of you." Bo Ah-ran jumped upon the roof and fought him. Lee Feng-jii blocked her attack and forced her back down.

Among the six Kung Lung casualties, five with minor wounds were servants and assistants. The one dead was Brother Miu, who had tried to slash Lee on the back. Miu and Feng had worked together for more than twenty years. Feng was sad at the loss and ashamed of the complete defeat.

Pan Zhi-sam said, "Let's see what he has written. We might get a clue." He thumbed through Lee's poems, and he yelled, "Ah! Lee Feng-jii is *Szechwan Dragon* Du's student." Feng said, "What? Didn't *Szechwan Dragon* pass away a long time ago? How could he teach a student in Beijing?"

Bo Ah-ran and the others all asked, "Who is this *Szechwan Dragon*?"

Two Swordmasters & Two Women

"*Szechwan Dragon* Du and *Dragon Knight* Gi were two superb masters thirty years ago. They were equally formidable and were known as the Two Dragons of Szechwan."

The news of those twenty Kung Lung members suffered a terrible defeat in the hand of one lone young scholar spread all over Xian. Feng preserved Miu's casket in a vault at a nearby temple so that all Master Bo's students and friends could have time to come to the funeral later.

Lu Zhi-chun arranged a duel with Lee Feng-jii. He said, "Mr. Lee, you've injured my nephew. You also killed one of my sworn brothers. We will have a duel tomorrow morning to settle the score."

Lee said, "The whole gang again! I do not want to wound more of you."

"Just you and me."

A crowd gathered around an empty field beside the Ba Bridge the next morning to watch the duel. Lu declared that he alone would duel with Lee Feng-jii, but Uncle Pan and the whole Kung Lung members, more than 30, ganged up on the lone Lee Feng-jii even before the duel. Lee Feng-jii wounded a few of them quickly and forced the rest of them to quit. Soon there were only Lu Zhi-chun and Bo Ah-ran. Both of them could not gain an inch. About ten passes later, Lee Feng-jii was just about to pierce Bo Ah-ran's shoulder, another short young man with a sword rushed in and blocked Lee's thrust. Two young men and two swords locked in a swift duel. Lee Feng-jii started to show signs of defeat, and he ran with the newcomer chasing him. The newcomer hit Lee's shoulder with the flat of his sword slightly and called a halt. Lee rode away, his face red. The new winner stopped Bo Ah-ran, who wanted to chase after Lee. "Miss, let him go. He knows he is beaten. So many of you fought one lone man. You're in the wrong. He is tired, and he is alone."

Lu Zhi-chun agreed, "It was supposed to be a duel between Lee Feng-jii and me. We should not have ganged up on one man. we have lost shamefully."

Feng thanked the young man and asked his name. The young man answered rather proudly, "I'm Gi Kon-jii. I'm *Dragon Knight* Gi's grandson."

"Master Gi, please come to our security station and let us thank you properly over drinks."

"Thanks. I'll be in town for three months. I'm sure we'll meet again." Gi Kon-jii stole a glance at Bo Ah-ran. Lu Zhi-chun noticed it and frowned.

"Where will you be staying, Mr. Gi?"

"At my uncle's shop temporarily."

On their way back to the station, Bo Ah-ran said, "Lee Fong-jii fought us a long time, and he was tired. I am going to find Lee Feng-jii and fight him alone. I also want to challenge that arrogant Gi Kon-jii." She did not want to admit, even to herself, that Uncle Lu had to help her to fight Lee, and that Lee almost wounded her. However, she cried when she was back in the woman's court. All the attendants and servants were subdued and quiet at Feng's security station.

Feng sighed, "What a shame! Our Kung Lung School's thirty-some year of good reputation is lost. One lone Lee Feng-jii killed and wounded twelve of our men in two days. If Gi Kon-jii had not come to our aid in time, we probably would have more casualties. How can we keep our security business going?"

Lu said, "It's no use to dwell on the defeat. In the world of martial arts, there will always be someone who will win. We still have to run our business and deal with our friends or enemies as the occasion arises. If and whenever Chiang Shiao-ho shows up, we'll have to fight him. That is more important."

Feng said, "Don't talk about that renegade. Right at this moment, I'm too ashamed to face anyone!"

Lu Zhi-chun sighed, "But I will say that Chiang Shiao-ho is the real problem. Gi Kon-jii's skills seemed to be superior to Lee Feng-jii's. Knowing that we were wrong to gang up on Lee, Gi Kon-jii still came to our aid. I'm convinced that young Gi Kon-jii is heroic in the heart. I suggest that we be friends with him. He could help us if Lee Feng-jii comes back for a fight, and he could also come to our aid whenever Chiang Shiao-ho comes back to seek revenge. What do you think?"

Feng disagreed adamantly, "I don't agree, and I don't think our proud Master Bo will agree either." Suddenly, his eyes lit up, "Wait! Gi Kon-jii could marry Bo Ah-ran. Didn't Master Bo send her out to see the world and to find herself a husband?"

"Gi Kon-jii is a good match. The only thing that bothers me is that Gi Kon-jii seems to be arrogant and showy. I have considered at first that Lee Feng-jii might marry her. That's why I wanted to duel with him to solve our differences. Anyway, Lee is very young, and he is also too scholarly to tolerate our ill-mannered and spoiled niece. Lee's family must be of the upper class, and he does not like Bo Ah-ran. Gi Kon-jii is a better match."

Feng said, "Gi Kon-jii is young, and he is entitled to be proud. I think Master Bo would be thrilled to have the famous Dragon's grandson in the family."

Lu Zhi-chun said, "Bo Ah-ran's father should be here soon. He could decide his daughter's marriage."

Feng said, "We don't have to wait for her father. We are her uncles. We could arrange her marriage."

Gi Kon-jii's uncle managed a small, crowded shop. Gi Kon-jii and a clerk had to sleep on a platform behind the counter after the shop closed. Gi Kon-jii was not happy about it. When Feng came to visit, they went to a teahouse where Feng inquired about Gi Kon-jii's family.

Gi Kon-jii told Feng, "My father passed away at a very young age. My grandfather, the one known as *Dragon Knight*, was disappointed with the constant killing and revenge business of the world of martial arts. He encouraged my father to study the literary arts only. Unfortunately, my father died right after he passed the second level of the civil services examination. Grandpa realized that merely studying literature arts would weaken the body. I'm his only grandson. He taught me both the literary arts and martial arts. He wanted me to have a strong body, and he also wanted me to make a living with martial arts if I failed the civil services examinations. I passed the first level of the examination but failed the second level twice."

Feng said, "I hope you'll stay in town longer so that we can get better acquainted. Master Bo, our teacher, will be here soon, I'm sure that he would like to meet you. You know that your fame has reached far." He continued, "We're all grateful for your help. Bo Ah-ran is Master Bo's granddaughter. She praised your superior skills and said that she would like to meet you and compare martial arts learning with you."

Gi Kon-jii said happily, "Really! Can I visit you soon?"

"Of course! You're most welcome. Come have supper with us."

Feng immediately ordered a banquet and a guest room to be prepared for Gi Kon-jii. Many guards from other stations came to visit, and he told them that he had met Gi Kong-jii before and that Gi Kon-jii's grandfather and Master Bo had been longtime friends. Most of the visitors had been at the duel, but they gracefully acknowledged Feng's face-saving boast.

Feng told Bo Ah-ran, "My good niece, Master Bo, and your father will be here soon."

Bo Ah-ran said, "Good. Grandpa and I will go to the East together, and I don't suppose that any of you dare to stop us from going." Then she asked, "Where is that little rooster Gi Kon-jii? Didn't he declare that he would like to challenge us? I'm ready and willing."

Feng smiled, "We should not listen to rumors. Gi Kon-jii wants to be our friend. He is an accomplished young fighter and a scholar, too. He's twenty-four years old, and his uncle has a shop here. I'm inviting him to stay with us for a while. I ask him to show us some of the legendary Dragon Knight's skills. He'll come to dinner tonight, and you'll have a chance to talk to him."

Bo Ah-ran pouted, "I don't want to talk to him."

" Ah-ran, now you're out to see the world, it's not necessary to stick strictly to Confucius's rules of propriety. It's all right for you to talk to Gi Kon-jii. His grandpa and your grandpa were old friends. You and he are almost like siblings, and it's appropriate for you two to get acquainted. Gi Kon-jii asked me about you, and I told him that you're Master Bo's granddaughter. He said right away, with admiration, 'no wonder you fight so well.'" Bo Ah-ran was happy to hear that. She shook her head, "No, I don't want to talk to him unless he would want to have a match with me. Grandpa had never mentioned that he knew some famous Dragon!" She noticed Uncle Feng was somewhat a braggart, just like his son.

"Yes, he did. You're too young to know."

Gi Kon-jii came to the station wearing a long formal robe, proper thick white-soled boots, and held an expensive scholar's fan in his hand. He tucked his sword, with the red silk cord, at the waist. It was custom to have a friend present when one invited an important person over for a formal dinner. Feng, Pan, Lu, and their friend Mr. Chu formally welcomed Gi Kong-jii to a spacious dining room. Gi Kon-jii looked around and was awed at the wealth on display. The intricately carved windowpanes, the polished heavy redwood and oak furniture, the exquisite table settings, and everything else he looked at told him that there was plenty of silver here. *'They are rich. Feng asked many questions about my family, and Bo Ah-ran wears her hair in two braids. She is not married. Am I dreaming that they want me to marry her? She is not very beautiful but not ugly either. Also, she is the first young woman I know that has excellent martial art training. We'll be a formidable team. I think I like the idea, yes. Indeed, I like it very much.'*

Gi Kon-jii said politely, "I did not expect to come to a formal dinner." Lu Zhi-chun thought, *'You sure did. You dressed for it.'*

Feng said, "This is our first meeting, and it should be formal. Later, when we see each other every day like a big family, there will be no more fussing."

Gi Kon-jii smiled and took off his long formal robe. He did not hesitate to take the seat of honor. He told them in detail about his famous grandfather's heroic deeds. He also told them how he won his duels with a famous sword master, Master Lin, and the well-known '*Tien Hsueh*' expert, Master Kac, at Kaifeng. When Feng asked him about Lee Feng-jii, he said, "I've heard a lot about him. Lee is also a scholar who failed the civil examination and that he is Szechwan Dragon's student. Lee Feng-jii indeed fights well with a sword, and he had accomplished quite a few heroic deeds in the East."

Feng said, "Brother Gi, it's all right that you didn't want to injure Lee Feng-jii and let him walk. Somehow we have to find him and fight him. He wounded my son and a few others and killed my sworn brother Miu. I've sent word everywhere to request aid from my friends. All of my sworn brothers will be here to attend the funeral of our deceased Brother Miu. We'll fight him again."

Gi Kon-jii thought, '*So you can gang up on him again.*' He said instead, "When the time comes, I'll help you."

Lu Zhi-chun asked, "Brother Gi Kon-jii when you were in the East, did you ever hear something about a young fighter by the name of Chiang Shiao-ho?"

"The name sounds familiar. What is this Chiang to you?"

Feng sneered, "Chiang is an enemy of our Kung Lung School. Someone told us that he had a great teacher. He might come to fight us."

Gi Kon-jii said, "When he comes to fight you, I will be on your side."

When Feng offered him the guest room for an extended stay, Gi Kong-jii accepted without hesitation. He was disappointed that Bo Ah-ran did not come out to meet him.

Lee Feng-jii moved out of the inn after he paid for the damaged window. He stayed at the library of one of his teacher Dragon Du's friends when he heard that Gi Kong-jii had moved in with the Kung Lungs. '*It is no fun and no purpose fighting with the Kung Lung gang and now Gi Kon-jii.*' He left Xian for the historical famous Middle Peak.

One afternoon when Bo Ah-ran back from her afternoon ride, she heard her Grandpa's booming laugh.

"Grandpa, you shouldn't have traveled in this heat!" Bo Ah-ran rushed to him.

"Bo Ah-ran, I'm so angry that Lee Feng-jii killed your Uncle Miu and ruined the good name of my Kung Lung School. I rushed here to challenge him. Where have you been? I don't like you going out alone."

"I went out for a ride. And I heard that coward Lee Feng-jii had run to the East, Grandpa."

Master Bo sighed, "Shame on us. Lee Feng-jii humiliated us, and we had to have Dragon Knight's grandson repel him for us," He continues, "I worry about you, you are so young, and you don't have any experience. Then your Uncle Yu came to fetch me. Ah-ran, you should listen to your uncles!"

"Grandpa, did you have lunch? I have not even had breakfast yet." Bo Ah-ran changed the subject.

"Greeting! Honorable Master Bo." Gi Kong-jii walked in.

The stout Master Bo stood up laboriously and greeted Gi Kon-jii, "Thank you for helping us, Mr. Gi Kon-jii."

Gi Kong-jii bowed low and said respectfully, "Please call me Kon-jii. It's my honor to meet you, Master Bo."

Master Bo talked noisily with Gi Kon-jii. The news of Master Bo's arrival spread, and many guards came to greet him. Some of them stayed for the inevitable banquet and listened to Master Bo's reminiscence of his past adventures and Gi Kon-jii's anecdotal stories of his grandpa, the famous *Dragon Knight*.

Master Bo told his pupils that he intends to arrange the marriage between Gi Kong-jii and Bo Ah-ran. Carrying out Master Bo's orders to be the middleman, Pan Zhi-sam talked to Gi Kon-jii over drinks in a tavern. Gi Kon-jii agreed readily.

Master Bo walked into Bo Ah-ran's room. She greeted her grandpa with a lovely smile, "Grandpa, it's so hot! Did you have a nap?"

"No, the heat does not bother me. I have not left home for twenty years. Now I'm out, and I feel young and energetic." He sat, stroking his white beard, and smiled, "Ah-ran! I've come to tell you the good news."

"Tell me. Are we going to the East soon?" Bo Ah-ran had not seen her grandpa so cheerful for a long time. She pouted, "Don't make me wait."

" Ah-ran, you remember how I told you to come out to see the world, and also to meet a suitable young man to marry? Now I think that young Gi Kong-jii is every bit qualified to be your husband. You'll marry him as soon as possible." Bo Ah-ran lowered her head cheerlessly with tears swimming in her eyes. She was just ready to protest when her grandpa continued, "Ah-ran, don't be shy. Listen, I have something to tell you, and it's for your ears only. You know that I'm getting old. Your father and all your uncles do not fight well. We have made countless enemies through the years, and now we have new ones. Lee Feng-jii's skills are superior to ours. If Gi Kong-jii had not come to our aid, the Kung Lung School would be finished. Besides, rumor has it that Master Hsu from Szechwan wants to challenge us again soon. If we cannot find someone with better skills to help us, we will soon be humiliated. This young Gi Kon-jii is good at both literary and martial arts. He may be a magistrate or even a governor someday. Besides his admirable skills, his family name is to our advantage too. I also think that his looks and his age are your matches. If I had such a young master to be my grandson-in-law, no enemies of ours would dare challenge us. Bo Ah-ran, I know it's a hasty decision." He looked at Bo Ah-ran with sad, old pleading eyes. Bo Ah-ran sobbed a while, and she tried a couple of times, but she could not tell her Grandpa that she loved Chiang Shiao-ho, a family enemy. Finally, she wiped her tears and agreed.

Master Bo said happily, "Good. I'm seventy-six now. Your future is a big worry on my mind, and now, even if I were to die this minute, I could breathe my last breath in peace knowing your future is settled."

Uncle Feng ordered an elaborate banquet for the announcement of their engagement. Gi Kong-jii kowtowed thrice to Master Bo and once to each uncle. The guests congratulated Master Bo and him in unison.

The jubilant Gi Kong-jii visited Master Bo and Uncle Feng's friends in Xian every day and thoroughly enjoyed his newly acquired affluence. On the contrary, the usually lively and boisterous Bo Ah-ran became quiet. She stayed in all the time now. Master Bo and the uncles did not pay too much attention to the sudden change. They thought that she was shy. The maids and Feng Junior's wife noticed that Bo Ah-ran wept often. They could not understand why she should be sad. It was a wonderful marriage. They talked about it, but none of them knew Bo Ah-ran's dilemma. They could not tell Master Bo and Feng about their concerns.

Bo Ah-ran missed her mother. She was too young to understand her feelings toward Chiang Shiao-ho before her mother died. But she believed that her mother knew, or at least guessed, about her feelings. Her mother often told Bo Ah-ran to be submissive and to accept what fate would bring. Bo Ah-ran recalled that once, she had argued with her mother about her uncle's abusive behavior. Her mother said something like this, *'We, women, are expected to be submissive. Anyway, we have very little say about our future, and about the way we live. Many women carried their dreams to their graves.'*

Lu Zhi-chun sensed that Bo Ah-ran was not happy about the marriage. More than once, he noticed that Bo Ah-ran was both sad and angry whenever someone mentioned Shiao-ho's name. He wanted to talk with Bo Ah-ran, but he knew he had no right and no way to question Master Bo's decision. Besides, it's not proper for him to talk to a grown-up niece alone.

Most of Master Bo's students came to attend the funeral of Brother Miu whom Lee Feng-jii killed. Bo Zhi-an lamented the death of his sworn brother but rejoiced at his daughter's good marriage.

The evening after the funeral, they all sat around a big banquet of four tables. Master Bo, his elder son, the young couple, two guests, Feng and his wife, sat at the head table. After a couple of rounds of toasts, Lu Zhi-chun expressed his concerns about the possible confrontation with Lee Feng-jii and Master Hsu of Szechwan.

Gi Kong-jii declared with a toast, "Toast! Grandpa and Uncles, please let me handle Master Hsu and Lee Feng-jii. I'm confident that my sword will repel them both and any other enemies. Bo Ah-ran and I will glorify the name of Kung Lung School."

"Bravo! Let's drink to that!" Uncle Feng stood up and cheered aloud, "Let all of us respectfully propose three toasts to Master Bo, two toasts to Brother Bo, the father of the bride, and one Toast each to the young couple."

"Congratulations! Good Fortune!" Everyone stood and joined the jubilee. The beaming Master Bo accepted the full cup from Feng, emptied it promptly for Feng to fill it again.

Lung Zhi-chi, the one who killed Chiang Shiao-ho's father, came in with his traveling clothes covered with dust. "Teacher, I have urgent news…"

Master Bo stood up nervously and demanded, "What? Tell me!"

Lung Zhi-chi took out an envelope and said somewhat disjointedly, "It… It's Chiang Shiao-ho! I got a letter from him. He is on his way here to avenge his father's death." Pounding the table, Master Bo demanded, "Read it to me."

Uncle Pan read it aloud, "This letter is to ask the Lung brothers of Zie-Yin City to notify Master Bo of Chengba my intention of revenge. I, Chiang Shiao-ho, have not let a single day pass by without having the bitter memory of your cruel killing of my father. Ten years ago, I was too young and too weak to resist your treachery and almost died at your hand. Now I'm grown, and I'm confident that I can complete my revenge. You killed my father, split my family, and exploited my youth. Except two, the rest of you Kung Lung gang are all my enemies. This letter is to warn you that I'm on my way and offer you ample time to prepare your defense against me. I promise that I will only kill my father's murderers. Signed, Chiang Shiao-ho." Pan noticed that the writing was rough, and the words were simple. A hired letter writer did not write it. Chiang Shiao-ho probably wrote it himself.

Master Bo's face turned from deep red to a deathly pale. Gi Kong-jii unsheathed his sword and pounded the tabletop with it. He yelled, "Grandpa and Uncles, I beg you not to worry. I don't think too highly of that damned Chiang Shiao-ho. I promise you that I'll slay him within five sword strokes!" Only a few applauded. Everyone was nervous.

"Who delivered this letter?" Uncle Lu asked.

"An herb merchant from the South. He told me that Chiang Shiao-ho had made quite a name for himself there along the Yangtze River. Someone said that Chiang Shiao-ho might challenge Gi Kon-jii."

Gi Kon-jii sneered, "Not Bad! He knows my name! I'll teach him a lesson with my sword." He was puzzled to see Ah-ran's expression and could not tell whether she was angry or sad. Bo Ah-ran left with an excuse that she had a stomachache. Watching her melancholy retreat, Master Bo suddenly remembered a trivial incident more than ten years ago. He remembered a snowy night when the fourteen-year-old Shiao-ho dueled with the twelve-year-old Bo Ah-ran. On that cold, snowy night, Chiang Shiao-ho failed in his first revenge attempt, and Ah-ran tried to punish him. Master Bo had kept Shiao-ho at his home as a servant for a while and even contemplated letting him marry Bo Ah-ran with the hope that the animosity between the two families would be resolved. But his son abused Shiao-ho, and the boy fled. Master Bo pulled his thoughts back to the present with an effort and wondered whether Gi Kong-jii could fend Chiang Shiao-ho off. The sorrow, the worry, the drinking, and the heat finally got to him, Master Bo collapsed. He came to a while later and told his anxious pupils, "I'm fine. Don't be afraid of Chiang Shiao-ho. When he comes, I'll meet him and let him kill me only to settle the score. All of you, please listen carefully to my words of advice: don't ever be too ruthless, be kind to your opponents, lest you have regrets in your old age. You're still young. Please take my words to heart." He turned his head to face Gi Kon-jii, "You're my future grandson-in-law and one of my families. I want you to hear what I have to say. If Chiang Shiao-ho comes before my death, let me face him alone. If he comes after my death, promise me that you will reason with him politely before fighting him. Otherwise..."

Gi Kon-jii interrupted, "Grandpa, you worry too much! Chiang Shiao-ho can't be so omnipotent, can he? Could his teacher's skills be superior to the *Szechwan Dragon's* and my grandfather's? I don't think so."

Master Bo sighed deeply, "You are all too young to know that thirty years ago, the two Dragons were called the two Zeniths in the world of martial arts. *Dragon Knight* and *Szechwan Dragon* Du retired suddenly at the same time. Not many people knew why. The truth is that there is another master, superior to both the Dragons, who would punish the two haughty Dragons and Steel Rod Monk at will with his phenomenal skills. I was young and had full capabilities, I was defeated completely when I met this short scholar. You may not believe, but I, Bo Kung Lung, was as powerless as an ant in front of him..."

"Is he Chiang Shiao-ho's teacher?" Gi Kong-jii asked anxiously.

Master Bo sighed, "If Chiang Shiao-ho had any other teacher, I wouldn't have been worried and scared to death for all these years."

Uncle Feng told everyone what happened ten years ago when the old Scholar rescued Shiao-ho. He had seized Feng's extra heavy Kung Lung saber with two fingers and broke it into pieces with one foot. Uncle Feng's voice shook as he vividly remembered the humiliation he suffered that day.

Total silence. Finally, Gi Kong-jii said, "Grandpa, you don't have to fight him yourself. Let me go to the East to meet him." He continued, "But I do not know him. I want to go with someone who knows him well enough to point him out to me." Old Bo decided that Uncle Chen, who knew Shiao-ho very well, and the One-eyed Yu would accompany Gi Kong-jii on his mission to seek Chiang Shiao-ho. Master Bo and Bo Ah-ran would go to Lu Zhi-chun's guard station at Da-Sam Fort to wait.

6

It was a hot summer, and the Yellow River puffed out hot steam. The thick forest and a clear creek at the foot of the Middle Peak had kept the unbearable heat away. Lee Feng-jii had a room at the White Pin Temple. He was a born poet. His great-grandfather was a high-ranked official of the Ming Dynasty and died fighting the Manchu. So his grandfather and father were all very good at literary arts but vowed never to work for the invaders, the Chin Dynasty. Lee Feng-jii's father and mother died when Lee was only three years old, and his baby brother was one. Lee was twelve years old when his uncle abused them. His older brother and Lee Feng-jii left home with a trusted servant. Not far from Beijing, the bandits killed his brother and the servant. When they tried to rape him, Lee Feng-Jii struggled wildly. An old Tao priest came, '*Tien Hsueh*' *(*attack vital points*)* the bandits, and took Lee Feng-jii to Beijing.

The Tao priest taught Lee Feng-jii martial arts and literary arts. He died two years later. At his death, He gave Lee a manual of advanced Martial Arts, some silver certificates, and told Lee Feng-jii that he was Szechwan Dragon Du and said, "I did not get the silver the honorable way, but I want you to use it wisely. My Teacher was a renegade Tao Priest from Wu-Ton Mountain. I had bad company, so I did a lot of senseless killing. I want you to remember that there always is someone who has better skills than you. Don't ever be conceited. Thirty years ago, a short scholarly-looking super master caught me in my atrocity act, punished me severely, and forced me to retire. Five years ago, Steel Rod Monk chased me out of Szechwan. I want you to be a kind person. You could disable your enemies but maim and kill them only when it is unavoidable."

Szechwan Dragon Du only taught Lee the rudiments of the '*Tien Hsueh*' technique. He said, "'*Tien Hsueh*' is a deadly technique. Not many people know how to do it, and the one who knows how to do it eventually will make more enemies. I'll only teach you the basics; you can use it to cure the sick and, if necessary, to make a living. Of course, you also need to know enough to avoid being killed or crippled by someone who knows '*Tien Hsueh.*'"

On this beautiful summer morning, Lee wandered down the hill to the almost finished rooms that he and a half-witted man nicknamed Big Fool had built. In two days, he would marry the maiden he had rescued from some roughnecks. Her widowed grandma was dying, and she wanted to see her granddaughter married to Lee right away. Lee heard the pleasant sounds of a bell. A small bell tied to a horse's neck, and the rider was a tall young man with a heavy long sword. '*This is no ordinary temple worshipper. and I bet he is very good at martial arts.*'

It was lunch hour. Big Fool pointed to a huge bundle of firewood, "I sold the first one and bought some meat. Stay here and have Lunch with us." Big Fool was a good son to his blind and crippled mother.

The tall young rider whom Lee had seen earlier came down from the temple. He seemed to be lost.

"Friend, can I help you? It's easy to get lost around here." Lee Feng-jii asked.

"Yes, friend! Can I ride down the valley on this narrow path?"

"It's too rocky and narrow for a horse. Friend, there are few houses down there. Are you looking for someone?"

"I am looking for an older scholar living in this mountain. My Teacher asked me to deliver a letter to him."

"You can keep your horse here and pick it up later."

"Thanks. How do I address you?"

"Lee Feng-jii. What's yours?

"Chiang Shiao-ho." The name sounded familiar.

"I'm from Beijing. Brother Chiang, you talk like a Southerner." Lee asked.

"Brother Lee, I'm originally from the North, and I've been in the South for ten years."

"You carry a heavy sword; you must be very good at martial arts. Who's your teacher?"

"My teacher is an old scholar from the South."

Lee thought, '*So you do not want to tell me your teacher's name yet, I will not impose.*' Chiang said, "Brother Lee, I know it is odd, but I do not know my teacher's name. He does not talk much. I lived with him for ten years, but he never told me his name."

Ten years ago, the old scholar saved Shiao-ho from the Kung Lung gang. The old scholar applied the '*Tien Hsueh*' technique to stop the boy's bleeding and put the boy to sleep on the horse's back, and he walked. He bought some herbs and treated Shiao-ho's multiple wounds at night in the inns they stayed on their long journey south. They crossed the mighty Yangtze River and finally reached the old scholar's home in a deep recess on the high Joe-hue Peak. A few acres of tea crops surrounded a small house. A mute kept the house and tended the tea trees.

The mute could not talk, and the old scholar never did tell Shiao-ho a thing about his identity, but Shiao-ho knew that the old scholar possessed the highest martial arts skills. Shiao-ho was determined to learn well, but the kind old scholar did not teach him any martial arts. At first, he merely ordered Shiao-ho to gather firewood and to tend the tea crops. Half a month later, he told Shiao-ho to collect rocks, small or big, from near or far. Shiao-ho worshipped his Teacher, and he was so grateful that he would do anything to please him. His teacher gave him a place to live, to have plenty of rice and fish to eat, and decent clothes to wear. After his father's death, it was the first time Shiao-ho was safe and had a home. His Teacher had never once lost the patience to listen to Shiao-ho's telling of his tragic past. Somehow, Shiao-ho did not tell him about Bo Ah-ran. He was shy. His father was killed for his trouble with a woman. Shiao-ho was afraid that his Teacher would condemn him and not accept him anymore if he told him his strong feelings for Bo Ah-ran.

He obediently gathered rocks and considered it a test like lifting the steel rod at Master Hsu's place. He had muscular arms from his blacksmith training, and in two months, he almost cleared the surrounding areas of rocks and piled them mountain high behind their hut. The old scholar, sometimes with the mute, would leave the peak for days. Shiao-ho had never been lazy when there was no supervision.

When his teacher saw the two high piles of rocks, he told Shiao-ho to empty them. "Shiao-ho, get rid of all the rocks in ten days. Ten Days! Don't throw them in the ravine. Don't block the creek and the mountain paths." Now Shiao-ho could hold two huge rocks in his hands or two baskets full of smaller ones and carried them to the top of the mountain quickly. He worked hard and completed his mission in less than seven days.

The old scholar praised him, "Good, you have a strong mind, and you have the determination to succeed. I will teach you now." The first things he taught Shiao-ho were 'breathing and concentration' and some simple boxing and jumping exercises. He stayed home for a year and a half to teach Shiao-ho, and he also taught him how to read and write.

For jumping exercise, he ordered the boy to hop up the high peak or down to the deep ravine at all hours. In the beginning, besides teaching and demonstrating, his Teacher often worked out with Shiao-ho, his movement was ever so graceful, and Shiao-ho tried to emulate him. When the tea flowers were blooming in the spring, he wanted Shiao-ho to catch butterflies alive and not damage any flowers and leaves. The exercise Shiao-ho liked the best was to catch small finches alive and then set them free.

At the beginning of the third year, he handed Shiao-ho a boxing stylebook and walked the boy through all the steps a few times before leaving for a long trip. Shiao-ho stayed behind, and he practiced diligently. The forms and styles were not many but very difficult. A few months later, Shiao-ho found that he could block and defeat the boxing styles that he had learned from his father and Uncle Ma very easily with this new form. *'It's just great. Now I can beat the Kung Lung students in boxing.'*

His Teacher came back and handed Shiao-ho an extra heavy sword and a few books on swordsmanship. He ordered Shiao-ho to memorize the instructions by day and practice at night. Shiao-ho could recite every line in less than a month, and then the old scholar took the books back and left again.

Shiao-ho continuously practiced by memory arduously regardless of whether his Teacher left home with the mute or not. Every month or two, the old scholar would check up on Shiao-ho's progress or correct his mistakes. He also urged Shiao-ho to practice swimming in the ice-cold mountain creeks at all hours. In the eighth and the ninth year, the old scholar stayed home to teach Shiao-ho *'Tien Hsueh'* and other sophisticated skills. He also taught Shiao-ho geography with a map. Sometimes Teacher and student would have a long discussion about any subject. He treated Shiao-ho as an equal and encouraged Shiao-ho to express his ideas. They also talked about ethics and the code of behavior. Shiao-ho learned the value of morality and good manners first from Master Hsu when he was in Szechwan and now from this great Teacher. He learned self-respect and also the value of genuine respect for others. His Teacher seemed to be pleased with Shiao-ho's progress.

Shiao-ho thought about his family and Bo Ah-ran often. In the first two years, Shiao-ho often cried when he thought about his unspeakable sufferings at the hand of Master Bo and his son. The old scholar always listened and let him cry and talk and then consoled him. When he got older he was ashamed of shedding tears in front of his Teacher and the mute. He would go up the high peak or go down the deep ravine to let out his grief. He wept when he thought about his mother's soft hands and her singsong voices to lure him to sleep at night. He grated his teeth when he remembered the abuses he had endured at Master Bo's place. The few trees on the high peak would shake their leaves, and the grass spurting between the rocks would weave to accompany his ranting. The creek in the deep gorge would also sigh along with his heart-wrenching yell or soft sobs. The wildflowers would look extremely pretty through his tears when he thought about Bo Ah-ran. Somehow his Teacher and the mute knew that he had been sad and they would be extra nice to him. The Mute would give him some delicacies to eat. He liked the way the Mute ruffled his hair and his Teacher's soft tone.

Three months ago, the old scholar asked Shiao-ho, "You've been with me for ten years now. Do you think you have learned well enough to face your enemies now?"

He was anxious to go home and to fight the Kung Lung s, Shiao-ho replied, "Teacher, I believe that I have learned well all of the skills that you have."

"Oh! No. Far from it. You may have learned almost one-half of my skills, less than the Mute. He is your classmate, your brother. He probably has learned sixty percent of my skills."

Shiao-ho broke out in a cold sweat. He could not believe that the Mute knew any sophisticated martial arts skills. He thought, *'Ah! The mute. It seems to me that he can't even move a heavy rock.'* He sat rigidly in awe when he thought, *'I am too blind to see it. Didn't the mute carry huge bags of rice and walk up the mountain so fast that I had to do my best to follow him? Didn't we always have wild birds he caught to eat? Didn't he always catch more fish when we fish together? And didn't…'* He heard his Teacher said, "Shiao-ho, you're right. He is highly skilled. He is your big brother and a good example of modesty for you to emulate. We, the Wu-Ton School of martial arts, concentrate on inner strength and mind training. We strive for harmony and moderation, not the outward show of skills and strength. In your case, it calls for some allowances. You have suffered so much at a young age, and you're entitled to avenge your father's death. Listen carefully to my instructions: First, you can only kill your father's murderers, and you must harm no others. I prefer that you forgive them, but I know it will be difficult for you to forgive and forget. They did mistreat you. Second, you can challenge other martial arts masters for a match so you can learn different skills, but you must not injure your opponent needlessly. If you must fight your enemies, you can only maim or kill when it is inevitable. Third, you have to help the weak and subdue the evil. You have to help the young and old and women. In a word, martial arts skills are designed to protect you and enable you to help others, NOT for self-indulgent material gains and fame. You may meet some other warriors of Sho-Lin School and Wu-Ton School of martial arts. Treat them as your brothers. A monk from India founded the Sho-Lin school, and Wu-Ton School's founder was the legendary Taoist Chang, and we're a branch of the Wu-Ton School. Both schools emphasize internal strength training for self-defense and obtaining harmony. The inner strength increases our capacity of endurance and also our capacity to resist the temptations of greed and other harmful desires. Remember my words well and OBEY them. You can leave any time. You have the gold and silver you had before, and I'll give you some more and a letter of credit for you to get silver from some tea companies doing business with us. There are frequent natural disasters in the North; you can help them with some silver and also Uncle Ma and others in need."

Shiao-ho knelt and begged, "Can I stay with you longer to learn more?"

The old scholar laughed, "Oh, no! If you learn more, no one could curb you. Now you can defeat the two Dragons at will if they were still alive. Master Bo will be an infant in your hands. All the others, they are less than worms to you. Are you not satisfied? I would have let you leave a few years earlier, but you were young, and your enemies, the Kung Lung, are strong. Now is the time for you to go out into the world to start some real learning. You better leave soon. I hope you will forgo your revenge. But I also know that you will have to do what you think is right for you. I suggest that you inform Master Bo of your intention of revenge ahead of time so that he could be prepared. He might have repented and changed."

Shiao-ho kowtowed thrice to his Teacher, once to the mute, and started going down the mountain. Half a *lee* (about one-half mile) later, the mute soundlessly appeared in front of the startled Shiao-ho. The mute handed him two letters for him to deliver. Then the mute smiled and rubbed his chin, pointed two fingers skyward, and shook his head vigorously. It meant his Teacher forbade him to use the deadly '*Tien Hsueh*' technique. He nodded. The Mute taught Shiao-ho a round of swords fighting styles, which Shiao-ho had not yet learned.

It was late spring, and many peasant girls worked hard in the fields. Shiao-ho thought about Bo Ah-ran. He wondered if Bo Ah-ran was married already and whether she forgot all about their innocent pledge of marriage under the big willow tree. He thought about his mother and speculated about how tall his baby brother had grown. He was happy that he could read and write, could now fight well with superior martial arts skills. He also had silver, and he was not the same destitute orphan boy of ten years before. He regretted that he did not tell his Teacher about Bo Ah-ran, and he almost doubled back up the peak, but he was shy, and so he didn't.

A huge boat took him across the mighty Yangtze River to Nanjing on the north bank, and he delivered one letter. Then Shiao-ho bought a horse and hung a small silver bell to the horse's neck. Master Hsu had given him this silver bell ten years ago when they were on their way to challenge the Kung Lungs. '*I was so hopeless after Old Bo had wounded Master Hsu. All the Kung Lung members wanted to kill me, and luckily I met my Teacher, and here I am.*' Shiao-ho was so happy and wanted to sing. '*I wonder if I could lift the heaviest steel rod at Master Hsu's place with ease now.*' He smiled because he knew he definitely could. However, his heart ached when he thought, '*What am I going to say to Bo Ah-ran that I will kill her grandpa.*'

On his way to the North, Shiao-ho had won many friendly matches with well-known martial arts masters. He heard about Lee Feng-jii, and he wanted to meet him someday. At Kaifeng, he defeated the famous '*Tien Hsueh*' Master Kac, and he also met his old friend Nan who had helped Shiao-ho a lot when Shiao-ho was in Szechwan ten years ago.

"Shiao-ho! I know that you have suffered gravely at the hands of the Kung Lung gang, but I would not like to see you become relentless and bitter. You know that harboring hatred and thoughts of revenge can only bring us sorrow in the end. I hope you can forgive that Old Bo; he must be almost eighty now." Nan advised him.

A sudden summer shower came when Lee Feng-jii tried to fix an old table.

"Ahe! Ahe! Master Lee Quick... help!" Big Fool shouted.

Lee rushed outside and saw, through the mist of the curtain-like heavy rain, a woman with a baby in her arm and a little girl was falling fast to the ravine from the slippery winding path above. It was a hopeless situation. Then a huge form flew through the mist, Big Fool yelled, "Ahe!" Chiang Shiao-ho, holding the woman and baby in one arm, the girl in the other, landed in front of Lee's hut. Lee Feng-jii was speechless, and the little girl was too scared to cry.

"Brother Chiang, Your martial arts skills are super!" Lee Feng-jii said.

"My classmate the Mute and I did something like this kind of rescue before. Brother Lee, I have a super teacher. But I don't know his name. He did not tell me himself and my classmate is mute."

Lee thought, '*So, he is not conceited. He had not many people to talk to for ten years. No wonder.*'

It was dark and cold. Lee took out some silver and asked Big Fool to buy some supper. Chiang Shiao-ho watched the rain and frowned.

"Brother Chiang, it's raining hard. Let's talk and drink all night long, how about it? I'd like you to stay for my wedding, the day after tomorrow."

"Thanks, but I'm anxious to go to Xian."

"You won't go far today in the rain. It may be clear tomorrow, and you can ride fast."

There was a rough bench and a table in the grass hut. Shiao-ho and Lee Feng-jii sat on the warm *kon (bed)*, drank in turn from a cracked bowl, and ate peanuts and coarse rice balls.

Lee said apologetically, "I did not know you'd be here today. I sent Big Fool to get us some supper."

"Brother Lee, this is good enough for me. Besides the old Scholar and the Mute. I have been alone for a long time. I'm glad to have a friend. Ahe! It's warm and comfortable sitting on the *kon* (bed) during a rainy day like today. I've been in the South too long. I almost forgot about the warm *'kon.'* It's warmer down South, and we don't need it."

"It's the first time I let the hot air and the smoke from the kitchen fire go through the hollowed-out part of it. The earthen *'kon'* actually is cool in the summer and warm in the winter. We must have some very clever ancestors to build it. Brother Chiang, you don't look like a Southerner to me. You are too tall. Where do you come from?"

"You're right. I'm not a Southerner. I came from Chengba Town, at the south end of the Shaanxi Province."

Lee was startled. "You're Master Bo's neighbor. You know some Kung Lung members."

Shiao-ho pounded the table so hard that the wine spilled. "Don't mention that Bo Kung Lung," he continued, "Brother Lee, ten years ago, I stabbed Lung Zhi-tin, one of the old Bo's students. I was fourteen."

"What? So you're not on friendly terms with the Kung Lung guards."

"Not! Besides Uncle Ma and Uncle Lu, the Kung Lung members are my enemies. My father was Master Bo's student. Master Bo and the Lung brothers killed my father and forced my mother to remarry. That's why I did not want to stay here too long. I want to complete my revenge quickly. I did not go to Chengba directly because I want Master Bo to hear about me first. I sent him a letter. I want him to be prepared and to gather all his students and friends to his aid. I don't like the others to think that I'd take advantage of Bo's being an old man without any help."

"I fought the Kung Lung gang alone in Xian last month. I killed one of Master Bo's students and wounded six or seven others. Indeed, I did not fight Master Bo himself, but I have fought Feng and Lu. They do not fight well, and their so-called Kung Lung saber system is clumsy. The only ones that count are Gi Kong-jii and a young woman."

"A young woman? What's her name?" Shiao-ho asked anxiously.

"I don't know, but I'm sure she is one of them. She fights better than all of the other Kung Lung members."

"How old is she? What does she look like? What is her hairstyle?"

"Come on, Brother Chiang, I did not pay close attention, and I was too busy fighting all of them. I guess she is about twenty-something. She had a scarf on. I couldn't tell whether her hair was in braids or not. But I do know she is conceited and obnoxious." Lee Feng-jii told Shiao-ho what had happened between him and the Kung Lung gang. Shiao-ho gulped down the wine fast. *'It must be Bo Ah-ran.'*

It rained even harder. Shiao-ho said, "Rain or shine, I must leave tomorrow."

Lee Feng-jii agreed with sympathy, "A son must revenge. A son must avenge a father's death. I can see that you're eager to go. I want to fight Gi Kong-jii again; I'll go with you."

"How could you? You're getting married. If you want to go after Gi Kon-jii, you better wait until I have finished my business. You see, if we go there together, no one will say that I could win without your help."

Shiao-ho browsed a page of one of Lee Fong-jii's anthologies.

"Brother Chiang, do you like poetry?" Lee asked.

"No. My teacher taught me how to read and write simple stuff. I only know enough words to get me by. I want to learn more. It's vital to know more words."

Lee said, "There are benefits of knowing how to write. I don't want to be a security guard fighting roughnecks, and I don't want to be an official working for the Manchu, the Chin Dynasty, either. I make a living with writings. I write deeds for the locals, copy lists of herbs for the doctors, and religious doctrines and prayer scrolls for the monks and Tao priests. There are many temples around here."

"My late father did that. Uncle Ma, my father's sworn brother, raised me after my father's death, and he taught me the trade of blacksmith. I guess later, I can be a blacksmith. But, first, I have to take care of the business of revenge." They talked more about the eccentric Master Bo. Shiao-ho told Lee that Master Bo had defeated the conceited Master Hsu. Lee thought, *'Master Bo defeated the famous Master Hsu. He must be a hundred times better than his students. I wonder whether Shiao-ho can match up to the old but experienced Master Bo, with Gi Kong-jii and that young woman to help him.'*

A neighbor told Lee that Big Fool was in trouble in the village, and Lee took an umbrella and went to get Big Fool home.

It stopped raining. Shiao-ho went out for a walk around the seemingly deserted village because of the cold rain. His mother always told him stories on a rainy day to keep him in. The memory of it made his chest hurt, and he silently renewed his oath of revenge. '*I just have to kill the old Bo, but what will Bo Ah-ran do?*'

An old man pointed to a shabby hut nearby and said, "Miss Chen lives there with her grandma. Her father was a hunter. He died two years ago from a fall. Now, Master Lee will marry her, and everything will be fine."

"Master Lee is a good man," Shiao-ho said. Then he suddenly thought that he should at least buy Lee Feng-jii a wedding present. On the way to a nearby town, Shiao-ho thought about what gift he should buy. He could not buy any cosmetics since he knew nothing about it, and it was also not proper for him to buy anything for the bride. He could not buy books for Lee either because he did not know the words enough to buy a good book. Finally, he decided that he would buy some chickens. Lee could use them for the wedding feast or raise them.

Chiang Shiao-ho bought two fat hens and one rooster. He saw a lively gander stand tall in a cage, Shiao-ho liked the look of it and bought it as a sign that Lee would have a strong boy soon. '*There must be some snakes in the hill, a goose will eat the small snakes, and it can also guard the yard.*'

He tied the chicken, their legs and wings bound up, to his saddle. Because the goose's legs were too short, Shiao-ho had to hold the struggling animal with one hand and rein with the other. The noisy birds made the horse jittery, and it was hard going through the crowd. A short dark form moved out of a corner. The startled horse bolted and galloped away with the chickens. Shiao-ho jumped free, holding the bellicose goose.

It was a short monk, wearing a cone-shaped straw rain cape. He stood there and laughed at Shiao-ho, holding tight to a flapping and honking goose.

"What's the matter with you? Don't laugh! You scared my horse away! Ah! You know how to '*Tien Hsueh.*'" The short man swiftly closed in and suddenly pointed his two fingers at Shiao-ho. Shiao-ho pushed the Monk away. The Monk fell onto the muddy street.

"You! Get up. Wait!" The Monk looked familiar, "Do I know you?"

"I know you, too! You are a renegade. Master Hsu did not want to teach you and..." The short Monk ran away when someone led Shiao-ho's horse back to him. Chiang Shiao-ho tried to remember where he met the Monk. Lee and the indignant Big Fool were at home when he got there.

Lee said, "Ah. Did you buy chickens? Thanks."

"These are your wedding presents. Is your big friend here alright?"

Lee laughed, "He is big, isn't he? Call him Big Fool; he doesn't mind. He beat up someone. He got beaten up too. Anyway, we brought supper home."

"I met a nasty short monk in town. He attacked me." Shiao-ho said.

"A monk from the White Pine Temple uphill?"

"I don't think so. This monk knew me, and I think I knew him from the past too. But I can't remember who he is. He fights well, and he also knows '*Tien Hsueh.*'"

"He knows '*Tien Hsueh*?' That's strange. Besides my teacher and Gi Kon-jii grandpa, Master Kac of Kaifeng, I do not know anyone else who knows '*Tien Hsueh*.' I only learned some of the basics to cure but not enough to fight. Gi Kong-jii did not use it, so I don't think he knew how to. I wonder who else knows this deadly technique." Shiao-ho did not want to tell Lee that there was even more secret, more advanced, and more deadly skills unknown to the masses.

Big Fool ate and drank with them and asked for some food to bring back to his mother. Lee lit a makeshift oil lamp.

"A toast, Brother Chiang. I'm glad to know you. You're highly skilled, and you're modest, not like that braggart Gi Kong-jii who tells just about anyone how great his grandpa was. The Kung Lung guards are even worse. I can't understand how they earned their name."

The mentioning of the Kung Lung gang saddened Shiao-ho. He thought, *'That young woman Lee told me about must be Bo Ah-ran. Is she married? Does she hate me? I'll be sad if she is married, but somehow I'll let it go. But if she is not married yet, it will be a dilemma for me. How can I want to kill her grandpa and, at the same time, want to marry her? What can I do?'* He sighed, pushed his drink away, and said, "Brother Lee, I can't drink anymore. Tomorrow I'll go even if it pours. I may not live up to my act of revenge."

"Why? If you think you are not Gi Kong-jii and Master Bo's match, I will go with you and help you. The wedding can wait."

"Ten Bo Kung Lung, sixteen Gi Kon-jii, I can beat them all. There is something else, in some way, connected with the revenge that has worried me all these years. It's more difficult than killing my father's murderers."

"Tell me your problem. I'd like to help, I lost my older brother years ago, and I'd like to have you as a brother."

Shiao-ho said happily, "I'd like that very much. I'll be twenty-five soon."

"I'm twenty-two now. So you are an elder brother, and I'm a younger brother."

Chiang Shiao-ho almost blurted out that Bo Ah-ran was also twenty-two.

They recited a simple oath of brotherhood on their knees, and then they kowtowed once to the sky, once to the earth, and once to each other. At last, Shiao-ho stood solemnly to receive Lee's, the younger brother's, kowtow.

"I'm glad that we do not have to drink the ceremonial wine mixed with our blood. Sincerity is good enough. I have a younger brother. Although I've not seen him for eleven years, I'll tell him to honor you."

"I also have a younger brother at home, and he should be nineteen now. I have not seen him since the day I ran away from my abusive uncle, and my late teacher saved me. We have a lot in common."

"Now that we are sworn brothers, I don't want to keep anything from you. But I can't tell you my trouble in a few words, and I don't believe you can help me even if you knew. I promise I will tell you the whole truth later. Please forgive me. Right now, I'm too troubled to be pleasant. Let us sleep," Shiao-ho said.

Lee sensed that Shiao-ho's trouble must have something to do with that Kung Lung woman. He figured that they must have loved each other ten years ago. '*No. It's not possible. Both of them were very young then.*'

He cleared the food when Shiao-ho whispered urgently, "Blow the light out! Someone is out there!"

"I heard nothing. It's just the leaves," Lee said. He grabbed his sword.

"It's nothing serious. The Monk I met today has come for me."

"Are you sure? I heard nothing but the raindrops on the leaves."

"I heard someone push the gate open slyly. I'm confident to say that I can hear a needle dropped ten steps away."

It might be a dog pushing against the gate." Lee was not convinced.

Shiao-ho said, "Go to sleep. It's nothing to worry about at this moment. I may catch the short Monk tonight."

"Good. It's your show." Lee wanted to see how good Shiao-ho's skills were.

The nervous Lee waited for something to happen; all he heard was Shiao-ho's soft snoring. Then Lee heard footsteps outside. He sat up, and Shiao-ho said, "Stay. It's Big Fool."

Big Fool yawned loud. Lee laughed, "You're right! Let him be the watchdog." No reply. Lee finally closed his eyes. Suddenly, Shiao-ho jumped out of the room and started to fight someone even before Big Fool's yell stopped. The intruder had applied '*Tien Hsueh*' on Big Fool. Lee knew how to reverse the technique. He patted Big Fool's leg hard a couple of times. Big Fool stood up.

Chiang Shiao-ho was dueling empty-handed with a short man brandishing a steel rod fiercely. The Monk tried vainly to attack Shiao-ho with '*Tien*

Hsueh' twice. He was ready to run away again. Shiao-ho caught him and said, "Friend, you don't have to leave in a hurry. You shouldn't use *'Tien Hsueh'* freely, for that alone I will punish you. Who are you?"

"Chiang Shiao-ho, let go of my arm. I admit that you're better than me."

"You know my name. Ahe! You're Brother Yuan. I met you ten years ago when Master Hsu took me to your home. We were both children then. Your father was very kind to me." Yuan was the skinny boy he had met ten years ago when Master Hsu took him to challenge Master Bo.

Shiao-ho continued, "Brother Yuan, did you go to Master Kac to learn how to *'Tien Hsueh'*? At that time, I was so jealous of you."

"My teacher is Steel Rod Monk. Nine years ago, bandits killed my father and burned my home. My teacher saved me. You're the cause of my father's death. I came to fight you."

"How could I be responsible? I was a homeless boy then."

Monk Pure said, "Everyone knew that Master Bo defeated Master Hsu. Master Hsu kept his promise and stayed away from that area afterward. Without his protection, all the bandits had a free run, and they robbed the rich, and you know my family was rich." The Monk continued after they went into the room and sat down, "A faithful servant saved my mother and me and hid us in his home. My father had always been generous with his donation when Steel Rod Monk came around. He killed the bandits and got back some silver for us. I became his student, and he called me 'Monk Pure.'"

"Monk Pure, why didn't you tell me that you knew me earlier? You didn't have to come here like a thief."

"I just wanted to challenge you and see how good you are. Everyone knows that you have a super teacher. Chiang Shiao-ho, I better tell you that Gi Kong-jii came to the East to apprehend you for Master Bo."

"Arrest me. I'm no criminal. Is Gi Kong-jii a law officer? Who told you that?"

"He posted posters of *'Chiang Shiao-ho – wanted'* everywhere. He's in An-Yin town now. Two men are traveling with him."

Lee Feng-Jii said, "That's Gi Kon-jii's way of forcing you to come out in the open."

Shiao-ho told Lee, "Younger brother, I'm going to find Gi Kong-jii now. I can't wait."

"Chiang Shiao-ho, I can understand that you want to go after Gi Kon-jii immediately. I want to warn you. Gi Kon-jii indeed fights well; he is the famous *Dragon Knight's* grandson, and he is cunning and evil. Please don't take him lightly." Monk Pure said.

7

Shiao-ho resented Gi Kon-jii's posters of "Chiang Shiao-ho wanted." *'How dare he blemish my reputation? I'm not a criminal, and he is not an officer.'* His teacher told him to think through the cause and effect of a problem first. An understanding of the 'why' helps find the right solution. *'The posters are Gi Kon-jii's an odd but effective way of forcing me to fight him first. Ahe! It's so true; the posters have angered me so much that I'm trying to find him. Gi Kon-jii is cunning, and he is winning. Bo Ah-ran is in Xian. Ahe! Bo Ah-ran, how can I face her? Certainly, Old Bo should have received my letter by now, and he is not stupid enough to stay in Chengba. I better go to Xian. And…and…the posters might be Gi Kon-jii's trick to draw me away from Xian! What if my* teacher *saw the posters, and he might think I'm a thief. I must stop Gi Kon-jii.'*

His teacher wanted him to be on friendly terms with the two Dragons' students. They were also the students of the Wu-Ton School of martial Arts. "If you ever meet them by chance, you should consider them as your brothers and schoolmates," his teacher said. Shiao-ho thought, *'Teacher,* you *also said that the disciples of the Wu-Ton School should be modest. Gi Kong-jii is not.'*

Lo-Yang, a magnificent capital of the Chou and Han Dynasties some fifteen thousand years ago, was the biggest city Shiao-ho had ever been. The wall of the city gate was at least ten feet thick. There were more than ten gates. He entered the Northwest gate and went to the first security station he saw to get some information about Gi Kon-jii.

"Master Gi Kon-jii is not here. A few days ago, Gi Kong-jii and two Kung Lung guards came…"

"Where are they now? "

"Gi Kong-jii stayed in town for two days, and he put up the "Wanted" posters everywhere."

"Where did Gi Kong-jii go? Do you know?"

"Someone said that he headed south to Nan-Yin City."

On the route to Nan-Yin City, a huge wanted poster was chiseled deeply, probably by a sword, into a section of the ruins of the old Great Wall. Shiao-ho had to stop and scrape the words off one at a time with his sword. His wrath toward Gi Kon-jii increased a notch each time when he obliterated a word.

An innkeeper informed him, "Three chaps stopped here for lunch yesterday. The short one wrote the wanted poster on our wall. We thought that he was an officer and dared not stop him. But we scraped it off after he left. You can still see the traces of it."

Shiao-ho frequently stopped to ask about Gi Kon-jii's whereabouts. Once, he felt a lump in his throat at the sight of a huge willow tree adjacent to a creek. *"Good Shiao-ho! Please go up and get my kite down for me. Please! Please..."* He could almost hear Bo Ah-ran 's sweet little voices and see her standing under the tree. But when he rushed over, there was no one. *'Bo Ah-ran! Bo Ah-ran!'* he murmured in a trance and almost fell off the horse. *'What am I doing here? I should go hunting Master Bo. But the posters...'* Now he decided that he would kill Gi Kon-jii. For once, he would disobey his teacher's order that he cannot kill anyone but his father's murderers.

Shiao-ho arrived at Nan-Yin City at early dawn. There was a crowd of poverty-stricken farmers, children, and feeble elders everywhere: on the street, at someone's door... All of a sudden, everyone ran to the southern part of the city. Afraid his horse would bump into them, Shiao-ho dismounted and asked one of them, "Where are you going?" The stranger shouted an answer and did not stop. It was a different dialect, Shiao-ho did not understand. Someone told Shiao-ho, "They are refugees from the North, Shandong Province. The Whee River flooded and washed away homes and crops. Yesterday, a kindhearted guest of an inn gave some of them a bit of silver. That's why they were rushing there today to beg for more."

'Didn't my teacher tell me to help the weak and the poor? I can help them with some silver too. Of course, I will keep enough for my mother.' Another man sighed, "It's so true that it's not easy to be benevolent. Yesterday, that kind young man had changed five ounces of silver into small cash to give to the refugees. Now all of them rush to him to beg. He does not seem to be rich; maybe he knows how to create unlimited amounts of silver. Now even if he had five hundred ounces of silver, it won't be enough!"

He paid a store owner to keep his horse and started to follow the crowd. "Buddha! Merciful Buddha! Please give me some coins too! My eighty-year-old mother is dying of hunger! Please..."

"Save my son! Please! We have not eaten for two days..."

The hungry crowd amassed at the gate of an inn. The scared innkeeper kept the gate closed. A short young man stood upon the wall and shouted, "I have no more silver. Sorry! I have given away all of my silver and also my friends."

Looking at the young man's fine clothes, Shiao-ho thought with admiration, '*He must be rich, and he's kind also. I can give him my silver. He looks like a scholar, is he…?*' Two middle-aged men jumped up on the wall, stood on each side of the young man. One wore an eye patch, and the other shouted down at the crowd, "Go! You hear! Go now and come back tomorrow morning!"

'*Ahe! I know both of them. Aren't they Master Bo's students? Uncle Chen and One-eyed Yu. Ahe! the young man must be Gi Kon-jii*.' Shiao-ho walked away, '*Oh! No. I can't kill him now. He is kind.*' Later at the restaurant, Shiao-ho heard, "That benevolent young man must be an important detective incognito. He and his companions placed the '..wanted' posters everywhere. The criminal is someone surnamed Chiang."

'*Now, what am I going to do? I can't beat the kindhearted Gi Kon-jii now. If he defends the Kung Lung gang, I will have another dilemma.*' The waiter told Shiao-ho, "Mister! I wouldn't go out after dark. Refugees are sleeping on the streets. They are waiting for the morning to beg for silver from that generous young man." Shiao-ho wondered from where Gi Kong-jii could have gotten the silver tonight. From what Lee Feng-jii had told him about Gi Kon-jii, Shiao-ho did not think that Gi Kon-jii was very rich.

Shiao-ho asked a clerk, "Are there any millionaires around here?"

"Yes. Ku of the Ku's Village to the west has more than a million ounces of silver."

"Why does this rich Ku not help the refugees?"

The clerk sneered, "If he's not a miser, how can he be rich? Ku won't give anyone even the smallest coin. Everyone calls him Miser Ku." Shiao-ho thought for a while and said, "I'd like to pay you now. I may leave very early tomorrow."

Shiao-ho squatted among the sleeping refugees on the street across from the inn where Gi Kong-jii stayed and waited. When the night-watcher sounded the midnight call, Shiao-ho saw Gi Kon-jii dressed in a short, tight black set and pair black cloth-soled shoes, walked fast to the west. He grinned knowingly and discreetly tailed Gi Kon-jii.

They were close to a high-walled villa. '*I am right. The righteous Gi Kong-jii is going to steal from the rich to help the poor. I may give him a hand, but I want to see how good he is.*' There were prickly throne branches and pieces of glasses on top of the high stone wall. Gi Kon-jii walked along the walls, and it looked like he was trying to find a lower part to jump over. Shiao-ho tied his straw sandals and jumped over the fence, landing soundlessly on the roof. Most of the rooms in the sprawling complex were dark but one. Shiao-ho went to it and hung himself, bat-like, from the roof. With a moistened finger, he punched a hole through the paper windowpane and looked in. '*I am lucky that I had learned this kind of skill from the guards in Szechwan when I was fourteen. Thankfully, my teacher is not here to scold me.*' An old, fat, richly dressed man, who must be the millionaire Ku, called out the quantities of various piles of silver and bills on the desk. A weary-looking clerk tallied the sums up with a weathered abacus. They were recording the daily account. '*He is indeed a miser and a loan shark too. One-third of his daily income will be enough to feed the refugees. I guess since he won't part with his silver voluntarily, I'm willing to give him a hand.*' Shiao-ho obeyed his teacher's taboo of not hurting and scaring ordinary folks with the martial arts, and waited. Finally, Miser Ku and the clerk finished their accounting and stored the bags of silver and bills in a chest with a heavy lock. The yawning pair blew out the lamp, chained, and locked the door.

No locks could stop Shiao-ho. He twisted the locks off the chest and took three bags of silver and a bundle of bills, assuming they were notes of loans. He hopped over the wall and waited for Gi Kon-jii outside the high walls. He did not wait too long when he heard loud alarms and men shouting; and many torches. Gi Kong-jii sprinted past Shiao-ho's hiding place, turned back to parry with two armed guards.

Shiao-ho watched them fight for a while and saw that one of the guards was adept with the saber. Gi Kon-jii seemed to have a hard time getting free. He wanted to rescue Gi Kon-jii first, but then he thought, '*It is just great. Gi Kon-jii wants to arrest me. It will be a laugh when he gets caught for stealing.*' He threw all the loan contracts into a deep, rushing creek, went back to Gi Kon-jii's hotel, sat on the roof, and waited.

It was quite a long time before Gi Kong-jii came back. He looked tired and carried no bags. He was just ready to jump over the wall and into the yard of the hotel. Shiao-ho threw the heavy bags at the exact spot in front of where Gi Kon-jii would land with precision and a low laugh. Gi Kon-jii immediately jumped upon the roof, but Shiao-ho had already left.

At dawn, Shiao-ho heard the refugees babble on cheerfully on the streets. He knew that Gi Kong-jii had indeed distributed the silver that he had stolen last night. He quickly dressed and saddled his horse just in time to catch the gloomy-faced Gi Kon-jii, Chen, and One-eyed Yu riding fast to the northwest.

Shiao-ho rode after them. '*They are heading to Xian. Why should I follow them? I was angry at Gi Kon-jii for posting the wanted signs and wanted to beat him, but now I know that Gi Kon-jii is an eccentric but kind man, and I should not think about beating him anymore. I should go to Xian to talk with Bo Ah-ran. How can I tell her that I have to kill her grandfather and, at the same time, I want to marry her? What should I do? I wish I told my teacher about Bo Ah-ran. That was the only thing I held back, I was too shy to tell him. Maybe I should go back to ask my teacher's advice before I go to Xian. I know for sure that my teacher will want me to be forgiving. My friend Nan at Kaifeng also wanted me to be forgiving. But, how can I make my father's soul be at peace? How can I forget about the abuses I had when I was young? They had hunted me down mercilessly. Ahe! Bo Ah-ran, let me know what I should do. And also, why does the heroic and kind Gi Kong-jii want to help the Kung Lung gang? What's the catch? For silver or …no! Gi Kon-jii is after Bo Ah-ran … Maybe Bo Ah-ran wants to marry Gi Kon-jii. I need to find out. I should be happy for her. Gi Kong-jii is a scholar, and if he passed the examination, Bo Ah-ran could be a lady. But what could I do?*' Shiao-ho was confused.

At noon, he stopped at a roadside eatery.

"Whose horse is this?" One of the two uniformed officers shouted, and the two guards who fought Gi Kon-jii the night before stood by.

"My horse, officer."

"Sergeant, Not him. He is too tall," one of the guards said. They got on their horses and were ready to leave.

"Wait. I was having a meal when you called me out to ask me. I think I deserve an explanation," Shiao-ho demanded. The short guard, the one who fought well, replied apologetically, "Sorry! We saw your horse and a sword so we thought that Gi Kong-jii was here. Last night, he stole more than seven hundred ounces of silver from my employer, Master Ku. I'm one of Ku's hired security guards. My name is Yan Hen. My colleague and these two officers are after the thief Gi Kon-jii."

Shiao-ho thought, '*This man fights well. With two officers to help them, they could arrest Gi Kon-jii. But I'm the real thief. I better go after them and see to it that they will not arrest Gi Kon-jii for a crime I have committed.*' He followed them discreetly. At the next town, he spotted more wanted posters.

"Pardon me. Who wrote these posters?" Shiao-ho asked a storekeeper.

"Mr. Gi Kon-jii. He paid for the right to write on the walls everywhere." Shiao-ho thought, '*Gi Kon-jii kept some of the silver I stole for him and used it to insult me. Somehow I'll find a way to punish him. I'll tease him.*'

The Guard Yan Hen stopped him, "You, my young friend! You thought that I did not know you were tailing us. Why? Are you Gi Kon-jii's friend?"

Shiao-ho said, "No. I'm just curious to see if you can catch Gi Kon-jii."

One officer accused, "Are you his accomplice?" We better arrest you first."

"How could I not know the famous Buddha Gi Kon-jii? I did not know he was a thief. I'm just curious, that's all!"

Guard Yan Hen held his angry colleague and the two officers back. He glanced at Shiao-ho's sword and said, "My young friend, you can watch us fight with Gi Kon-jii as long as you stay aside." He turned and whispered to his companion, "He must be Chiang Shiao-ho. I heard that Chiang is tall and carries a sword."

Shiao-ho heard it, and he sneered, "So what? I'm Chiang Shiao-ho. I better warn you that Gi Kong-jii is Dragon Knight's grandson."

The other guard was angry, "You must be a thief, too." He chopped at Shiao-ho savagely. Nobody had time to see how and when Shiao-ho caught the saber and broke it into two pieces with one hand. He laughed and galloped away.

The next day, he followed Gi Kon-jii's group to the Province of Hubei through heavy fog. A talkative hotel clerk told Shiao-ho, "Everybody here knows about the famous Master Gi Kon-jii. We heard that he had helped the refugees. He offered a reward for any information about a criminal named Chiang and posted the wanted posters everywhere. Oh, yes. He is famous."

"Where is this Hero Gi Kon-jii now?"

"He left earlier with two Kung Lung guards. They wanted to visit the famous Wu-Ton Mountain. They are probably staying in the small town at the foot of the mountain. You see, he does not know that he has to wait for a clear day to go up the mountain. The god will seal the passes with dense fog for days. Sir, do you know that fellow Chiang? Mr. Gi Kong-jii also told us to inform Chiang Shiao-ho that he can find him at a famous Kung Lung security station in Xian."

"I know about Chiang Shiao-ho He is not a criminal," Shiao-ho said.

Shiao-ho's teacher once told him, "Wu-Ton Mountain is where the Wu-Ton School of martial arts originated. The Tao priests there know martial arts. If you have to pass there by chance, be extremely respectful and careful."

Shiao-ho asked the clerk, "How far is Wu-Ton Mountain from here?"

"Sir, not far at all. Less than a day's ride to the north from here."

"I'd like to visit the Wu-Ton Mountain and to light a stick of incense for the legendary Master Chang."

"Sir, I advise caution and sincere reverence lest you be severely punished."

"How? What are the taboos?" Shiao-ho asked.

"Sir, first and foremost, you have to leave your sword behind."

"Why?"

"That's the rule. There is a "Swords Depository Pond" at the entrance from this side. Everyone, even the most prestigious general, has to throw his sword into the pond. If he does not do it, the spirit of Lord Chang or the Tao priests there will punish him severely." The waiter lowered his voice and continued conspiratorially, "Once, a most powerful general refused to give up his sword. He kept on going up the mountain, wearing his sword and…" the clerk stopped for suspense.

"What happened?" Shiao-ho asked with feigned anxiety.

"A huge boa constrictor appeared miraculously and literally scared the general to his deserved death. Sir, you see, the snake is Lord Chang. You know, Sir, even on the portrait of Lord Chang, he is holding no sword but a long-handled broom. How can anyone else be allowed to carry a sword? All the Tao priests there carry a sword, though."

"How many skilled priests are there? Do you know?"

"There are at least a hundred armed ones plus the famous seven swordmasters. Sir, please remember to leave your sword behind if you want to visit the mountain. Otherwise, the least of your troubles will be suffering a case of bad diarrhea."

"Thank you for your advice. I'm here to show my respect. How can I not obey the rules?"

'I wonder the conceited and arrogant Gi Kon-jii would know about the business of leaving his sword behind. If he goes up the mountain with his sword, it would be fun to see how the great seven swordmasters punish him. I better go and follow Gi Kon-jii up the mountain. Ahe! A good opportunity to tease him.'

The small village seemed to have a good business from the worshippers. It had three inns and two restaurants. He inconspicuously followed the impeccably dressed Gi Kon-jii, a white silk top and black silk pants, to the biggest restaurant.

Shiao-ho sat in a dark corner and waited for an imminent fight with Gi Kon-jii if Chen came in later and pointed him out. Gi Kon-jii drank alone and murmured something that sounded like a verse.

"Waiter! Bring me a pen and ink! I want to write a poem on the wall," Gi Kon-jii called.

"But, my Lord! The wall is newly whitewashed, and it would not look nice with writings on it. I can bring you paper, and then I can paste your poems on the wall. How about it, my Lord? Sometimes other guests will buy a well-written verse from us. We surely will appreciate the opportunity to earn some coins."

Gi Kon-jii sneered, "Are you afraid that you will not earn some silver if I write the poem directly on the wall? Here is one ounce of silver. You don't have to wait for someone to come along to buy it. Go and fetch me the writing tools; I'll even pay you a bit more if you prepare the ink for me."

Shiao-ho swore silently, *'Damn you, you're certainly very generous with the silver I stole for you.'*

Gi Kon-jii wrote "Chiang Shiao-ho -- Wanted" on the wall. Gi Kon-jii had a flair for calligraphy. Shiao-ho looked on with admiration. He thought, *'He sure writes well. I don't know enough to judge, but I think Gi Kon-jii writes better than my teacher and Brother Lee. Ahe!. My father wrote beautifully, too.'* Sadness and hatred washed over him, and Shiao-ho renewed his determination for revenge.

He did not fully understand the three lines Gi Kon-jii had written, but he knew enough to tell it was something about his heroic deeds. *'He is a braggart all right.'* Shiao-ho chuckled and praised aloud, "Great. Fit for a hero!" annoyed at the interruption of his flow of thoughts, Gi Kon-jii turned around and looked at Shiao-ho angrily. He saw that Shiao-ho was poorly attired, bare-footed with a pair of straw sandals, and carried no sword. Gi Kon-jii decided that it would not be worth his effort arguing with an ignorant simpleton. He paid for his drinks and left, not knowing that Shiao-ho had followed him.

Gi Kon-jii lit the oil lamp on the wall in his room, and he began to compose the fourth line to complete the poem. He wanted to use this poem as his "*morning after*" poem to impress his bride Bo Ah-ran that he was good at both martial arts and literary arts. He could not concentrate. He thought, *'I had never dreamed about marrying a rich woman when I left home. If I could capture that damned Chiang Shiao-ho and take him to Master Bo, Bo Ah-ran and the others will praise me to no end. I have written so many wanted posters in many towns, but I cannot find him. He must be afraid of me and keeps hiding. But I don't understand why Chen and One-eyed Yu changed their attitude and refused to sleep in the same room with me now. Ever since that night, someone delivered the silver to me to help the refugees, both of them are jittery. Chen is probably too scared to identify Chiang Shiao-ho for me, even if we come face to face with that rascal. There's no point in prolonging my search and keeping Bo*

Ah-ran waiting. I will go back to her after visiting the famous Wu-Ton Mountain and seeing how good the famous seven swordmasters are. I may even challenge one or two. After the wedding, I will have Bo Ah-ran accompany me to look for Chiang Shiao-ho and the unknown person who stole the silver.'

Gi Kon-jii did not even bother to wash the ink off his favorite pen brush. He blew out the light and slept fully clothed. It was bright when Gi Kon-jii woke up. He noticed the ink spots on the bedding and thought, '*I was too tired to wash my hands last night. The ink on my fingers stained the bedding. I better remember to wash the ink off before I sleep every time from now on.*'

"Waiter! Fetch me water!" Gi Kon-jii opened the tightly closed door and called.

The waiter put down the washbasin and just stood there staring at Gi Kon-jii's back.

"Fetch me breakfast. Did you hear me, and what are you looking at? Are you stupid or deaf?"

"Nephew Gi Kon-jii, do you still want to go up the Wu-Ton Mountain today? I…" One-eyed Yu said as he walked into Gi Kon-jii's room. He stopped talking and stared at Gi Kon-jii's back, "Why did you write the wanted poster on the back of your nice white shirt? You've ruined a nice shirt."

Gi Kon-jii broke out into a cold sweat and quickly took off his white top and looked at the writings on it. '*Who dares write on my top while I'm sleeping? I did not feel a thing. Ahe! This man could have killed me.*' His forehead dampened suddenly. However, Gi Kon-jii said with a forced nervous laugh, "I write them again and again. I must have written them last night after I had too much to drink. I'm tired of this business of catching Chiang Shiao-ho."

"It's a useless chase; let's go back to Xian and wait for him there. Who knows what will happen there if we stay out too long. The Kung Lung School needs your help to defend us from that renegade," One-eyed Yu agreed.

"Let me think about it. I'll talk to you later," Gi Kon-jii dismissed One-eyed Yu impatiently.

Gi Kon-jii examined the poorly written words on his white top closely. '*The writer is no scholar. That tall young man whom I met last night might have written it. When he praised my verses last night, I thought he was pretending that he knew the words. Maybe not so. Didn't they all say that Chiang Shiao-ho is tall? I'm going back there to have a drink, and maybe I can find out something about that young man. I need a drink anyway.*'

"You braggart! I spared your life." Someone had added a line to the poem he wrote yesterday with these words.

For the second time, cold sweat rushed over him. Gi Kon-jii yelled at the waiter, "How dare you let someone else ruin my poem? Who wrote this?"

"Sir. I don't know how to read. He gave me two ounces of silver to write it. More silver than what you gave me. Mercy! Don't hit me. Please."

"What does he look like?"

"A tall young man, he was here yesterday when you were here." Then both of them heard the shouting. "Gi Kon-jii, shame on you!" Gi Kon-jii rushed downstairs and caught sight of a tall man on a black horse galloping toward Wu-ton Peak. He went back to the inn to fetch his horse.

"Kon-jii, where are you going?" One-eyed Yu and Chen asked.

"Wait for me here!" Gi Kon-jii did not spot Chiang Shiao-ho hiding behind the trees waiting to make sure he was going to the Peak. Now Shiao-ho rode back to Gi Kon-jii's hotel.

"Chen Zhi-pi. Come out!" Shiao-ho shouted.

Chen and One-eyed Yu had concluded that there must be a highly-skilled martial arts master who had followed them. One-eyed Yu said, "You know, I don't think that mysterious master wants to kill Gi Kon-jii. But, from the way he humiliated Gi Kon-jii last night, he is not a friend either. Someone is calling you."

"I'm Chen, my young friend. Why? …. Hay! Are you…?"

"Right on, I'm Chiang Shiao-ho! I want to talk to you."

"Shiao-ho, you surely are grown. You are even taller than your father. We have heard that you have learned martial arts well."

"Right on again. Let's find a place to talk. Follow me! And relax! You know I could have killed all of you last night or at Nan-Yin City."

Shiao-ho took Chen to an empty field. A barrel-thick stone post was half-buried.

"You know that Master Bo and the Lung brothers killed my father, and you also know Bo's second son abused me when I was a vulnerable boy. Although you did not torture me, you did not help me either. I think you're neither my enemy nor my friend. I will show you a bit of my strength now, and you can tell the others. I don't want to wound anyone lest he's in my way." Shiao-ho pulled the half-buried stone post out and threw it about thirty feet away with ease.

"You …you indeed learned well. Shiao-ho, please understand that One-eyed Yu and I did not come with Gi Kon-jii willingly. It was Master Bo's order…"

"I do understand. Don't worry! My teacher instructed me that I can only kill my father's murderers: Master Bo and the Lung brothers. I only come to ask you not to identify me to anyone," he then sneered, "not that I'm afraid. I just want to tease that braggart a bit longer."

"You could have killed Gi Kon-jii many times. I will not point you out."

"Good! I'm sure that braggart is provoking the wrath of the famous Wu-Ton swordmasters now. I better go up to rescue him."

Through the lingering dense fog, Gi Kon-jii entered the Wu-Ton Mountain. When he galloped through the mountain pass, he thought furiously with a bravado he did not feel, *'Who dares tease me? I'm the grandson and the successor of the famous Dragon Knight. I will teach this person a lesson.'* Gi Kon-jii was scared. He knew that someone could have killed him twice already. Once by the person who stole the silver for him, and then by the young man who teased him last night. Was there only one man or two men? Anyway, this man, or two men, definitely were no friends. *'Is he afraid of the power of Master Bo and the Kung Lung School? Or is he afraid that I might have some highly skilled classmates?'*

He came to a waterfall. The words "Remove Swords Pond" were carved into the cliff. He did not remove his sword. A tall Tao priest with a black beard, standing beside an old pine tree on a high ridge, looked down at him and shouted something, but Gi Kon-jii could not hear him over the sound of the cataract. He tied his horse to a tree and hopped over a few rocks. The Tao priest shouted angrily, "No sword is permitted here! Drop your sword. If you don't, Lord Chang will punish you. Didn't you see the sign 'Remove Swords Pond'?"

"My name is Gi Kon-jii. My grandpa was the famous *Dragon Knight* Gi."

"Your grandpa visited Wu-Ton Mountain several times. Every time he removed his sword reverently."

"Oh! Time changes. No need to follow the antiquated rule." Gi Kon-jii refused to remove his sword.

"No one has dared to come here carrying a sword, and you are the first one to break the rule in two hundred years. I'll arrest you." They fought, and soon five priests were fighting Gi Kon-jii. Another three priests entered the melee. Gi Kon-jii ran uphill and hopped on a huge rock. None of the panting priests could get close.

A graybeard priest called a halt and said, "Ten years ago, Steel Rod Monk came to provoke trouble here, and we repelled him. Since then, no one has dared to come here to give us trouble. Did your grandpa tell you that? There are seven superior swordmasters here. I'm the fourth one." Graybeard alone fought him and was a strong opponent. Gi Kon-jii's arm was sore from blocking the graybeard's powerful thrusts. He fought and retreated backward toward the cliff and fell back down the deep ravine.

When Gi Kon-jii came to, he realized that the same tall young man he'd followed was washing his head with cold water. Gi Kon-jii slapped the young man hard and shouted, "You tricked me. You knew the Tao priests are too many for me to fight." Chiang Shiao-ho dropped Gi Kon-jii into the rushing creek. Gi Kon-jii was floundering in the swift current. Chiang Shiao-ho fished him out.

Gi Kon-jii asked, "Friend? Foe? Who are you?"

"I'm Kao Joe-hua." Kao means high, Joe-hua was the name of the peak where his Teacher taught him.

"You must not be famous. I thought that you were Chiang Shiao-ho, the one I want to catch."

"If I were Chiang Shiao-ho, you can bet I wouldn't save you, and you'd still be hanging from the tree up there," Shiao-ho laughed and pointed up. Gi Kon-jii looked up and thought, *'He must be very good. It's not easy to get up there and fetch me down.'*

"I followed you from Nan-Yin City. I wanted to see how good you are, that you think you can catch Chiang Shiao-ho. you're just a braggart."

Gi Kon-jii retorted, "There were too many damned Tao priests." He continued conciliatorily, "You stole silver for me, and now you save me. If you're not Chiang Shiao-ho, I'd like to be your friend."

"Good"

"Where is my sword?" Gi Kon-jii said.

"There!" Gi Kon-jii looked up at the sword caught in-between the tree branches. Shiao-ho climbed up and got it. He threw it down to Gi Kon-jii and shouted, "Catch!" He jumped away swiftly like a monkey. *'He has followed my every step, and I knew nothing about it. He is so much better than me. If he is Chiang Shiao-ho, I don't think I'll have a chance. Why did he tease me? He is no friend.'* Gi Kon-jii thought.

Chen was worried about whether Shiao-ho had killed Gi Kon-jii. Gi Kon-jii and Shiao-ho walking in. Gi Kon-jii started the introduction. "Brother Kao, please meet One-eyed Yu and Chen, two famous Kung Lung guards traveling with me."

"Nice to meet you, Brother Kao."

Gi Kon-jii observed when Chen and One-eyed Yu greeted Shiao-ho. There was no sign of recognition. Gi Kon-jii relaxed and thought, *'So, this Kao is indeed not Chiang Shiao-ho. And that damned Chen even afraid of his own shadow now.'* He did not notice that Chen was very nervous.

Gi Kon-jii said cheerfully, "Brother Kao, it's cool out in the yard. I'll wash up and be back." Chen got up and wanted to accompany Gi Kon-jii, but Shiao-ho held his arm and said, "Let's wait here. It's cool here. I am flattered to meet two famous Kung Lung guards." He slightly increased his squeeze on Chen's arm.

"Yes! Yes! It's cool. Cool here…" Chen stammered. Chen was sweaty and pale from the pain.

One-eyed Yu asked with concern, "Chen, does the heat ill you? Sit and try to relax."

One-eyed Yu then politely asked Shiao-ho, "Brother Kao, where do you come from? Are you new to this area?"

"I came from the South. While I was visiting Wu-Ton Mountain, I saw Tao priests fighting Brother Gi Kon-jii. Brother Gi fell, and I saved him." Gi Kon-jii claimed indignantly, "Brother Kao, there were too many of them. Let's go back and demand a fair one-to-one duel. I'll show you that I can beat any one of the so-called seven swordmasters."

"Bravo! But it won't be easy. The Tao priests are not braggarts." Shiao-ho laughed. One-eyed Yu and Chen agreed, "They must be good. They are very famous."

Gi Kon-jii sulked a while and then asked, "Where are you going?"

"Xian."

"Business or sightseeing?"

"You could say it is business, and there are a few people who owe me a lot ten years ago. I am going to call in the debt, principal plus interest."

"We'll go to Xian together. I'd like you to meet my newly acquired family. Did you ever hear about the famous Kung Lung School? They're my family now."

Shiao-ho laughed, "If I want to challenge someone, I'll surely choose Master Bo. I don't want to take advantage of his old age; I'll fight his heavy Kung Lung saber with my bare hands. If I cannot grab his saber in three passes, I'm no winner."

Gi Kon-jii smirked, "Do not brag. I bet his granddaughter Bo Ah-ran can beat you easily." Hearing Bo Ah-ran 's name, Chiang Shiao-ho's face turned red and then pale. He sipped some tea and asked, "Is she in Xian now?"

"She will be there soon."

"Brother Gi, does she fight better than you?"

"We did not have a match. But I assume that she is a bit inferior. For instance, she fought Lee Feng-jii, but she didn't win. I did. Lee is *Szechwan Dragon's* successor," Gi Kon-jii gloated.

Chiang Shiao-ho tried hard to control his mixed feelings of hostility for Master Bo and his longing for Bo Ah-ran. His facial expression kept changing, and his hand holding the teacup shook. One-eyed Yu and Chen thought that Shiao-ho seemed suddenly older. Finally, thinking he had his emotion in check, Shiao-ho asked, "Is she promised to be married?"

Like most self-centered men and a bully, Gi Kon-jii ignored Shiao-ho's changing countenance. He was excited about his upcoming marriage to Bo Ah-ran. He said, "Indeed. She is promised."

Chiang Shiao-ho asked hastily, "To whom?"

Gi Kon-jii roared, "It is not your business. How dare you ask about her affairs. You're neither her brother nor her family. All right! If you must know, she is mine. We'll be married in the fall. Damn you!" Gi Kon-jii hurled the teacup at Shiao-ho. Chiang Shiao-ho dodged and pointed two fingers at Gi Kon-jii's chest. Gi Kon-jii slumped to the ground.

"Did you kill him?" One-eyed Yu yelled.

"Shiao-ho, you promised that you wouldn't harm Gi Kon-jii. Brother Yu, he's Chiang Shiao-ho," Chen shouted.

Shiao-ho thought, *'What have I done? My Teacher forbade me to use 'Tien Hsueh' I better get hold of myself.'*

"I did not kill him. Is it true that Bo Ah-ran is going to marry Gi Kon-jii?"

"Yes. Shiao-ho, please be merciful." Chen pleaded.

Shiao-ho freed Gi Kon-jii and left.

Chiang Shiao-ho wanted to be in Xian fast; however, he was hurt all over. Somehow he managed to get on his horse and let the horse canter ahead by itself. His chest hurt, and he was confused and dazed. He did some deep breathing exercises to steady himself.

"Chiang Shiao-ho, you coward! You even dare not use your name. Do you dare fight me squarely with your sword? You..." Gi Kon-jii caught up with him.

"Gi Kon-jii! I don't want to fight you. Sorry, I should not have used *'Tien Hsueh'* on you. I am not against you. We are students of the Wu-Ton School and should be friends and brothers, not enemies. I could kill you. You must know that, don't you? My enemies are Master Bo and the Lung brothers only. I would kill no one but them to avenge my father's death."

Gi Kon-jii thrust his sword forward, "I, Gi Kon-jiii, won't allow you to harm anyone affiliated with the Kung Lung School."

Shiao-ho raised his sword seemingly lazily, only to block Gi Kon-jii's thrust. His strength numbed Gi Kon-jii's arm. Soon Gi Kon-jii's arm was too sore to fight with the superior styles anymore; he could only thrust wildly and haphazardly.

"Stop! Gi Kon-jii! I don't want to harm you." Shiao-ho retreated.

Gi Kon-jii came after Shiao-ho ruthlessly. Shiao-ho pierced at Gi Kon-jii's chest lightly, not to kill but only to draw blood. He said, "Gi Kon-jii, go back home. Go back to your grandpa's tomb and learn more before you fight me again."

The white-faced Gi Kon-jii looked down at the tiny cut between his breasts. There was a small bloodstain. He thought, *'Why! Chiang Shiao-ho could have killed me again. He controlled his sword and pierced me with such meticulousness.'* He recalled the numerous reprimands from his grandpa whenever Gi Kon-jii beat up someone and then bragged about his skills.

"Remember! Kon-jii, martial arts is for self-defense. I'm sorry that your mother and I spoiled you. Learn to be modest. I cannot live forever to protect you when you offend someone better than you. Don't you know that there will always be someone superior to you? I want you to copy this every day for a month until you remember it well." *Dragon Knight* continued, "There are some deadly techniques - '*Tien Hsueh*' can inflict or delay death at will. I'm not going to teach you now until you shape up your manners and behavior."

Gi Kon-jii remembered that he wrote the following sentences many times: *'Both the Sho-Lin School and Wu-Ton School of martial arts equally emphasize pacifism over violence. Both schools teach the most refined self-defense, unarmed or armed, fighting techniques. Martial arts' philosophical essence should be: Learn the ways to preserve rather than destroy life. Avoid rather than check; check rather than hurt; hurt rather than maim; maim rather than kill. For all life is precious and cannot be replaced.'*

Dragon Knight died soon afterward, and Gi Kon-jii never learned '*Tien Hsueh.*' *'That damned Chiang Shiao-ho knows all of the other techniques too. How can I fight him?'* Gi Kon-jii was fumed with frustration and humiliation and took his anger out on Chen. "I brought you along because you know him, and you can identify him, but you pretended that you didn't know him. Are you conspiring with him and let him play a dirk trick on me?"

One-eyed Yu intervened, "Gi Kon-jii, you can't blame Brother Chen. He knew Chiang Shiao-ho when he was a boy. It's been ten years. How can Brother Chen recognize him right away?"

"Nonsense! I know you, all of you so-called mighty Kung Lung guards are afraid of Chiang Shiao-ho. Master Bo would faint whenever Shiao-ho's name is mentioned. If it were not for Bo Ah-ran 's sake, I wouldn't help you."

One-eyed Yu retorted, "Gi Kon-jii, that's not true. My Teacher is now old and feeble; he also has regrets. Brother Chen must have known that the three of us together have no chance of surviving if we were to fight Shiao-ho. That's why he did not identify him."

"Chiang Shiao-ho could only harm me when I'm not prepared. Oh! Well! He must have escaped quickly; I missed him." One-eyed Yu and Chen stared at the now spreading bloodstain on Gi Kon-jii's beige-colored top and said nothing.

Gi Kon-jii continued, "Chiang Shiao-ho must be on his way to Xian now. He does not know that Master Bo and Bo Ah-ran are staying at Uncle Lu's. We should go and warn Master Bo. Master Bo should find a place to hide for a while; we'll fight Shiao-ho in Xian. Get ready to leave now!"

One-eyed Yu agreed, "Exactly! We better be on our way before it's too late."

One-eyed Yu counseled the dejected Chen, "At least Gi Kon-jii is still willing to help us to fight Chiang Shiao-ho."

"Are you completely blind? Even with one eye, you must have seen the bloodstain on Gi Kon-jii's chest. Shiao-ho did not intend to kill Gi Kon-jii. That's all. Last night and this morning, Shiao-ho had many opportunities to kill Gi Kon-jii. Shiao-ho is not conceited like his father. He is better than his daddy."

Looking at One-eyed Yu's eye patch, Chen continued, "You know, it's true that old Master Bo was cruel, ruthless, and stupid. He should not have had Shiao-ho's father killed in the first place. After that mistake, he should have killed Shiao-ho when he was young and not *'Let the root growth.'* But Shiao-ho's father, Chiang Shiao-ho Zhi-shen, was to blame too. He was very conceited, and he did insult Master Bo. Shiao-ho must have a good teacher who taught the boy well, not only skills but good manners too. Shiao-ho wants only to kill the Lung brothers and Master Bo. Twelve years ago, Master Bo and the Lung brothers hunted Shiao-ho's father down and killed him."

One-eyed Yu advised, "Let's hurry. Maybe we can all go into hiding. We can convince Master Bo to lead us into hiding in Szechwan."

Chen said, "You forget that Master Hsu's there. Master Hsu indeed is not Master Bo's friend."

Gi Kon-jii rode fast ahead, but One-eyed Yu and Chen dwindled. They were afraid of catching up with Chiang Shiao-ho soon. Gi Kon-jii became very impatient. At the next town, Millionaire Ku's guards and the officers caught up with them. Gi Kon-jii fought them and got away. They arrested Chen and One-eyed Yu.

8

Lu Zhi-chun was surprised to see that Gi Kon-jii came back to Da-Sam Fort alone, "Nephew Gi did you meet Chiang Shiao-ho? Where are One-eyed Yu and Chen?"

Gi Kon-jii shouted, "They are slow. I must see Grandpa Bo and Ah-ran immediately." He dashed to the inner court where Bo Ah-ran, in a pretty pink silk short set, practiced her Kung Lung saber skills diligently. "Miss Bo, I caught Chiang Shiao-ho at Wu-Ton Mountain. We fought and he jumped into the creek and escaped." Gi Kon-jii bragged.

Master Bo was not pleased that Gi Kon-jii joked with his granddaughter before marriage. He coughed to show his disapproval and asked, "Kon-jii, tell me everything."

"Grandpa, I posted "*Chiang Shiao-ho -- Wanted*" posters everywhere. He avoided me. A few days ago I met him at the foot of Wu-Ton Mountain. He fooled me with a feigned name and wanted to be my friend. Uncle Chen wouldn't identify Chiang Shiao-ho for me, even though he recognized the culprit. I almost fell into the rascal's trap. I wounded him. He jumped into the creek and swam away. I suffered a slight wound on my chest too. Chiang Shiao-ho said that he is coming to Xian to kill you only. Grandpa, I suggest that you find somewhere safe and go into hiding for a while. Bo Ah-ran and I will fight Chiang Shiao-ho at Xian, I need her help."

Master Bo hid his fear and sneered, "I'm not going to hide. Where? My tomb? I'll wait for him at Xian and fight him. He can only kill me once. Get my horse ready!"

Bo Ah-ran begged, "Grandpa, you cannot go! I'll go. I want to talk to Shiao-ho first before I kill him. I want to know whether he still remembers…" Bo Ah-ran cried.

Lu Zhi-chun said, "Teacher, you and Bo Ah-ran should wait here a few days. Kon-jii and I will go to Xian and have a council with Brother Feng. Besides, I may be able to talk Shiao-ho into his senses."

Master Bo thought, '*Yes, I always knew that you had helped him to escape.*'

Gi Kon-jii opposed, "Not good enough! I'm not afraid of Chiang Shiao-ho if I can fight him face to face, but I'm no match for his trickery. His swordsmanship is just so-so, but he's very good at leaping and wall climbing. At night, I cannot beat him. He will be in Xian soon. If he knows that Grandpa is here, how can we prevent him from sneaking in here at night to assassinate Grandpa? I insist that Master Bo should go into hiding for a while. Bo Ah-ran and I, together, will beat him in Xian."

They had a lengthy discussion. Uncle Lu summarized, "Gi Kon-jii's idea seems to be the only solution for now. I will accompany Master Bo to hide at a trusted friend's villa in Henan Province. Chiang Shiao-ho cannot find us there." Master Bo seemed to be swayed at first, but he objected, "No. I can't go there myself and let Shiao-ho kill all my students; I won't be able to live afterward."

Gi Kon-jii insisted, "If Grandpa is not here, the rest of us will be safe. In his letter to you, and he told me again in person, that he won't kill anyone but the Lung brothers and… and Grandpa."

Old Master Bo recalled the pitiful scenario of when Shiao-ho's father was killed. '*Chiang Zhi-shen's clothes were torn, his feet were bleeding. It was a pitiful sight. He had left his young family behind. I was cruel to have ordered him killed. Now, his son comes back to avenge his death. I do deserve to die.*' Huge tears rolled down his wrinkled cheeks, he said, "I was merciless. Shiao-ho has the right to kill me."

They discussed more and finally, Master Bo agreed, "Lu Zhi-chun and I will go into hiding. Get someone to warn the Lung brothers. I'll ask my life-long friend Master Lee to help. Master Lee has a lot of students."

Gi Kon-jii said, "I'm certain that I can curb that rogue all by myself. I'm only afraid that Lee Feng-jii will come to fight us too. I'm sorry to say that none of your Kung Lung guards can be of any help. I need Bo Ah-ran to be at my side and to help me to fight him, only she can help me."

Master Bo agreed, "Of course, she will go with you, but…" he hesitated and continued, "Without a proper marriage, it won't be fitting for you and Bo Ah-ran to travel together… It's still early. If we hurry, you can be married tonight."

Bo Ah-ran sobbed and went to her room. Master Bo followed her into her room and said, "Don't feel sorry for me. It's my fault. I am too cruel.

I'm only sorry that my students and you, Gi Kon-jii, are all going to suffer because of that. To tell you the truth, I truly admire Chiang Shiao-ho; he is determined, brave, and resourceful. Tomorrow I'll go into hiding. If we can live through this, we'll see each other again. Otherwise…"

"I'm going with you"

"No! Gi Kon-jii will need your help to fight Shiao-ho, and probably Lee Feng-jii, in Xian. For you two to travel together properly, you'll marry him tonight."

"No! Grandpa, No! …I don't want to…I like…I love…"

"I know you love me and don't want to leave me. Please obey me. Otherwise, I won't be able to die in peace …You're the one I worry about the most. Knowing that you have a good husband, I'll feel better…even if I die."

Uncle Lu's wife was not at the station. The wives of his assistants and friends all eagerly pitched in to help. They worked diligently to decorate the bridal suite in the frontcourt. A few younger women crowded into Bo Ah-ran's room to help her into a borrowed wedding gown. They undid Bo Ah-ran's maiden-styled braids first and then piled her black glossy hair high to form a woman's hair-do held with gold and silver combs. Everyone said the necessary good wishes. Bo Ah-ran kept on sobbing.

One woman said with a trace of envy, "Why, isn't it grand that you're going to marry a good-looking scholar who fights well too? Don't cry. You don't want your handsome groom to see that your eyes are red and swollen tonight, do you?"

Others joined the teasing. Bo Ah-ran could not endure it any longer; she pushed them away, tore free her elaborated hair-do, threw her red embroidered jacket away, and wept.

Master Bo came in and asked, "My precious Ah-ran, what's the matter? It's a hurried wedding, and I don't like it either. I'd like you to have a grand wedding, too. But now we don't have time. Ah-ran, you know that I'm forced into marrying you off without a well-planned ceremony; you don't even have a new gown made. But I insist on having a proper marriage. Before my departure, I'd like to see you happily and formally married. I know you're sorry for me, and it's not fitting to marry you off in haste, but…" Master Bo begged.

"Grandpa, I'm sorry. I don't want to … I only love… It's just that they are making such a fuss. I…"

"But, a wedding is supposed to be noisy and festive. Besides, laughter and noise are supposed to repel the evil spirit. We're so unfortunate now;

we need a noisy one, *Ha! Ha!"* He sounded nothing but cheerful, "My good Ah-ran, let them help you get dressed up again."

He asked the women, "Please help her dress up again. My family is facing a very difficult time. Please pardon my granddaughter's bad temper." The women dressed Bo Ah-ran up in silence.

Gi Kon-jii appeared to be electrified. He repeated his victorious fight with Lee Feng-jii and Chiang Shiao-ho to the visitors. With each subsequent telling, he would add on more details. To the listeners, it was a matter of fact that Gi Kon-jii, the successor of *Dragon Gate* Gi, should beat the obscure Chiang Shiao-ho easily. But Lu Zhi-chun was uneasy, *'A cut on his chest! Shiao-ho did not want to kill Gi Kon-jii.'* He wondered why Gi Kon-jii had not come back together with Chen and One-eyed Yu. Gi Kon-jii's excuse of wanting to be here fast seemed flimsy. Besides, Lu Zhi-chun noticed that Master Bo looked over every younger visitor with apprehension. Master Bo did not quite believe Gi Kon-jii's telling either.

At the wedding ceremony, the pair kowtowed to the symbolic nameplates of Gi Kon-jii's ancestors first, to Master Bo and Uncle Lu second, and to each other last, to complete the ceremony. A big square of red silk completely covered Bo Ah-ran's head and face. Nobody could tell whether she was pleased or not, but the two now subdued women, on each side of Bo Ah-ran to guide her, saw tears dropping down onto her red wedding slippers. They all wondered why and hoped that their husbands would take them home quickly, away from this seemingly doomed family.

Gi Kon-jii drank and talked about his victories throughout the hasty wedding banquet. Then Lu Zhi-chun announced, "Thank you all for coming. By now I expect that everyone here knows that we are preparing to repel an enemy or enemies. Tomorrow morning, the newlywed couple will go to Xian to intercept the enemy. Master Bo and I must leave early tomorrow to make necessary arrangements too. Thank you all for coming." Uncle Lu also forbade the three younger assistants to play the customary pranks on the newlyweds.

It was dark and quiet. Only the pair of huge red candles in the temporary ceremonial hall, and a small oil lamp in the bridal suite kept burning. They were supposed to burn all night long as the customary token of a long and happy marriage.

Gi Kon-jii, freshly groomed in his pajamas, coughed aloud to announce his entrance to the bridal suite. Suddenly, the lamp of longevity went out. In pitch-dark, Gi Kon-jii nervously laughed to repel his superstition, "Don't be bashful! Bo Ah-ran, don't you think we have seen each other often enough....

Ouch!" he bumped his head on a heavy chair barring the door to the bedroom, and said, "Oh! My precious Bo Ah-ran, you're teasing your bridegroom before..." *Clang Clang*... Gi Kon-jii then tripped on a basin half-filled with water. He pushed the closed bedroom door hard and shouted, "It's too much. Bo Ah-ran, don't spoil our wedding night. Open the door NOW!"

Bo Ah-ran shrieked, "You dare come to my room? If you dare push again, I'll..."

"What's the matter with you? Of course, I'll come to OUR room. Are you not my bride? OPEN THE DOOR!" Silence.

Gi Kon-jii stooped down, pushed the bedroom door at the bottom. The door gave in and two chairs leaning against the door inside collapsed. But he jumped aside free, barely avoiding Bo Ah-ran's saber. He laughed tensely, "Duel first before..."

He gripped Bo Ah-ran 's wrist, trying to relieve her of the saber, but a vicious kick to his eye numbed him. He hit his head on the corner of a heavy dresser. Bo Ah-ran chopped at him again and somehow he managed to back out of the wedding suite.

"Why, do you want to kill me? I'm your husband."

Bo Ah-ran cried, "Get away. Get away. I don't want..."

Gi Kon-jii stood dumbfounded and at a complete loss of what he should do next. Lu Zhi-chun came out holding a lamp and said, "Kon-jii, please be patient. Ah-ran indeed has a bad temper. Now her grandpa is forced to hide, and she may not be able to see him again for a long time. It's too much for her right now. She will come to terms soon."

"Uncle Lu, I understand. But she should not..." Gi Kon-jii intended to say that Bo Ah-ran should not chop at him so viciously, but he only said, "All right. I'll be patient." Gi Kon-jii's new pajamas were wet and dirty, and he had one swollen and blackened eye. It looked funny. Lu Zhi-chun smothered a laugh. Master Bo was drunk and exhausted from worry. He did not hear the commotion from his room at the inner court. Others kept quiet even when they heard it.

Gi Kon-jii said to the closed door, "Bo Ah-ran, your grandpa wanted us to get married. Why do you reject me? Besides, you don't think that I, Gi Kon-jii, could not find a wife? You're not the only young woman I have met. I do admire you and your skills. I understand your dilemma and I'll be patient." Bo Ah-ran sobbed even harder. Gi Kon-jii pulled two chairs together to make a temporary bed in the front room and slept. When he saw Bo Ah-ran the next morning, Gi Kon-jii forgot all his trouble from the night before.

Master Bo told them, "Now you two, as a young couple, will face the enemy for me. I'm worried about your safety too. By the blessings of the gods, I wish we will see each other again soon."

"Grandpa, don't worry. Don't think that you'll have to hide for long. Think of it as a vacation and have a good time. Don't worry. Bo Ah-ran and I will win."

Master Bo sighed and handed Gi Kon-jii two sealed envelopes. "The letter writer wrote these two letters for me. This one, you'll give to Uncle Feng. That one…you keep it. When and if he defeats you, Give Chiang Shiao-ho the envelope."

"I'll obey your order. Good luck and goodbye."

Bo Ah-ran said in tears, "Grandpa, Uncle Lu, goodbye. We'll see you soon." She turned back again and again on horseback until she could not see the sad Old Bo, her Grandpa, any longer.

9

Bo Ah-ran had traveled on the same route alone two months ago, and now she rode behind Gi Kon-jii as a wife should. She thought, *"I will see Shiao-ho soon. I will fight him to the death if only he insists on killing grandpa. He can kill the Lung brothers. They are wicked anyway. Somehow I have to let him know how much I miss him yet hate him. I am married now, how can I talk to him alone? How can I tell him I'm not truly married yet, it was only a ceremony? How can I tell him something like that? Will he or any other man believe me if I tell him that? What am I going to do?"* Her tears came.

Gi Kon-jii said, "Bo Ah-ran, why? You're a crying baby. Are you afraid? Honestly, I'm afraid, too. You have to be strong to help me fight Chiang Shiao-ho. Now that we are married, I'll tell you the truth that I, alone, can't fight him off. I need your help." No reply.

Gi Kon-jii sighed, "Last night should have been our memorable wedding night. You spoiled it. If I were not patient, we would be eternal foes instead of a newlywed couple. You must understand that I'm not afraid of you. I care for you very much. Now that we are traveling together, I expect you to behave as a wife should. I don't want you to fight me every night and make us laughingstocks. We must be a team when we fight Chiang Shiao-ho. I'll take you to my home and present you to my mother later. Oh! How she wishes to have a grandson soon. I'll go to Beijing to take the civil examination. I promise that you'll be a lady soon."

Bo Ah-ran pouted, "No more nonsense! You better hurry up." Gi Kon-jii smiled happily at the way Bo Ah-ran addressed him as "YOU." At dusk, Bo Ah-ran insisted that they keep on going.

Gi Kon-jii said, "We better find a hotel for the night. We have to cross the Wei River, and I'm not sure how late the ferry will run. Besides, even if we could reach Xian tonight, we have to wait for the city gates to open in the morning." Reluctantly, Bo Ah-ran agreed. A raised earthen *kon* (bed), but no other furniture, in their room. Bo Ah-ran sat on the bed with her Kung Lung saber beside her.

The innkeeper brought them basins of water to freshen up. Gi Kong-jii ordered a meal and wine. He handed Bo Ah-ran a cup of wine and said cheerfully, "A toast, and my precious. Let's have a new beginning." Bo Ah-ran pushed it away, and the wine spilled all over the bed and Gi Kon-jii's new clothes. He protested, "What's the matter with you? You could have told me that you don't want it. You treated me with no respect. Do you loathe me? Do you not want to be my wife? You know that you don't have to marry me, and I am sure that I can find another young woman to marry."

Bo Ah-ran reached her saber and shouted back, "Who's your wife?"

Gi Kon-jii laughed, "You! You're my wife. We were properly married yesterday. You are my wife, consort, and lover." He leaned forward, wanting to kiss her. But Bo Ah-ran unsheathed the saber, and Gi Kon-jii ducked immediately, barely having time to avoid the blade.

'How dare she treat me this way? I'm going back to Master Bo to demand an annulment.' Gi Kon-jii rushed to the stable and started to saddle his horse. As soon as he put the saddle on, he took it off again. *'No! I can't do that. We will be foes. There are indeed other young and prettier women who also know martial arts, but where can I find one as rich and skillful as Bo Ah-ran. Besides, I can't back out now. All of them will think that I'm too afraid of Chiang Shiao-ho to marry into Master Bo's family."* He went back to their room.

Pushing the door open slowly, Gi Kon-jii told the sobbing Bo Ah-ran "I know now that you don't like me, but I don't understand why you married me. Marriage will not buy my loyalty. It's not only for you that I want to help the Kung Lung School to fight off Lee Fong-jii and Chiang Shiao-ho. I do it because I think it is unfair to let some young upstarts humiliate Master Bo at his age. Chiang Shiao-ho is very good at the deadly *'Tien Hsueh'* skill. I am not. His running, leaping, and wall climbing skills are all superior to mine, even though his swordsmanship is not as good as mine." Gi Kon-jii felt his face hot. He was bragging, "The outcome of the impending fight to the death between Chiang Shiao-ho and me is anybody's guess. Who knows which one of us will die? If I'm the one to die, I'll have no regrets since I died for a good cause of defending Master Bo. If by chance I live, I will go away and grant you the freedom of marrying someone else." Bo Ah-ran whined, "Who grants you the right to kill Chiang Shiao-ho? He's my family's foe; no need for you to kill him. If you kill him, I'll kill you. I don't want to talk to you."

Gi Kon-jii chuckled first and said seriously after a long sigh, "I don't want to talk to you either. Let's be husband and wife in name only for now. Someday you'll know that I, Gi Kon-jii, am a champion, and you're not the only one who is proud." He ate in silence and then slept on the bed apart from Bo Ah-ran. At midnight, he woke up and saw that the oil lamp was almost out of oil. In the flickering light, Bo Ah-ran looked extremely attractive and seductive. Gi Kon-jii's heart pumped fast, and he reached out his hand ever so slowly, wanting to take Bo Ah-ran's saber away first and then overpowered her. At that moment, Bo Ah-ran opened her eyes. Gi Kon-jii pretended that he was dreaming and shouted, "Chiang Shiao-ho!" while moving closer to his unapproachable wife. By then, Gi Kon-jii's head was very close to Bo Ah-ran's red-embroidered socks, and his fingers nearly touched her saber. Bo Ah-ran moved farther away.

The following day, Gi Kon-jii deliberately ignored Bo Ah-ran, but his heart kept pounding at the sight of her grooming with a small mirror. Gi Kon-jii suppressed his urge to talk to Bo Ah-ran. He wanted to find a way to make her long for him.

Bo Ah-ran wore the new matron-styled hairdo and a red silk outfit. Uncle Feng welcomed them as a couple. "Congratulations! Now we're truly a family. Kon-jii, did you meet Chiang Shiao-ho? Where are One-eyed Yu and Chen?" Gi Kon-jii bragged again how he indeed defeated Chiang Shiao-ho and how he rushed to Da-Sam Fort alone to inform Master Bo of Shiao-ho's impending arrival.

Gi Kon-jii complained, "Uncle Chen would not identify him for me. They are afraid of that renegade, and they probably won't come to Xian soon. Uncle Feng, here is a letter Grandpa wanted me to give you." However, Gi Kon-jii did not tell Feng about the other one addressed to Chiang Shiao-ho.

Inside the thick envelope, Feng found a short letter and another unsealed envelope addressed to Chiang Shiao-ho. It briefly stated the hasty marriage necessary so that Gi Kon-jii and Bo Ah-ran could come to Xian together to fight Chiang Shiao-ho. Master Bo also said that he was not afraid of Shiao-ho's revenge, but Uncle Lu and Gi Kon-jii insisted that he should hide somewhere temporarily. Uncle Pan also read the unsealed letter addressed to Shiao-ho. It read, "Shiao-ho, I truly regret killing your father twelve years ago, even though your father did covet his neighbor's wife and deserved to die. Shiao-ho, now you're grown. If you can be understanding and forsake the act of revenge, we can be friends. Otherwise, if you insist on revenge, I am willing to surrender myself if you promise not to harm my students and family."

"We must not give Chiang Shiao-ho this letter… We'll…"

"We'll fight Shiao-ho until the very last one of us dies." "We will never give him this letter!" All the uncles and their students shouted in unison their willingness to defend Master Bo. Bo Ah-ran started to weep.

Feng calmed everyone down and said, "When that villain shows up, we will not fight him at once. We'll let him read this letter..."

Uncle Pan interrupted, "You want our reverent teacher to surrender without a fight?"

Feng argued, "Of course not! We would rather die first before he can reach Master Bo..."

"Why do we have to give him this letter first?"

Feng continued, "It's an order, and we must obey. As soon as Shiao-ho comes, we'll show him this letter. Lieu Zhi-an, you are the only one here who knows the past. You tell Shiao-ho the details: his father's immoral behavior, sacrilege, and the intolerable insults to Master Bo. I expect that the grown-up Shiao-ho would be reasonable and understanding."

Lieu shouted, "He should remember that Master Bo was kind to him and fed him for a while." Bo Ah-ran cried, "My uncle abused Shiao-ho. Whenever he shows up, let me talk to him first. I want to ask him..." Gi Kon-jii wondered, *'Bo Ah-ran is on his side. Is this why...'* he knew that Bo Ah-ran could not repel his advance in front of all the uncles. He put an arm around her and hugged her.

Feng Zhi-pan said, "Not to worry! I have many friends in high official positions. If Shiao-ho comes, the net will be tight; he'll have no way to escape."

Bo Ah-ran pleaded urgently, "We should not ask the officials to arrest him. It's not fair."

Gi Kon-jii also argued, "We should not get the law involved."

Feng said, "We're not going to get him arrested right away. We'll talk to him first. But, if he's not reasonable, I'll have to ask for the officials' help. Indeed I value my thirty years of reputation of not involving the officials. But, if it's the last resource to save our Kung Lung School, I'll arrange to have him jailed. If I can't have Shiao-ho beheaded, at least he'll be jailed for life. You'll see."

Pan said, "Put him in jail for a year or so, and he will lose most of his training without proper daily workouts."

Gi Kon-jii objected, "Uncles, we can't do that to him or anyone in our circle of martial arts brotherhood. It's not fitting. I will fight him and win or lose the honest way." Bo Ah-ran looked at her new husband and thought, *'He is righteous. He is better than Uncle Feng and Uncle Pan.'*

Feng quickly changed the subject and said, "First, let's celebrate and congratulate the newlyweds. It's a happy event."

All the uncles joined in on the teasing and well-wishing. Bo Ah-ran's cheeks turned flamingly red, and she ran to the women's quarters. The usually talkative Gi Kon-jii had something else on his mind. He thanked the uncles. And talked excitedly for a while, then said he would go to see his uncle. He did not go to his uncle's shop. Instead, he went into a blacksmith's with a sign advertising to forge all sorts of weapons. There were sabers, swords, and daggers hanging on the walls of the shop.

"What do you want us to make for you, a sword or a saber?" The storekeeper asked Gi Kon-jii.

"Do you have any steel darts?" Gi Kon-jii asked.

"No. We don't have steel darts on hand. You have to order them. Which security company sent you to us?"

"Feng's."

"I know everyone who works at Feng's. Oh! You must be the famous Gi Kon-jii. Didn't you go to the East to catch Chiang Shiao-ho? Did you catch him?"

Gi Kon-jii said, "I'm in a hurry. If you don't have steel darts, I'll go somewhere else."

"For you, we have, Master Gi Kon-jii. Please wait. We have some in the back." He showed Gi Kon-jii a box of assorted steel darts and said, "We forged these twenty years ago. Twelve years ago, Master Bo's son, your father-in-law, lost a convoy to the bandit Dart Hu Li. All the blacksmith shops in Xian were ordered not to forge and sell any darts."

"My grandfather, *Dragon Knight*, was famous for his swordsmanship. Not many know that he was also very good at throwing darts. The darts we use are much better than these. I don't have any with me."

"If you give us the specifications, we can forge them for you."

Gi Kon-jii drew the specification and ordered twenty. He paid the deposit, bought five darts and a leather carrying pouch.

A huge half-buried stone post with words chiseled on it at an empty lot next to Feng's station. Gi Kon-jii picked up a stone, aimed at a stroke of a written word, and threw the stone at it. The rock hit the target. He picked other marks, and again he hit the target squarely. A crowd gathered to see him throwing stones and cheered every time he hit the target. So he announced his target before each throw and gained more cheers.

There was a formal banquet to honor the newlywed. Gi Kon-jii laughed happily, but he was puzzled by Bo Ah-ran 's attitude. She just sat there silently, ate, and drank nothing. She looked sad.

Feng's daughter-in-law looked tired. She was heavy with the child. She tried to be cheerful and congratulated the bride, "Congratulations, Sister Bo," then she whispered, "How was it? If I were you, I would train him to be more considerate of you when he is most mellow now. Give in a little and control a lot. Ah." Red-faced Bo Ah-ran said, "Please don't tease me. You know that my grandpa arranged this marriage. I'm not..." Barely halting her tears, she continued, "Because it's convenient for us to fight Chiang Shiao-ho together."

"You know, it's convenient now but not for long. We women just cannot go out to fight enemies as freely as men can. There will be times when we're just not available." Bo Ah-ran guessed that her sister-in-law was talking about having a child. She blushed. Somehow, she did not want to go back to their room lest the loathsome Gi Kon-jii would be there. All of a sudden, she sobbed.

"Why? Did I say something wrong? Sorry, I'm just joking. I didn't mean to upset you," Feng's daughter-in-law apologized.

Bo Ah-ran said hurriedly, "No, it's not you. Sorry. It's just that I don't want to marry..." A maid called, "Mistress Gi, Master Gi Kon-jii wants to take you to visit his uncle. The carriage is waiting."

Gi Kon-jii told Bo Ah-ran, "We're going to visit my mother's only brother, our uncle." Gi Kon-jii's uncle and aunt welcomed the bride, and Gi Kon-jii was proud.

Uncle Feng invited two officials to dine with him and told them that Chiang Shiao-ho was a thief and asked their help to apprehend him. Chief Ting offered the assistance of his whole detective force and declared, "Unless this Chiang Shiao-ho has six arms and eight legs, he can't get free. I'll have my men ready to come in whenever you sound the alarm." Gi Kon-jii disagreed; he thought a hundred soldiers would not be enough to catch Chiang Shiao-ho. He alone knew Shiao-ho's ability. His only hope lay in the few steel darts he carried. He thought, '*If Chiang Shiao-ho could be here a few days later, I will have my specially ordered darts ready on hand. I'm confident of my accuracy and speed, and I'm sure that he can't escape if I had the chance to surprise him.*'

Bo Ah-ran sat on the bed and brushed her shiny black hair cascading over her shoulders, Gi Kon-jii watched her with aching longing. He dared not make a pass lest Bo Ah-ran would fight him and make him a laughingstock again.

When Bo Ah-ran changed her hair back to two thick braids, the style of a maiden, Gi Kon-jii protested, "Bo Ah-ran. Why did you change your hairstyle? Do you deny that you're married? I demand you to change it back…" but upon seeing Ah-ran's breasts revealed through her sheer undershirt, the mesmerized Gi Kon-jii continued, "Well, you sure look pretty this way. I guess it's all right at night when we're alone, but you should wear your hair in the matron style during the day." No reply. Gi Kon-jii tentatively reached out, took Bo Ah-ran's hand, and asked, "Please tell me why you don't like me. We're married, are we not?" Breaking the silence, Gi Kon-jii continued, "I don't think Chiang Shiao-ho will be here tonight. If he does show up, I won't let him get away again." No reply.

Bo Ah-ran, saber in hand, went out and jumped up on the roof. Gi Kon-jii followed her, and they landed on the roof simultaneously.

"Thief! Thief!" an assistant guard on watch duty yelled and struck a gong.

"You fool! It's us. Didn't you see us come out?" Gi Kon-jii slapped the offender. The whole household aroused, and all the guards, Feng, Pan…were out fully armed. Also, the town detectives rushed in to help.

"Where's the thief?" "Is anyone injured?"

Uncle Feng did not want to admit that it was a false alarm. He told the soldiers, "We heard someone on the roof, but we did not see him. The thief must have run away. Thank you for coming."

Back in their room, Gi Kon-jii opened Master Bo's sealed letter addressed to Shiao-ho, the one he did not give to Uncle Feng earlier. It read, "Chiang Shiao-ho if you would insist on taking revenge, I'm at Ho's farm in Nan-To town, Henan Province. I'm willing to give you my white-haired head if you spare my family and students." Gi Kon-jii explained the message word by word to Bo Ah-ran. He said, "Grandpa ordered me to give Chiang Shiao-ho this letter if I am defeated. I won't hand him this letter even if his sword pierces my chest. I'll never reveal grandpa's whereabouts. To tell you the truth, I'm no match for Chiang Shiao-ho. I promised to help you Kung Lung School, and I'll defend you to my death whether you love me or not." He tore the letter into pieces, burned it, turned around, and slept without saying another word. Bo Ah-ran was touched. Looking at the sleeping Gi Kon-jii, her husband in name only, she thought, '*Why, he meant it. He would fight Chiang Shiao-ho to the death to shield Grandpa and me. Without him, Lee Feng-jii would have injured more Kung Lung members. I'm married to him, but I treat him as an enemy. It's not right.*' She moved closer to Gi Kon-jii, wanting to pour her heart out to him, but a fleeting remembrance overtook her. She sat and wept. Gi Kon-jii heard her but did not comfort her. If he had, she would have succumbed and cried on his shoulder.

A "BOOM" sounding like a ton of rocks startled everyone.

Gi Kon-jii rushed out, a sword in hand, ahead of Bo Ah-ran and the others. A huge stone pole dented the hard-packed earthen floor. It was the same one that Gi Kon-jii had practiced throwing his darts on earlier. Gi Kon-jii shouted, "It's him! Chiang Shiao-ho is here!" Everyone could jump on the roof; Chief Ting and his detectives rushed in to help but found no trace of any intruder.

Bo Ah-ran noticed that the front hall was dark. *'That's strange!'* She knew that the room stored important documents and was always lit and guarded. She entered the room cautiously with her saber ahead of her, but she did not sense any danger. She lit the lamp and started to search under the table with a sense of uncertain and urgent anticipation.

"What's amiss?" Gi Kon-jii followed in with a torch.

Bo Ah-ran spotted a long strip of paper with words hanging down from the ceiling and jumped up to reach it. Gi Kon-jii grabbed it first, and they each had half of it.

She threatened Gi Kon-jii, "Give me the other half! Now!" Gi Kon-jii ran out to the yard with his half.

Bo Ah-ran's half note read, "Bo Ah-ran. Ten years...we...talk…tomorrow… Shiao" Chiang Shiao-ho wanted to meet her tomorrow, *'But where and when?'* She burned it.

Gi Kon-jii's half note read "… morning at Ba Bridge. miss … ho".

"Bo Ah-ran, how could you burn it? I'm helping you Kung Lung School to protect Grandpa… Anyway, I think that Chiang Shiao-ho wants to fight me tomorrow morning at Ba Bridge." The uncles crowded into the room. Gi Kon-jii quickly tucked the note in a fold of sash tied his pajama.

"Uncles, Chiang Shiao-ho invited me to a duel tomorrow morning at Ba Bridge. He left a message."

"Where's the message?" Uncle Pan asked.

"It sounded rude, so I burned it."

"Too bad! It's a piece of evidence."

Gi Kon-jii said, "Never mind. Chiang Shiao-ho's night skills are truly incomparable. I will depend on my steel darts to defeat him; Too bad. I don't have my specially designed ones at hand yet."

"Let's plan then. We could search for him and arrest him for breaking in," Chief Ting continued, "But Chiang Shiao-ho did not commit any major crime. After we've caught him, we can't put him to death legally."

Feng agreed, "Of course we can't hang him. We'll just have to jail him for a few years. He'll lose his skills and strength. That stone post must weigh a ton. He was able to pull it out of the ground, carry it and hop up the roof, and throw it down. His strength alone is frightening enough."

Gi Kon-jii protested strongly, "We can't do this to him. It's cruel. It's not honest. It's against the code of integrity. How could you even think about it? Are we not all brothers of the circle of martial arts warriors?"

"Nephew Gi, you're right. It's just that I am too angry now to think clearly. We'll catch him and then persuade him to forget his revenge. It's getting late. By the way, better keep Bo Ah-ran out of it. Kon-jii, you should be with Ah-ran now. Don't let her go out tonight to seek Chiang Shiao-ho on her own," Feng wanted to get Gi Kon-jii out of the way so he and Chief Ting, Uncle Pan could plot.

"Bo Ah-ran, don't cry and don't worry about the duel," back in their room, Gi Kon-jii said, "If Shiao-ho defeats me tomorrow, I don't think he will kill me. I think I can talk him out of hurting Grandpa. You stay home tomorrow and let the uncles and I handle him." No response.

It was drizzling early the next morning. Bo Ah-ran pretended to be sleeping when Gi Kon-jii covered her with a blanket and left. At Ba Bridge, Gi Kon-jii helped the Kung Lung s repel Lee Feng-jii not too long ago.

It was misty at Ba Bridge, with only a few pedestrians holding umbrellas.

Uncle Feng said, "We're here too early."

Lieu said, "It might be a trick to get us here, or he's afraid to come."

Pan said, "He is not afraid. If Chiang Shiao-ho could throw that heavy stone post last night, he's not afraid of us. Let's wait at the tea house over there." The teahouse had a crowd of husky farmers, fishermen with long hooks, and armed travelers. They were Chief Ting's detectives and soldiers in disguise. Feng and Pan exchanged a knowing smile. Gi Kon-jii did not notice it. He touched the pouch containing the five steel darts. His eyes on the two ends of the Ba Bridge, and he was ready.

Chief Ting, dressed as a wealthy merchant, carried a birdcage. He whispered to Feng, "The net is complete, and the surrounding area is all covered. The renegade can't get away unless he has wings. Chiang Shiao-ho checked in a hotel in the west section of Xian, but he did not go back to his room last night. We'll catch..."

A tall young rider with a wide-brimmed hat got on the Ba Bridge from the east. "It's him. It is Chiang Shiao-ho!" Lieu recognized Shiao-ho. Gi Kon-jii was already on the bridge. Chief Ting slipped away. Gi Kon-jii told

Feng urgently, "Be careful and don't make a hasty move. Chiang Shiao-ho swims well, if he jumps into the river, there is no way we can ever catch him."

"Brother Gi Kon-jii, nice to meet you again," Shiao-ho greeted Gi Kon-jii friendlily.

"Brother Chiang Shiao-ho, let's start the duel right away. We could fight on horseback or foot. You choose."

"A duel? Who set it up? Ah, that's why you came with bodyguards."

"You did. You left a note last night, did you not? Don't pretend that you did not, coward!"

"I did, but I did not invite you."

"Did you not write the message to invite me here to fight? Don't lie."

"I certainly did write the note, and it's not for a fight, and I did not invite you!"

"Whom? Whom did you invite?"

"Bo Ah-ran. I invited her here today. It's not your or anyone else's business."

"Of course, it's my business. Bo Ah-ran is my wife." Gi Kon-jii advanced and slashed at the suddenly paled Shiao-ho furiously. Shiao-ho blocked Gi Kon-jii, and then Feng, Pan, and the whole Kung Lung gang joined in to fight Chiang Shiao-ho.

Bo Ah-ran was on the bridge from the west. Shiao-ho saw her and called, "Stop, all of you! I'll fight you all after I talk with Miss Bo." He forced back all his attackers. They met in the middle of the bridge. Shiao-ho's cracked voice trembled when he greeted Bo Ah-ran, whose hair was in braids, "Miss Bo, ten years is a long time. Do you still remember me?" The drizzle turned into rain. Bo Ah-ran was pale, her eyes wide with tears, but she could not cry. Her mouth was agape, her lips quivered, but no words came. She sat stiffly on the horse and her whole body tensed. The rain poured down her hair, her face, but she did not move. She just stared at Shiao-ho, and he stared at her. Gi Kon-jii and the others were there in between them. Their silence and their grief-stricken looks mesmerized everyone around. For a while, no one moved.

Then Gi Kon-jii thrust again, but Chiang Shiao-ho blocked it. The sound of the two swords clanging broke the spell. All of the Kung Lung gang and soldiers ganged up and charged at Chiang Shiao-ho with all kinds of weapons.

Bo Ah-ran 's shrill voice pierced the air. "Stop! All of you! Uncle Feng, Gi Kon-jii... stop! I'll ask him."

"Yes, Bo Ah-ran, We have to talk. It's between our families. It has nothing to do with the others," Shiao-ho blocked the attacks from all sides.

"Bo Ah-ran is my wife. Chiang Shiao-ho, it's not fitting for you to talk to her. You can't insult me. She is my wife. I'll kill you, or I'll die first," Gi Kon-jii shouted and attacked savagely.

"But… your hair… Bo Ah-ran, is it true? Are you married? But you wear your hair in braids. You and I better talk first and sort things out. It's been ten years, and I have got a lot to say. After you hear me out, then we can decide whether I should seek revenge or not," Shiao-ho said coarsely.

"Shiao-ho, I want to talk to you about…the past ten years. Let's talk. Let's go there." She turned her horse around and rode to the grassy field under the bridge. Chiang Shiao-ho rode behind her. No weapons could stop him.

"Bo Ah-ran, YOU are my wife. I forbid you to talk to him. Chiang Shiao-ho, you are morally wrong," Gi Kon-jii was furious, and he kept attacking Chiang Shiao-ho.

"Wait, let them talk, we'll…" Feng Zhi-pan held the enraged Gi Kon-jii back with force. "Let them talk." He signaled everyone with his eyes.

"Miss Bo, don't talk to him. It's not fitting. You have a husband," someone shouted. Chiang Shiao-ho and Bo Ah-ran rode fast. Gi Kon-jii aimed and threw a steel dart at Shiao-ho's back, but Shiao-ho dodged it. Gi Kon-jii threw another dart, Shiao-ho caught it with two fingers. When the third dart sped toward him, Shiao-ho tossed the dart in his hand and knocked the third dart down.

"Gi Kon-jii, you have more?" Shiao-ho did not slow down.

Chief Tong's men waited. They let Bo Ah-ran's horse pass and attacked Shiao-ho from all sides with long sharp hooks. Three of them hooked onto the horse's legs, and one clamped onto Shiao-ho's right arm. With his left hand, Shiao-ho pulled the hook out. It came out with a chuck of flesh and a stream of blood. He jumped free from the falling horse, dodged two rapid darts. The Kung Lung gang now surrounded him for the kill.

"No!" Gi Kon-jii shouted. He slashed at the soldiers' hooks and cut a few in half.

Bo Ah-ran heard the noise and turned around, and saw that wounded Shiao-ho was in danger. Shiao-ho had already chopped down Lieu and Pan. He ran toward Bo Ah-ran on foot, Gi Kon-jii was in hot pursuit on horseback.

"Uncle Feng, Please stop the soldiers! Don't you see that he is injured? Please stop," Bo Ah-ran pleaded.

"It's an ambush. I despise you," Shiao-ho shouted, and he pierced Gi Kon-jii, knocked Gi Kon-jii down from the horse. He then jumped onto Gi Kon-jii's horse and galloped past Bo Ah-ran's horse. He looked at her with anger and accusation since he thought that she was a part of the plot to trick him.

"Shiao-ho, wait!" Bo Ah-ran kept on calling. She cried.

Shiao-ho shouted back, "Bo Ah-ran, you set up an ambush to capture me. You forget our pledge. You help them to trap me. You are the bait…"

"Shiao-ho, I swear I did not know about the ambush. Wait! Come back! I swear."

Chiang Shiao-ho spurred Gi Kon-jii's horse and overran all of his pursuers.

They gathered around the three wounded: Gi Kon-jii, Lieu, and Pan. None of the three had severe wounds. Gi Kon-jii suffered a bloody flesh wound inside his left thigh. He shouted, "Bo Ah-ran, why do you want to talk to Chiang Shiao-ho? See, my blood is red like the color of your wedding robe. But, I have no regret. I'll defend you and the Kung Lung School again; someday, I'll cut and wound Chiang Shiao-ho deeper."

"Kon-jii, take it easy. Chief Ting and his men will surely catch Chiang Shiao-ho. He is bleeding, and his wound might be serious. He can't run too far." Bo Ah-ran worried about the injured Shiao-ho, and at the same time, she worried about Gi Kon-jii's wound.

"Kon-jii, we'll seek the best doctor," Bo Ah-ran comforted Gi Kon-jii.

"It's nothing. It's just a flesh wound. Don't worry. But Ah-ran, why did you want to talk to him?" Gi Kon-jii moaned. No reply.

Gi Kon-jii blamed Uncle Feng, "You set the ambush, a dirty trick. shame on you Kung Lung school." Feng Zhi-pan said nothing.

Chief Ting came to Feng's, "Did you catch the renegade?" Feng asked.

"No way! He is the most cunning and slippery man I've met in my twenty years on duty. He is a master of horsemanship. Gi Kon-jii's horse is an ordinary one, but Chiang Shiao-ho turns it into a champion. We chased him through forests, across rivers, yet somehow he shook us off and disappeared in thin air. How could he know this area better than my men? Don't worry. We'll catch him tonight if he shows up." Chief Ting reported.

"Ahe! He's free! We'll have endless trouble now. I'm sure of it," Feng whined.

10

Feng asked Lieu, "Only you and Chen know about the past. Was there anything between Shiao-ho and Bo Ah-ran ten years ago?"

"I'm not sure. But, it sure does not look right how Shiao-ho and Bo Ah-ran looked at each other on the bridge this morning. Ten years ago, Shiao-ho was fourteen, and Bo Ah-ran was twelve. They played together often."

"Ahe! They were not adults, but they were not children either."

"They were very young. Ahe! I remember now. Bo Ah-ran hates Chiang Shiao-ho. She gnashed her teeth and cursed him when Chiang Shiao-ho led Master Hsu to challenge Master Bo. I saw it with my own eyes. It also seems to me that Bo Ah-ran and Gi Kon-jii are a loving couple. You worry too much."

"I hope you're right," Feng was not convinced.

In the evening, Feng went to Gi Kon-jii and Bo Ah-ran's room. He stood outside the window and asked, "Bo Ah-ran, is Kon-jii better? Dr. Lee's preparation should help. Please don't get up and open the door for me. I won't stay."

"Uncle Feng, Gi Kon-jii's sleeping. Is there something important?"

"I'm coming to tell you and Kon-jii not to worry; there are a dozen soldiers here to help us tonight. Besides, Chiang Shiao-ho was injured, and he lost a lot of blood. He dares not come tonight."

"Uncle Feng, come in. I'm awake. I'm waiting for Chiang Shiao-ho. He'll come tonight, wounded or not because he has to find out whether Bo Ah-ran and I are married or not. A hundred detectives can't stop him or an ambush. I'm ready to fight him again. Bo Ah-ran, I order you to put your hair up right now!" Gi Kon-jii pretended he was not in pain and continued, "When he comes, I'll deal with him."

Uncle Feng was surprised to see Bo Ah-ran started to change her hairstyle. He thought, *'She did obey Gi Kon-jii's order. Maybe she will be a good wife from now on.'*

Bo Ah-ran worried about both Gi Kon-jii's and Chiang Shiao-ho's injuries. She felt wretched with regrets that she had treated Gi Kon-jii like dirt. She respected Gi Kon-jii's gallantry to defend her family even though he knew he would be wounded or even killed. She also noticed that Gi Kon-jii fought against the soldiers with the hooks. It was apparent that Gi Kon-jii strongly disapproved of Uncle Feng's treachery. He was righteous. She truly worried about Gi Kon-jii's wound and decided that she will be nice to him from now on. *'We are women, and we don't have any say about our future, about how we want to live or to whom we want to marry. Some women will take their wild dreams and wishes silently to their graves,'* her mother told her before, and now she must accept this arranged marriage. But she also kept seeing Shiao-ho's bleeding right arm with a chuck of dangling torn flesh. She thought, *'It's his right arm. Is he disabled? He was mad at me. He thought I played a part in the ambush. He probably hates me now. I know he has not forgotten our pledge under the willow tree. He did not know that Grandpa coerced me to marry Gi Kon-jii. Besides, how could he know that Gi Kon-jii and I merely completed the ceremony? I am not Gi Kon-jii's wife in reality. How can I tell him...?'* She wept.

Feng inspected the security everywhere. He felt a raindrop and wished that it would pour so that Shiao-ho wouldn't come. Sitting on his bed, Feng took off one shoe and saw a hand holding a sword reach out from under the bed. Feng yelled and tried to run, but Shiao-ho pushed him back on the bed.

Lieu heard Feng's shouts and asked, "Brother Feng, is something wrong?"

Shiao-ho's sword was at Feng's throat. Feng called, "It's nothing. I'm all right. Good Night."

"Feng Zhi-pan, I don't want to hurt you or anyone else. I only want some information. Then I'll leave." Shiao-ho said.

"I'll tell you, but you will have to free me first."

Feng got up and sighed, "Shiao-ho, you don't have any grievance against me..."

"No grievance against you? If my teacher had not rescued me and scared you stiff ten years ago, you would have me dead. Never mind, it's not important now. I'll only kill my father's murderers. That's all. Tell me now! Is it true that Bo Ah-ran is married? Where is Master Bo? Chen lied to me; he said that Master Bo is here, but he isn't. Tell me the truth now. Where are old Bo and the Lung brothers? Tell me NOW!"

"The younger brother is at home. The older one-Lung Zhi-chi, the real killer, was here a few days ago; I don't know where he is now. That's the truth. Master Bo is in hiding at one of his old friends' place. Bo Ah-ran is married. She said that her Grandpa did not want her to know where he went. That's the truth."

"How convenient. Feng Zhi-pan, I'll…"

"Wait, Shiao-ho! There's a letter from Master Bo addressed to you. I kept it in the front hall. I'll get it for you."

"I want to read it. We'll go together. You're my shield. You should understand that I'm not afraid of however many fighters you have out there, but I don't want to harm anyone unnecessarily, especially the soldiers. Let's go!" There were many soldiers on the roof with long hooks, and guards with weapons crowded the courtyard.

"Feng Zhi-pan, don't worry! You're the buffer. They dare not attack me, and I promise that I won't harm you. Go!"

"Everyone listen to me! Listen! Chiang Shiao-ho only wants to read Master Bo's letter," Feng handed a string of keys to Lieu, "It's in the big chest. The front hall. Hurry!"

Bo Ah-ran hid behind a door and watched and decided, '*Grandpa's pathetic letter begs for Shiao-ho's forgiveness. I'll wait and see. If Shiao-ho is moved and forsakes his revenge, I will go to him and pour my heart out to him. I'll even tell him that I'm still a maiden.*' she forgot her resolution to be nice to Gi Kon-jii a moment ago.

"Chiang Shiao-ho, here it is. I'll ask Pan to read it aloud."

"Please do! I have to guard against any contingent ambush or steel darts." Master Bo's plea in his letter moved Bo Ah-ran to tears. From the mist, she saw Shiao-ho's expression change from melancholy to anger.

"Master Bo is cunning, isn't he? Now he begs for mercy. When my father sneaked back home and gulped down cold rice before his escape, Master Bo did not pity him and hunted him down like an animal. Twelve years ago, he did not pity my father. How can he ask me to forgive him now? No! I won't. Master Bo made my infant brother orphans and me, used me as a servant, and allowed his son to abuse me. He also waited in the wheat field to kill me. How can I be forgiving? No way!" Shiao-ho's hatred was naked for everyone to see.

"Chiang Shiao-ho, I'll kill you first." Bo Ah-ran rushed in and slashed at him.

"Wait. You helped your uncles to ambush me this morning, and now you want to kill me. I can't believe that you have turned into such a fraud. I don't know you anymore." Shiao-ho blocked her saber.

Gi Kon-jii rushed to fight Shiao-ho, and all of them joined the melee. Shiao-ho wounded a few and seized the sabers from Bo Ah-ran and Pan and the sword from Gi Kon-jii. Then Bo Ah-ran rushed at his sword hysterically. Shiao-ho repelled the others with his injured right arm, swept up the struggling Bo Ah-ran with his left arm, and jumped up on the roof.

He shouted, "Stop! I don't want to hurt anyone unnecessarily. I'll..."

"Chiang Shiao-ho, set my wife free, I'll..." The wounded Gi Kon-jii tried to leap onto the roof too. He couldn't and fell.

"Bo Ah-ran, I'll take you somewhere. I know you're married now and I want to talk to you for the very last time. Ough. Don't..."

Bo Ah-ran bit down hard on the arm holding her and cried, "Let me go! How dare you insult me like this. I don't want to talk to you. I hate you. You want to kill my Grandpa. How can I not hate you? Let me go!"

Shiao-ho released Bo Ah-ran and escaped through a maze of hooks and throwing darts.

Feng Zhi-pan gathered everyone two days later and said, "It's no use to keep up the tight security anymore. Chiang Shiao-ho could come and go at will. Now I know why Master Bo is afraid of him. However, he did make it clear that he'll kill no one but Master Bo and the Lung brothers. We will thank Chief Ting and make sure that his soldiers would get the compensation."

Uncle Pan said, "Now Shiao-ho knows that Lung Zhi-chi was the killer, and Brother Lung probably found a safe place to hide already. I suggest that we let Bo Ah-ran lead us to see Master Bo. If Master Bo wants to fight, all our Kung Lung members will fight Chiang Shiao-ho to the death. If Master Bo wants to hide, we'll accompany him to Beijing. The Manchu Emperor won't allow anyone to get away with killing. We will be safe there."

Uncle Feng disagreed, "No, we can't go to Master Bo's hiding place. What if Chiang Shiao-ho follows us there? I bet that bastard is just waiting for us to lead him to Master Bo. It seems to me that Chiang Shiao-ho is not short of silver; he can afford to watch us and wait. We better stay put for a while and let him search for Master Bo. China is a big country." Feng did not tell them that he had asked a friend to offer Shiao-ho many silver and a top-paying guard position. Chiang Shiao-ho politely refused but said again that he would only kill his father's murderers.

Gi Kon-jii's injury worsened. The continuous rain and his impatience were no help either. He loathed the way Feng had bribed the officials to help, and he could not make anyone believe that he honestly did not know the plot. *'Now everyone, especially Chiang Shiao-ho, will certainly despise me. All of them will think that I'm a deceitful coward. I have blemished my Grandpa's good name. This marriage is a sham, and my greed had led me blind to it. Every one of the Kung Lung group, except Lu Zhi-chun, had convinced me that Chiang Shiao-ho is truly a villain. But now I think he is a man of standards. He could have killed me over and over again, but he only teased me. He has the right to be angry with me because of these stupid 'Chiang Shiao-ho -- wanted' posters. On Ba Bridge, he could have easily cut off my whole leg in anger when he thought I was a part of the ambush. If I had not gotten mixed up with the Kung Lung gang, I might have had the opportunities to make two new friends: - Lee Feng-jii and Chiang Shiao-ho.'* He moaned and cursed in pain.

Bo Ah-ran now acutely felt Gi Kon-jii's pain as her pain. Chiang Shiao-ho insulted her in front of the others, wrongly accused her of participating in the ambush at the Ba Bridge. *'He took advantage of me when I was twelve. He knew then that I wanted the kite and tricked me into calling him 'my husband.' That's blackmail.'* She felt that her anger and hatred toward Chiang Shiao-ho were justified. Somehow her justified anger did not last. She couldn't get him out of her mind. She missed his sad look and the feel of his arm holding her. *'Why did I bite his arm? He said that he wanted to take me somewhere to talk and it will be the last time. Didn't I want to talk to him, too? I wanted to tell him my feelings and that I'm not married. He would believe me. Maybe I can talk him out of revenge, and then I'll go away with him. Oh! I missed the opportunity to talk to him. No! How about Gi Kong-jii? I could not do this to him. Gi Kon-jii is a good man, a little flamboyant perhaps. He yelled at Feng for setting up a wicked trap to catch Shiao-ho. I wish someone could tell me what to do.'*

Gi Kon-jii groaned in his drugged sleep. She went closer to him, and Gi Kon-jii jerked himself awake to subdue a moan.

"Kon-jii, do you feel a bit better now? Does the medicine help?"

"Don't worry. I won't die, and I'll fight Shiao-ho again. Now I understand that you and he were sweethearts. You stared at each other at the Ba Bridge, and he carried you up to the roof tonight. I'm a fool. I'll go and ask Master Bo to release me from this miserable false marriage. I come from a good family, and I'm sure that I can find another wife. But, I will fight Chiang Shiao-ho. He insulted me, and I cannot live with the shame."

Bo Ah-ran wanted to tell Gi Kon-jii the past - how her uncle abused Chiang Shiao-ho, and how the proud boy had silently taken it all, how her pity gradually turned into love and their childish pledge of marriage. But she could not bring herself to tell Gi Kon-jii or anyone about it. *'No, it's too embarrassing to tell anyone my deepest feelings. Besides, Grandpa adamantly prohibited an affair between a man and a woman. Isn't it the very misconduct* that caused Shiao-ho's father to die? Grandpa will die from fury if he knows that I secretly love Shiao-ho, an enemy. Now he thinks that I'm truly married, and he will consider it adultery. He might kill me. No, I can't tell Gi Kon-jii or anyone else.'

"You're wrong. How could I love an enemy? I cried this morning because I was angry and ashamed that I couldn't beat him off. He insulted me tonight, and I can't do anything about it. He is tougher and stronger than all of us. That's all."

"He is super, isn't he? I admit that his leaping skills and strength are superior. If I'm well and I have the specially designed steel darts, I believe that I might have a better chance of winning."

"You can't spread rumors that I love him. I forbid you."

"I won't, Bo Ah-ran. It's too shameful for me to mention it. If it's true, like you said, that you don't have any feelings for Chiang Shiao-ho, I want to know why you don't love me as your husband. Most brides never met their bridegrooms in an arranged marriage. After they are married, the wife will love her husband anyway. We knew each other a while before we're married. After the ceremony, you have never allowed me to be close to you and be your husband. I want to know why you dislike me that much. If I had not been injured today from defending you, Kung Lung School, would you still ignore me and not talk to me. Why?"

"Grandpa coerced me to marry you. I did not want to marry anyone, and I want to stay with Grandpa. My mother died when I was fifteen, and since then, I have been very close to Grandpa. That's all."

"It's too bad. Chiang Shiao-ho won't let your Grandpa live. Besides me, you can't find another fool who is willing to die to defend you. We may as well consider each other strangers from now on. Good night."

Gi Kon-jii's sarcastic remarks infuriated Bo Ah-ran. *'It's no use to depend on Gi Kon-jii, an outsider. We have to face our problems ourselves. Grandpa's cruelty deserves retribution anyway. It's not worth living under the constant fear of Chiang Shiao-ho and now the contempt from Gi Kon-jii.'* She decided that she would go to her Grandpa's hiding place alone the next day, and then together, they would face their peril and death honorably.

It drizzled again early next morning when Bo Ah-ran wanted to leave before the others were up. Gi Kon-jii was not awake, but he was frowning and moaning in pain. Looking at him, Bo Ah-ran hesitated. *'Whether I like him or not does not change the fact that he's my husband, and he was injured because he wanted to protect my family. I can't leave him without discussing with him first. Besides, if I go to Grandpa alone, he will be angry with me, and he will order me back here.*' She dawdled a while, and then the whole household woke up. "Bo Ah-ran, a cup of tea," Gi Kon-jii murmured.

"Here it is." Bo Ah-ran carefully put the cup close to Gi Kon-jii's mouth and waited on Gi Kon-jii tenderly.

"Thank you. Bo Ah-ran, please forgive me. I shouldn't have made those awful remarks last night. I love you so much, and I'm afraid of losing you. I let jealousy get in the way. Now I think the way you stared at him was because you wanted to accuse him of your family's peril. Chiang Shiao-ho has been your family's enemy for a long time. He induced Master Hsu's attack on your family ten years ago and Grandpa beat Master Hsu. Do you know what I believe? I think that Grandpa's skills could be higher than that renegade. Master Bo's fear is from his old age, and he is afraid of Chiang Shiao-ho's omnipotent teacher, that's all. With help and encouragement from both of us, Grandpa may very well defeat Chiang Shiao-ho. Last night, I was out of my right mind. I was frustrated, and I was rude last night. I'm sorry."

Bo Ah-ran felt wretched that she couldn't forget Chiang Shiao-ho and be Gi Kon-jii's wife. Ten years ago, when Chiang Shiao-ho and Master Hsu challenged Master Bo, she truly hated him then. Later, she missed him and pitied him all the time. Yesterday morning when she and Chiang Shiao-ho had their painful reunion, their longing for each other overwhelmed her. She knew that she loved Chiang Shiao-ho, and she was sure that Chiang Shiao-ho truly loved her. Her anger at Chiang Shiao-ho's improper action was real but short-lived. Chiang Shiao-ho's sad expression and his handsome face haunted her, and her feelings for Chiang Shiao-ho have become a permanent barrier between Gi Kon-jii and her. She felt guilty, and so she talked extra nicely and tenderly to Gi Kon-jii.

Bo Ah-ran wished that Uncle Lu were here in Xian. She would tell Uncle Lu the intense love between Chiang Shiao-ho and her without any reservation. She would even boldly tell Uncle Lu that she had never gone to bed with Gi Kon-jii. Uncle Lu might find a way to end this phony marriage. Uncle Lu might convince Chiang Shiao-ho that killing the Lung brother would be enough to avenge his father's death. Then she and Chiang Shiao-ho could get married and live happily ever after like a happy ending of a story.

11

Chiang Shiao-ho was thinking and wishing Uncle Lu were in Xian, too. Uncle Lu and Uncle Ma had protected him and, in many ways, had kept him alive ten years ago. Sometimes, Uncle Lu would slap or yell at him first in Bo Zhi-lin's presence. Chiang Shiao-ho hated Uncle Lu then until one day Uncle Ma told him, "Shiao-ho, Bo Zhi-lin was very jealous of your father. He insisted that Master Bo should kill you lest you would avenge your father's death when you grow up. We all knew that your life was in danger. Uncle Lu hit and punished you whenever you did something wrong. He wanted to protect you whenever there might be a cause for the sadistic Bo Zhi-lin to punish you severely or kill you. He tried his best to make sure you weren't alone with Bo Zhi-lin." Chiang Shiao-ho will never forget how Uncle Lu had helped him to escape. Now he thought, *'I could tell Uncle Lu of my love for Bo Ah-ran. In the last ten years, not a day has gone by that I did not think about Bo Ah-ran and our secret pledge of love. It hurt so much when I knew that Gi Kon-jii married her. I was so jealous, and I had behaved improperly. Now I cannot talk to Bo Ah-ran anymore, and I'm sure that she must hate me now since I wounded her husband. I can ask Uncle Lu to tell Bo Ah-ran that I'm truly sorry. Uncle Lu can say to her that I won't bother her anymore. I can also seek Uncle Lu's advice on the matter of revenge.'* Chiang Shiao-ho stayed in his hotel room all the time. He could not eat, and he could not sleep. He lost Bo Ah-ran now for sure. This kind of pain felt even worse than his injured arm and all the beating he got ten years ago.

Nothing happened for a couple of days, and Feng Zhi-pan relaxed a little. A friend of Feng's brought him some of his family's secret preparation to treat Gi Kon-jii and Pan. This friend also mentioned that he had information that Lee Feng-jii might be back in Xian soon.

Gi Kon-jii collected his specially ordered steel darts and started practice. He was happy that Bo Ah-ran was finally nice to him.

Feng visited the young couple one evening. He told them, "Lee Feng-jii and Chiang Shiao-ho marred Kung Lungs' reputation. Lately, we have had hardly any customers come to buy our protection. Everyone knows that Master Bo must hide from Chiang Shiao-ho. How can anyone trust us to escort their valuables? We may as well close our business."

"Uncle Feng, you're right. Grandpa should not hide. Now we don't know whether he's well or not. Sooner or later, Chiang Shiao-ho will find him. It will be better if I go and ask him to come out. We will fight that renegade together," Bo Ah-ran said.

"No, we should not let Master Bo face the danger. His hiding place is very secure and it won't be easy for Chiang Shiao-ho to find him," Feng said.

Gi Kon-jii said, "All of us will stand and help Grandpa to fight Chiang Shiao-ho. But his hiding from Chiang Shiao-ho is not good for business. We can't let this affair drag on too long. Uncle Feng, you're rich, but a lot of your employees will starve if all the Kung Lung Security Stations close their doors."

"Right! Uncle Feng, you can't close your station. We just can't let Grandpa's thirty years of accomplishments fade away." Bo Ah-ran said.

"I don't mean that I'll close the security station. I just want to be fully prepared to face Chiang Shiao-ho. There is no information about his whereabouts lately. We're not sure the elder Brother Lung is still alive, or Teacher Master Bo... I'll go to Han-Chun City soon," Uncle Feng said.

Bo Ah-ran asked, "Why?"

"I'd like to ask your father to be our leader. We'll gather all the Kung Lung members and friends together to fight Chiang Shiao-ho."

Gi Kon-jii said, "Bravo! My father-in-law should be the one to lead us to fight. We'll go with you."

Gi Kon-jii was riding in a carriage. He was impatient with the slow pace and insisted on riding. The almost healed wound on his inner thigh ruptured. When they stopped at an inn on the first night of the trip, Feng had to help Gi Kon-jii dismount and get to bed.

Bo Ah-ran's mind was in turmoil. She started to get used to being married, and they would be a real couple when Gi Kon-jii got fully recovered. But she was not sure that she could ever forget her first love and the pledge under the willow tree.

"Bo Ah-ran, don't worry about my wound. You look tired. I'm fine. You better go to sleep. We will get up early tomorrow," Gi Kon-jii said. He looked at Bo Ah-ran with all the love he could express. He was happy, and he did not know anything about Bo Ah-ran's troubled thoughts.

"I'm not sleepy yet," Bo Ah-ran said and rearranged Gi Kon-jii's pillow.

She heard someone outside the window sigh softly. She opened the door quickly. Gi Kon-jii struggled to get up, readied his sword, stood beside her protectively. They only saw some other travelers sleeping on the ground under the bright moon. It was cooler outside.

"Bo Ah-ran, did you see someone? Hear something?"

"I'm not sure."

Gi Kon-jii spotted a black form on the roof across from where he stood. He threw a dart at it. "Mew!" He hit a black cat, and the dead cat fell off the roof and landed on the ground. Someone cursed. With difficulty, Gi Kon-jii walked over and collected his dart from the dead cat. He apologized sincerely for the disturbance. Gi Kon-jii did not know that he had changed, and now he was nicer and more considerate to others.

They reached Lu Zhi-chum's security station at Da-Sam Fort two days later.

"How is Grandpa?" Bo Ah-ran asked anxiously.

"Let's get Kon-jii comfortable first. I'll tell you after supper," Lu said.

"How is Grandpa? I want to know now," Bo Ah-ran once again asked as soon as they had helped Gi Kon-jii to bed. She sat beside Gi Kon-jii on the bed, and the uncles sat around the table.

"Bo Ah-ran, promise me that you won't cry. Master Bo and I got to Ho's ranch safely. Mister Ho is over eighty. Master Ho prayed to the Buddha all day long, and his two sons were in charge. There are grandchildren too. They were all rude to us. Master Bo decided to leave and ordered me not to follow him. I tried, but he insisted that he go to Szechwan alone to visit his old friend Master Lee. I got back two days ago."

"But, Master Hsu is in Szechwan. He's no friend of ours," Bo Ah-ran sobbed.

"I don't think Master Hsu will harm Master Bo. I believe Grandpa wants to fight Chiang Shiao-ho alone. That damned Chiang Shiao-ho has forced Grandpa to become homeless. We'll..." Gi Kon-jii said. He struggled to sit up and put his arm around Bo Ah-ran 's trembling shoulders.

"I can't take it any longer! I'm going to find Grandpa, and we'll fight Chiang Shiao-ho together. Kon-jii! Sorry, I can't wait for you to get well," Bo Ah-ran shrieked. Gi Kon-jii held Bo Ah-ran's hand.

"Bo Ah-ran, calm down! Master Bo knows Szechwan well. He..." Uncle Lu said.

"Grandpa has not set foot there for thirty years. He is too old to travel alone. Besides, Master Hsu is Chiang Shiao-ho's first teacher. He'll detain Grandpa for Chiang Shiao-ho."

"Master Hsu won't do something like that. He was grateful that Master Bo had spared his life ten years ago."

"I will fight Master Hsu if he would act against us." Gi Kon-jii said.

Bo Ah-ran stopped crying, but Uncle Lu and Feng were afraid that Bo Ah-ran would leave alone during the night again, and they dared not sleep until just before dawn. Bo Ah-ran sneaked out at dawn and rode fast on the deserted mountain pass.

"Bo Ah-ran! Bo Ah-ran!" Uncle Lu caught up and said, "Let's go back. You can't travel Tu-Nan Mountain Range alone from this side. So many trails branch out from the main one, you will get lost, and you may wander a month and still cannot find your way out of the mountains. Besides, Dart Hu Li and his two sons have been very active lately. They knew that we Kung Lung had met defeat."

"Please don't force me to go back, Uncle Lu. I'm worried to death about Grandpa. He is old and should not be alone."

"I'm sure Master Bo is safe. Please come back with me. When Gi Kon-jii's leg is better, I'll go with you two."

"Uncle Lu, I know you care about my safety. Why can't you accompany me?"

"I have no weapon and no silver. You wait here! I will go back to get them."

"I'm not a child anymore. I don't think you can stall me. Besides, if you go back, Gi Kon-jii will insist on coming, and he will slow us down. I have some silver. When we get to my father's place, we'll have more silver."

"Let's hurry then. When we meet with Chiang Shiao-ho, I can talk him out of wanting revenge. Ten years ago, I had pointed out the right route for him to escape. I'm his father's sworn brother, and I did not think that his father deserved to be hunted down and killed like an animal. I did not want Chiang Shiao-ho to die when he was only fourteen years old. Later, I helped him to escape from Lung Zhi-chi again. I have saved Chiang Shiao-ho twice. He will listen to me." They rode through increasing heat until they were almost out of the mountain range.

"Uncle Lu, where can we find some water?"

"Not so loud. Soon we'll be at my friend's place. We can rest a while there. I'm going to ask my friend to send a message to Feng and Gi Kon-jii. They must be worried about us."

When they were close to the checkpoint where Dart Hu Li's bandits guarded the pass to the next peak, Uncle Lu warned, "Ah-ran, be careful now! Our arch-enemy Dart Hu Li controlled this mountain area. He's deadly accurate at throwing darts, and he wounded your father twelve years ago." Bo Ah-ran thought Uncle Lu was too cautious. She was not afraid of the bandits, but she did not want an encounter that might delay them. So she kept quiet and followed Uncle Lu obediently. Uncle Lu was both amazed and sad to see that the once spirited yet spoiled Bo Ah-ran had suddenly matured. '*Poor child, she has gone through a lot lately. I wish that she could confide in me and tell me her true feelings about Shiao-ho. Feng told me what had happened when Shiao-ho and Bo Ah-ran met at Xian. It's the first time they saw each other in ten years. I had my suspicions when I noticed that she honestly did not want to marry Gi Kon-jii. She rejected him on their wedding night. Oh, that's something even a father cannot ask his daughter. If she had told me the truth, I might have talked to Master Bo about it. A marriage between Shiao-ho and Bo Ah-ran will dissolve the animosity between them. Then the Kung Lung School would be number one again for sure. Ah! It's wishful thinking. Anyway, it's too late now. Bo Ah-ran is married. I noticed that she's pretty attentive to Gi Kon-jii's wound.*'

Hu Li's second son ogled Bo Ah-ran openly and blocked the narrow passage with his men. He said, "Bo Ah-ran is gorgeous. I only want to ask her to have a drink with me. Is anything wrong with it? It does not mean that I want to bed her..." Bo Ah-ran cut off his right shoulder and arm. Hu Jr. died instantly. She also killed Black Bear, another bandit leader. Uncle Lu urged, "Hurry, the whole gang will be here soon." The dead man's brother threw steel darts at Bo Ah-ran and Uncle Lu but missed, and Uncle Lu slashed off his two fingers. Dart Hu Li came, and the first dart he threw lodged in Bo Ah-ran 's right shoulder. Dart Hu Li threatened, "Lu Zhi-chun, I order you to fetch Master Bo and Bo Ah-ran 's father here to see me in five days. On the sixth day, if they are not here, I'll cut off this wicked woman's head and send it to her father."

"Your son insulted my niece first. She's Gi Kon-jii's wife. Your son should not have insulted a married woman," Lu Zhi-chun argued.

"Don't threaten me with Gi Kon-jii's name. I demand that Gi Kon-jii accompany the Bos, father, and son, here with one thousand ounces of silver and kowtow to my sons' caskets. Black Bear was also a son to me. I'll extend the time to ten days," Dart Hu Li continued, "Hurry! It's good enough that I spare your life." Uncle Lu watched helplessly as the bandits dragged Bo Ah-ran away. Feng and Gi Kon-jii-Kong-jii met him.

"Where's Ah-ran?" Gi Kon-jii shouted from afar; he could not ride fast.

"Bo Ah-ran killed Dart Hu Li's son and a lieutenant. Hu Li wounded her with a dart and captured her. They took her up the peak."

His defeat at Chiang Shiao-ho's hand, his wound, and now his wife's capture drove Gi Kon-jii mad.

"Nephew Gi Kon-jii, be patient! They've got Bo Ah-ran, and they may kill her," Lu Zhi-chun warned Gi Kon-jii, "Hu Li's darts are deadly accurate."

Gi Kon-jii barked, "Who's afraid of his darts. I have darts too."

They decided that Uncle Feng and Gi Kon-jii go uphill with no weapons to negotiate, not fight. Uncle Lu would wait.

Feng whispered, "This peak is named Hawk Fall, meaning even the hawk can't fly up to its top. With his unerring darts, Hu Li and his men have held it for over thirty years. Even the Manchu Army could not dislodge him. More than two hundred desperadoes are up there. If they want to fight, two of us won't have a chance to survive, and Bo Ah-ran will die for sure." He continued, "Don't worry! Nobody dares touch Bo Ah-ran, or even look at her for now. Dart Hu Li and Master Bo both respect a married woman and hate lust and adultery. Master Bo ordered Chiang Shiao-ho's father killed because Shiao-ho's father committed adultery."

They left the horses and walked up on foot.

A piercing whistle signaled dozens of men to circle tightly around Gi Kon-jii and Feng. More were coming out from the caves like mice.

"Gi Kon-jii! Bo Ah-ran's life or death is in my hands. You, Master Bo, and Bo Ah-ran's father must kowtow to the two coffins. Give me five thousand ounces of silver and a hundred good horses." Hu Li hissed.

"I'd like to see my wife."

"Come with me!"

All the caves, resembling mouse holes, were carved into the mountain. Some of them were very deep with windows. Two caves with rusted iron bars were prisons, and they were darker than the other caves. Bo Ah-ran was in one of them. There was dried blood on her right arm.

"Uncle Feng, Kon-jii, you are here!" Bo Ah-ran sobbed.

"We're here to save you." Gi Kon-jii said, "Master Hu, release my wife now, and I promise that I'll deliver the silver."

"I will hold her as a hostage. No ransom, I will kill her. These are my final words. You see this huge padlock here and the thick bars on the door. Even a leopard couldn't get free; if you come back at night to save her, you'll die. I warn you."

Gi Kon-jii reached for his concealed darts, but the experienced Hu Li had noticed the slight bulge around Gi Kon-jii's waist earlier. He dodged. His men rushed at Feng and Gi Kon-jii at once. Feng Zhi-pan was down immediately, but Gi Kon-jii snatched a saber and cut down four bandits. Hu Li aimed well and threw his dart, hitting Gi Kon-jii's wounded leg. Gi

Kon-jii stumbled. The bandits tied up Gi Kon-jii and dragged him past Bo Ah-ran's jail.

"Kon-jii let them kill us together now. I'll be your true wife in the underworld," Bo Ah-ran sobbed. "Bo Ah-ran, I've no regrets. I'm only sorry I could not kill Chiang Shiao-ho to keep Grandpa safe and to restore the Kung Lung School's glory." Gi Kon-jii and Bo Ah-ran looked at each other.

"Master Hu, please kill us now, or put us together in one cell," Gi Kon-jii said.

"No way. I will lock you in a cave close to hers. You may not be able to talk to each other, but I'm sure you'll hear her screaming. *Ha! Ha!* I have captured Dragon Knight's grandson. My son's souls will be pleased," Hu Li laughed, but tears welled in his eyes, and his voice cracked.

Hu Li told his men, "Treat their wounds. Gi Kon-jii is Dragon Knight's grandson. Dragon Knight may have other students. The Kung Lung gang is not completely sunk yet. Fetch Feng Zhi-pan here."

"Brother Feng, we don't have any grudge against you."

"From now on, I will not be part of anything between Bo Kung Lung and you," Feng said.

"Good! You better keep your word. You're free to leave."

Feng told Uncle Lu what had happened up there, and then he said, "I told Hu Li that I will be neutral from now on. I hope I can live my old age in peace."

Uncle Lu argued, "You cannot quit on us! We have to stick together to help Master Bo. You know the saying, *'one-day teacher-father, lifelong teacher-father.'* Besides, our oath is that we are to be loyal to our teacher and each other forever."

Feng sneered, "You do that. For me, I don't want to stay on a sinking boat."

Uncle Lu hired a carriage to take Feng back to Xian. Then he hurried to deliver the bad news to Bo Ah-ran's father. He felt sorry for old Master Bo. *'Master Bo does not treat his pupils equally. He was merciless when he ordered Brother One-eyed Yu to cut off one eye and killed Chiang Shiao-ho's father. Master Bo falls for flattery. He is blind to the corrupt Feng Zhi-pan and the Lung brothers. Feng got his wealth through embezzlement, and Lung Zhi-chi had many women, and he is nothing but evil behind Master Bo's back. Master Bo needs all of his students' help and support now. Feng quits, and Lung Zhi-chi had escaped. I can't complete Hu Li's demand in ten days, and I don't even know where Master Bo is at the moment. I think the only one who can save Bo Ah-ran and Gi Kon-jii is Chiang Shiao-ho. He will save Bo Ah-ran. But how about Gi Kon-jii? Yes, Shiao-ho will save him too simply because he is Bo*

Ah-ran's husband. He must love Bo Ah-ran a lot. From what Feng Zhi-pan told me, Shiao-ho could have cut off Gi Kon-jii's leg and killed more people when at Ba Bridge. Gi Kon-jii's wound was not fatal. In the heat of the fight, he controlled his anger and used his sword to pierce but not maim. It's not easy. He could have killed Gi Kon-jii-Kon-jii when they met at Wu-Ton Mountain. As far as I know, Shiao-ho did not kill anyone yet. His teachers taught him well, not only martial arts but also the true meaning of 'right' and 'wrong.' I'm sure he had trailed after Bo Ah-ran, and the poor black cat was a victim. He might have wanted Bo Ah-ran to take him to Master Bo or simply because he wanted to have a look at Bo Ah-ran. He is around this area. He is famous for what he did in Xian. I hope I can find him.'

Hu Li and Master Bo were alike in their firm belief that the worst evil is '*Lust.*' His men could rob but not rape. He did not kill Bo Ah-ran because his dead son was in the wrong. The only women in the camp are the wives of some older bandits. Red-faced was thinking about Bo Ah-ran, the first young woman he had met for a long time. He wanted to take advantage of her. He did not have the key of the heavy padlock to the jail, and he decided that he at least could talk to her and tease her a bit.

He dismissed the two bandits on watch and whispered, "Bo Ah-ran! Bo Ah-ran!" No reply.

"Bo Ah-ran, I'm the third-ranked man here. I can save you and your husband if I can have you for one night. I'm young and strong, and I'll make you happy. *Ha! Ha!*"

"Scoundrel!" Bo Ah-ran shouted.

"I promise I'll save you and your husband and send you home after you bed me. Ahe! Who is..?" Someone choked him from behind and smashed his head against the iron bars.

Bo Ah-ran tried to find something in the cave to hit Red-faced. Ants and centipedes were crawling on the damp ground, and she dared not to search the ground in the dark with her bare hands. Suddenly, she heard muffled sounds and watched Red-faced slump down. Then, someone tall twisted the lock and opened the door.

"Who... who goes there?"

"Hush! It's me. Chiang Shiao-ho. Bo Ah-ran, come with me quickly."

"No, I'm going nowhere with you. It's your fault that we were captured. Go away!"

"Bo Ah-ran, there's not a moment to spare. Hurry! I'll save you first and rush back here to save your husband. Sorry, I won't hold you too tight." Shiao-ho seemed to be able to see in the dark like a cat. He swept Bo Ah-ran up and said, "Hush! Don't cry! If the bandits awaken, it'll be difficult for me to save Gi Kon-jii. They may kill him." He kicked the inert Red-faced away and jumped nimbly over the rough terrains, peaks, and ravines. Bo Ah-ran held tight and closed her eyes a couple of times when she thought that they would fall. In his arms, she felt his warm body, and she knew that she loves no one but Chiang Shiao-ho.

"Ah-ran, sit here and wait! I'll bring Gi Kon-jii here soon." Chiang Shiao-ho left Bo Ah-ran sitting on a big rock surrounded by tall trees.

By now, torches shone all over the camp, and hundreds of bandits searched everywhere like an army of ants. Chiang Shiao-ho knew that they must have moved Gi Kon-jii to another cave. He stood on a rock halfway up the peak and watched. Soon he spotted Red-faced, with a bandage wrapped around his head, and a few others standing afar beside an obscure niche. He disabled them.

"Chiang Shiao-ho cut me loose, and I can escape myself. They tied me extra tight after you saved Bo Ah-ran. Too bad I was sleeping when you came to save her," Gi Kon-jii shouted. He was bound tight like a cocoon, and now Shiao-ho held him under his armpit.

"Maybe they've drugged you. Brother Gi Kon-jii, there is no time to untie you, and you can't move very fast anyway," Shiao-ho shouted amid the uproar. More than a hundred bandits fought them. Shiao-ho held Gi Kon-jii with one arm, cut down several bandits with quick sword thrusts, and swiftly jumped upon a rock halfway to a peak. Neither he nor Gi Kon-jii was hurt. While catching his breath, he dodged a few steel darts thrown up at him. He looked down and spotted a grey-bearded man aiming another dart at him. He knew this man must be Dart Hu Li. He held Gi Kon-jii under his left arm; Shiao-ho tucked the sword into the sash at his waist to free his right hand. He caught one of Hu Li's darts and threw it back. His aim was good, and he killed Hu Li.

They got to the rock where he had asked Bo Ah-ran to wait. She was not there. Shiao-ho set Gi Kon-jii on the rock and quickly searched around. Nothing.

"Bo Ah-ran! Bo Ah-ran!" Shiao-ho shouted, and the mountain echoed. He untied Gi Kon-jii and continued calling Bo Ah-ran, and so did the echo.

"Where's Bo Ah-ran?"

"I told her to wait for us here. It did not take me long to save you, but she is gone! Bo Ah-ran!..."

"Bo Ah-ran, don't be afraid. I'm here. I'm your husband, Gi Kon-jii." Both of them searched and kept calling. No reply.

"Did they capture her again?"

"No, that's not possible. There are no easy paths up here. No one but me can climb so high!"

"But…a tiger? A leopard might have snatched her. Are there any huge animals up here?"

"I don't know," Shiao-ho's voice trembled.

They tried to search for any trace of blood and paw prints, but they could not see very well in the dark.

"Let's go down and have a look. Bo Ah-ran might have thought that it's not safe here and went down. She may be waiting for us down there," Gi Kon-jii said.

"No! Impossible. In front of us is a deep ravine full of sharp rocks. Behind us is a rushing creek. Either way is a long drop. She could not manage it."

"Chiang Shiao-ho, it's all your fault. If you had not come to save us, somehow I would have found a way to escape with her. It is not your business anyway. How did you know that we got caught?"

"I shadowed you from Xian at first. I know I shouldn't have done it, but I thought you would lead me to Master Bo. I went to Su-An town after you killed the black cat. There I met Uncle Lu. He told me that you and Bo Ah-ran were captured and asked me to save you. Uncle Lu had saved me twice when I was running away from the Kung Lung s ten years ago," Shiao-ho sighed.

He did not want to talk about how he had spied on and followed Gi Kon-jii and Bo Ah-ran when they left Xian. He could not help himself from wanting to have a glance at his love. He told himself, *'I want to have a look at her, that's all. I want to find out whether she loves Gi Kon-jii or not. If I see that she is not happy as Gi Kon-jii's wife, I may have another chance to win her over.'* He knew this was wishful thinking, and he behaved foolishly, but he could not stop it. That night he saw through the window that Bo Ah-ran was very attentive to Gi Kon-jii's need. He was so disappointed and gave up the impossible hope.

"Why? Bo Ah-ran is your enemy's granddaughter. Why do you want to save us?" Gi Kon-jii asked.

"Uncle Lu asked me to save both of you. Brother Gi Kon-jii, I don't consider you my enemy. Yes, I was furious when you posted the ridiculous thief-wanted posters everywhere. I wanted to kill you then. I changed my mind because of the refugee business. I even stole silver for you."

"Chiang Shiao-ho, who is your teacher? I heard that he is a skinny old scholar. What's his name?"

"I don't know his name. Honestly, he does not talk a lot. He is a good listener, and I cannot even begin to tell you how superior his skills are. I'm a little afraid of him, and I never asked him about his identity."

"Chiang Shiao-ho, Bo Ah-ran is my wife. Are you after my wife?"

"Bo Ah-ran and I liked each other a lot when we were young. I was hurt when I knew that you two are married and I was very jealous. Now I respect the fact that she is your wife. But I feel that I'm responsible for her being missing. I'll find her for you. You're not capable of searching for her among the high peaks and deep ravines here. It's not an insult. It's the truth."

"I'm injured now. I'll come back to punish the bandits, and I'll challenge you again, Chiang Shiao-ho."

"That's up to you. Now I'll carry you down to where my horse is. I should say 'your horse,' the one I had snatched from you at Ba Bridge. Go to Su-An Town. Uncle Lu is there. After I find Bo Ah-ran, I'll send her to Su-An town, too. Please don't be suspicious. Bo Ah-ran is your wife, and that's that. I'll never be infatuated with a married woman. If I did, my teacher would punish me severely. Besides, you're a scholar, and Bo Ah-ran could be a lady someday."

"I see; you do care for her a lot, Brother Chang."

Gi Kon-jii let Chiang Shiao-ho carry him over precarious ravines and helped Gi Kon-jii to get on the horse. Gi Kon-jii said, "You need a horse too."

Chiang Shiao-ho chuckled, "I'm a wanted thief, am I not? I will steal one." Shiao-ho handed Gi Kon-jii his sword and said, "Take it! You may need it to fight off bandits on your way out. I'll pick it up at Su-An town or later at Uncle Lu's guard station."

Now Gi Kon-jii was truly moved, he said, "Brother Chiang Shiao-ho, I would be honored to be your friend. I'll try to get you and the Bos to reconcile and dissolve your animosity. No matter what, I'll never help the Kung Lung s fight you again. By the way, I would like you to know that I knew nothing about the ambush at Ba Bridge."

"I never thought you did, Brother Gi Kon-jii. You're a braggart, but you're a man of integrity. If I thought you had been a part of the dirty plot, you wouldn't be alive. Brother Gi Kon-jii, you better hurry. It will be dawn soon."

"Brother Chiang Shiao-ho, if you find Bo Ah-ran, you must tell her to come to Su-An town. She did not… We're not… I must talk to her. It's important." Chiang Shiao-ho did not understand what Gi Kon-jii had intended to say.

Back at the peak, Chiang Shiao-ho searched again but found no sign of Bo Ah-ran. He thought that either a huge animal had mauled her or Bo

Ah-ran had committed suicide. He did not find any traces of blood or paw prints the following day. So he jumped down to the rushing creek and found it was not deep. Then he waded downstream and found one of Bo Ah-ran's red embroidered slippers jammed between two rocks, and he scrutinized everything along the creek for miles. At first, he was elated that he did not find a body and thought that Bo Ah-ran probably was alive. Then he started to think that an animal ate her body, or the bandits captured her again.

"Bo Ah-ran! Bo Ah-ran!" he kept calling when he met two hunters.

"Did you see a young woman around?" he asked.

"A young woman? Here? What does she look like?"

"About twenty, and probably wore something blue, had only one shoe on." Shiao-ho was wet through, moss-covered his hand, and his left hand grabbed one red woman's shoe. The hunters thought Shiao-ho was deranged and tried to get rid of him quickly.

"We hardly ever see any women around here. Men don't walk around here early in the morning either."

"Are there dangerous animals?" Shiao-ho asked.

"Oh yes, all kinds - rabbit, fox, wolf, tiger, leopard." They left with a smirk on their face, but the troubled Shiao-ho did not take notice. He thought, *'Bo Ah-ran must be dead. She was wounded, and she did not have any weapon to fight off an animal. A tiger or a leopard must have dragged her to its lair, and that's why she lost one shoe. She's my enemy's granddaughter and Gi Kon-jii's wife. It's not my business to save her. I better concentrate on the revenge business.'*

He met White Tiger, who gave him a horse and said, "We know all about you. Master Bo killed your father and forced your mother to remarry. You should go after your father's murderer. That's a son's duty. Instead, you rescued your enemy's granddaughter. I'm sure you can kill all of us easily, but I don't think you can hold your head up high for too long. Did you accomplish anything regarding a son's duty to avenge his father's death? I don't think so. We're afraid of you. We'll give you anything: a horse, silver…"

"A horse will do, thanks." *'White Tiger is very cunning. He wants a clash between the Kung Lungs and me and hopes that both parties will suffer. But he is right; I should take care of the business of revenge first.'*

At Su-An town, he told Uncle Lu that he could not find Bo Ah-ran, "An animal probably got her. I loaned my sword to Gi Kon-jii, and please get it for me." Shiao-ho did not want to face Gi Kon-jii because he wanted to keep Bo Ah-ran's shoe, and he knew very well that it should be handed to the husband.

Uncle Lu handed Shiao-ho the sword and then said, "Shiao-ho, I'm repeating myself. Master Bo is old now. I beg you to forgive and spare him. Lung Zhi-chi was the real murderer; you have the right to kill him."

"But...All right, Uncle Lu, I'll try to be merciful." Shiao-ho had told Uncle Lu about the past ten years and his love for Bo Ah-ran. Uncle Lu had told him, "Shiao-ho, you should have come to me earlier, I could have… any way it's too late now. Brother Feng should not have enlisted the official's help to ambush you. And that braggart Gi Kon-jii also made things worse. By the way, Bo Ah-ran told me that Gi Kon-jii had nothing to do with the ambush. Shiao-ho, go home! Go home to see your mother and Uncle Ma. Your stepfather sold your brother to be an apprentice somewhere in Shandon, and your mother is not well. Uncle Ma has a hard time, too."

"Uncle Lu, I will go home. Gi Kon-jii is not that bad. He likes to brag, but he is kind and generous." They laughed when he told Uncle Lu the silver he had stolen for Gi Kon-jii was given to the refugees.

On his way to Xian a month ago, at Su-An Town, he met Black Leopard, who had saved him when he escaped from the jail ten years ago in North Szechwan. Black Leopard had suggested that Master Bo must have hidden somewhere close to home. Now Shiao-ho knew that Master Bo was traveling somewhere in Szechwan from the conversation between Uncle Lu and Feng. He did not like to admit that he had done some eavesdrops.

He had promised Uncle Lu that he might spare Master Bo's life. However, he was not sure that he could contain his hatred and be truly merciful when he finally caught Old Bo. The closer he came to his hometown, the more he recalled Bo's cruelty. His heart hardened again. He wanted revenge.

Chengba town looked dilapidated and small to Shiao-ho now. His legs leaden, his chest ached, and his eyes misted...when he led the horse through the streets Many people crowded the narrow streets, some of them must have been Shiao-ho's friends, but none seemed to recognize Shiao-ho.

His hands trembled when he tied his horse to a post in front of Uncle Ma's shop. The shop stood dark and old.

"Uncle Ma! Uncle Ma!" Shiao-ho called.

"What do you want to buy, a pot?" a sleepy apprentice asked. The sight of the young boy reminded Shiao-ho that he had once been an apprentice. He was suddenly hungry as he was back then when Aunt Ma never gave him enough to eat.

"Will you tell Master Ma that Chiang Shiao-ho is here?" There were only a few dusty pans and pots on the wall in the shop. Business was not good.

"Shiao-ho! Shiao-ho! Is that you? Stand up! You are tall." Uncle Ma was thin and old. He coughed and pulled the kneeling Shiao-ho up.

"Uncle Ma, how are my mother and my baby brother? How are you?" Shiao-ho sobbed.

"Come inside. Shiao-ho, let me have a closer look at you. You've grown." Uncle Ma coughed again and then led Shiao-ho to a thin woman and said, "Woman, do you know who this young man is? He's our Shiao-ho!"

"Aunt, greetings!" Shiao-ho kowtowed.

"Shiao-ho, you've grown. Sit, your daddy would have been proud. Your mother is sick. Ton does not treat her well. I'll go and get her. She misses you."

"Uncle Ma, how is everything?"

"Not good. We had famines and drought, and business is poor. I'm a night guard for a rich landlord. My two boys are apprentices, and their masters feed them. Oh well, at least we are not starving." Uncle Ma coughed again and then whispered, "Who's your teacher? Did you fight Gi Kon-jii? Master Bo is in hiding. He hopes that Gi Kon-jii will beat you."

Shiao-ho told Uncle Ma everything.

"I'm so proud. You're the number one now, Shiao-ho!"

"I heard that Master Bo is in Schwann. I will beat up that mean son of his."

"Shiao-ho, be forgiving! You cannot revive the dead no matter what. Your mother has a hard time too. Ton lost his business, and he blamed your mother for bringing him bad luck. Your brother, Chiang Shiao-leo (Little Loon), is about twelve years old now. Two years ago, a merchant from Shandon province took him away to be an apprentice. Your mother had three more children. Two died. The young one is not well."

"Shiao-ho! Oh! My Shiao-ho! It's you, not a dream. You must avenge your father's death. He came to my dream often and asked for cold rice..." Shiao-ho's bony mother coughed and cried, "I should have remained a widow. Ton cursed me every day and said that I brought him bad luck. He abused your brother. Two years ago, he sold your brother Shiao-leo to a merchant from Shandon. That kind man gave me his address; you must go to Shandon to see your brother. I don't have long to live now, but I'll die in peace knowing that you'll kill your father's murderers and find your brother. Your poor father came home that night to eat some cold rice and then he was killed."

"Mother, I promise I'll kill my father's murderers. Here! I have some silver for you to see a good doctor. Mom, you will get well soon. My teacher owns a profitable tea farm. You'll never be impoverished. I can't wait any longer; I'm going now to Bo's village to beat up Bo Zhi-lin."

Shiao-ho cried and kowtowed to them and said, "I'll be back soon."

"Shiao-ho, wait! Your mother just got here, and I want to talk to you, too!" Uncle Ma shouted, but Shiao-ho rode off fast toward Bo's village. His chest hurt so much that he almost fell off the horse. *'If I cannot find Master Bo, at least I can kick Bo Zhi-lin. He kicked me every day when I was fourteen.'*

Bo's village was also dilapidated. Shiao-ho's old home was a relic now. Master Bo's training field now became rough and uneven. However, they reinforced the enclosing wall, built it higher, and sealed the side door through which Shiao-ho had escaped. Shiao-ho pounded on the tightly closed gate.

"Who's there?"

"I'm Chiang Shiao-ho. Open the gate! I'll kick it open or jump over the wall. You think the high wall can stop me?"

"Master Bo ordered me here to guard his home, Chiang Shiao-ho, I could call the officials and have you arrested. You have to fight me first," Master Bo's latest student Su Zhi-mi shouted.

Shiao-ho jumped over the high wall. Su Zhi-mi fought him, Shiao-ho blocked Su's heavy saber and wounded him just enough to immobilize him.

"Bo Zhi-lin, come out!" Shiao-ho shouted.

"Shiao-ho, please spare him. I was nice to you, and I always begged him not to abuse you," Bo Zhi-lin's wife begged.

"Aunt Bo, I won't hurt you. You know how mercilessly he had abused me. He treated me worse than he treated the dogs and pigs. I won't kill him. Bo Zhi-lin, come out! No use to hide behind a woman."

No reply. Shiao-ho dragged Bo Zhi-lin out from under the bed.

"Shiao-ho, please forgive me. I beg of you. I was evil to abuse you before; please spare me." Shiao-ho halted his sword. He could not kill a cripple. Shiao-ho's teacher disabled him with *'Tien Hsueh'* ten years ago. Shiao-ho kicked Bo Zhi-lin once and sent him rolling.

"Aunt Bo, you know that I have the right to kill him. Master Bo and he wronged me cruelly. But, I cannot kill a cripple. Bo Zhi-lin, tell me the truth! Who killed my father?"

"Shiao-ho, be merciful, don't kill your Uncle Bo." Uncle Ma rushed in. He coughed and tried to catch his breath.

"He is no uncle of mine." Shiao-ho sneered.

"Brother Ma, ask him to spare me. He'll obey you. Shiao-ho, Everyone said that it was Lung Zhi-chi who killed your father. But Lung Zhi-chi told me later that it was my father who killed your father."

"That's not true. Shiao-ho, Lung Zhi-chi killed your father. Master Bo had a stroke when your father insulted him and fought him. He did not have to order me to fetch the Lung brothers here to do the killing if he was well. He could easily do the killing himself," Uncle Ma said.

"I won't exonerate Master Bo and Lung Zhi-chi," Shiao-ho said.

"Shiao-ho, I beg you not to kill Master Bo! He's old. Your father won't revive even if you kill all the Kung Lung members. Do you want to kill me, too? By oath, I have to defend my teacher, Master Bo. By oath, Bo Zhi-lin is your uncle. He and I, your father, Uncle Yu, Uncle Lu Zhi-chun, and Feng Zhi-pan are all sworn brothers. Do you want to kill every one of us? We all are under oath to obey and to protect Master Bo with our lives. If I had to fight you, would you kill me? Would you kill your Uncle Lu, too? He saved you and helped you escape, and I raised and sheltered you because we are your father, Chiang Zhi-shen's sworn brothers. You see, we are all connected. I don't think you want to kill me, but I'm obliged to fight you," Uncle Ma said.

"But, Uncle Ma, you heard my mother…" Shiao-ho argued.

"If you kill Master Bo now, someone from the Kung Lung School will take revenge on you later. Why not have mercy and end the animosity. I know you're not evil. You could have killed me or wounded me a lot worse," Su Zhi-mi said.

"My teacher told me that I could only kill the murderers. I'm going now to find Lung Zhi-chi and Master Bo. Uncle Ma, tell my mother I will bring their heads back." Shiao-ho left.

He went to the tall willow tree where he and Bo Ah-ran had pledged their young love. He heard young girls singing. For a split moment, he thought Bo Ah-ran was among them. The girls were ready to run when they saw Shiao-ho on his big horse.

"Don't be afraid, little ladies. I'm from this village too."

"No! You're not. We don't know you," a bold one said.

"I left home ten years ago. Do you know old Master Bo?"

"We don't want to talk about the Bos," one said angrily.

"Master Bo is not here. His granddaughter left a while ago too. We don't like Master Bo's son. His granddaughter is nice," the bold one explained.

Two other girls nervously looked around and said, "Say no more, we don't want trouble." The Bos were feared and hated.

"I knew Bo Ah-ran. Tell me, how nice she is?" Shiao-ho asked, but the girls just stared at him and followed him to the willow tree.

"Don't be afraid. My name is Chiang Shiao-ho. I grew up here. Your brothers and your uncles may know me."

"You? You're Chiang Shiao-ho?" The girls came closer.

"Yes. Your elder brothers probably played with me before."

"We heard about you. We all hoped that someday you would come back to punish Master Bo' son, the Hunchback. He's evil."

"Especially his student Terror Lung Zhi-chi, Master Bo backed him up all the time. Last year, Terror Lung crippled a farmer, yet nobody dared to tell the officials."

"Terror Lung beat my father up pretty bad. When Master Bo asked my father why he was limping, my father dared not tell him."

"Go home and tell your folks that I'll kill the Lung brothers. What happened to this tree? Who has chopped it again and again?"

"Miss Bo Ah-ran did. She rode every day, and she came here often. She cried and chopped the tree, sometimes twice or thrice. See, how many cuts? They looked like scars. My brother said that the tree might die soon."

"Why? Why did she cut the tree?"

"She told my elder sister that she hates this tree. Why? Are you ill?"

"Look at his face. He's whiter than my Grandma when she was dying. He must have seen a ghost."

"A ghost? Let's get out of here."

They shrieked and fled like a pack of birds. Shiao-ho quivered and leaned on his horse. '*Bo Ah-ran hates this tree. She has hated me since that day. She hates me, and she hates the time we spent together. Ahe! I'm a fool. How can I care whether she's alive or not anymore? Poor Father, his soul must be in agony. Mom said that his spirit came to her in her dream to ask for cold rice. Father, I'll kill your murderers.*'

Shiao-ho rode listlessly across the Ba Mountain in the dusk. He lingered at the rushing creeks and waited for any signs and signals from his father, whose body was at the bottom of the creek. He also remembered that twice he had dashed across this mountain to safety. The second time he was with Master Hsu's group. His first desperate escape came the night after he stabbed Lung Zhi-lin. Uncle Lu caught up with him and pointed out the correct route for him. He had ravenously gobbled down the dumplings that Bo Ah-ran had stolen for him. Ah! Bo Ah-ran! Everything led back to her. Her image and words came flashing back.

"*Shiao-ho, please! Get my kite down for me.*"-- A sweet little girl so long ago.

"*Shiao-ho, wait! I'm not a part of the ambush.*"-- At the Ba Bridge at Xian.

"*Shiao-ho put me down! You want to kill my Grandpa! How can I not hate you?*"-- On Feng's roof at Xian.

"*I'm going nowhere with you. It's your fault that we were captured.*" -- At Hu Li's camp.

'She does not hate me. From how she stared at me at Ba Bridge, I know she remembers our pledge of love very well. But now I have to kill her beloved Grandpa. We both are in a dilemma.' Shiao-ho thought.

Shiao-ho wanted to rush back and look for Bo Ah-ran again. Then he realized that even if he could find her, she was forever out of his reach. She was married, and she won't forgive him for wanting to kill her Grandpa.

Ten years ago, Master Hsu had taken Shiao-ho to Zie-Yin City. He was young and scared. Now Shiao-ho walked directly into the Lung brothers' security station.

"Stop right there, you! You cannot go in," Lung brothers' student shouted.

Shiao-ho pushed him away, and other guards came to fight him. Kao came out. Shiao-ho remembered that Master Hsu had stabbed Kao ten years ago.

"Uncle Kao, do you remember me?" Shiao-ho said.

"Ahe! It's Chiang Shiao-ho. All of you, stay away! Don't come close. Don't fight him! It's no use to fight him, and we cannot win. Get back and put down your weapons! Now!" Kao ordered the armed guards not to fight Shiao-ho.

"I won't kill the innocent. Better stay out of my way," Shiao-ho laughed.

"Chiang Shiao-ho, you must be a reasonable man. Your Daddy Chiang Zhi-shen was my sworn brother, too."

"It's true that Lung Zhi-chi killed my father?"

"Yes, they searched everywhere in Chengba for three days and could not find your daddy. Bo Zhi-lin must have watched your home because he knew your father came home one night. The impatient Lung Zhi-chi killed your father before Master Bo could stop him. That's the truth, Chiang Shiao-ho!"

Lung Zhi-tin rushed out from the living quarters and shouted, "Damn you, Kao, you're a coward. You're afraid of Chiang Shiao-ho, and now you try to name us the killers." Uncle Lung Zhi-tin charged at Shiao-ho.

Chiang Shiao-ho forced Uncle Lung Zhi-tin back.

Kao shouted, "Stop, Shiao-ho, go after Lung Zhi-chi. He's the real killer. Master Bo did not have the heart to kill your father. Now Lung Zhi-chi escaped to North Szechwan. Shiao-ho, leave now before the officials come here to arrest you," Not wanting to hurt anyone, Shiao-ho brandished his sword in a tight arc to force everyone back and then rode away.

12

Lung Zhi-chi killed Chiang Shiao-ho's father. He was Master Bo's most favored student. Behind Master Bo's back, he committed adultery, snatched pretty married women. In front of Master Bo, Lung Zhi-chi was ever so obedient and righteous. Master Bo did not know that he terrorized his neighbors at Bo's village.

Chiang Shiao-ho's imminent revenge tore Lung Zhi-chi away from his new concubine and he escaped to North Szechwan. He feared and hated Chiang Shiao-ho. When he heard about Gi Kon-jii's 'wanted...' postcards, he thought, *'Great, I will get Shiao-ho arrested and hanged.'* He started to steal and rob and told his victims that his named was Chiang Shiao-ho. He robbed a rich merchant's wife while she was on her way to join her husband. She hanged herself before he could rape her. Officials were now on alert to catch a middle-aged, fat, beard, and brutish bandit named Chiang Shiao-ho in North Szechwan. Lung Zhi-chi hid from the law in the hills for a few days and then met with Master Bo who traveled alone on route to his old friend Master Lee in South Szechwan.

Master Bo said, "I will stay in hiding no more. I'll go after Shiao-ho and fight him to the death. An honorable death is better than humiliation. Last month, Lu Zhi-chun accompanied me to my old friend Ho's farm to hide. Ho's children humiliated me. I want to fight Shiao-ho alone. I had his father killed and now it's my punishment to be killed. I'm not afraid to die. I'll find him, but I'll only allow him to kill me only. All the gods and ghosts will not allow him to kill my sons and students." His eyes were huge and his white beard spiked. Lung Zhi-chi feared that Master Bo was losing his mind.

Master Lee has many students and many grandchildren. Everyone was courteous, not very warm, to Master Bo and Lung Zhi-chi, and let them stayed in a separate court. Master Bo enjoyed a long rest and had time to think and remember.

Master Bo sighed, "Zhi-chi, I had his father killed but truly I was not unkind to Chiang Shiao-ho. He was homeless and I took him in ten years ago. I could have killed him ten times over. I should have *'weeded the root'* to eliminate the potential danger of his revenge. At that time I wanted to be a kind person and I didn't kill him though my son urged me to kill Shiao-ho time and time again. Now Shiao-ho came back and forced me to flee home at my old age. I did not have time to give Bo Ah-ran a proper marriage ceremony. He forced me to separate from my family and I'm not sure if Gi Kon-jii and Bo Ah-ran are still alive. Oh! My hair and my beard are all white now and I can't stay at home to enjoy my remaining years."

Lung Zhi-chi thought, *'You deserve it. You're the one who ordered us to hunt Shiao-ho's father down and bring you his head. You're the one who split Chiang Shiao-ho's family and made him an orphan, and you're the one foolish enough to allow a pup to become a killer wolf and put all of us in danger.'*

"Teacher, somehow we will trudge through this. The supreme god won't allow Chiang Shiao-ho to get his way for long," Lung Zhi-chi feigned sympathy.

When Master Bo heard the news of Chiang Shiao-ho's alleged crimes, He said, "Fighting Chiang Shiao-ho is no longer a personal issue. He is evil. I will fight him to my death to rid this criminal of innocent people. It might be true that I'm merely afraid of his teacher. I'm old but I still have good skills and strength." Master Bo went out every day to look for Chiang Shiao-ho and he loved to hear the news of Shiao-ho's criminal behaviors. He was in high spirit. His favorite student Lung Zhi-chi hid in his room all the time. Lung Zhi-chi worried every day that he would be identified as the one who impersonated Chiang Shiao-ho and arrested him. He also was afraid that the real Chiang Shiao-ho would come and kill him. *'Master Bo is an old fool. It was on his order that I killed Chiang Zhi-shen. He turned soft and would not kill the son. Now the cub has grown to become a killer. Damn that old fool! It serves him right to be hunted like a homeless dog. Damn old Fool!'*

Master Hsu and his son came to visit Master Bo and declared, "I cannot believe that Chiang Shiao-ho became a low criminal. We will join you to purge Chiang Shiao-ho. My daughter-in-law is Dragon Du's granddaughter. She is highly skilled in martial arts and she will be back soon from North Szechwan. She will help us." Old Bo was glad and Lung Zhi-chi was scared.

Chiang Shiao-ho was not well. The constant fighting, the acute misery of losing Bo Ah-ran, the pressure, and the conflicting ideas of revenge…had caused him poor appetite and sleep. At a small town in North Szechwan, he was very sick and fell into a stupor at the first inn. He did not notice the inn keeper's odd expression at hearing his name. The officials arrested him and he would have been jailed if the carriage driver did not clear him. "It is not him. This young man is tall and slim. The criminal is not as tall, fat, almost fifty, dark complexion, has a bushy thick beard and a big head. Maybe they have the same names. Ahe! I remember that the criminal sometimes calls himself 'Lord Lung.'" The detective also noticed Shiao-ho's southern accent and found in Shiao-ho's bag a letter of introduction from a reputable tea company in Nanjing. He released Shiao-ho.

Shiao-ho thought, '*Did Lung Zhi-chi use my name? Isn't he in Szechwan?*' He recalled his teacher's words, '*Shiao-ho. Preventing and avoiding danger is important. Think ahead... anticipate...*' He asked the detective, " Could you write a notice to clear me. I don't want to be arrested again."

"Yes. I will also let all the other detectives know you have been framed. Where are you going?"

"I will go down south to visit Master Hsu."

This incident reinforced Shiao-ho's decision of revenge. He soon gained back his health and earned his new estimated status for being the hero who killed the notorious Dart Hu Li with one of Hu Li's darts.

Shiao-ho waited for his friend Black Leopard and he did not wait too long.

Master Hsu's daughter-in-law came home from North Szechwan and told everyone the news that the villain Chiang Shiao-ho was still at large. One of her relatives was a victim and she wanted to catch Chiang Shiao-ho.

Master Hsu also heard the news that Dart Hu Li was killed. He wondered, '*Chiang Shiao-ho cannot be both a lowly villain and a hero. Not my Shiao-ho! The courageous boy I knew ten years ago.*' He went to visit Master Bo one evening. While they were drinking and talking, a screaming and bloody Lung Zhi-chi ran out of his room. Someone had cut off Lung's left arm and half of the left shoulder. A small person dressed in black escaped from the roof. Master Hsu made a half-hearted chase. He recognized the killer was his daughter-in-law.

Six officers with lanterns came. One asked excitedly, "Is Chiang Shiao-ho caught? Where is he? Someone told us that we can capture Chiang Shiao-ho here."

"It's him. Ah! He fits the description perfectly; tall, fat, a bushy beard, and a big head." One of them looked at the inert Lung Zhi-chi.

"He's not Chiang Shiao-ho. He's my pupil, Lung Zhi-chi," Master Bo shouted angrily.

"No mistake. The robber sometimes called himself 'Lord Lung' and sometimes said his name was Chiang Shiao-ho." Master Bo kicked the chain out of the detective's hand and aimed his saber at them.

"Halt! Do you dare attack the law? Captain Fee, should we chain this old rascal up, too?" the sergeant yelled.

"It's outrageous. Lung Zhi-chi is my best student." Master Bo said.

"Lung Zhi-chi called himself Chiang Shiao-ho, committed all the crimes. The real Chiang Shiao-ho was framed. My colleague up north had arrested and released the real Chiang Shiao-ho." Captain Fee said.

"If anyone dares insult me and my student, I will kill him. My student would never rob and lust after a woman. You hear?" Master Bo roared like an enraged lion.

"Shut up, old man!" The detectives wanted to arrest Lung Zhi-chi.

Master Hsu quietly handed the captain some silver and asked that they do not arrest Lung Zhi-chi. He said, "He is dying anyway. Please let him stay. Maybe there are two impostors. We need a witness."

"Master Hsu, we will put him in your custody for now"

Master Hsu loathed Lung Zhi-chi and he knew Lung is truly wicked. He pitied the old homeless Master Bo. *'When Chiang Shiao-ho-ho comes, he can have Lung Zhi-chi's head.'*

Master Bo stood there, a sad and hopeless old man.

"We cannot be responsible for our students' evil doings. When I see Shiao-ho, I will talk him out of taking revenge. Take care." Master Hsu left.

Master Bo knew that Shiao-ho would be here soon, he was on alert. He tore a pair of pants into strips to bind tight his flabby stomach and thick thighs. He practiced and worked out more. He was waiting for the imminent fight with Chiang Shiao-ho. *'Did Ah-ran and Gi Kon-jii fight with Chiang Shiao-ho already? Did Chiang Shiao-ho spare their lives? I have taught so many students and now I'm alone at my old age.'* Master Bo held his tears back with tremendous effort.

Master Lee's students and family did not want to get involved, but Master Hsu almost came to be with old Bo every day. He invited the detectives to dinner, trying to get them not to arrest the wounded Lung Zhi-chi. The banquet was on the second floor of the biggest restaurant in town. Master Bo arrived and carried his Kung Lung saber. He insisted that Lung Zhi-chi was innocent.

"My student would not rob and steal. You cannot accuse an innocent man." Master Bo roared.

"There is no mistake. The witness, the carriage driver, had met the real Chiang Shiao-ho and said Chiang Shiao-ho was not the robber. The real Chiang Shiao-ho is young and tall. He is not fat. He does not have a beard and his head is not big. If you offer some silver…" The corrupted detective said.

"I swear it with my life. I guarantee it with my reputation. My student Lung Zhi-chi is innocent," Master Bo shouted again. Nobody listened; they were all staring at the tall young man just coming upstairs.

"Shiao-ho, be merciful. Master Bo is old," Master Hsu called.

"Master Bo, it's between you and me. Let's go somewhere else to…" Chiang Shiao-ho said.

"Enemy!" Master Bo chopped savagely at Chiang Shiao-ho. He failed.

"Shiao-ho! You cannot kill him!" Master Hsu and his son rushed in to intervene. Master Bo took this opportunity to run to the stairs. Chiang Shiao-ho dodged Master Hsu's and his son's swords, he ran down and caught Master Bo. He threw the heavy old man onto the horse's back and ran with the horse in a flash to the waiting Black Leopard.

"Brother Wu, don't hurt him. I'll go now to finish the other business." Shiao-ho said. Master Bo struggled; Black Leopard hit his head with a rock and tied him up.

"Bo Kung Lung, you old bastard! All these years you permitted your students to terrify us. You'll pay for their wickedness now." He dumped Master Bo roughly on the cracked floor of a deserted temple and waited.

Chiang Shiao-ho returned soon and handed Black Leopard a bloodstained bag and said, "Please tie it to your horse." He put Master Bo on a horse and called, "Let's go. I'll bring Lung Zhi-chi's head to the creek where my father was killed. You don't have to slow down your horse. I walk fast."

Master Bo looked Chiang Shiao-ho over and saw that Chiang Shiao-ho was taller and more muscular than his father. He sighed when he recalled that once he had wanted to see him and Bo Ah-ran get married.

"Shiao-ho, I'd like to see my two sons and Ah-ran once again before my death. Did you, tell me the truth, did you kill them all already?"

When he heard Bo Ah-ran's name, Chiang Shiao-ho sighed. He cut loose the cord that tied the old man and helped Master Bo sit straight on horseback. He replied, "No, I did not kill them."

"Shiao-ho, you… you are not going to kill me? I regret…"

"Of course I'll kill you, Master Bo! Ten years ago, I was a boy and you plotted to kill me in the wheat field. You killed my father. How can I let you live? But you're old and alone, so I won't kill you right here. I'll take you home and give you plenty of time to gather your sons and students. Then I'll duel with you and kill you squarely in front of your sons and students."

"Very well! I do regret it. It's no use to say anymore."

"Listen, old monster! You indulged Lung Zhi-chi; you let him terrorize your neighbors. Don't you know that they call him 'Terror Lung'? Lung Zhi-chi committed crimes and wanted to get me arrested. If the witness had not cleared me, I would be in jail. I will bring his head to my father's memorial."

Black Leopard led them north on some less-traveled roads and stayed in some meager village inn. The dejected Master Bo kept quiet but sighed often. They hardly ever met other travelers.

Black Leopard said, "We better kill the old rascal now. There was a mean Tao priestess in Win Town. We have to pass there to enter the mountain path. Master Bo might call for help and we'll have trouble."

"A Tao priestess who knows martial arts? I'm not afraid. Let's cross the mountain before nightfall. Master Bo, I'll kill you the minute you call for help, you hear!"

"Shiao-ho, I am not a coward, and I won't call for help. My Kung Lung School is down in luck now, and everyone jeers at us. As long as one member lives through this catastrophe, someday he will take revenge on you."

"I've told you again and again that I'll only kill my father's murderers," Chiang Shiao-ho said furiously. He was angry at his indecision. He should kill Master Bo now. Instead, he delayed with the excuse of wanting to take Master Bo home first. The truth was that he simply could not kill this old man whom he used to call Grandpa Bo. His heart squeezed and hurt whenever Master Bo sighed. Besides, every hair of Master Bo's white beard seemed to beg him to be lenient. Uncle Ma and Uncle Lu had asked him to be merciful. His Teacher advised him to be forgiven. Bo Ah-ran 's tearful face mirrored in Master Bo's unyielding but pathetic old eyes.

"Bo's village is just on the other side of the mountain. I'm not afraid of their future revenge, but you may want to avoid it. Let's part here." Chiang Shiao-ho told Black Leopard.

"No, Shiao-ho, I hate the Kung Lung gang and I want to see the end with pleasure."

Black Leopard led them astray; he was trying to avoid Win Town and the Tao priestess. It was pitch dark, yet they still rambled along the curvy, rocky route. The horse slipped and threw the heavy Master Bo off. Chiang Shiao-ho caught the falling old man but not his bag of clothes. He hastily gathered the scattered articles up. He did not see Bo Ah-ran 's shoe. When Black Leopard hit the old man, he said, "Leave him alone, it's not his fault. We better find shelter for the night." He wanted to walk back to find the missing shoe.

"Look! A shed with a light on over there! Let's go, Shiao-ho! It's dark. Can you wait till tomorrow morning? What did you lose?"

"It's nothing important. You take him up there first. I'll have another look," Chiang Shiao-ho said. He did not want to tell Black Leopard that he must find Bo Ah-ran's shoe. He had carried it all the time. It was the only tangible article connecting him to Bo Ah-ran.

"Look, this nice hunter's wife has a pot of millet cooked."

"I'll be back." Chiang Shiao-ho traced back along their trek but found no shoe. He hated himself for the absurdity of looking for a shoe, but he was compelled to find it. He bent his head and strained his eyes in the dark till his back and eyes hurt.

Two horses were tied to a tree with their bags on it. *'Black Leopard should take the bags in.'* Chiang Shiao-ho searched his bag one more time and found no shoe. He took the bags and walked up to the faintly lit shed.

"What?" Black Leopard, the hunter, and his wife are all dead. Someone cracked their skulls. Blood everywhere, but no Master Bo, only a pot of millet steaming.

"Old Brute, you killed them all!" Chiang Shiao-ho cursed. His heart pounded, and hairs on his arm stood up and vomited. Two horses were still tied up. *'Old Bo cannot escape far on foot'*. He dodged just in time. The end of a heavy steel rod had stroked the spot where Chiang Shiao-ho was, and a towering monk attacked him with a heavy steel rod. Shiao-ho met the famous Steel Rod Monk. Chiang Shiao-ho threw his sword away and used his two hands to grab the steel rod. The monk could not free his rod, and neither could Chiang Shiao-ho gain an inch. Chiang Shiao-ho had met his match.

"You captured a feeble old man, and you robbed and nearly raped a woman in Szechwan. You're evil. I will kill you," Steel Rod Monk roared. The mountain echoed back evil ..evil .. kill .. kill.

"Lung Zhi-chi committed the crimes, not me. He told everyone his name was Chiang Shiao-ho. I almost got jailed, a witness cleared my name. Your student Monk Pure is my friend. Please hear me out. Master Bo and Lung Zhi-chi killed my father ten years ago. I caught Master Bo, but I don't want to kill a lone old man on the run. I'm taking him back home to his sons and pupils..."

"Don't beg for mercy! Are you afraid of death? *Ha! Ha!* I won't spare you tonight."

"Who is afraid? I just want you to know the truth. That's all," Shiao-ho shouted back.

Chiang Shiao-ho was too smart to fight Steel Rod Monk with strength alone. He let go of the heavy rod and fought with agility and jumped free whenever the monk's rod struck at him. They fought for quite a while and

Shiao-ho pushed the exhausted Steel Rod Monk, holding the heavy rod, down the hill. He heard a piercing shriek. *'He must have cracked his head on the rocks and died.'* Shiao-ho gulped for air when he heard a horse neigh, and found one horse, the one with Lung Zhi-chi's head on it, was gone. He wondered, *'It's possible that Steel Rod Monk did not die and he took the horse. Master Bo might have had stolen the horse when I was fighting Steel Rod Monk. Or the frightened horse broke the cord and ran away. I know that none of these reasons are good.'* Chiang Shiao-ho was also exhausted. He was afraid that some other warrior might be lurking in these unknown hills; he hid between two rocks and slept.

Chiang Shiao-ho woke up and found his sword among the bodies. *'I should have listened to Black Leopard and killed Master Bo yesterday. The hunter and his wife, Black Leopard, all died because I hesitated.'* He sighed and walked down the hill. When he took a closer look at the huge body, he found that Steel Rod Monk did not die from the fall. Someone had slit his throat with a sword or a knife. Who? Chiang Shiao-ho did not have his sword last night. Another scare awaited Chiang Shiao-ho when he found the cord that tied the horse had been cut. He knew that someone with even higher martial arts skills was around last night. This person was neither a friend nor an enemy. If he were a friend, he would have helped him fight Steel Rod Monk. If he were an enemy, he could have killed the exhausted Chiang Shiao-ho. However, this person must have saved Master Bo.

Not far from Steel Rod Monk's body, Chiang Shiao-ho spotted the red embroidered shoe. He stared at it for a long time, hating it. His compulsory search for it last night had caused three persons' lives. He decided not to pick it up and ride away quickly. Black Leopard's old mount would not move fast. Anyway, Chiang Shiao-ho felt like a fool when he doubled back and picked up the red shoe.

Shiao-ho found the path to Win Town and ate at a crowded noodle shop.

"Mr. Wong, did you feed Steel Rod Monk today?" someone asked the owner. Chiang Shiao-ho strained to hear the answer above the noise. "Not today. I hope he will go to Lee's shop to beg. Yesterday he ate eleven bowls of noodles here. He eats so much. He'll ruin my business at this rate; I may as well close the door," the owner complained.

"Why? He does not pay you enough?" Chiang Shiao-ho asked.

"Pay? Not even a small coin. He bars the door with that heavy rod of his and demands to have noodles to eat. He has been around here for a month now. I heard that he stays at a monastery up the hill, but they can only afford to feed him one meal a day," the owner grumbled.

"I bet you don't mind offering a meal to the Tao priestesses when they come to beg. A couple of young ones are pretty," another customer teased.

"Don't blaspheme! It's not funny. The Tao priestess only asks for a little," the owner rebutted.

Chiang Shiao-ho concluded that whoever had saved Master Bo must have sent him to a monastery or a temple. It was also possible that an enemy of Steel Rod Monk waited and killed the monk and stole the horse last night. The other possibility is that Master Bo might have known this area well and escaped to a temple.

On his way uphill, he met two young boys herding pigs and sheep. They seemed to be afraid of telling Chiang Shiao-ho anything about the temple and convent. Chiang Shiao-ho recalled that Black Leopard had mentioned a mean Tao priestess was around here. *'The monks and Tao priestesses here might have harassed the farmers.'* He felt that he could smell the odor of pig shit on him again. The memory of his suffering at Master Bo's ten years ago came back vividly. He saw himself as a young boy through his tears, with pig waste all over him again. The young boy held a kite and looked down at Bo Ah-ran's small lovely face from a high branch of the willow tree.

In this dream-like mist, he let his horse trample through the hills and woods. When he had a glimpse of the frightened Master Bo on the run around the corner of a convent, he was not fast enough to catch him. It was a big convent with many courts. Chiang Shiao-ho pounded on the closed gate, but no one answered. He then jumped up on the wall and saw a young woman, wiping the tears from her face with a scarf, was on her way to open the gate for him. Chiang Shiao-ho did not want to be rude to watching a woman; he jumped down from the wall and waited at the gate. He wondered whether this convent might be a corrupted one that would hold ordinary women hostage. The gate opened. When the woman took away her tear-soaked scarf, Chiang Shiao-ho was speechless to see Bo Ah-ran 's sad and bitter face.

"Bo Ah-ran, is that you, am I dreaming?" Chiang Shiao-ho murmured.

"It's you. You drove me here. Do you want revenge? Good! But you cannot kill my old Grandpa. You can only have one life." She rushed at the paralyzed Chiang Shiao-ho and held onto his arm. The numbed Chiang Shiao-ho lost all his strength.

"Bo Ah-ran, please hear me out. I. I'm so confused. I don't know what to do anymore."

"My family wronged you and abused you, and you had suffered a lot. You must have revenge. But you can only kill one of us. One of us is enough to compensate for your father's death. One to one! You hear!" With tremendous strength, Bo Ah-ran pulled Shiao-ho's sword hard against her chest. Her blood gushed.

"Bo Ah-ran! Bo Ah-ran! You mustn't die…"

"I have to die. It's for the best. It's my homage to Gi Kon-jii, Grandpa, and YOU… Are you not satisfied, Chiang Shiao-ho? You are the cold and heartless one. I waited for you for ten years. Grandpa forced me to marry Gi Kon-jii, but I'm not his wife in reality. You know, Shiao-ho, ten years ago I promised to marry you, and I have never forgotten it…" her voice weakened. Chiang Shiao-ho wept.

"Chiang Shiao-ho, you can kill my granddaughter, but you can't embrace her. She's not your wife. It's sinful and unethical. Put her down! I'll fight you," Master Bo roared.

"Grandpa, you're cruel. I have loved Chiang Shiao-ho since I was twelve. If you had been kind … If you had not allowed my uncle to abuse Shiao-ho, we would be a happy family now. You're very cruel…Why did you force me to marry Gi Kon-jii…Ah! Shiao-ho! Hold me! Let me die in your arms. I love you… Shiao-ho."

Master Bo stared at the wounded Bo Ah-ran and the weeping Chiang Shiao-ho.

Ten years ago, he had wanted them to get married once. The memory of Shiao-ho's father's death flashed vividly back. He truly regretted his cruelty now, but he shouted with added venom, "Bo Ah-ran, I renounce you. You're no longer my granddaughter. Chiang Shiao-ho, I know you can kill me at will. But let me tell you that Lung Zhi-chi killed your father before I could stop him, and I gave your mother the silver that I found on your father's body. Everyone else advised me to kill you, but I did not. I'd like you to know the truth. That's all. I'm going to find Gi Kon-jii to nullify the marriage." Master Bo walked away without a second look at the heartbroken couple.

13

An elderly Tao priestess bandaged Bo Ah-ran's chest.

"Reverend Mother, when did she come here?" Shiao-ho asked.

"Steel Rod Monk and his student took her here. He knows our Head Priestess Keen. He told us that a bandit was chasing her and her Grandfather. She had wounds on her shoulders and legs when she first came. Yesterday, Steel Rod Monk took her Grandfather here. We cannot have a man here, so he stayed at a shed where we kept some deer. Poor girl."

"Shiao-ho, you better leave. You and me, we're doomed. I don't want to see you or my cruel Grandpa anymore," Bo Ah-ran whimpered.

"I'm so sorry. I... I'm wicked, and I don't deserve your forgiveness. Please get well. I..." Shiao-ho sobbed. No answer. Shiao-ho waited a while and then said, "I'm going to get some medicine for your wounds. I'll be back soon." Bo Ah-ran had a deep cut on her chest. It was a tricky place to use the '*Tien Hsueh*' technique to stop the blood. A wrong move might kill her; Shiao-ho was afraid to apply it. He wished his Teacher were here.

He scooped some dirt to cover the bloodstains near the gate, and he could not find his sword. He left it at the gate when he carried Bo Ah-ran to her room. He did not want to look for it further, so he ran downhill, and his horse was missing, too. There was only a pile of droppings. '*Master Bo must have stolen my sword and the horse.*' Shiao-ho ran to Win Town.

No doctor specializing in cuts and no good medicine was available at Win Town. He bought some mint-like herb and hoped it could at least reduce the pain. Then he thought about Bo Ah-ran 's husband Gi Kon-jii. He wondered, '*What should I do now? Bo Ah-ran told me that she always loved me. If Bo Ah-ran gets well and marries me, how could I face Gi Kon-jii? My Teacher will certainly punish me. I won't have a leg to stand upon; everyone will loathe me. I can't marry her. Now I can't kill Master Bo either. How can I face my mother and my dead father's soul? What shall I do?*'

The gate of the convent was bolted from inside. Shiao-ho did not want to wait, so he jumped over the wall. When he landed, something hit his left elbow; he fell and dropped the package of medicine. He stood up at once and dodged the second and the third egg-sized iron balls rapidly hurled at him.

"Who is it? Come out! No more dirty tricks!" Chiang Shiao-ho shouted.

"Bastard! You killed my sworn brother Steel Rod Monk. Now I'll kill you!" A tall and malicious-looking middle-aged Tao Priestess charged at Shiao-ho with a curved saber.

"Steel Rod Monk killed my friend, an innocent hunter, and his wife. He fought me, and I won."

"They are not hunters. They are bandits, and they deserved to die. You tortured old Master Bo."

"Master Bo killed my father, split my family, and abused me ten years ago."

He evaded the Tao Priestess's lethal saber thrusts, but another iron ball from her bow almost hit Shiao-ho on his head when he tried to pick up the package of medicine. No longer defensive, Shiao-ho seized her steel bow and used it as a sword to fight. The Tao priestess had great strength, and she fought better than Gi Kon-jii. Shiao-ho wanted to end the fight quickly; he applied the '*Tien Hsueh*' (vital points press) technique and disabled her, left her sprawling on the ground and yelling obscenities.

He put some medicine on Bo Ah-ran's wound and hoped it would work.

"Shiao-ho, you should not hurt Priestess Keen. Steel Rod Monk saved me, and she is very kind to me. I…" Bo Ah-ran closed her eyes and the tears came. She told Shiao-ho her story between sobs and moans. When she was sitting on the big rock waiting for Shiao-ho to save her husband Gi Kon-jii from Hu Li's camp, her thoughts were so tangled and jammed even the finest comb could not detangle them. She could not be a good wife to Gi Kon-jii because she secretly harbored her unquenchable love for Shiao-ho. She could not truly love Shiao-ho, knowing that he wanted to kill her Grandfather. There were no feasible answers. Only death could set her free. She wanted to die, so she threw herself from the cliff down into the rushing creek.

It was a long drop, but she did not die. Her years of martial arts training and her survival instinct saved her. Her ankle twisted, clothes torn, and knees bleeding, and she lost one of her red shoes when she landed on the rocky river bed. She hopped and crawled to a nearby mud house and knocked on the closed door. A woman pulled her in, pushed her to the corner, and whispered, "Silence."

A man knocked on the door and shouted, "Did you see any strangers, a man, and a woman, around?"

"No."

The woman handed Bo Ah-ran some old clothes and a pair of shoes. She told Bo Ah-ran, "Dart Hu Li is dead. A young man who saved your man and killed Hu Li. Somehow they knew that you're still in the mountain, and they are searching for you. Hurry, walk to the back of the house and turn to your right. You can get out of the mountain through the trees. Good Luck."

Some bandits saw her. She fought them, but they were too many, and she had a bad ankle. At the crucial moment, Steel Rod Monk came and saved her. Monk Pure, Steel Rod Monk's student, carried her first on his back and then hired a carriage for her to get to this Taoist convent.

Monk Pure said, "I know you are old Bo's granddaughter. Last night Chiang Shiao-ho killed Hu Li and saved your husband, too. Now he probably is hunting for your Grandfather. Your Grandfather cannot hide forever; sooner or later, Shiao-ho will kill him. I met Chiang Shiao-ho ten years ago when Master Hsu took him to fight your Grandpa." Bo Ah-ran cried, she needed someone to talk to, so she told Monk Pure about the past and her dilemma.

Monk Pure blamed her, "You should have insisted on marrying Chiang Shiao-ho. Then, he definitely would not want to kill Master Bo."

Steel Rod Monk and the skinny Monk Pure would come and go. From their conversations, Bo Ah-ran learned that her Grandfather was at Szechwan, and she also guessed that Lung Zhi-chi, not Chiang Shiao-ho, was the criminal. She tried to explain, but Steel Rod Monk would not listen and vowed to save Master Bo and kill Chiang Shiao-ho.

Bo Ah-ran's talk of wanting to die knifed Shiao-ho's heart. *'She is right. We, she and I, are doomed. I wished that I had told the Teacher about Bo Ah-ran. He would tell me what to do.'*

He told Bo Ah-ran, "I met Monk Pure about a month ago. I'll release Priestess Keen now. She and Steel Rod Monk saved you, but they are not authentic clergymen, and they are ruthless. They have the same Teacher. And I don't know why one is a monk, and one is a Tao priestess. Once, my teacher told me that Buddha and Taoism are two different religions. I'm sorry that Steel Rod Monk is dead. We fought; I did not kill him. It's all very complicated."

"Shiao-ho, go and release Priestess Keen, and I want you to tell her that you are sorry. Please. Could you do it for me? Then come back, I have so much to tell you."

"I want to talk to you, too. I want to tell you all my dreams and longing for you ten long years."

"Shiao-ho, I missed you and worried about you every day after you escaped ten years ago."

Shiao-ho apologized and told Priestess Keen again that he did not kill the Steel Rod Monk. He freed Priestess Keen. Unexpectedly, Priestess Keen jumped up the minute she was free and tried vainly to '*Tien Hsueh*' Shiao-ho. He pushed her away.

"Chiang Shiao-ho, do you dare go up to Wu-Ton Mountain to fight me there? I don't think you have the guts to go."

"You have friends there? Please don't scare me with the Tao priests. I'm not afraid of the famous seven swordmasters and all the armed priests. I've been there."

"I'll wait for you there. We'll see whether you're a coward or not." She left. Chiang Shiao-ho thought, '*She fights better than Steel Rod Monk, and she is very powerful. She is a woman, and she is older, but I had a hard time to defeat her.*'

The same elderly priestess came out with a meager supper for Bo Ah-ran.

She told Shiao-ho, "Sir, you mustn't mind Priestess Keen. She looks mean, but she's not all bad. We're all afraid of her, but we have to obey her. She is not an authentic Tao Priestess, and she does not know the doctrine well. But she is rich. She had the convent repaired, and she subsidizes us. She also protects us."

"No wonder she swore. Was she here last night?" Shiao-ho asked.

"No, she came back this morning and told us that you killed Steel Rod Monk. Sir, you can stay here a little longer, but you can't stay here overnight. No man can stay here overnight."

Shiao-ho wondered who the mysterious stranger out there last night was. He thought, '*I was lucky. If she were there and helped the Steel Rod Monk to fight me, I would have had a hard time to escape or be alive...*'

"Shiao-ho, you better leave. It's late. Come back in the morning," Bo Ah-ran said.

"Can I stay with you a little longer? Now I hate my father too. If he had not deliberately broken Grandpa's Bo's rules, we might be happily married now. It's fate. Gi Kon-jii is a good man. It's not proper that we are together, but you're not safe here. That vicious priestess might come back tonight. Let me carry you downhill to Win Town. After you're well, I promise you that I'll find Gi Kon-jii..."

Bo Ah-ran interrupted, "No! Don't. I.. ten years ago, I hated you when you brought Master Hsu to fight my Grandpa, but I could not hate you for long. I missed you, and I never forgot our secret marriage vow under the willow tree. I told you before that I did not... I'm not truly... Gi Kon-jii's real wife yet. Although I can't forget him, I don't want to see him again. Shiao-ho, I want. I want...ten years ago, when my uncle kicked you and abused you, my heart ached. Every day and every night, I was worried. I knew that my Grandpa wanted to kill you. They all wanted to kill you, and I was afraid for you. I missed you all the time after you escaped," Bo Ah-ran moaned.

"Bo Ah-ran, you see, I found your shoe. I searched and searched up and down that creek when I tried to find you. I found one of your shoes. I did not want to hand it to Gi Kon-jii, your husband. Because of you, I did not kill your Grandpa, and I did not let my friend Black Leopard whip him. I want..."

"Shiao-ho, it's late. You better leave. I understand everything now," Bo Ah-ran sobbed.

Halfway to Win Town, Shiao-ho thought, '*Bo Ah-ran g said that she is not, in fact, Gi Kon-jii's wife. Gi Kon-jii hesitated to tell me something like that, too. Ah! They are married in name only. I pierced Gi Kon-jii's thigh, and he couldn't... I guess I can marry Bo Ah-ran.*' He rushed back excitedly to Bo Ah-ran's room. It seemed that she was waiting for him.

"Bo Ah-ran, I have had only two wishes on my mind the last ten years. One was revenge, and the other was to marry you. Master Bo told me that Lung Zhi-chi killed my father. Now that I have killed Lung Zhi-chi, I think my father's soul should be satisfied. Yesterday, your Grandpa said that he would find Gi Kon-jii to end your marriage. I think we can keep our vow and get married after you're well. Your Grandpa would give us his blessings eventually. Please say yes...I won't blame you if you say no, Bo Ah-ran!"

"Shiao-ho, you know that I have always wanted to marry you."

"Good! Good! I'm going to Win Town tonight to hire a carriage. I'll get the seat well-padded. Bo Ah-ran, I'm so happy."

"Shiao-ho, don't cry. I'm happy, too. Hold me! I wish you could stay with me," Bo Ah-ran sobbed also.

"I'll be back with a padded chair to carry you downhill early tomorrow morning." He did not want to go, but he had to. He was excited and very tired; he did not detect two pairs of eyes watching him as he ran downhill.

Bo Ah-ran was excited too. Their sweet young love in the past and a happy future kept her awake. She worried for Shiao-ho when she remembered that Monk Pure had told her both Steel Rod Monk and Priestess Keen wanted to kill Shiao-ho. Now Steel Rod Monk was dead, but Priestess Keen wanted to kill Shiao-ho even more.

Priestess Keen was Steel Rod Monk's classmate of the Sho-Lin School. They could not stand anyone who fought better than they do. They fought the aged Szechwan Dragon Du twenty years ago and forced Du into hiding in Beijing. Dragon Knight Gi retired, and he was also a student of the Sho-Lin School. They left him alone. Steel Rod Monk demanded silver when Master Hsu could not lift the heavy steel rod. Only Shiao-ho's Teacher and the mute punished them frequently. They hated and feared Shiao-ho's Teacher intensely. Of course, they wanted to kill Shiao-ho.

Steel Rod Monk asked old Bo, "Old Bo. Chiang Shiao-ho captured you, and you've been on the road with him for a few days. Do you think Chiang Shiao-ho's skills are higher than mine? If I fight him, which one of us will win? Tell me!"

Master Bo hesitated for a while and then said, "Chiang Shiao-ho's strength might be comparable to yours, but he is more agile. If you two fight, Chiang Shiao-ho probably will win. That's the way I see it."

Steel Rod Monk roared furiously. He then sent Monk Pure to fetch Master Bo's students from Chengba to take Master Bo home.

Bo Ah-ran knew Shiao-ho had killed Steel Rod Monk and overpowered Priestess Keen. She was worried that her friends, the militant Tao priests at Wu-Ton Mountain, would harm the lone Shiao-ho. She also thought about Gi Kon-jii and her Grandpa, and finally, she moaned and slept.

Someone walked into her room. Bo Ah-ran asked sleepily, "Shiao-ho, you're back already? Don't worry; I won't change my mind again. I'll marry you."

"Gi Kon-jii is your husband, whore! Now you want to marry your enemy," Priestess Keen sneered.

"Reverend, you don't know that Shiao-ho and I had a promise of marriage ten years ago. Please don't hurt me. Please!"

Priestess Keen tied Bo Ah-ran up roughly. The coarse straw rope cut deeply into Bo Ah-ran's chest wound, and she fainted. Keen carried her downhill. Priestess Keen stole Chiang Shiao-ho's sword, hid, and watched Chiang Shiao-ho went downhill and came back once and left again. So, she waited until she was sure Shiao-ho would not return and then snatched Bo Ah-ran. For a long time, she wanted to have a female student with a sound martial arts foundation. In this area, only two young women knew martial arts well: Fairy Du and Bo Ah-ran. She could not snatch Fairy Du, Master Hsu's daughter-in-law. She had the homeless Bo Ah-ran until the damned Chiang Shiao-ho showed up. Now they wanted to get married. She would not allow it. She must take Bo Ah-ran to somewhere remote to teach Bo Ah-ran all her skills.

Bo Ah-ran came to and realized that Priestess Keen was carrying her on her back. Keen's every step jerked Bo Ah-ran's abrasion and caused her excruciating pain. She moaned. However, Keen ran even faster as though someone was chasing her. Bo Ah-ran hoped that Shiao-ho was pursuing them.

The sound of a horse came from behind when they came to a bridge. Priestess Keen jumped down from the bridge and stood in the knee-deep water. She warned Bo Ah-ran, "Don't you dare moan. I'll kill you." The pursuer went over the bridge. Priestess Keen waited for a long time and then crossed the bridge too. Bo Ah-ran assumed that Shiao-ho must be the one who chased them. She was too sick to yell or even to whine. She fainted again. At daybreak, Priestess Keen stopped when she saw a horse with no rider at the roadside. She looked around cautiously and then put Bo Ah-ran roughly on the horse's back. A man came out of the high grass and charged at her. She recognized the Mute, her feared enemy.

The Mute snatched Chiang Shiao-ho's sword from Keen's hand and kicked Priestess Keen away. He held Bo Ah-ran in one arm, mounted the horse, and rode fast.

Bo Ah-ran asked her middle-aged rescuer, "Who are you? Did Chiang Shiao-ho send you here to save me?" No reply. However, the rider dismounted a short distance away and gently cut Bo Ah-ran loose, and then put her back on the horse. With one hand, he steadied the Ah-ran and ran alongside the horse until they reached a grand villa. Servants and maids hastened to put Bo Ah-ran on the bed and called a doctor.

"Where am I? Who saved me?" Bo Ah-ran asked.

"Is she your wife?" different voices asked.

Bo Ah-ran's rescuer tapped her shoulder first and then pointed to his nose, pushed a thumb up, flapped his arms like a bird, and wiggled his little finger. Someone told Bo Ah-ran, "He's a mute. Only the master understands his signs."

A richly dressed old gentleman exchanged a few hand signals with the mute first and then told Bo Ah-ran, "Miss, my name is Cus. He is a mute, his Teacher, and he saved me twice. From his signs, I gather that his younger brother's name means a bird. You're his brother's wife. A bad woman wounded you. He wants me to take care of you while he goes to get your husband. He's brilliant. He can read facial expressions."

"I see, thanks." Bo Ah-ran was too weak to explain that she is not Shiao-ho's wife yet. They moved her to a nice room and laid her down on a well-padded bed. A maid served her, and a doctor tended to her wounds. Mister Cus's wife and her daughter-in-law came to stay with Bo Ah-ran for a while. They make Bo Ah-ran comfortable and helped Bo Ah-ran into clean clothes. The maid combed her hair, too. The doctor's medicine soothed her pain a little, and Bo Ah-ran fell into a drugged sleep.

Mister Cus wondered, *'How could the mute know that his brother's name means "a bird"? does not know how to read and write.'* Indeed the Mute was illiterate. But he was very smart. Once he and Chiang Shiao-ho tended the tea plantation together, Shiao-ho pointed to the soaring eagles and then pointed to his nose. That was how the Mute knew that Shiao-ho's name had something to do with a bird.

Shiao-ho's Teacher found the baby mute in a deserted shed, hired a woman to help him to raise the mute. When the mute was five years old, the old scholar started to teach him martial arts and sign language. The Mute accompanied the old scholar on frequent trips; he remembered every route, every place they had traveled. The old scholar mapped out a few trails, marked a few places, and sent him to trace Chiang Shiao-ho. The old scholar knew that Shiao-ho's skills were good enough to beat most adversaries. However, he was worried that no one could curb Shiao-ho if he would commit any evil.

The Mute went to Bo's village, the first location his Teacher marked, and could not find Shiao-ho. He could not ask anyone, but he spotted Steel Rod Monk and Priestess Keen. It seemed that they were also looking for Chiang Shiao-ho. These two were highly skilled and cunning, and the Old Scholar made sure the mute understood that Shiao-ho might not be able to defend himself against them. He followed them to the Taoist Covent and found a secular young woman staying there and decided to stay around. One night he followed Steel Rod Monk and spotted Shiao-ho and his prisoner, Master Bo. He watched Shiao-ho desperately search for something in the dark. He was too late to save Black Leopard, the hunter, and his wife. He watched Shiao-ho fight Steel Rod Monk, pushed the Steel Rod Monk downhill. The Mute killed Steel Rod Monk stole a horse and threw away the bag containing Lung Zhi-chi's head. Later, he watched Shiao-ho picked up a woman's red shoe. He watched Shiao-ho and Bo Ah-ran and assumed that the young woman must be Shiao-ho's wife. The Mute also spotted Priestess Keen stealing Shiao-ho's sword and was in hiding. When he woke up from a short sleep and saw that Priestess Keen had kidnapped the young woman, he then followed the Tao Priestess, used the horse as bait to trick Priestess Keen, and saved Bo Ah-ran, and took her to the Cus' village.

The Mute knew that Chiang Shiao-ho would go back to the Tao convent to look for Bo Ah-ran. So he hurried back to the convent. When he got there, the quiet yard of the convent was full of men. Lu Zhi-Chun, Ma Zhi-min,

Gi Kon-jii, and Master Bo's two other students were all there questioning the elder priestess about Master Bo and Bo Ah-ran's whereabouts. The Mute found no Shiao-ho. He tapped Uncle Ma's shoulder first and then imitated a bird flying. He was asking, "Where's Shiao-ho?"

"Get out, you crazy! Are you a bird? A butterfly? Get out! You hear!" Gi Kon-jii tried to push the Mute away.

"Wait! I think he is a mute. He wants to tell us something. Don't hurt him!" Ma shouted.

The Mute did not budge. Instead, he snatched Gi Kon-jii's sword and threw it away. He also kicked Gi Kon-jii.

"How dare you kick me? Who are you? Ah! You have Brother Chiang Shiao-ho's sword." Gi Kon-jii recognized the sword, and he wanted to charge at the Mute again. Lu Zhi-Chun held him back and said, "He's mute, and I think he's also highly skilled. Let me try to guess what he wants us to know."

Lu Zhi-Chun smiled at the Mute friendlily. The mute pointed to the Tao priestess, imitated someone carrying something on the back, and then imitated a woman's walk.

Uncle Lu thought a while, and then Uncle Ma said, "I think he's telling us a Tao priestess carried Bo Ah-ran away."

"Where? Can you ask him, Uncle Ma?" Gi Kon-jii asked.

Monk Pure walked in, and his eyes were tearful. He had just buried the Steel Rod Monk's remains. As soon as he saw the Mute, he wanted to escape. But the Mute grabbed him, patted his shoulder, and smiled. He was saying, "I came as a friend."

"I know him. He's a mute. He is Chiang Shiao-ho's classmate. He fights almost as well as their Teacher," Monk Pure said, and everyone was scared, speechless. The Mute drew a bird, a few lines on the ground with Shiao-ho's sword.

"He's asking us where did a bird...an eagle...a crane... Ah! Shiao-ho (Little Crane) goes. Before you came, he tried to tell us a priestess carried Bo Ah-ran away. Chiang Shiao-ho must be on the chase now, but where?"

"Priestess Keen and my Teacher, Steel Rod Monk, were taught by the same Teacher. She fights better than my Teacher. She wanted Bo Ah-ran to be her student. If she kidnapped Bo Ah-ran, she would take her to Wu-Ton Mountain. She knows many militant priests and the seven famous swordmasters there."

"I've been there. Let's go," Gi Kon-jii boasted and gave the Mute a friendly pat. He then pointed to the picture of the bird and nodded. He was telling the Mute that he would lead the Mute to Shiao-ho. "Uncle Lu,

Master Bo must not have gone far. You will find him. I'll take the Mute to Wu-Ton Mountain," Gi Kon-jii said.

"Brother Gi Kon-jii, when you meet Priestess Keen, please be nice to her. If you're rude, she might kill Bo Ah-ran. By the way, please tell Chiang Shiao-ho if you meet him, that I'm still his friend even though he killed my Teacher. I'm going to retreat to a monastery to study Buddhism."

The Mute was a Southerner. He was even shorter than Gi Kon-jii. On their way to the Wu-Ton Mountain, the usually dominating Gi Kon-jii found that he had to obey the Mute. If the Mute wanted to stop to eat, he dragged Gi Kon-jii off his horse. If the Mute wished to go, Gi Kon-jii was not allowed to sit. Gi Kon-jii cooperated. He knew that he had to depend on the Mute's help to fight and get Bo Ah-ran back. He missed Bo Ah-ran. He often thought of what Bo Ah-ran had told him when they were prisoners at Hu Li's. "*I will be your true wife in the underworld.*" He wanted to ask Bo Ah-ran whether she still wanted to be his wife, now that both of them were alive. '*Bo Ah-ran loves me, at least a little. If not, she won't say something like that.*'

They met Lee Feng-jii at the foot of Wu-Ton Mountain. Gi Kon-jii told Lee Feng-jii everything. Lee said, "I'd like to join you. Chiang Shiao-ho is my sworn brother."

The inn clerk served them dinners and advised, "Young masters, and No one is allowed to go up there now. A tall young fellow is raising havoc there. He killed one of the seven swordmasters, one guard leopard, and at least wounded five others."

"Bravo! Brother Chiang Shiao-ho is great," Lee Feng-jii said excitedly.

"We, the folks around here, all know that one of the famous seven swordmasters is a bad lot. He knows a mean-looking Tao Priestess. Behind the back of the noble Abbot and the other good Tao priests, the two of them had done crimes. The Tao priestess must have kidnapped a young woman, but the good Tao Priests did not know about the kidnapping. The young man did not believe them and argued with them first and then fought them. I heard now the Abbot began to investigate the case. I hope he'll get rid of the evil pair."

14

There was dense fog when Chiang Shiao-ho reached Wu-Ton Mountain. The Tao Priests were annoyed when Chiang Shiao-ho asked them again and again about a missing woman. They fought, and Shiao-ho killed a leopard. Its owner fell off a cliff and died. The priests ganged on him, Shiao injured a few more and escaped to the woods.

Priest Quey stopped Shiao-ho and said, "Brother Chiang Shiao-ho, I am not a local. I killed someone and came here to hide three years ago. I tell you this because I was hoping you could believe me. I know of Priestess Keen. She indeed comes here once in a while but not lately. You can find her at Uennan Province down south or at Chin Mountain Range at Shaanxi up north."

"I just came from Shaanxi. She kidnapped a young woman and challenged me to be here." Shiao-ho had the impression that Quey was not telling the truth and trying to send him on a wild goose chase.

He was starving and smelled cooking. An old Tao Priest at a shabby temple offered him a meal and told Shiao-ho that not all the Tao priests at Wu-Ton Mountain know martial arts. He also said that Quey was a bad lot, and he indeed had some shady deals with a Tao Priestess. Another priest told Shiao-ho the location of the village where he thought Priestess Keen might be hiding. "Get rid of her. We want to get the peaceful mountain back soon. You may stay here tonight."

It was raining, and the mountain paths were dangerously slippery. Shiao-ho found the village. It was a challenging and lengthened fight. He finally pierced the Priestess Keen with the skills the Mute taught him on the day he left his Teacher.

"Tell me where Bo Ah-ran is. Quick! I won't kill you."

"Your...the Mute grabbed Bo Ah-ran...I..."

"My brother the Mute! Where?" Priestess Keen died.

All the bells of every Taoist Temple on Wu-Ton Mountain were ringing again to alert the priests of intruders. He half dragged, half carried the dead Priestess Keen to the center court. 'This is the proof; Maybe The Abby can force Priest Quey to tell…"

All the priests stood with their mouths open, eyes bulged, and Gi Kon-jii and Lee Feng-jii were there. The Mute and the Abbot, number one swordmaster, were engaged in a duel. The two combatants slowly circled each other; their two swords moved slowly and never came close to each other. Shiao-ho knew that it was a hair-raising, to the death duel.

"Chiang Shiao-ho, where is my wife?" Gi Kon-jii demanded.

"The Mute knows where she is. Watch! We have to wait," Chiang Shiao-ho said. His mouth opened as he watched intently. Just when he thought the barefooted Mute was going to win, the white-bearded Abbot fell.

Most of the Tao priests went to the wounded Abby, and some priests looked at the Tao priestess's body.

"Ya Ya…" the Mute hugged Chiang Shiao-ho and handed over Shiao-ho's sword, which the Priestess Keen had stolen. Then he reached up and slapped the puzzled Shiao-ho hard, pointed out his two fingers. Shiao-ho understood that the Mute punished him for applying the 'Tien Hsueh' technique to Priestess Keen. Now everything came to him clearly, and he knew that the Mute had killed Steel Rod Monk, stole the horse, watched his every movement, and saved Bo Ah-ran.

"Brother Chiang Shiao-ho, Priest Quey is under house arrest…" Lee Feng-jii said.

"Where is my wife?…" Gi Kon-jii demanded.

"My brother the Mute saved Bo Ah-ran. He'll take us to her," Shiao-ho told the impatient Gi Kon-jii. The Mute pulled Shiao-ho to the horses.

When Shiao-ho was locked in the critical fight in the village with Priestess Keen, Gi Kon-jii, the mute, and Lee Feng-jii wanted to search the mountain with the accusation that the Tao priests had hidden Bo Ah-ran. The two sides decided to have a duel, and the winner will have the last word.

The Mute impatiently wanted to take Shiao-ho to Master Cus's villa. He did not understand why Gi Kon-jii insisted on joining. He pulled Gi Kon-jii off the horse and threatened Gi Kon-jii with fists. Shiao-ho repeated talked to the Mute with his hands, and finally, the Mute allowed that Gi Kon-jii to join them.

When they reached Cus's villa, Bo Ah-ran died two days ago. Mister Cus took them to the elaborate coffin and said, "Poor Miss Bo, the cuts on her chest were deep and extensive. Two doctors tried very hard, but they could

Two Swordmasters & Two Women

not save her. Which one of you is Shiao-ho? She called 'Shiao-ho' often and with her last breath."

"I'm Chiang Shiao-ho. But her husband is Gi Kon-jii...." Shiao-ho sobbed.

"Stop it, Chiang Shiao-ho! I'm leaving. Your dead father must be proud of you. You forced an old grandpa to be homeless, caused his granddaughter's death. *Ha! Ha*! Bo Ah-ran called your name with her last breath. I was never really her husband. I am just a clown playing the role of her husband. That's all. I'm leaving. It's your turn to be her husband now. Bye!" Gi Kon-jii left with a deranged laugh. Mister Cus, the Mute, and the maids all stood stunned. Shiao-ho managed to stop crying long enough to draw a route and ask the mute to go to Bo's village to fetch Uncle Ma. Mister Cus was a good listener. Between sobs and over drinks, Shiao-ho told him everything.

Mister Cus sighed, "It's all predestined. The three of you are in an eternal triangle. There is nothing more to say. But I wish to see the practice of 'revenge' come to an end. You should have listened to Uncle Ma and Uncle Lu and be forgiving. They were right to say that you cannot revive your dead father even if you kill all the Kung Lung members. I wish that all the warriors learn a lesson from your tragedy and no more acts of revenge. We must stop the vicious circle of killing for revenge. Shiao-ho, you killed Lung Zhi-chi because he killed your father. He was evil, and your revenge was justified. Are you not afraid that one day that Lung's son, if he had one, or a family member of his will try to kill you for revenge?" He then continued, "It is ridiculous to say that *'it's a son's duty to kill his father's murderer, to please the dead father's soul.'* I would think a dead father's soul, regardless if he was murdered or died in bed, would rather see his sons and daughters have a good life. A son's primary duty to his parents should be to have a successful life, to have a loving family. I think that is the wish of any parent."

Uncle Lu and Uncle Ma arrived at Cus's villa with the Mute. They consoled Shiao-ho, "Its fate, there are only two persons to blame: Master Bo and your father. But it's useless to dwell upon it anymore. We'll take care of everything."

The Mute pulled Shiao-ho aside, pointed to the sky, and imitated the action of stroking one's beard. He was saying, "Shiao-ho, go home, go to see our Teacher now. He'll take care of you." The mute understood Shiao-ho's pain. Shiao-ho shook his head, touched his little finger, and made other signs. He was saying, "I'll go home later. Now I want to see my little brother."

The Mute nodded. He walked like a woman, waved his hand, and wiped his eyes. He was saying, "I know your wife is dead. Please don't cry anymore. It's no use to cry." He then reached up and ruffled Shiao-ho's hair fondly.

On the way to Bo's village with the coffin, Uncle Ma told Shiao-ho that his mother died.

"Shiao-ho, your mother hired some Buddhist monks and Tao priests to conduct a memorial for your father with the silver you gave her. Her husband, Ton, repeatedly accused her of wasting silver. Then your stepsister died. Shortly after, your mother died. She told me to tell you that you must find your brother and take care of him," Ma continued, "Shiao-ho, you should have come home directly to see your mother. You should be frank about your wish that you want to marry Bo Ah-ran. Master Bo would gladly have you marry Bo Ah-ran and dissolve the animosity. It's too late to be sorry now. Go to see your brother and look after him. I know you will."

"Thanks. I'll see to it." He did not say that he would look after Uncle Ma and his family too.

He went to the big willow tree.

"Mister Chiang Shiao-ho, you're back with your big horse. Miss Bo likes to ride too. She is not home yet." A village girl said.

He went into town and lay on a lice-infested bed for three days without eating. On the fourth day, he went to Uncle Ma's shop to find out where his mother's tomb was and his younger brother's address.

"Shiao-ho, have you been sick? Don't be too hard on yourself. Life has to go on, and it's no use to weep over the past. Will you stay for the double funeral?"

"Double funeral? Who else died, Uncle Ma?"

"One-eyed One-eyed Yu and Feng Zhi-pan brought Master Bo's casket back. He killed himself." Uncle Ma sighed.

Master Bo was too ashamed and remorseful to go home to face his students. He found a Buddhist monastery and wanted to be a monk. There were so many regrets: the regret of killing so many persons, sometimes with no reason to kill, the guilt of indulging the Lung brothers while punishing other students harshly, the shame of allowing his second son to abuse Shiao-ho. He wanted to see his crippled son one more time before he became a full-fledged monk. When he found out that he had no more silver and was too old to rob, steal…and at the end, he hanged himself.

After the funeral, Shiao-ho shamefully admitted that he was, not Gi Kon-jii, who stole the silver to help the refugees.

One-eyed Yu laughed, "Chen and me knew. Gi Kon-jii could never steal or carry nearly seven hundred ounces of silver and jump up a roof. You should see how unhappy and nervous he was when he distributed the silver to the refugees the next day. You should see how scared he was when he found out that you wrote that ridiculous 'Chiang Shiao-ho (江小鶴) -- wanted' poster on his back." Then One-eyed Yu told Feng, Uncle Lu, and others in detail how Chiang Shiao-ho had teased Gi Kon-jii. They talked about the past and the tragedy. No one condemned Shiao-ho and they all agreed that it was predestination.

Feng and Bo Ah-ran's father were shrewd businessmen. They wanted to have Shiao-ho as a friend. Shiao-ho also knew that his beloved Uncle Ma and his family would need to have the Kung Lung member's goodwill. They parted amicably. Shiao-ho burned incenses and paper silver nuggets for the deceased to use in the underworld, at the site where his father died, and at his mother's tomb and under the dying willow tree for Bo Ah-ran. He cut off a piece of the tree bark as a keepsake.

His younger brother was a well-liked and very honest twelve-year-old apprentice at a fabric shop. The owner liked him and treated him like his own son. The boy cried at their mother's death, but Shiao-ho did not tell him the details of their father's death.

He told his Teacher everything. His Teacher listened to him with patience and consoled him with a long philosophical talk. "Shiao-ho, there are two equally cruel and unreasonable traditions. All the women are the victims of the foot-binding custom, and you are a victim of the tradition that all sons must avenge their father's death. We were told and taught to follow them. I was to blame, too. I could not break off from this evil tradition; otherwise, I would have forbid you to do it. It's no use to regret it now." In the following days, Shiao-ho did his chores, practiced martial arts listlessly, and lost weight. The mute looked at him with concern and coerced him to eat more.

His Teacher said, "Shiao-ho, don't live in the past. I know you cannot forget your painful past. But, life goes on. No one can turn back the time to correct the wrongs. You owe it to yourself and the people who care for you, deceased or alive, to be happy. Nobody said life is fair. We have to grasp the beauty, the pleasure, and the joy of being alive. Your late parents and Bo Ah-ran (飽阿鸾) would be disappointed if you let the bitter past prevent you from enjoying any small doses of happiness you can get out of life. Shiao-ho, be happy for me, for the mute, for your brother, for Uncle Ma and Uncle Lu. You are fond of martial arts so learn it well. Put your passion into it." His Teacher then taught him the highest martial arts skills and agreed that he would help Uncle Ma with the proceeds of the tea plantation.

His Teacher passed away five years later, Shiao-ho wore a white armband as a true son would. Years later, he also wore white as a true son for Uncle Ma and Aunt Ma. Every three or four years, Shiao-ho would repeat the same trip. He would visit his brother and return to his hometown to see Uncle Ma first and then burn incense at his mother's grave and the site where his father died. He would stand a long time besides the site where the big willow tree was. It was there under the big willow tree where he and Bo Ah-ran (飽阿鸾) pledged their love. A piece of the tree bark and one of Bo Ah-ran's red shoes accompanied him everywhere.

-End-

II

A Living Widow
Lee Mo-bai (李慕白) and Yu Ceo-lian (俞秀蓮)

List of characters

A Chinese name -- A Chinese name has 2 or 3 characters. One word, one sound, no alphabet.
The first word is the Last name (surname)- about 150 to 200 surnames in China. There are thousands Chinese with the same last name: Lee , Chang, Lung, Wong. The other 2 words (sometimes only one) are chosen for meaning randomly from all the Chinese words. One word would be the "generation word". Example

Mon Zhi-an (孟 志 安-)--Yu Er (俞二) Yu Ceo-lian's (俞秀蓮) fiancé
Mon--Last name. **Zhi**-- the 'generation word.' **An**--meaning safe.
Mon Zhi-chi -His brother

Lee Mo-bai (李慕白)
Yu Ceo-lian (俞秀蓮)
Mon Zhi-an - (Yu Er)
Violet (Chi Mi-neon)- a beautiful prostitute.

Lee Feng-jii - Lee Mo-bai's father
Chiang Nan-ho (江南鶴)**--Uncle Chiang** -(aka- **Chiang Shiao-ho** (江小鶴)
Gi Kon-jii- Lee Mo-bai's teacher

Friends
Da Wu (Master Da-ti) Lee Mo-bai's best friend.
Prince Te - possible future Emperor
Viscount Chiu
Fat Shih (Mountain Lizard)
Feng Four –Saber King His brothers **Feng Five**
Brother Su
Enemies
Dart Mew
Jao (golden spear) –husband of She-Devil
She-Devil
Monk Pure
Thin Buddha Hwang

Prologue

The birds were quarreling, and the dew was sparkling. Lee Mo-bai (李慕白) finished the morning workout and murmured,
 'In the big gradual and turbulent world,
where can I use my talent to achieve?

He felt the same frustration that a demoted minister wrote two hundred years ago. Twenty-four years old Lee Mo-bai was depressed ever since his teacher Gi-Kon-jii passed away four years ago. He was good-looking, taller than average and lived comfortably as the nephew and heir of a landowner. He was an expert at both the literary arts and martial arts.

His ideas of his future and marriage were different from his dominant uncle's, and the burden of being the only heir made him feel trapped like a caged tiger.

Lee Mo-bai (李慕白) wanted to win fame and fortune with his martial arts skills; he wanted to see the world and rid it of bandits. Doing anything was better than staying home and getting served, literally, from mouth to foot. His uncle wanted Lee Mo-bai to pass the second level of civil services examination and be an administrator. He tried to keep Mo-bai safe. The highway robbers killed his son, Lee Mo-bai's only cousin.

1

His aunt said after breakfast, "Mo-bai, the matchmaker found you a good wife. Miss Pu is seventeen, and her feet are tiny." She understood Mo-bai's restlessness and thought a good wife would keep him happy, and she wanted to have grandkids soon.

His uncle said, "Her family is very much like ours. Since you're a scholar with a promising future, we would expect that she would bring us a good dowry. It's a good match. You've rejected two marriage proposals. Don't you know how much it cost us to pay that greedy matchmaker?" Lee Mo-bai said nothing.

His aunt pleaded, "We want to have a grandson soon to carry on the bloodline. Her sister had two sons in four years, so Miss Pu is likely to have children soon. This girl has tiny feet, true *'golden lilies.'* Think it over."

No reply.

His aunt sighed, "Maybe we should not be afraid of letting you leave home; you may find a wife yourself." His uncle said in a conciliatory tone, "Mo-bai, I know you want to have a wife who knows martial arts. Where could we find someone like that? Maybe we can arrange for you to have a look at Miss Pu."

"Let us wait for a while. I will try hard to pass the examination in the fall." Lee Mo-bai (李慕白) said. His uncle and aunt smiled.

Lee Mo-bai thought, *'Who cares whether she has tiny feet or not. My mother had tiny feet, but my father always wished that her feet were bigger, so they could go to places together.'* He missed his parents and Uncle Chiang Shiao-ho (江小鶴), his father's sworn brother. His parents died when he was eight years old.

His classmate Tu came, "Mo-bai, you better thank me first. I have found you a perfect wife."

"I'm in a bad mood. My aunt is trying to arrange a marriage for me again."

"It's for real. This pretty maiden knows martial arts well."

"She knows martial arts? Who is she? Tell me."

"*Ha Ha*. I bet you're interested. Be patient. I'll tell you in my own time. The famous Master Yu, nicknamed '*Iron Wings*,' has a pretty daughter."

"Our late Teacher Gi praised him highly. He must be close to seventy now."

"He's old. His daughter is about seventeen years old and very beautiful."

"The folks of a small town like to exaggerate. Besides, a fair maiden hardly ever shows herself in public. How do you know that she is pretty and knows martial arts well?"

"It's true. On Spring Memorial Day, Master Yu and his family went to visit their ancestors' graves. On their way back, four young men attacked them. Yu Ceo-lian (俞秀蓮) seized an attacker's saber and wounded one. That's why the folks know that she is pretty and fights better than men."

"Ahe! She's truly one in a thousand," Mo-bai praised.

"I told you so. Miss Yu also beat up our classmate Brother Lu pretty bad."

"Why? She likes to fight?"

"Brother Lu was there when Yu Ceo-lian and her father fought off the enemies. He was obsessed with her. Brother Lu went to Master Yu's house at night to peep at her. He got caught, and she nearly killed him."

"It served Brother Lu right. But, his defeat will certainly tarnish our Teacher's reputation."

"Only you can fight her and let folks know that Master Gi's students are good. You can kill two birds with one stone, be famous and fulfill your dream of marrying a pretty girl who knows martial arts well."

"How can I go there and challenge a maiden? Besides, Master Yu must have arranged a marriage for her already." Lee Mo-bai sounded disappointed.

"She is not promised. You fight her, you win, and you will have a wife. Master Yu pledged that whoever could beat his daughter in a friendly match would be his son-in-law. With your good looks, Yu Ceo-lian might admit defeat. *Ha! Ha*! Mo-bai, you're not afraid, are you?"

"I told you twice already that I'm in no mood for jokes."

"I swear it is true. If you don't believe me, ask Master Yu yourself. I want you to gain back our Teacher's good name."

"You want me to fight her. That is it."

"I got it from a reliable source that Master Yu truly wants to find a capable son-in-law who can help him to fight off his enemies. He did say that his intended son-in-law has to fight better than his daughter. You have to challenge her; you may very well win a wife with your sword."

"Four young men attacked an old man! Master Yu may have more enemies. I would help Master Yu. I don't want to see a true hero suffer defeat at old age."

"That's the spirit. Do you want to have a look at her? The day after tomorrow, the seventh day of the Fourth Month is Buddha's birthday. Everyone will go to the temple to ask for blessings. Tomorrow we can stay overnight at my father's shop in town. Then we can go to the temple to have a look at her." Mo-bai agreed.

Tu rushed home and sent a servant to town with a letter to his friends. He wanted his friends there to help him play a trick on Lee Mo-bai. Though Tu and Lu were also Master Gi's students, only Lee Mo-bai learned well. Tu and Lu were jealous of Mo-bai's achievement, and they thought Lee Mo-bai is conceited.

The next day, Mo-bai told his uncle that he wanted to go to Lu Town to buy some books and stay overnight. His uncle agreed readily. His uncle always wanted Mo-bai to be friends with the well-to-do Tu and Lu.

Tu took Mo-bai to dine at a teahouse. They met two friends of Tu's. One said, "Brother Tu, did you know there are a few young martial arts fighters in town already. They came to challenge the pretty Yu Ceo-lian."

Tu said, "Has anyone won the trophy yet?"

"Not yet. Someone mentioned that Master Yu would rent the field behind the temple for the match after tomorrow. Tomorrow is Buddha's birthday."

"I think that Master Yu wants to save a dowry for his daughter and get someone to help him to fight off his enemies. He probably will want his future son-in-law to move in and live with him. He even might hope the young chap will reopen his security company. I think it's a kind of wishful thinking of his." another friend of Tu's said.

Tu said to Lee Mo-bai, "You may have to forgo the whole thing. Your uncle wants you to earn an office with your pen."

Brother Lu's friend asked, "Brother Lee, do you want to challenge her?"

Lee Mo-bai said, "I don't want anyone to think Teacher Gi has no good students."

Tu said, "Brother Lee sure will win and get a pretty wife."

"Really? Does he fight better? Miss Yu (俞秀蓮) is not easy to win."

Lu said, "Brother Lee Mo-bai (李慕白) will win. Let's have a toast."

A crowd gathered at the temple; slender maidens wore new outfits, portly matrons dressed in somber colors. Many idle young men walked around to watch the pretty girls. Tu pointed out Yu Ceo-lian (俞秀蓮) for Lee Mo-bai, and it was love at first sight. They followed Yu Ceo-lian and her mother home.

Su, Master Yu's student, wielded a heavy saber at Tu and Lee, "You rascals. Go away!" Tu left.

Lee Mo-bai said to Su, "I came to visit Master Yu."

Su sneered, "No, you're not. You followed Miss Yu from the temple. Get away from here, you HEAR!"

They fought. Su could hardly defend himself, and then Yu Ceo-lian came out. She had on a short outfit, and a pink scarf covered her two braids. She shouted, "You rascal, I won't fight you on the street. You dare come inside?"

"Certainly."

The robust Su insisted on helping Yu Ceo-lian, but he could not keep up with the fast moves. Carrying a birdcage, Master Yu rushed home at a neighbor's urging. He saw right away that his daughter was not the young man's match, and the young man fought in defense only.

"Stop!" Master Yu ordered. Lee Mo-bai obeyed instantly but not Yu Ceo-lian (俞秀蓮). She advanced and slashed, scissors-like, at Lee Mo-bai with her two sabers. Lee Mo-bai jumped free with her scarf on the tip of his sword. Yu Ceo-lian cried and rushed inside.

"Teacher! He and another young rascal followed Sister Ceo-lian from the temple." Su said.

Master Yu asked, "You don't look like a rascal. Why do you come to fight my student and my daughter?"

Lee Mo-bai sheathed his sword, bowed respectfully low, and said, "Reverent Master Yu. Please forgive me. I behaved impulsively. I'm Lee Mo-bai of Nan-kon Village."

"You fought with genuine Wu-ton style. Ahe! You must be the late Master Gi's student."

"Yes. I am."

"Oh! You must be Master Lee Feng-jii's son. Once I had a drink with your late father and Master Chiang. You're almost a nephew to me. Come in, and we will talk over a cup of tea. May I ask why do you come here to fight us, Mo-bai?"

"I won." Lee Mo-bai bowed, with the girl's scarf in hand. He was wishfully thinking that Master Yu would accept him as his son-in-law.

"Indeed you have. Master Gi taught you well. I want to know why you came to fight us. What do you want to do with my daughter's scarf?" Master Yu tried to hold his anger in check.

"But…But Uncle Yu didn't you…" Lee Mo-bai stuttered at first, and then his words gushed out, "didn't you say that whoever could beat your daughter in a match could marry her?"

"Ha Ha! Someone duped you. Someone played a dirty trick on you. You're a fool." Su laughed.

Master Yu also chuckled and said, "I've never said such a thing. Your young friends played a prank. We arranged her marriage five years ago. She would marry my good friend Master Mon's second son. This fall, I will take her to Da-ton, Shanxi Province, to be married. Nephew Lee, you're welcome to come to visit us any time. If I know of a suitable maiden, I'll be the middleman."

Lee Mo-bai's face turned red first and then pale. His flame of hope a moment ago turned into ice. He managed to murmur, "Reverend Uncle, I'm sorry. Please forgive me."

"Let's forget it. I'm glad to meet you. Come to see us again."

Lee Mo-bai thought about nothing but Yu Ceo-lian's pretty face and her graceful, agile movements. He composed verses and verses praising her beauty and lamenting his misfortune. Sometimes in his dreams, he would fight a faceless young man or rescue Yu Ceo-lian from a brutal husband and a mean mother-in-law. He was lovesick and getting thinner and decided that he would find an excuse to leave home soon. *'There are many martial arts masters out there, and they must have daughters who are good at martial arts. If I stay home, I would never find another one like Yu Ceo-lian.'*

His servant suggested that he could copy Buddhism scriptures and verses for devotees and earn some silver. They paid him well for his beautiful calligraphy. His writing style was a perfect mix of his father's graceful strokes and Master Gi's powerful ones. Once he was mechanically copying the religious verses, his mind wandered from Yu Ceo-lian to Teacher Gi and Uncle Chiang. *'Were they ever enchanted by pretty girls when they were young? Have they ever been brokenhearted like me? Daddy used to brush my mother's beautiful long hair tenderly. From reading the poems my father had written, I knew he adored my mother. Teacher Gi married and had children though he hardly talked about them. How about Uncle Chiang? Why wasn't he married?'*

His aunt noticed his melancholy and thin face. She worried, and she knew that Mo-bai was bored at home. She sent a letter to her cousin in Beijing and asked him to find a position for Lee Mo-bai.

Yu Ceo-lian (俞秀蓮) was worried because her father was worried. She noticed it even before she had to help her father to fight off the attackers. Ever since her father's student Brother Wei from Henan Province visited them during a blizzard two months ago, her father started practicing and teaching her martial arts in earnest. He even brought a horse and rode often. She sensed that there would be dangers, so she practiced more. When she fought these four vicious men who attacked them, she was scared but she helped her father fight them. That night when a young man came to her home, she chased him away. Since then, she had been on alert, and she knew that she needed to practice more after Lee Mo-bai took her scarf away. '*Ahe! He could have killed me. Luckily, he is no enemy.*' Her face felt hot whenever she thought about that incident.

Then Brother Wei came again. Their enemies were closing in.

Su suggested, "Teacher, I'll go to Nan-kon Village to fetch Lee Mo-bai (李慕白). We don't have to worry about anything if we have him here to help us."

"No, we cannot. It's not fitting for Ceo-lian to meet him again. Lee Mo-bai's uncle wants him to be an administrator, and he certainly won't want his nephew to marry the likes of us. I heard that Lee's uncle is greedy, and he probably wants to have a huge dowry." Master Yu said.

"But, he wants to marry Ceo-lian very bad."

Master Yu prepared to take Ceo-lian and her mother to her betrothed's.

A letter came from Uncle Kao saying there would be an opening for a minor clerk. Mo-bai should be in Beijing soon. His uncle and aunt thought that if Mo-bai could find a job there, he could stay there and then take the civil services examination in the fall. Mo-bai was elated, and he promised that he would study hard for the examination.

His aunt supervised the tailor to make new clothes for Mo-bai. His uncle hired a reliable long-distance carriage to take him to Beijing. They consulted a fortune teller to pick an auspicious day for his departure. Lee Mo-bai gladly set out in the increasing summer heat. He secretly took his father's sword with him. He had three swords: his own, his father's, and Teacher Gi's.

At the first town north, Lee Mo-bai dismissed the carriage and bribed the groom not to tell his uncle. He brought a horse, a used saddle, and a wide-brimmed straw hat. He loved to ride, and he could ride very well when he was five years old. His uncle did not want to have a horse around, and this was the first time he rode after Teacher Gi's horse died. Now, he had a horse and felt free like a released caged eagle, and the dirty hotel room and coarse meals did not bother him at all.

"Mr. Lee, Nephew Lee, where are you going?" Master Yu was riding alongside a carriage. Lee Mo-bai (李慕白) caught a glimpse of Yu Ceo-lian (俞秀蓮) and her mother inside the carriage before she closed the curtain.

"Greetings, Uncle Yu. I'm on my way to Beijing."

"We're going to Da-ton. Glad to see you again. Have a nice trip. Nephew Lee…" Master Yu seemed to want to talk more when his daughter called, "Daddy, can we go now? It's hot."

Mo-bai said, "Goodbye, have a safe trip."

Lee Mo-bai thought, '*The whole family is going to Da-ton. Isn't that where Yu Ceo-lian's husband-to-be lives? Master Yu is anxious to see his daughter get married. I hope his decision has nothing to do with my ridiculous behavior a month ago. What did he want to tell me? They have to turn to the west after two or three stops. I'm going straight to the north. If I slow down and stay behind a bit, I won't meet them again. This is an embarrassing situation.*'

His meager fund got low after buying the horse. He remembered that Teacher Gi had told him about how to earn a free stay at the temple. So he found a Buddhist temple and copied some scriptures for the abbot. He earned a two-day stay and meals. On the second night, he thought wistfully, '*Maybe Old Yu changed his mind about his daughter's marriage. He called me in the middle of the road and tried to tell me that I may marry Yu Ceo-lian. She was too shy to let him finish telling me. I'd better try to catch up with them and find out.*' Another thought chased him on the road before dawn. '*Maybe he is afraid of his enemies. He wants to send his family to the in-laws to be safe. What if the enemies attack him now? I better hurry up to help them.*'

Four riders, three men and a woman, passed him in a rush, and their horses kicked up enormous dust. Lee Mo-bai's horse bolted, and he had a hard time getting the jittery horse under control. '*They might be Master Yu's enemies.*' He hurried.

When he was close to the next town, Lee Mo-bai saw a crowd and heard shouting and the sound of weapons clashing. Master Yu and his daughter were fighting the four riders who had passed him on the road. The woman shouted obscenities while fighting Yu Ceo-lian (俞秀蓮) and the other three men circled the old Master Yu. Lee Mo-bai dashed in; he injured one tall man, and the other two men fled. The crowd cheered when Yu Ceo-lian wounded the malicious woman. Lee Mo-bai turned pale at the sight of blood, and his hands shook when a good bystander brought his horse to him. It was his first real fight, and his sword had drawn blood. '*Taste the blood once; your sword would forever be thirsty for more,*' he seemed to hear Master Gi's words. He knew that he could no longer keep his promise to his dear aunt that he would not fight, and his promise of passing the examination… He was no longer living in a sheltered and pampered world anymore. '*This is real life.*' He felt good.

Soldiers came. They dragged the wounded man and the screaming woman to court. The Yu family and Lee Mo-bai were ordered to follow them to the court. Some bystanders followed them and told the Magistrate that the four riders attacked the Yu family first. Lee Mo-bai came later and helped them.

"My lord, this man, Yu, killed my father. We want revenge," Ho Su-an, nicknamed '*She-Devil,*' said.

"Silence! You cannot take the law into your hands. Put these two in jail. Sergeant, take the Yu family and the young man to a hotel and have them wait for further investigation." On their way out, a fancy-dressed young man ogled the pretty Yu Ceo-lian.

Mrs. Yu was sick. They found a doctor, bought the medicine and borrowed a small charcoal burner and a medicine bowl for Yu Ceo-lian to brew the herbs for her mother.

Master Yu came to Lee's room and explained, "You must have heard about the rule of '*weed out the roots*'; a person who killed someone has to kill the victim's children too, lest they perform their duty-bound revenge on their father's killer. I don't blame them for wanting to kill me. I killed their father. I was anxious to send my family to my in-laws, and then I can fight them alone. I knew they were after me. When I met you the other day, I wanted to ask you to help me then."

"Uncle Yu, you know I would help if I only knew." Lee Mo-bai refrained from asking the details of the animosity.

"Their father, Master Ho, and I were professional guards. We were good friends first and later sworn brothers. Right from the beginning, Master Ho's unscrupulous ways bothered me. We parted. I was poor then, and I had to move to where the jobs were. I lost two boys since we did not have a steady home. Gradually I made a name for myself and had my own security company. When Ceo-lian was five years old, eleven years ago, a young scholar and his bride bought my protection for a trip. The convoy carried the flags that identified my security company. I did not have to escort them myself; most bandits would honor the flag. Master Ho, a bandit leader, led his men to rob the young couple, and he raped the bride. She killed herself. I went to challenge Master Ho, and killed him. I took enough silver from his estate to compensate the scholar's family. However, I spared his children and his students. Then I started teaching Ceo-lian martial arts. Two months ago, Master Ho's two sons, two students, came to kill us. Ceo-lian helped me to repel them. I know they will come again soon."

"Uncle Yu, I will go to Da-ton with you lest they attack you again. I don't have to be in Beijing soon."

"Thank you, but no. Da-ton is not that far. By the time they could return with extra help from Kaifeng, Ceo-lian and her mother could stay with her new family and my in-laws will stand by me."

Lee Mo-bai's heart felt like a sharp dagger stabbed it; he thought, '*Oh yes, she will be married,*' He said, "They may have more help nearby. Please let me accompany you."

"That's not their style. If more of their team here, all of them would gang up on me already. Master Ho's children are mediocre. The woman is the most capable one, and Ceo-lian wounded her. The only one who might be difficult to fight is her husband Jao, nicknamed '*Golden Spear.*' Jao's uncle Mew's steel darts are deadly accurate. Mew was the late Dart Hu-Li's student. I'm telling you this so you will be prepared. You are their enemy now. Mo-bai, is this your first real fight?"

"Yes. I was scared at first, and I was clumsy."

"Master Gi taught you well, you have strength, skills, and speed, but you don't have experience. That will come. When you have to fight your enemy, you should not hesitate. Remember your enemy intends to kill you…"

A sergeant walked in, "Master Yu, I have good news for you…"

"Are we free to leave?"

"Soon. The bystander's report cleared you. The Ho woman admitted that they wanted to kill you. I'm bringing you great news. The Magistrate's only son wants to take your pretty daughter for a second wife, not a concubine. His first wife did not have children. If your daughter has a son soon, her position will be equal to the first wife. Magistrate Feng will pay you three hundred ounces of silver. You need not worry about the dowry. You're in luck, old friend."

"Sergeant, my daughter is already engaged to be married. We are on our way to her new home. Please thank Magistrate Feng for me."

"Master Yu, don't ruin your luck. You should think it over."

"My daughter is true to be married to Master Mon's second son. I can show you the marriage contract. Please intercede for me. Sergeant, here is some silver for your trouble."

"I'll try. But if I were you, I would reconsider it seriously." The sergeant accepted the silver and left. His threat lingered in the air.

Master Yu sighed and whispered, "It's preposterous. My Ceo-lian is not going to be some wealthy scoundrel's second wife. I'd rather marry her to…" he did not finish his statement, Lee Mo-bai's hope started to rise again.

"Uncle Yu, please don't be angry. The Magistrate must be a corrupt one. My Teacher always said that no honest men want to work for the Manchu. I'm afraid that he will find a way to detain us."

"Don't voice your opinion in public. The walls have ears. The Manchu have occupied us, the Han, for over a hundred years now; they were still wary of the resistance. Be careful."

Lee Mo-bai thought angrily, *'Beauty surely tempts evil'*. He remembered that his Teacher told him how to gather information. He put on his scholar's garb, went to a crowded teahouse, and sat at a dark corner. His keen hearing picked up segments of conversation above the noises.

--' *That woman bandit is indeed vicious. Lucky for the old man and the pretty girl, a young chap came to their rescue just in time....*'

--' *That young man looks like a weak scholar, but he sure knows how to wield the sword....*'

--' *The fighters of the internal Wu-ton School of Martial Arts never appear tough outward. You remember that Master Gi and Master Lee, before them the two Dragons, all look like weak and soft scholars. Rumors had it that they composed poems when they fought. Ha.Ha...*'

Lee Mo-bai thought, "*They are talking about my teacher Gi Kon-jii and my father Lee Feng-jii.*"

--' *I'm sorry for that pretty girl. She won't be safe now. Magistrate's son gaped at her..*'

--' *Oh. That devil won't leave any pretty young woman alone. ...I heard... Chen's wife...*'

Lee Mo-bai strained to hear more of the whispering, but he could not. He suddenly was afraid for Yu Ceo-lian.

"Brother Lee, please help us. The soldiers arrested my father. Please go and find out why," a tearful Yu Ceo-lian met him and pleaded.

"Yes, I'll go. Miss Yu, please stay in your room and wait."

He adjusted his scholar's cap first and asked a guard at the gate. At the same time, he inconspicuously handed the guard some silver. The guard told him that the officers arrested Master Yu because someone had reported that Master Yu is a bandit.

"Go to Captain Ta-di. He will help you," the guard whispered.

"The last name is Ta-di. A Manchu?" Lee Mo-bai also whispered.

"Captain Ta-di is indeed a full-blooded Manchu, but he is just. It was on his order that old Yu was put in a cleaner cell. He knows the Magistrate's son is a bad lot, and he will help you. Not all the Manchu are cruel and not all the Hans are nice either. Go to ask him quickly," the guard whispered.

Lee Mo-bai had to bribe another guard again before he was presented to Captain Ta-di.

"Master Lee, don't worry. They cannot hold him long. The woman insisted that she would not lie. She said, "Of course we want him dead. But it's against our ethics to indict him when he is truly not a bandit." I know that Magistrate Feng is very corrupt. I have sent a report to a righteous high-rank minister. Our Emperor is trying to get rid of the corrupt officials now. Master Yu will soon be released. You can visit him."

"Mo-bai, I'm grateful you are here. I'm jailed because…"

"Uncle Yu. Take it easy. Captain Ta-da said… I'll look after your family. I will bring you meals, too." They whispered through the barred window.

"Mo-bai, I don't know how to thank you…"

A guard came and said, "Visiting time is over," and told Lee to leave.

Lee Mo-bai bought a meal, and he had to bribe the guard to let him take the meal to Master Yu. He started to worry that he would not have enough silver to keep going. Yu Ceo-lian handed him some silver and said, "Brother Lee, we're very grateful that you are here to help us. I don't know what we would do without you. I don't know how to thank you…" she wept and so did Mrs. Yu.

Master Yu was released two days later. He looked a lot older. Two days in jail with constant worry and rage seemed to be longer than a year. He ordered his daughter to pack their belongings and paid for Lee Mo-bai's fare with extra if Lee wanted to stay another day.

"Aunt Yu is still not well enough to go in the heat yet. Besides, you need rest, too. Why not stay one more night? We'll leave tomorrow morning."

"Mo-bai, we're not safe here. The Magistrate can easily find something else to detain us with. Besides, you're right about how my enemies may have some help nearby. Someone visited the jailed '*She-Devil*' and her brother. I overheard that someone is on his way to fetch her husband *Golden Spear* Jao from Kaifeng. I'm not afraid of them, but I want to send my wife and daughter to Da-ton. They will be safe there," Master Yu whispered.

"Let me go with you. What if your enemies attack you soon? I'm not in a hurry to go to Beijing," Lee Mo-bai argued.

"No. Mo-bai, your position in Beijing awaits you. I'm sorry I delayed you already. I also don't want to drag you into this deeper. Master Gi told me that your uncle wants you to be an administrator. Ceo-lian and I can repel them before Jao arrives. Thank you again for everything. You can mention my name to Master Lieu. He is my friend and the owner of the Grand Security Station in Beijing. I'm sure he will help you if you ever need help. Safe trip."

Master Yu almost could not mount the horse if Lee Mo-bai had not helped him with a push. Master Yu was pale and sweaty.

Lee Mo-bai pleaded again, "Uncle Yu, please wait. I'll go with you."

"No, I said no. Thank you, we can manage. Bye."

Lee Mo-bai did not want to insist on accompanying them again lest they think he wanted to go after Yu Ceo-lian. The hotel owner overheard the exchange and said, "Young Master Lee, I would follow them discreetly. Master Yu is in no shape to travel in this heat. If something happens to him, how could that young girl manage? Her mother is not well, too."

"Yes, I will follow them. I leave tomorrow morning."

"They are traveling west. I would go north first and then west. You know, young man, you might be watched," the hotel owner whispered.

2

Lee Mo-bai wanted to save the silver, so he swam in a creek and stretched out on the grassy bank. The bright stars of a clear summer night blinked at him like Yu Ceo-lian's sparkling eyes. *'She is lovely but is off-limits to me. How can I forget her?'*

At midnight, he jumped up on the hotel's roof where the Yu family were staying and scanned the area. No sign of enemies. He deliberately made a noisy landing. No one came out to check it out. He sighed, *'Master Yu must be tired, and Yu Ceo-lian's a young girl. I better keep watch.'* His teacher told him about the unscrupulous trickery that one's enemy could do in the dead of night.

It was sweltering hot the next day. Through the mist of the hot air, he saw that Master Yu's group kept on traveling. *'Master Yu should not ride in the heat. H will soon be sick…'* Ahead, Master Yu's horse slow down suddenly, and the heavy old man was just about to topple. Mo-bai galloped ahead and jumped down from his horse to intercept the older man's fall. Both of them fell to the ground with Lee Mo-bai on the bottom.

"Ahe! You caught him. He did not break his neck." the carriage driver yelled and rushed over to help them up. The impact of the fall knocked the wind out of Lee Mo-bai. The groom pulled Master Yu's limp body away, and Lee rose shakily. His top shirt was torn and his back bruised.

He said to the weeping mother and daughter, "Don't. Worry. Everything will be all right." He asked the groom, "Help me carry him into the carriage. He should be out of the sun.

"Thank *Lou Tien Yeh* (God). You're here," Master Yu said weakly. White foam and blood covered his white beard. He closed his eyes and breathed hard.

The groom said, "I know a doctor who lives two miles from here, Master Lee."

"Let's go there."

Mrs. Yu sat on the footboard and sobbed silently. There was no room for Yu Ceo-lian to sit in the carriage. Lee Mo-bai brought Master Yu's horse to her. She cried, "I don't know how to ride. It's so tall. I'm…scared." Her tearful eyes were full of fright. Lee Mo-bai had to bite his lips to stop the impulse of holding her in his arms.

He said, "Miss Yu, don't be afraid. You know martial arts well, and you'll learn how to ride very quickly." He bent down and cupped his hands together and told her, "Step on my hands, I'll help you get on the horse. I promise that you won't fall." He gave her a hoist and adjusted the stirrups. With one hand, he steadied the girl, and with the other hand, he held the rein.

Dr. Ma took charge. Lee Mo-bai went to unsaddle the horses. The groom said, "Dr. Ma is very good, but I don't like the look of it. He may not pull through."

Dr. Ma said to Lee Mo-bai, "I don't think you're his son, but I have to tell you that it's bad. His vital signs are feeble. He must have been troubled and anxious lately. I can only make him comfortable. You should prepare for the worst. What's your relationship to him?"

"We are not related. Master Yu knew my teacher. I met them…" Lee explained.

"He is lucky to have met you. We will have to see to things then," Dr. Ma sighed and continued, "I'll get my men to prepare everything. You had a nasty fall; I'll treat it later. You go in now, and he wants to see you."

Master Yu told his wife and daughter between breaths, "I know the end is coming. Luckily we have Lee Mo-bai here to help you…"

He told Lee Mo-bai, "My good nephew, I cannot repay your kindness in this life anymore. I want to be your…horse to serve you …in the next life. Promise me…"

"Uncle, you'll get well soon. Tell me what you want me to do."

"Ceo-lian, kowtow twice to him. From now on, Lee Mo-bai is your brother. You'll obey and respect him as you will obey me."

Lee Mo-bai stood rigidly and accepted. Then he kowtowed to Master Yu once, to Mrs. Yu. Kneeling, he said, "Please order me!"

"Mo-bai, promise me that you will escort your aunt and sister to the Mon's. She is almost seventeen now. I want her to get married right away, no need to observe the customary twenty-seven months-long mourning period. Please don't refuse a dying man's request."

"I, Lee Mo-bai here solemnly promise that I'll escort my aunt and sister to the Mon's. I'll see to it that my sister Ceo-lian will have a proper wedding."

"Good," Master Yu coughed, spat blood and died.

They buried Master Yu beside a grove of willow trees behind the villa. Lee Mo-bai wrote a tombstone tablet to be chiseled and erected later.

When Mo-bai offered Dr. Ma silver for the expenses, Dr. Ma refused, "I'm glad to be able to do a good deed and hope it will please Buddha. Mo-bai, Buddha will bless you, too. You wrote beautifully. Would you please indulge me and copy a couple of lists of herbs for me?"

"I'd be honored." They stayed two more days there.

"Mo-bai, may I be blunt? You are depressed, are you not? Whatever it is that's eating you does you no good. Please let it go and learn to enjoy the precious small pleasure that our hard-living brings us. Look after yourself; you're thin for your height. You have a bright future ahead of you."

"Thank you, Dr. Ma. You're right. There is a big world out there. I'll make new friends and enjoy my stay in Beijing."

That evening Mrs. Ma complained to her husband, "Master Yu was a fool. He should let Lee Mo-bai marry his daughter right away. Her mother told me that they heard nothing from the Mon family for three years now. Who knows what has happened; the groom-to-be might be sick, might be ugly, and rude. Young Lee helped them so much, and he is good-looking, polite, and a scholar. If Lee passes the examination and gets a position, Yu Ceo-lian would be a lady then. Instead, Master Yu made them sworn siblings. He was an old fool."

Dr. Ma said, "Master Yu loved his only daughter, and he wanted her to be happy. She is a simple country girl, and Lee Mo-bai is too sophisticated and too educated to marry. You are right that Lee Mo-bai will be somebody someday. But Yu Ceo-lian is not groomed to be a lady. She would be completely out of place among the highborn, well-versed wives of other administrators. Lee Mo-bai could only be happy if his wife can compose a poem or read and write well. Yu Ceo-lian cannot read. Master Yu had to make them sworn siblings so that Lee Mo-bai could escort them to Da-ton."

Dr. Ma did not know that Master Yu said the same thing when his wife and his student Su suggested that he should let Lee Mo-bai marry his daughter.

Mrs. Ma sighed, "Poor Lee Mo-bai! He adores the girl, and he can't marry her."

"Yes, Lee Mo-bai is a born poet, and now he is bleeding inside."

"I think Ceo-lian loves Lee Mo-bai, too."

"I don't think so. Right now, Ceo-lian is in shock. She worships Lee with deep gratitude. I'm afraid she will also be hurt when she realizes that she loves Lee later on. I hope that her husband will treat her well."

His concubine chuckled, "Master, you're so wrong. I was only sixteen when you took me. She is seventeen, and she sure has feelings. From the way they looked at each other, both of them have feelings, and strong feelings, too."

Early morning they set out for Da-ton. Mrs. Ma had packed boiled salty eggs, steamed buns filled with meat fillings, bottles of tea, and pears for them to eat at the noon hour. Dr. Ma advised that they travel in the morning and the evening but take a rest at noon. Lee Mo-bai attached a loop to the foot-stirrups for Ceo-lian to mount the tall horse. He walked alongside her horse for a while to make sure Yu Ceo-lian had learned enough to ride independently.

At noon they rested at a thick grove of trees off the main road. While they were eating, Lee Mo-bai politely answered Mrs. Yu's inquiries about his family. Then Lee told Yu Ceo-lian, "You know that the '*She-Devil*,' her husband Jao, and the others are now your enemies. If you don't mind, I'll teach you martial arts."

Yu Ceo-lian said excitedly, "Yes. Please teach me. You've taught me how to ride already. Thank you." Mrs. Yu also agreed, "Mo-bai, teach her. She must be well-prepared for the impending troubles."

"The first thing you have to learn is how to control your breathing and the flow of your energy. It'll take time to achieve any noticeable progress. But, gradually, you will learn how to use your energy economically, conserve energy, and utilize your total reserved energy at will. A master of the internal martial arts can reach the stage of *'quiet like a maiden, fast like a dashing rabbit.'*"

Yu Ceo-lian interrupted, "Is that why you could recover from the fall so quickly when my father fell on top of you? You looked so white. I was afraid that you were sick, too."

"You have a keen sense of observation. At that moment, I spent all of my reserved energy. I'm still tired." Lee scrutinized the forest carefully and then continued, "I will teach you the technique of how to breathe effectively now. While you're practicing, I want you to be my guard even though I think we are safe here. I need one more session of meditation in the open air."

Lee Mo-bai showed her the proper sitting position and demonstrated deep breathing a couple of times, and then said, "You keep on practicing now, and it will help your sore legs. It's common the first time you ride. Watch over me. Wake me up only when you need help."

Yu Ceo-lian watched the eye-closed and seemingly breathless Lee Mo-bai with awe, and she saw a light sheen of sweat covering the thin face. Meanwhile, she tried to practice deep breathing. Her mother dozed, sitting against a big tree. It seemed a long time before Lee Mo-bai opened his eyes;

he looked refreshed and smiled, "Thank you. I feel better. Dr. Ma's *ginseng* pill helped too. I hope the breathing exercise does some good for your sore legs."

"Yes, it did help. But, I did not see you take any pill."

"Dr. Ma made some for Aunt, and he gave me two of them and said they would help restore my energy and lift my spirit. I took one before I started to meditate." Lee Mo-bai took out a small ball of herb to show her.

"I did not see you take it. I was watching your every move." Yu Ceo-lian continued, "Is this another magic trick of yours like the one when you took my scarf off?"

Lee Mo-bai said, "No magic tricks, just *'speed.'*" He stood up and stretched his arms. Ceo-lian stood up too, and she asked, "Are we leaving?"

Lee Mo-bai opened the palm of his right hand and laughed, "Sorry, little sister, you have to retie your hair." In his palm lay a strip of white cloth with which Yu Ceo-lian had tied one of her braids.

"How did you get it? I still have my scarf on. Daddy warned me that I should be wary of skinny Taoist priests or scholars. He said that they might be superb martial arts masters. Is that why you're so thin?" Yu Ceo-lian said with admiration.

"I'm only a beginner. I lost weight lately because of…a family problem. Aunt is awake. It's time to go," Lee thought, *'Because of you, Yu Ceo-lian, no food tastes good anymore to me, and sleep evades me most of the time. Now you're beyond my reach forever.'*

The next day when they stopped at noon, Lee Mo-bai told Yu Ceo-lian, "Uncle told me that one of the enemies, Dart Mew, can throw deadly accurate darts. I'll teach you how to avoid, throw and catch darts. Most honest fighters despise throwing darts. My teacher insisted that I learn it well. He and his wife were wounded and captured by a bandit who was good at throwing darts. It is an excellent technique to learn, especially for a woman. Throwing darts or pebbles can repel several enemies rapidly. Someone used a small bow and arrows."

They practiced with pebbles. Lee Mo-bai showed her how to hold a handful of rocks and throw one at a time at different targets with quick succession. He stood still and asked Yu Ceo-lian to throw pebbles at him, and he caught everyone. He said thoughtfully, "I should not show you how to catch it. Learn how to dodge and not to catch the darts that your enemy throws at you. The darts might be poisonous. Try to remember NOT to catch the darts with bare hands when you're in a real fight. I regret that I had shown you how to catch it." Yu Ceo-lian learned eagerly and laughed every time she hit a target. She did not know that the sound of her innocent laugh pierced Lee Mo-bai's aching heart just as severely as her tearful looks whenever she mourned for her father.

Lee Mo-bai also taught Ceo-lian throwing and dodging pebbles while riding at high speed. He taught her the almost soundless leaping skills in the evening. He behaved most properly, and Yu Ceo-lian simply worshipped him, and she also learned to be quiet whenever she sensed that Lee Mo-bai was sad.

One night Yu Ceo-lian wanted to practice her newly learned jumping skills. She opened the room door she shared with her mother and walked by Lee's window as quietly as she could. Through the rice paper window panels, she saw Lee sit and read. She jumped. Just as she was about to land upon the roof, she has pulled down the roof and was pushed into a room, and she heard Lee whispered, "Stay in the room and close the door. There is danger out there. I'll be back soon." She was in the pitch-dark room alone, and her heartbeat was so fast and loud that she could hear it. A low cough, she heard, "Come out and let me walk you back to your room."

She also whispered, "The enemies?"

"No. Only two thieves. I'll tell you tomorrow. No need to be afraid. Good night."

The next day Lee Mo-bai told her, "I heard you last night when you opened your door. I would not stop you, but then I heard a low whistle, a common signal among the thieves. That's why I pulled you down and pushed you into my room. I'm sorry. There were two thieves. Miss Yu, we have to be on our guard at all hours. From the books I read and what my teacher had told me, I learned that wicked men, who are good at night leaping skills, are looking for maidens to ra...to hurt. A woman has to be extremely careful." Lee Mo-bai changed the word 'rape' to 'hurt'.

Yu Ceo-lian sensed that he would say at first something more sinister than 'hurt', and she was scared. Noticing her paled face, Lee Mo-bai apologized, "Don't be scared. Sorry, I did not mean to scare you. I just want you to be cautious."

"My father used to tell me to be alert, too. Thank you. My father's spirit would be at peace knowing you are taking good care of us."

"It's my duty, and I'm honored." He thought, *I'm glad that I can be with you, to hear you laugh, talk and sob. I do wish this trip would never end. You'll be another man's wife soon when we reach Da-ton. I don't know how I can carry on without you.*'

Noticing Lee's melancholy, Yu Ceo-lian kept quiet, and they rode in silence.

Two days later, Lee Mo-bai said, "Aunt, we can sell Uncle's horse at the next big town before we reach Da-ton. That way, you'll have some silver."

"Let's sell the horse. You will need some silver to go to Beijing."

"Aunt, I have some silver. You and Ceo-lian should have some silver of your own. We also need silver to move Uncle's casket back to Lu Town." Lee sounded sad, and the women started to sob.

The next day they checked into a hotel before noon in a big town. Lee Mo-bai sold the horse and changed the silver into amount bearing certificates for Mrs. Yu.

Riding ahead of the carriage, Lee Mo-bai dismounted at Mon's security company gate, and said, "We are here to see Master Mon. I'm Lee Mo-bai of Nan-kon Village. I escort …"

A white-haired man came out and called, "Oh! Sister-in-law and Ceo-lian are here, but where is Brother Yu? What happened?" Master Mon asked when he noticed the women wearing white armbands; white strips of clothes tied in their hair. Lee Mo-bai had on a black armband.

"Ceo-lian's daddy passed away on the way up here." They sobbed. Mrs. Mon and other women took them into the women's quarter.

Lee Mo-bai took the bags out of the carriage and paid the groom generously. The groom said, "May all the gods bless you. Master Lee, you're a righteous and brave man, one in ten thousand. Good luck and goodbye."

Master Mon noticed that Lee Mo-bai had on a black armband. He said, "Master Lee, I did not know that Brother Yu had a nephew? Why did he have to travel in the heat?" Master Mon sighed, "I was going to visit him and tell him the problem myself, and now… let's discuss it over a drink."

Something was wrong. Lee Mo-bai felt it. He replied, "Master Mon, I am not related to the late Master Yu. My teacher and Master Yu were friends. Last month, I met…" He detailed the incidents leading to Master Yu's death and continued, "On his death bed, he asked me to escort Aunt Yu and sister Ceo-lian here to marry your second son. I'll be on my way to Beijing after Ceo-lian's wedding. Uncle Yu said that she should be married now, no need to wait for the twenty-seven months-long mourning period to end. I'm her sworn brother."

Master Mon exclaimed in agony, "That's the problem. There cannot be a wedding soon because…" It was Lee Mo-bai's turn to shout, "No wedding soon? Why! Uncle Yu told me that you and he arranged the marriage of your second son and Ceo-lian five years ago. Is your son sick? I can wait for a while."

Master Mon shook his head hard and said rather too fast, "My second son is not sick. He is missing. He ran away eight months ago. All my inquiries have failed. Nephew Lee, let me explain."

"Please do. Your son did not want to marry my sister?" Lee Mo-bai's heart skipped a beat. His wild hope rose high again.

"Zhi-an knows Ceo-lian is a pretty girl, and he wants to marry her. He is twenty-one years old. He always is a difficult and mischievous boy. His older brother and I tried very hard to discipline him. Maybe we were too hard on him. He ran away the first time when he was eight years old. Miraculously, he came back on his own six years ago and changed utterly. He also learned martial arts very well. But, he still could not get along with his elder brother and wanted to leave home again. Then Master Yu came to visit us and mentioned that his daughter Ceo-lian learned martial arts, too. I asked her hand for my second son, and we had a marriage contract. Mon Zhi-an knew about the marriage and he was happy about it. He stayed home, and all was well. Eight months ago, millionaire Ting, who had a relative held a high position in Beijing, raped his servant's pretty daughter. Both father and daughter hanged themselves. It was terrible, and it was not my second son's business. He went there and chopped both of Ting's legs off. Ting did not die. His gang and the soldiers came to arrest Zhi-an. He fought them off and ran away. We have not heard from him since then." Master Mon sighed and continued, "I'll raise Yu Ceo-lian as if she were my daughter. Zhi-an probably dares not come back. I'll take Yu Ceo-lian to him as soon as I know where he is. What else can I do? I wish to see my Zhi-an before I die."

Lee Mo-bai was dumbfounded at this unexpected twist of fate. He knew the rigid custom would demand that poor Yu Ceo-lian be a *'living widow'*. Without the news of the certainty of her fiancé's death, she could not bind by custom, marry another man. The only hope for her was that Mon Zhi-an could be found quickly, living or dead. Even if the death of Zhi-an could be confirmed, it would still be a problem for Yu Ceo-lian to marry someone else. Not many families would be free of superstition to marry a girl whose karma was so bad to have a fiancé dead. Lee Mo-bai mused, *'But if I know for sure Mon Zhi-an is dead. I'll marry her. I'm not superstitious. To be with her one day is worth more than living a long lonely life. I better leave tomorrow morning. It's not proper for me to see her or talk to her anymore. I can only imagine how hard Aunt Yu and she are crying at this moment. It's fate.'*

A short man came to the guest room and introduced himself, "I'm Hsu Mo-ti of Lu Town. I was an assistant guard at Master Yu's security company. Master Yu recommended I work here. Miss Yu used to call me 'Short Brother'. Poor girl. Mrs. Yu told me everything. Thank you." Hsu tried to kneel, Lee Mo-bai pulled him up and said, and "I only did what a decent man would do. Brother Hsu, please tell me everything you know. What does Mon Zhi-an look like? I'll make inquiries in Beijing. I hope I can find him for Miss Yu. You know I'm her sworn brother."

Short Hsu said, "Mon Zhi-an is of medium height and thin with a sallow complexion. He is not the sort of man whom folks would notice and remember. Wait, his eyes are big. His eyes are big but not very bright. It won't be easy to find him, like a straw among a heap of hay." Short Hsu sighed and continued in a sad tone, "Mon Zhi-an's mother was a concubine. Mrs. Mon abused her; she died. The first son, Mon Zhi-chi, is greedy. He coveted the family wealth, charmed his father, and forced his younger brother out of the family. The greedy elder son controls everything. Now even his father is afraid of him. His wife is a mean woman, too. I'm afraid that they won't treat Ceo-lian and her mother nicely. I'm worried. I know you cannot take them back to Lu Town. Could you send ward to Brother Su to come here to take them home? At least they will have their own home, and Brother Su will look after them."

"I'm in a very awkward position here. Master Mon told me that his second son is a wanted criminal and he dares not come back. Please tell me more. I need to know the whole truth to help Ceo-lian," Lee Mo-bai said.

"It's a familiar story. The wicked elder brother forced the younger one out. Mon Zhi-chi dared and manipulated his younger brother to go after the vile millionaire…" Hsu filled in the details.

Lee Mo-bai said, "Now we have to find her fiancé and then bring Yu Ceo-lian to him as soon as possible. I'll ask Aunt Yu whether they want to go back to Lu Town or not."

At the dinner in honor of Lee Mo-bai, Mon Zhi-chi subtly belittled his younger brother. Lee Mo-bai in turn also subtly praised Mon Zhi-an for his heroic deed and stated that he, as Yu Ceo-lian's sworn brother, would ask for a share of the family wealth for Yu Ceo-lian later. He told them that he would leave for Beijing early next morning.

In the evening, Lee Mo-bai asked the middle-aged Short Hsu to accompany him to visit Aunt Yu and Yu Ceo-lian. He handed Mrs.Yu the remaining silver and told them that he'd leave for Beijing the next day. Their swollen eyes pained him. He asked, "Aunt, do you want me to send a message to Brother Su and tell him to escort you back to Lu Town?"

"Let's wait for a year or so and hope they will find him," Aunt Yu said. Le Mon-bai handed her a piece of paper, "Here is my Uncle Kao's address in Beijing. I'm going to ask around and try to find Mon Zhi-an in Beijing. I'll come back to see you next spring." Lee Mon bai signaled Yu Ceo-lian to follow him to a corner and whispered, "Continue to exercise the breathing technique but do not practice your saber fighting and jumping skills when everyone is around. You can go over the steps in your head. Find something heavy to lift to pump the iron in your arms. It's not proper for me to talk to you like this. I know your difficult situation. Be strong and be careful."

Yu Ceo-lian cried and begged, "Can you stay a few days? You're the only one we have."

"No. It's not fitting for me to stay. My staying would cause scandal. If I travel, I can make inquiries about your fiancé. Uncle's friends at Beijing might know something."

Whenever Lee Mo-bai passed a security company, he asked around. Most of them knew about the crime, but they didn't know where Mon Zhi-an is. He would copy some scriptures to earn free meals and a night at a temple often; it saved silver and made it easy for him to do the required morning workout. The change of scenery and the freedom to travel fast lifted his spirit and stimulated his appetite. He harbored a secret hope, *'If we cannot find Mon Zhi-an for a year or so, or his death can be confirmed. I might have a chance to marry Ceo-lian after all.'* He was ashamed to have the thought of wishing someone died. No matter how hard he tried to forget, the image of Ceo-lian tantalized his mind day and night. In his agony, Lee Mo-bai wanted to provoke a fight with anybody, and he did just that when he had to go through the Gu-bai Pass of the Great Wall.

The number of travelers dwindled at the entrance of the mountain road before the pass. He rode alone for a while, and soon, he caught up to a convoy carrying a security company's triangular banners. A guard who sat on the backdrop of a cart called, "Hi, young fellow, you have the nerve to travel alone. Don't you know that Bandit Wu's gang controls this mountain area? Come along then. You'll be safe traveling with us. My master's name card will see us through."

"There are bandits? I'm not afraid of them. I'll beat them all off." Mo-bai said.

"Wu has more than two hundred braves, and Wu is famous for fighting with a heavy steel rod. But he respects my boss, Master Yan." The guard said proudly.

"Friend, do you know Mon Zhi-an? He is twenty-one, of medium height."

"Sure, we know him. Wasn't he on the run from the law? His brother tried to force him to leave home. His father, Master Mon, is blind."

"Ahe! That's the one. Do you know where he is now?"

"I don't, but my master may know…"

"Stop!" twenty-some rough young men rushed toward them.

"Brothers, we are Master Yan's party. Here is Master Yan's calling card and some silver for you to buy a drink." The guard greeted the leader. "I'll signal ahead, and no one will stop you again." The leader whistled for his men to leave.

"Wait! I did not give you silver and my calling card yet. I travel alone, and I have silver if you dare rob me." Lee Mo-bai shouted. The bandits rushed back and surrounded them.

The guard cried, "Are you crazy?" Turning to the bandit leader, he pleaded, "He is not one of us." The bandit leader ordered, "Let the convoy go, but not this crazy bastard. He has eaten a tiger's heart and thinks he is brave. Get him!"

Lee Mo-bai called, "Come! All of you. No need for me to draw my sword." He scooped a handful of pebbles and threw them at them. Every one of the bandits yelled with pain. The bandit leader, his forehead bleeding, ordered, "Get him. All of you!" He wielded his saber at Lee Mo-bai. Lee Mo-bai laughed, "Come on! All of you! I'll fight you with my fists." He jumped around and punched this one and that one. They all got hit and fled. Lee Mo-bai called after them, "My name is Lee Mo-bai, and I'll wait for your leader Wu at the first town on the other side of the pass." He laughed, and somehow he felt better. He deliberately rode slowly, but he met no more bandits. Black clouds gathered, and soon a sudden summer rain poured. His horse nearly slipped. He thought, *'I better get down and pull the poor old horse through.'* Leading the horse, he sloshed through the mud and puddles and checked into the first inn. It was a huge establishment with three courts. The room was comfortable with nice, clean bedding. He knew the price would be high, but he was too miserable to find a cheaper one.

It was early, he had a plateful of steamed dumplings, and he saw the tearful face of Yu Ceo-lian on each one. Lee Mo-bai thought, *'Poor Ceo-lian and Aunt, they must cry a lot.'* He did not feel like eating, but he forced himself to eat all the dumplings and a bowl of noodle soup. Then he took out a damp anthology to read. He found the one that the famous Madam Lee of the Sung Dynasty (12th century) wrote:

You, my dear husband, reside at the head of the Mighty Yangtze River,
And I, your wife, live at the end of the same river.
Every day and every night, I miss you, but I can't see you.
Although we drink the water from the same river.

Lee Mo-bai closed the book and thought, *'Did it rain also at Da-ton, where Yu Ceo-lian is? Which are more? The raindrops or her tears?* He woke up to angry voices.

"I can't wake every customer and ask him his first name. 'Lee' is a common last name. We have more than seven customers with this last name," a hotel clerk said. Customarily, the hotel register only listed the surname.

A guttural voice snarled, "This Lee is a tall, thin young man who looks like a scholar. He has a horse. He said he would wait for me at this town. I have checked all the other hotels. Wake them up and ask before I beat the shit out of you."

Another voice, "You can't harass a hotel clerk. You hear!"

The same guttural voice, "What if I do? What can you do?"

Lee Mo-bai said, "Are you looking for me? I'm Lee Mo-bai. I beat up your men yesterday. Are you the bandit leader 'Wu'?"

"No need to know my name, I'll punish you."

"I have nothing to do with the law. I want to know the name of the persons whom I will beat up. Fight me!" The stout Wu hit Lee Mo-bai with his steel rod.

Lee Mo-bai did not want to have his father's sword damaged. He avoided confrontation and slashed at Wu's hand holding the rod. Wu laughed, "You weakling, you're afraid, are you not? Ouch." Wu dropped the rod, and both of his hands were bleeding. He called menacingly, "We will meet soon again. Next time I will not be fooled by your soft scholarly looks."

"I'll be in Beijing soon. You can find me there."

Someone knocked at Lee's door and asked politely, "Master Lee, may I come in?"

"Please."

The middle-aged, portly man said, "I watched the fight, and I admire your martial arts skills. You must be a student of a top-notch teacher of the Wu-ton school?"

"You, my friend, have good judgment." The stranger looked like a Manchu, Lee did not want to tell him more.

"My name is Dae-ti Fu. In Beijing, folks called me Dae Wu (five). I'm the fifth son in my family. I would be honored to be your friend. I know Beijing well, and I'd be glad to be your guide."

The name is a Manchu name. Lee said politely, "Master Dae-ti, I'm honored to make your acquaintance."

"Master Lee, are you coming to Beijing to take the triennial metropolitan-level of civil services examination next spring? I'm sure you will pass it with flying colors."

"No, Master Dae-ti, I'm ashamed to admit that I failed the provincial level. I'll try it again this fall. A relative of mine might find me a clerical position in Beijing. I should have been in Beijing a month ago. I had to go to Da-ton first."

"I was hoping you could stay another day and we'll go to Beijing together. I lived there. I hope you will have a good position, and I'm sure we'll meet again soon."

Early that afternoon, Lee Mo-bai entered the mighty capital Beijing. The grand buildings and the crowd intimated him; he dismounted and walked beside the horse until he saw others, even a few women riders. He rode again.

Uncle and Aunt Kao welcomed him warmly and told him no job anymore. "You should have been here earlier. What was the delay?"

"I was sick. I'm sorry." He lied.

"Look at you. You are thin. Your aunt should have found you a wife to look after you a long time ago. I know a couple of nice maidens. I'll find you a good wife," Aunt Kao said. Uncle Kao said, "Mo-bai, come back tomorrow afternoon. I'll ask around. There will be other positions."

Lee Mo-bai went to Grand Security Company to see Master Lieu. He told him about Master Yu's death and asked him to make inquiries about the whereabouts of Mon Zhi-an.

"Ahe! That's bad. Where is his family now? I know that they have a daughter."

Lee Mo-bai replied, "Yes. Mrs. Yu and their daughter are staying with Master Mon at Da-ton."

"Mo-bai nephew, Master Yu would not recommend just anybody. If you want to be a guard, I would be glad to have you work for me here. Your teacher's fame is far-reaching." Master Lieu also told Lee that he would find a buyer for Lee's horse.

"Mo-bai, your Uncle Kao may introduce you to Master Dae Wu. Although he is a Manchu, he is very friendly and helpful to us, the Hans. He knows many people who are good at martial arts. He may help you. If this Mon Zhi-an had been caught and jailed, Master Dae Wu would know, and he may extricate Mon, too. Dae Wu is very resourceful."

"I have met him already. I don't have his address."

"Dae Wu is well-liked and well known. Everyone knows where he lives."

The next day, Uncle Kao handed Lee Mo-bai twenty ounces of silver and a few books. "Mo-bai, I heard that you wrote beautifully. It won't be difficult for you to pass the provincial level of examination this fall and then the highest level next spring. Don't be idle. The Manchu court needs talented young scholars." Lee Mo-bai thought, '*I should try to pass the examination. With a position and the authority that comes with it, I can help Yu Ceo-lian to get her entitled share of the family wealth. But why, every thought of mine turns back to her. Can I ever forget her?*

He tried to study. Every page he opened to read showed only Yu Ceo-lian's tearful face. Finally, he gave up and went out for a walk. He walked absently into a section with fancy bungalows and many carriages parked. It was the district of prostitutes. He heard, "Master Lee, I did not expect to see you so soon. Beauty sure draws young heroes. *Ha Ha*." It was Dae Wu. Lee Mo-bai blushed.

3

"Brother Lee, don't be bashful. It is normal for an elegant and romantic scholar to want to meet a pretty lady. I'm surprised that you found your way here so soon." Lee Mo-bai looked like a petty thief who just got caught.

Instead of explaining how he had absentmindedly walked into this district, he asked, "Brother Dae-ti, when did you get in?"

"Late last night. Call me Dae Wu. I'm so glad that I have run into you. I forgot to ask you where you would be staying in Beijing. Brother Lee, may I introduce you to my good buddy Master Yong? Call him Fatso Yong." Turning to the rotund, well-dressed Yong, Dae Wu said, "Lee is the young martial arts master I told you about."

"Nice to make your acquaintance. Brother Lee, take us to meet your favorite."

"I don't know anybody."

"Brother Lee. How about coming with me to meet my good friend?" Dae Wu suggested. Lee Mo-bai took the term 'friend' literally and presumed that they would meet another man. To his surprise, a heavily made-up, richly dressed woman welcomed them into her parlor and immediately started to flirt with them. Lee Mo-bai was embarrassed, and he felt completely out of place. He awkwardly accepted a cup of tea and kept quiet.

"Don't tease my young friend. He is new, and he is shy," Dae Wu told the woman and then asked Lee, "Where do you stay?"

"At Restful Inn, not far from here."

"I will visit you soon. Brother Lee, I'm outspoken, and I want to be your friend very much. Please don't mind my forthright manners."

"Please call me Mo-bai. I'm but a poor rural student. I'd be honored to be your friend, Brother Dae Wu."

"Mo-bai, I know you're not comfortable here. Let's get out of here." Dae Wu insisted on taking Lee Mo-bai back to the hotel in his carriage. He said, "Now I know where I can find you. We'll meet soon."

The oil lamp in his room attracted many mosquitoes. Lee Mo-bai blew it out, and sleep evaded him again. The man in the room next to his was singing a popular Chinese opera about a young woman lamenting her husband's death at the Great Wall two thousand years ago. The sad tone increased his melancholy. *'If I meet another woman, prostitute or not, she might free me from the thought of Yu Ceo-lian. A prostitute would be good-looking, but she would not know martial arts. It's my misfortune to know Yu Ceo-lian; I love her but cannot have her. How can I forget her and find someone good enough to replace her?'* Finally, he stood on his head, feet up and meditated to clear his tormented mind, and then slept.

The following day he woke up refreshed and felt he could start life anew. Unfortunately, his head did not stay clear for long when he realized that he had written Yu Ceo-lian's name again and again instead of composing an essay on current affairs. He tore the paper into pieces and used them to practice the darts' throwing skills. He had a hard time throwing the flimsy paper far or hitting the target, but he was getting better. He was proud of himself and exercised more when the hotel clerk led Dae Wu to his room.

Dae Wu saw the pieces of paper flying around and said, "A new martial arts technique? I hope that I'm not your target, Mo-bai." He took in Lee Mo-bai's scanty luggage and knew at once that Lee was far from wealthy.

"It's a stupid game. I'm bored."

"How are you getting along? Did you get the position?"

Lee Mo-bai sighed, "Someone had filled the position."

"Never mind. Other positions will come along soon. You can't study all the time. We will keep each other company. My office work is not demanding, and I'm free before noon every day. We can have *Wei Qi* (chess) or go to the theater in the afternoon. Boredom and the heat will make you sick."

"Honestly, I'm all right. I'm not distressed. I'm debating with myself whether I should work as a security guard or wait to take the examination."

"Mo-bai, it's all written on your face. You have to be patient. Don't worry about silver. I have enough for both of us, providing you're not a spendthrift. If you're happy and not worried, you will pass the exam easily with your beautiful calligraphy."

"You're right! Uncle Kao said so too. He wants me to study hard."

"Yes, you should, but not today. It's too hot. Let's have lunch first and then go to the theater later. You're welcome to my home to study in my library any time." Mo-bai missed his room at home with bookshelves lined along the wall. Everyone at the theater knew Dae Wu. They were offered very good seats at the front. Lee Mo-bai asked, "Brother Dae Wu, you're famous. Beijing. Master Lieu, the Grand security company owner, suggested that I ask your help to find the missing fiancé for a relative of mine. The young man's name is Mon Zhi-an." He told Dae Wu the situation.

"Mo-bai, I will try my best. But if this Mon Zhi-an does not want to be found, no one can find him. China is a big country, and Beijing is a big city. It won't be easy to find one person. Poor young girl, I feel for her. She cannot marry another man until her fiancé's death is confirmed. She is what you Han people called 'a *living widow*'. It's an unreasonable and cruel custom. If she is a Manchu, it won't be too bad, she only has to wait for a few months for his return, and then she can marry someone else."

Lee Mo-bai's heart started to ache again. On the stage was the opera of the legend of 'Sister Thirteen.' It is a girl who fights off a group of bandits and rescues a scholar in distress. The actress moved gracefully, and her small feature also reminded Lee Mo-bai of Yu Ceo-lian. Dae Wu noticed his melancholy and tried to draw him out of it. He asked, "Mo-bai, do you have a theater in your hometown?"

"It's a village. We have no theater. After the harvest in the fall, a troupe will play in front of a temple for two days. I hardly ever watch the show."

"Mo-bai, it sounds like you were bored at home, too."

"Indeed. My Teacher passed away three years ago. I don't have anybody to talk to about martial arts and poetry anymore. My Teacher was good at both martial arts and literary arts. He taught me calligraphy."

"Mo-bai, how many children do you have?" Lee Mo-bai did not want to tell him that he was not married lest Dae Wu would try to find a wife for him, so he replied, "None."

Noises and loud quarreling sounded at the back of the theater, a fight.

One man said, "Be quiet. Master Dae Wu and his friend are sitting in the front. Be quiet. Go out and fight outside."

An angry voice, obviously not a native Beijing resident, shouted, "I don't care about this Dae Wu. Even the high judge himself is here; I will insist on having the right to be respected. This Dae Wu better mind his own business."

Everyone looked at Dae Wu, waiting to see his reaction to the insult. He stood up and walked to the back. Five robust young fellows, not locals, encircled a junior office clerk whom Dae Wu knew well.

"It's too hot to fight. Friends, please indulge me and break this up so we can watch the show. I'm Dae Wu." Usually, a fight would cease when

Dae Wu spoke. But one tall man of the five yelled, "I don't care who you are. Who gives you the right to protect one of your Beijing folks when he is unreasonable? I don't have to obey you. What are you going to do about it? Shut up and mind your own business, you hear?"

Dae Wu shouted, "You rascals. All of you." He dodged in time to avoid the tea kettle hurling at him and continued, "You dare? Let's go out and fight."

"Brother Dae-ti, let me fight them," Lee Mo-bai said.

"Master Dae Wu, no need for you to fight them. Just give us orders." More than ten bystanders volunteered to fight for Dae Wu.

"Friends from out of town, there are five of you, and I'm alone. But I can gather more than ten men at once. You better choose one-to-one. One of you will fight me."

The tall one challenged, "It's between you and me. Only a coward will need help from others. Come on!" Dae Wu stopped Lee Mo-bai and said, "I don't need your help to beat up a worm." Their fists joined. The tall man hit Dae Wu a couple of times, and then Dae Wu's palm struck flatly on the stranger's bare chest hard and left an impression of his whole hand. The stranger faltered backward and vomited blood.

"Bravo! Master Dae Wu. No wonder you are called '*Iron Palm,*'" someone praised. The five troublemakers left, and Dae Wu laughed. However, he did not look too happy. One man he wounded is one of the Feng Brothers of Ba-tin Town. The five of them were guards working for Universal Security Company.

Lee Mo-bai said, "Brother Dae, you're a true hero, not a showy one. I did not know you fight so well. I have to emulate your modesty. I'll always be on your side, whoever you have to fight." He noticed Dae Wu's apprehension.

"Everyone can praise me but you. I know you're an expert. I think you can scale a three-story building easily. I don't think you have much experience of real fighting. Am I right?"

"You are right. The first time when I wounded a man, I was almost sick from the sight of blood. I had only fought a real fight twice in all my twenty-four years of life. I'm only a beginner. Please don't think too highly of me."

"Mo-bai, a young warrior like you should have someone like the famous 'Sister Thirteen' for a wife. Is that the cause of your sadness?" Lee Mo-bai sighed again, said nothing, but he looked very miserable. Dae Wu thought that he guessed right. A woman was at the root of the problem.

"Cheer up, Mo-bai. Let's have supper first. Then I'll take you to meet a heroic prostitute. She does not know anything about martial arts and can't fight, but she is courageous and generous. I think only an elegant young man like you could win her affection and friendship."

"Brother Dae-ti, be serious. I don't have a job, and I don't have silver. How can I afford to pay for her services?" Lee Mo-bai protested.

"Indulge me. Violet is indeed someone special. For instance, one of the prettiest call girls spent more than she could earn and was deep in debt. She wanted to kill herself. Our heroine heard about it and paid off all the debts for the poor girl and then helped her find a decent man to marry. Another time, she heard that a malicious pimp abused three young apprentice call girls. She gathered all the other righteous prostitutes and went to the law to get the pimp arrested. Then she found a rich family willing to take the three young girls in as maids. Not a heroine? What else do we call her?"

"Where did she get the silver to help others? Does not her pimp control her income?"

"She is an independent prostitute. She and her mother run the business very well. She keeps the earnings. She also holds high standards. I heard many rich men want to pay a lot to bed her, but she won't sell herself to just anyone. Rumor has it that so far, she likes no one enough to let him bed her."

The so-called heroic prostitute picked her artistic name '*Violet*'. She likes the color purple, and all her clothes are in different shades of purple. She and her mother have been in Beijing for two years. She would be the number one flower in Beijing with her beauty and artistry if she were not so proud and extremely picky about her clients. Only a selected group, mainly the literary class, would seek her out and pay highly for her favors, which she does not grant lightly.

Dae Wu and Lee Mo-bai found her place tastefully furnished. An older woman asked them to be seated and offered them tea. She told them, "Violet is changing, and she'll be out in a minute. Can you tell me your names?"

"My name is Dae Wu. My friend Lee Mo-bai wants to meet Violet." Lee Mo-bai scanned a few paintings and a poem artistically decorating the walls. The paintings and the poem all bore the signature and stamps of 'Violet.' She was indeed not an ordinary ignorant prostitute.

Dae Wu whispered, "Mo-bai, she does have a haughty air. She lets us wait. This is the first time I encounter one in her trade that lets the customer wait."

Le Mo bai whispered back, "The famous poet Bai Jiu-ee(白居易)of the Tang (唐)Dynasty wrote in the poem about the *Pi Ba* (琵琶行 guitar player); '*thousands of calls and thousands of pleas before she shows herself.*'"

They were not disappointed, though. Twenty-five-year-old Violet approached them gracefully. Her beauty and sophistication mesmerized Lee Mo-bai. Suddenly he was tongue-tied and nervous. This feeling was new to him.

Violet glanced at Lee Mo-bai and asked with a pleasing tone, "You're Master..?"

Red-faced Lee Mo bai found his voice and said, "Lee Mo-bai."

"Welcome, Mister Lee," Violet looked Lee Mo-bai over imperceptibly and then asked Dae Wu, "And you're Master..?"

"Call me Dae Wu. I'm here today to accompany my friend Brother Lee to visit you." He saw the by-play between the girl and Lee Mo-bai. He smiled and thought, *No more sadness. Mo-bai.*"

She said, "Welcome, Master Dae Wu, your fame is far-reaching. We're honored to have your patronage."

"Brother Lee is new in Beijing. I dared not take him anywhere else. I know you won't take advantage of my shy and honest young friend," Dae Wu said.

The old woman, her mother, chuckled, "My Violet is also shy and honest."

"That is why I bring him where. They are a pair. *Ha Ha.*" Lee Mo-bai blushed, but Violet chatted with complete ease and grace. In the beginning, Lee Mo-bai could only reply whenever Violet asked him something, but gradually he asked a question or two.

He asked, "Violet, would you please tell us your real name?"

"Chi Mi-neon. I'm from Kaifeng." Violet replied. She thanked Lee when he praised her paintings and poems. Nevertheless, Dae Wu subtly signaled a stop when he sensed that Lee Mo-bai wanted to inquire about her background.

A servant delivered a note written on a strip of elaborately decorated red paper. Lee Mo-bai did not know what it was, but Dae Wu knew that it was a note to summon Violet's services elsewhere. He said casually, "Mo-bai, it's late. I don't want to face a complaining wife." He put some silver beside the teacup.

Violet said, "Sorry, I have to go to the Grand Inn. Please come by tomorrow?"

Dae Wu stood up and said, "I can't. I promise you that Brother Lee will visit you tomorrow and the day after. I'm sure of it."

Back in his shabby hotel room, a feeling of emptiness weighed him down. Lee Mo-bai thought, '*How could a beautiful, classy lady fall so low to become a prostitute? Violet must have had some unspeakable experiences. That's why Dae Wu did not want me to probe further. She and I have something in common. Both of us are talented but not successful. Is it fate or a flaw of character that made us this way? Who knows?*' He paced and finally went to a nearby tavern to drink himself into a stupor to block his mind of two images; an innocent pretty girl and a beautiful mature woman.

He was still asleep the following day when Dae Wu's valet delivered a letter. It said, '*Mo-bai, I'm not well today. I cannot come to visit you. Mo-bai, you're talented but at present have met with difficulties which life itself has the habit of granting us once so often. Please indulge me with a bit of pleasure and accept the enclosed silver certificates. I'm looking forward to seeing you soon. Be happy.*'

Lee Mo-bai's (李慕白) eyes moistened, '*I have only known him, a Manchu, a few days, and he is so understanding and caring. Dr. Ma and Dae Wu are two of the kindest friends I have met.*' The thought of Dr. Ma brought his thoughts back to Yu Ceo-lian again. He wrote two letters: one to Mrs. Yu and one to Dr. Ma. He took the letters to Grand Security Company and asked Master Lieu to deliver them whenever there is a convoy going there. Master Lieu welcomed him, and they chatted about his Teacher, Master Gi, and Master Yu. Master Lieu asked him again whether he wanted to be a guard. He said he would consider it. He did not like the sight of blood, and he preferred finer things of life. He thought that he should study more since he had help now.

He strolled and tried to spot a medium-height young man with big eyes among the crowd. A carriage stopped beside him. Violet invited him, "Will you come to visit us tonight. I'll be waiting."

"I will be there."

Lee Mo-bai thought, '*Why did I promise her that I'll visit her tonight? I need to study. What would Aunt Kao, Uncle Kao, and Yu Ceo-lian think if they knew that I visit a prostitute? I'm not going. That kind of woman will not mind if I don't go.*' His empty hotel room and boredom sent him to Violet's parlor that evening.

Violet felt an unusual sensation of waiting and anticipation of Lee's visit. She thought, '*Lee Mo-bai does not look like a man who could afford to visit me. He may not come.*' Lee Mo-bai's thin face, modest clothing, and especially the deep melancholy of his eyes touch somewhere deep in her. She thought about her painful past and the constant fear she has, and her tears came. Her tears stayed on her long dark eyelashes like tiny crystals.

The doorman announced Lee's visit. Violet quickly retouched her hair and went out to welcome Lee warmly, "Master Lee, you're here."

"I said I would come."

Lee Mo-bai noticed that Violet dressed her hair in a different style. Her snugly fitting light purplish outfit with black trimmings showed her tall, willowy figure to perfection. He couldn't take his eyes off her.

Violet also had a pinkish glow as she asked, "Master Lee, you said you're staying in a hotel. Is your wife with you?"

"No," Lee replied but did not mention that he was not married.

"Are you a colleague of Master Dae Wu?"

"No. I'm still looking for a position. A relative told me there was a position a while back. I did not arrive in Beijing in time, and someone filled the position. I'm not sure what I want to do next; prepare to write the civil services examination in the fall or go down South to seek Uncle Chiang. But I have to find my sworn sister's missing husband for her first." Lee Mo-bai stopped, and he was surprised that he talked so much to a new acquaintance. He was embarrassed and picked up the teacup. Violet thought, '*He is indeed an honest man. It's refreshing to hear someone talk candidly when all the other clients of mine only brag.*'

"Master Lee, you're young. A setback at present does not mean much. I know you'll be successful soon."

"Thank you. It is the first time I have come to a prost...a nice place like yours."

Violet laughed, "I don't mind. I'm a prostitute. But I have a conscience. I don't want to see a young scholar like you fritter away time and energy in a place like mine." She sighed and continued with a low laugh, "But, on the other hand, I would like you to visit me often, Master Lee."

"Call me Mo-bai."

"Oh! It's not fitting. I know my place."

He looked gloomy, and she tried to cheer him up. She pulled Lee up to look at the bright moon out of the window. "Tomorrow we will have a full moon, and one month from now we'll eat moon-cakes and celebrate the Moon Festival. By then, you'll be an important official, and you will forget poor Violet completely."

He appreciated her effort to bring him out of the blue. Lee Mo-bai forced himself to be cheerful too.

Lee Mo-bai was not quite sure of where Dae Wu lived. He hired a carriage thinking the groom might know where the well-known Dae Wu lived. He was right. The carriage took him across town to a well-kept residential area with many grand mansions. They stopped at a mansion with two huge stone lions guarding a redwood gate. A uniformed servant came to answer the door and asked him his name.

"I'm Lee Mo-bai. I came to visit Master Dae-ti."

Dae Wu's valet rushed out to welcome Lee and escorted him to an elegantly furnished parlor.

Dae Wu welcomed Lee Mo-bai, "Glad to see you. Mo-bai." He had on a silk short set.

"Brother Dae-ti, you look well. Thank you for the…"

"Don't mention it. I had a slight case of diarrhea. Did you go to see Violet?"

Lee Mo-bai said, "Yesterday, she invited me, and I paid her a short visit."

Dae Wu laughed, "No need to explain. You can't sit in your hot hotel room alone all the time. I honestly think that Violet likes you. She was cheerful when we visited her too. These are signs that she valued your attention. I heard that many rich men paid her a lot of silver and still did not get any good words."

"I don't think I should go to that kind of place often," Lee Mo-bai said.

"I agree. No matter how nice and graceful Violet is, she is a prostitute. You have a bright future. We will do some sightseeing, and then we'll have supper with my family. I'd like you to meet my wife and my mother."

They met many of Dae Wu's acquaintances at the famous Yuan Ming-Yuan, Everywhere they stopped to rest, the waiters would offer them the finest seats, and others would greet Dae Wu warmly. Dae Wu was proud of his popularity. When Dae Wu greeted a thin, well-dressed man, "Master Hwang, a pleasant afternoon." Master Hwang kept on walking and ignored him. Dae Wu was very embarrassed.

Lee Mo-bai asked, "He is rude. He has no manners. Who is he, and what makes him think he is better than you?"

"Master Hwang, nicknamed '*Thin Buddha,*' is a philanthropist in Beijing. He knows martial arts very well. I'm neither rich nor very good at martial arts, but I'm more popular, and he cannot take it. You could say that he is jealous."

"So he is narrow-minded and arrogant. He has no right to humiliate you today. He deserves a beating."

"No, Mo-bai. He and I have mutual friends, Viscount Chiu and others, so somehow we have to get along and keep the peace."

"The surname '*Chiu*' does not sound like a Manchu name. Is he a Han?"

"Yes and so is Hwang. They are the descendants of the first group of the Han people who betrayed the last Emperor of the Ming Dynasty and accepted the Manchu. Emperor rewarded them with wealth and position. Viscount Chiu fights very well with a spear, and he is Master Yan's student."

"I will challenge Hwang to a friendly match, and I will not mention that I'm your friend."

Dae Wu said, "Hwang is very powerful, and he has spies all over Beijing. If you beat him, he'll find a way to discredit you and make it impossible for you to be successful in Beijing. It's not worth it to make this kind of rascal your enemy." He continued, "Let's go home, and I'll treat you to a Manchu-style home-cooked meal."

"If I'm used to eating Manchu-styled meals, what am I going to do when I go back home?"

"It's easy. Bring your family here and live with us. I'd be flattered."

"My aunt and uncle won't come."

"Take your wife here then."

"I don't have a wife."

"Really? You told me you didn't have children the other day. Mo-bai, be serious. Are you not married? You country folks usually marry at sixteen or seventeen."

"I'm the odd one. That's why I cannot get along with my uncle. He's so angry with me for not wanting to marry the girl he and my dear aunt had arranged for me."

"Ah, you're reticent. I'm your friend, am I? Why can't you tell me?"

"I've learned a painful lesson, and I learned to be reticent. You're a true brother, and I'll tell you everything."

Dae Wu's mother and wife liked Lee Mo-bai right away. They told him that he could visit them at the inner court anytime.

Lee Mo-bai told Dae Wu everything.

"Brother Dae, let me tell you my first and painful lesson. I was so naïve that I honestly believed that I could win a wife with my sword." Lee Mo-bai told in detail that his friend tricked him into winning a wife with his sword."

Dae Wu roared with laughter, "That was absurd. Mo-bai, you're gullible. How could you be so stupid?"

"I had a sheltered and pampered life at home. This trip is the first time I left home. Now I realize that my Teacher Gi Kon-jii was a brag, and…"

"Mo-bai, you never told me you're Master Gi's student. What else did you not tell me? Your surname is Lee. Are you Lee Feng-jii's son?"

"Yes. I'm telling you everything. I need to talk to someone."

"That made sense now. Master Gi taught you all his skills without any reservation. Did you know your father and your teacher were good friends?"

"Yes, I know, and Uncle Chiang Nan-ho is my father's sworn brother. Teacher Gi was a braggart. He made me believe that I can win anything with my sword. He taught me for nine years and I was very close to him."

"Wait a minute, and something is missing. Master Gi was from Szechwan. Why did he move to the East to teach you?"

"I don't know. Teacher Gi told me a lot of his heroic deeds, about how many fights he had won. He did not talk about his family much."

"Tell me from the beginning. Please."

"My father, Teacher Gi, and Uncle Chiang resisted Manchu's rule in the beginning. But when my father realized that only the Manchu Emperor could stabilize the country and let the Han people have a better life, he offered his service to a famous general. I grew up in an army camp in Nanjing with a sister and a brother. Uncle Chiang visited us often. He and my father taught us martial arts. I learned well, and I also rode well. When I was seven, my father's company went to the Southwest to put down the Muslim rebellion. During a skirmish, my father lost a leg, but he managed to put my mother and me on a horse and told me to run. My brother and my sister were on another horse, and both of them died. Uncle Chiang saved my father from the enemies' camp. But my parents died shortly afterward. Uncle Chiang took me to my father's only brother's home and asked permission to adopt me as his son. My uncle refused and kept me. Five years ago, my cousin was killed and had left no child. I became the only heir. My uncle wants to keep me at home and get married. But I vowed to marry a girl who knows martial arts well. That's why I fell for a trick." Lee Mo-bai then told in detail what led him to become Yu Ceo-lian's sworn brother.

He sobbed, "I promised her that I'll find her fiancé. I wish that I had never met her. Now I live in a state of perpetual agony. I can't have her, and I can't forget her. Sometimes I want to be a Taoist priest if I did not have an obligation to carry on my father's and my uncle's bloodline."

They sat in silence for a long time. Then Dae Wu said, "Mo-bai if we cannot find Mon Zhi-an in a year, I will go to Da-ton to have a candid talk with Master Mon. He cannot let Yu Ceo-lian be a living widow forever. I'll be the middleman and arrange the marriage for you and her." He then added, "Of course, we'll try our best to find Mon Zhi-an. You're a very virtuous man, one in ten thousand. You are drunk. Stay here tonight. Tomorrow we will bring your luggage here."

"1 don't want to impose on you. Ask your groom to take me back to my hotel. I need to be alone."

The next day, Uncle Kao's valet came to the hotel to summon Lee Mo-bai.

"Mo-bai, it's too expensive and too noisy for you to stay in a hotel. I made arrangements for you to have a room in a temple. The old monk there once told me that someone broke in and stole the silver his devotees donated. He would like to have you there to help him to repel any thieves and also to copy some scriptures for him."

Lee Mo bai could have a quiet court for himself. The room needed repair. He could practice martial arts anytime, and he was anxious to move.

A wounded Dae Wu was in his hotel room. He said, "Remember the fellow Feng whom I had hit the other day at the theater? He and his brother gathered ten roughnecks and waylaid me down the street. They wounded me, but I cut down two of them before the soldiers came."

"Where can I find them? They cannot get away with this."

"The tall one whom I hit the other day is Feng Three. There are many brothers. Feng Five is a guard at Universal Security. Feng Four, nickname *Saber King,* fights with two heavy sabers superbly. It's said that Viscount Chiu, Thin Buddha Hwang, and the bandit Wu whom you had wounded are all not his equal. That's why the other day I started to worry when I knew who they were. I avoided this section of town."

"Is Feng Four the one who wounded you today?"

"Not him. He is not in Beijing. If he were here today, there would be no ambush. He is just and righteous, and he won't allow his brothers to do this."

"I'll go and beat them off. They've gone too far. If I don't punish them now, you will not be able to walk on the streets without fear from now on," Lee Mo-bai said.

"You're right. I'm coming with you."

"Dae Wu, Stop!" Feng Five shouted, and his long spear almost touched Dae Wu's chest.

Lee Mo-bai broke the heavy spear into two, "I won't fight you here on the street. Let's go out of town. I'm Lee Mo-bai. Whoever dares harm Brother Dae Wu will have to fight me first. If you're afraid, go home and get *Saber King* here to fight me."

They went out of the city gate. There they ganged up and wanted to upturn the carriage with the wounded Dae Wu inside. None of them was free of some slight sword wounds from Lee Mo-bai's lightning-speed sword thrusts. Most of them fled. Feng Five's neck was bleeding, and he knew that Lee Mo-bai had spared his life. He shouted, "Lee Mo-bai, we'll fight you again."

"You'll find me at Peace Temple on East Street. Tell *Saber King* to come to fight me!"

Lee Mo-bai told Dae Wu about the room at the temple.

"Good, Mo-bai, I came to ask you to move into my house, but I think you'll feel less restricted living in the temple. If you don't like it there, you're always welcomed to move into my home."

"Thank you. You're a true brother to me."

4

Tall walls circled the temple. Lee Mo-bai could practice martial arts in the court. There was a well in a corner. The old monk was very pleased with Lee's calligraphy and suggested that they set the table in the frontcourt for Lee to write letters for the illiterate devotees. Lee Mo-bai felt for the first time that his life was somewhat regulated.

The room needed repair; the once whitewashed wall had cracks, one corner of the earthen raised *kon* (bed) was potholed. The nice bedroll Mo-bai's aunt prepared for him looked out of place. Dae Wu wanted to send a servant to help him tidy the room, but Lee Mo-bai refused. He was embarrassed. Thinking of his comfortable room at home, Mo-bai laughed lest he would cry. He felt better after he told Dae Wu everything. Now he did not feel that he was utterly alone anymore. He could talk openly with Dae Wu about his confused thoughts.

"Mo-bai, I was right to say that Thin Buddha Hwang has spies all over. He knows that you've fought Feng Five and won. He wants to meet you." Dae Wu said.

"That's preposterous! How dare he summon me? Does he think he is an emperor, a lord? I don't want to meet him."

"Of course, you don't have to meet him. Mo-bai, you better stay away from him. He could use his silver to set you up and incriminate you…"

Lee Mo-bai interrupted sarcastically, "You don't mean that silver can do everything."

"Of course, silver is indeed power. One of Violet's regular clients is Huge Bo, who owns six pawnshops. Hwang and Huge Bo are the wealthiest men in Beijing; even the ministers have to be cordial to them and do their biddings because they owe either Huge Bo or Hwang silver." Dae Wu sighed and continued, "Believe me, Mo-bai, the rich Hwang can use the weight of his wealth to hire someone to trick you or ambush you. I heard that he is the real owner of Universal Security Company. You've wounded Feng Five, one of their guards, so you've damaged their business standing. Hwang will think of you as his enemy. I'll be out of town on official duty soon, and I want you to stay low for a while. I want you to be careful."

"I'm not afraid of them. Don't worry."

"Mo-bai, just remember this: *'It's easy to win an open-handed battle, but it's hard to avoid a dart coming from the dark.'*"

Lee Mo-bai was mildly drunk when he got to Violet's place.

"Long time no see. I'm glad that you still remember me." Violet said.

Lee Mo-bai stammered, "I. I've been busy. I moved and..." he added quickly, "I have not come to see you for three days, longer than three years to me."

"I know you won't forget me. It's raining. I'll sing for you." She stood up, reached up to the top shelf and took down a *Hu chin* (二胡t two-stringed guitar) in one smooth movement, and started to play. Lee Mo-bai was puzzled, *'She moves with unusual agility. It almost looks like she has some martial arts training. Is it possible?'*

Violet sang a Sung Dynasty poem about a lonely woman missing her traveling husband during a rainy day. Lee Mo-bai tapped his teacup in harmony with the song. The haunting verses mesmerized both of them. Yu Ceo-lian's tearful face came to his mind, and his melancholy touched Violet. She said, "It's wrong of me to sing a sad song. It's the rain. When the sun comes out tomorrow, everything will be fine. Master Lee, you should not miss your wife in my presence. I'll be annoyed."

"I'm not married. That's part of my problem. I am half drunk. The rain and your enticing song made me temporarily forget myself. Sorry."

"Do you want to talk about it, Master Lee? Letting it out will help you feel better. I'm a good listener. It's my job to listen."

"I met the girl of my dreams, but she is engaged to someone else already. It's silly of me to pity myself." He thought, 'You're *the most beautiful woman I have met. But you are a prostitute. I can't, and I don't want to marry you.*' Violet thought about her unspeakable sufferings in the past. They sat in silence. The sound of a neighboring prostitute's lamenting singing came through the partially curtained window.

Her mother came in with a note summoning Violet. She said, "Master Lee, don't leave in the rain. There are books and anthologies you may want to read."

"I'll leave when it clears a bit." Lee Mo-bai pulled a thin volume down from a shelf on the headboard. A long, narrow wooden box fell and exposed a shining eight-inch-long dagger. He put everything back and pondered,

'That's why Violet looks sad. Sometimes she has a look that she is ready to flee. She must have an awful past, and her enemies are chasing her. I may be able to help her. Oddly, I met another woman who knows martial arts. She is a prostitute. I won't marry her, and I can't afford to support her anyway. Besides, I can't forget Yu Ceo-lian.'

It poured when Violet came back. They talked and read some poems. The half-drunk Lee Mo-bai stayed overnight. He left at dawn and felt miserable and guilty. He wondered now how he could face Yu Ceo-lian? How disappointed his uncle and aunt would be if they knew about his visiting a prostitute? However, he visited Violet almost every day. When he asked her about her past, Violet only sobbed.

Dae Wu asked Lee over for supper and said, "Mo-bai, I know you like Violet very much, and she likes you, too. But, please keep in mind that she is a prostitute, and silver is important to her. You can't trust a prostitute. I heard either Vice Minister Hsu or Huge Bo would buy her out. Either one can wipe you out at will. Jealousy is a powerful emotion." He continued, "Mo-bai, you're young, and you are lonely. I want you to be careful. I will be away for at least two months. Please be careful. *Thin Buddha* Hwang likes to stab you in the back and…"

Lee Mo-bai interrupted, "But, I can't keep quiet and do nothing if someone challenges me to a fight."

"Mo-bai, I'm sure you will win if they fight you openly. I'm not worried about *Saber King*; he is a man of principles. The others may ambush you or frame you. Who knows what schemes they may harbor? Maybe you should leave Beijing and go to the South to seek your Uncle Chiang. You could come to meet me at Yin-kin Town in Shanxi Province two months later. Yin-kin is not far from Da-ton. You can go to visit Miss Yu."

"I can't if I want to write the examination, I'll be careful. Besides, I have to wait for *Saber King*. I don't want them thinking that I'm scared and run."

"Mo-bai, here is a passbook of silver for you to draw on. If you refuse, I'll consider that you don't respect our friendship."

"Ah!.. thank you, and have a safe trip."

Lee Mo-bai did not want to leave Beijing and could not resist the lure of wanting to visit Violet. It was a scorching afternoon. Lee Mo-bai sat on a straw mat under the shade, watched the floating white clouds, and threw pebbles to knock down a leaf. Three men came. The thin one was Thin Buddha Hwang.

Lee Mo-bai asked, "Are you looking for someone?"

"Are you Lee Mo-bai?" Hwang asked.

"That's me." Lee Mo-bai wondered why Hwang came without being invited.

"I'm Ku An-chi. I heard that Dae Wu, with your help, considers that he is number one in Beijing now. I also heard that you defeated Feng Five. You boasted that you would duel with Saber King. Am I correct?"

"Yes, I said all of that and more, Mister Ku. I would also like to step on a well-known hypocrite and coward call '*Thin Buddha.*'" Lee Mo-bai despised that Hwang did not use his name.

"Thin Buddha is kind and generous. You insult my friend. I'll punish you."

Lee Mo-bai knew that the cunning Hwang did not use his name in case he would lose. "I don't care you are a coward, a fake. Lee Mo-bai is at your service." He deliberately let Hwang complete the whole sequence of a set of boxing moves but never let his fist even come close. Master Shih, the owner of a nearby eatery, walked in to watch the duel.

Lee Mo-bai called out, "Watch out. I'll hit your left shoulder." Hwang staggered back a few steps and was sweating from the pain. Master Shih called, "Bravo!"

Lee laughed, "You're Thin Buddha. Coward. You dared not use your name." Thin Buddha and his men left.

"Master Lee, you are the number one in Beijing now, and you must have a very good martial arts teacher," the portly and short Shih said.

"I'm a beginner, Master Shih. Do you know martial arts?"

"Call me Fat Shih. I'm too fat to brandish a saber. I love to watch a duel. Master Lee, I would be very careful and watch my back all the time if I were you. Beware of Thin Buddha and his kind."

"Thanks. Tell me what you know about Thin Buddha Hwang and Huge Bo."

"They are rich and wicked. Thin Buddha helps the poor often to buy a good name. Huge Bo is a miser. He only uses the power of his wealth to do evil and to control many high positioned officials who owe him money. All the poor trollops, high or low, are afraid of Huge Bo. Ah! I don't know martial arts well; otherwise, I would beat up that wicked Huge Bo."

"I think you're modest," Lee Mo-bai said. Shih laughed and left.

Lee Mo-bai thought, '*Money is indeed power. I fight well, and I write well, but I don't have silver, and I can't find a satisfying job to support myself. And the two women I love are out of my reach. I cannot marry Yu Ceo-lian because there is a faceless man called Mon Zhi-an. I'm even willing to lower my standards and rebel against my uncle to marry Violet. Where can I find the silver to buy her out? Besides, she is used to luxury, and she doesn't want to marry a poor man. Maybe I will be a guard for a while to earn some silver.*' He knew that 'indecision' was his worst enemy; there were too many 'maybes' and too many 'ifs. He couldn't make a clean cut. He practiced sword fighting. The bluish blade of his sword looked frosty cold and mirrored his mood.

It was hot and crowded at Shih's eatery. Many customers stared at Lee Mo-bai. They seemed to know that Lee Mo-bai had hit Thin Buddha. Master Shih set the table for Lee in the backyard.

"Master Lee, the owner of Fu-An fabric shop, hanged himself," Fat Shih said.

"I was there, and it looks prosperous. Why did the owner kill himself?"

"Huge Bo charged him an exorbitant interest that compounded monthly. The good profit from his shop was not enough to pay the interest. That wicked Huge Bo pressed him to pay; he wanted to seize the business and his pretty daughter."

"Maybe I'll teach him a lesson he won't forget." Lee Mo-bai said.

He walked around town aimlessly to hold back his urge to visit Violet. In the end, he gave in and went to her parlor. A servant stopped him and told him that Master Bo was visiting Violet. He heard robust laughter mixed with Violet's pleasant voice. He was jealous and angry, and his taut nerves snapped.

"Huge Bo, you murderer. You forced a man to hang himself. I'm here to punish you!"

"Who is here looking for trouble? I'll get you arrested." A fat man shouted down from upstairs. Lee Mo-bai jumped up, threw Huge Bo down.

Violet shouted, "Lee Mo-bai, you beat my client. You'll ruin my business!"

"I'll marry you. I'll support and protect you and your mother," Lee Mo-bai declared.

"Can you support us? Yes, you can fight with your fist. But, tell me what you will use to support us? You only know how to make our lives more difficult." Violet cried. She slammed the door shut. The news of two of the wealthiest persons in Beijing being hit in one day spread fast, and Lee Mo-bai became a celebrity.

Lee Mo-bai decided that he would leave Beijing. When he went to say goodbye to Uncle Kao, the valet politely turned him down.

"My relative won't see me anymore; a prostitute won't see me anymore. I'm going to leave Beijing soon." Lee Mo-bai told Fat Shih.

"The sooner, the better. It's dangerous for you to stay. Even if you decide to write the civil services examination, they will find a way to ban you. Where are you going?" Fat Shih said.

"Everywhere and nowhere. I need to find a missing person for a relative. You've been around. Have you ever heard of a young man called Mon Zhi-an? He had run away from the law. His father owns a security company at Da-ton, Shanxi Province."

"No, but I will ask around. Da-ton is part of the area called Inner Mongolia. He may have escaped to Mongolia or even Russia. You may find some information in Xian, or he might be hiding right here in Beijing. Have you heard the saying, '*Beijing is a place full of hidden dragons and crouching tigers*? Look at you, before yesterday; were you not an obscure fighter veiled behind your scholarly look? Oh! You can't leave Beijing yet. I heard *Saber King* is on the way here to fight you. If you leave now, folks will think you're afraid and run away."

"That's right. I'll wait three days. Then I will meet Saber King on my way home. I have to pass through Ba-tin."

"Saber King and Golden Spear Jao are equally famous. They are different like day and night: Feng Four, Saber King is righteous, and Golden Spear is wicked. If Saber King finds out that his brother was in the wrong, he will not fight you. Perhaps you can resolve the animosity between you and him. Master Lee, to have a friend is better than to have an enemy."

"It's up to Saber King. Now I'd like to go to bid Violet farewell. I mean to end it."

"I heard Violet is a nice lady. Why don't you buy her out? If she loves you, she won't mind a modest lifestyle. She is no longer young. To have an elegant husband like you is not a bad choice."

"Ah! I can support her and her mother only if I want to be a guard. I cannot make up my mind about her and my career."

Violet offered Lee Mo-bai a cup of tea nonchalantly.

"I'm leaving Beijing soon. I came to say goodbye."

"Master Lee. Where are you going? When will you be back?" She was no longer cold.

"I'll go home first and then to Da-ton and Xian. I won't be back soon. Violet, I truly care for you and intend to save some money to buy you out and marry you even if I choose an unsatisfying job. But you've given me the cold shoulder. I should not beat up Huge Bo. I was so jealous."

"I care for you, too. But…" Violet said.

"I know you consider me a poor and bad-tempered bully now. You don't know how long I have been in agony over you and Yu Ceo-lian, the other girl I told you. By now, you probably know that I'm a highly trained martial arts fighter. If anyone wants to marry you by force, or your enemy wants to kill you, I will be back to fight them off. I'll protect you whether you want to marry me or not."

Violet threw herself into his arms and kept on sobbing. Finally, she said, "Mo-bai, you know I love you, but I know you are in a constant state of indecision. I'll wait for you to make up your mind. No matter how long I have to wait. Oh! It's my karma to be a prostitute and that you met Yu Ceo-lian before you met me."

On his way home, Lee Mo-bai heard a noise and acted on it.

"*Ouch*! Let me go, Master Lee." Fat Shih tried to waggle out of Lee's grip.

"It's you. What are you doing here at this hour?"

"Your enemies are waiting for you at the temple. I came to warn you."

"Who are they? Saber King?"

"Yes. Be careful. Saber King is a powerful man, and his sabers are heavy and deadly. But, he won't play a dirty trick."

At the gate of the temple, Lee Mo-bai heard, "Mister, are you Master Lee Mo-bai?"

"I am. Who are you?" One of them held a lantern, and another one held some weapons and the reins of three horses. The empty-handed one bowed politely, "Master Lee, I'm Feng Four of Ba-tin Town. You said you want to fight me."

"You're the famous Saber King. Why do you await me in the dark?"

"You're right that I should have waited for the morning. But I'm angry, and I want to meet you as soon as I came into town. See, I'm empty-handed. Please come to Universal Security tomorrow morning with your friend Dae Wu. We'll fight then."

"Dae Wu is out of town on business. I'll be there."

He could not sleep and thought, "*Violet is right. I simply cannot forget Yu Ceo-lian. Of course, Violet does not want to marry me, knowing that I have another woman on my mind. That Saber King seems to be a good man. Whether I win or lose tomorrow, I can ask for his help to find Mon Zhi-an.*"

Lee Mo-bai rode one of Fat Shih's horses. When he passed Grand Security, a guard stopped him, "Master Lieu would like to have a word with you."

"Mo-bai, I heard about the duel, and I'd like to talk to you."

"Uncle Lieu, guide me. I never had a formal duel with anyone before."

"Is that right? You will win. I'm asking you to be lenient when you fight Saber King. He is not your equal. He is proud, but he is a real honest man. Please indulge me in an unreasonable request. I want you to spare him a humiliating defeat."

"King may defeat me. I'll not be aggressive if I have the upper hand. Is this what you want to advise me?"

"Yes. Mo-bai, we'll go there together."

All the guards and the martial arts fanatics in Beijing waited to see the duel. Saber King was rugged, compact, and robust. Lee Mo-bai was thin, pale, a tired scholar. Even the seasoned Master Lieu started to worry that Lee Mo-bai would meet a shameful defeat.

"Welcome, Master Lee. There is no real animosity between us. You have challenged me to fight you, so let's have an honest boxing match without any dirty tricks or hidden steel darts. Agreed?" Saber King bowed low and politely.

"Master Feng, we'll fight fair and square. Weapons are sharp, and we can have a match without them." Lee Mo-bai bowed equally low and polite.

"Bravo. Master Feng is a true hero," said one onlooker.

"Lee Mo-bai bowed like a courtier or an opera actor," another spectator.

"There's a saying that *'when two tigers fight, one will die.'* I'm on friendly terms with both of you. Please indulge an old man's suggestion that you two talk over your differences." Master Lieu stood between Lee and Mo-bai and Feng Four. He pleaded that they don't fight.

"Sorry, Uncle Lieu, I cannot obey you today. Lee Mo-bai boasted that he would defeat me. I rushed here in the heat to meet his challenge. If he apologizes now, we'll have a truce," Saber King said.

"Uncle Lieu, I can't obey you either." Lee Mo-bai said.

Someone shouted, "Master Feng, chop him up with your sabers. He is afraid of your sabers, and that's why he agrees to have a boxing match." But the powerful Saber King knew that the skinny Lee Mo-bai was not an easy contender.

"We'll have a boxing match first." They bowed once to each other and started to fight. Saber King hurled at Lee with fast and powerful fists and kicks, each of his powerful movements came with whooshing sounds. Lee Mo-bai moved seemingly slow and gracefully. Lee Mo-bai let Saber King's fist or foot hit him once in a while because he did not want to humiliate him with a quick and apparent defeat. All of the audience applauded loudly whenever Saber King hit Lee Mo-bai. Only Saber King himself knew that Lee Mo-bai had spared him. His powerful strokes seemed to lose power when they touched Lee's body, and Lee's strokes at him were harmless. Sweat poured from Saber King, and he hauled at Lee with all the strength he could muster. Lee waited until the last second and jumped three feet high, descended bird-like with a one-foot kick that sent Saber King rolling.

Saber King yelled, "Lee Mo-bai, dare to fight me with your sword?"

"Certainly." Lee Mo-bai had a sword, and Saber King had two heavy sabers. Lee Mo-bai bowed and said, "Master Feng, you're the host. Please start."

Three sharp weapons moved too quickly for the lesser skilled guards to see which is which. Lee Mo-bai never let the heavy sabers clash with his lightweight sword. Saber King took it that Lee was afraid of his strength and the heavy sabers. He gained confidence and fought ferociously. Lee Mo-bai kept the same principle of not embarrassing Saber King, and he delayed his sure victory. They fenced for a while, and suddenly Lee Mo-bai shouted, "Stop!" and jumped aside. He bowed and said, "Thanks. It's a good fight."

"*Lee Mo-bai lost*," someone shouted.

"*Bravo, Saber King*." Many voices shouted.

Feng Five yelled at his brother, "Why didn't you chop him down. Don't be merciful."

"You fool. Lee Mo-bai spared my life. Thank you, Master Lee. You will have my unyielding gratitude, and I wish to be your friend." Saber King raised his arm and showed everyone that a slight sword cut pierced his clothes, which could have sliced his right shoulder off very well.

"Master Feng, it's a hard fight for me, too. You're a tough contender. If you can forgive my earlier offensive remarks, I'd be honored to be your friend," Lee Mo-bai said with sincerity. He knew now that he had forgotten the rule of modesty when he openly challenged Saber King.

"Well said. I'm proud to have two worthy nephews," Master Lieu said.

Saber King laughed, "I had a torn sleeve, and I get a friend. Fighting is a thirsty business. Let's drink and eat." He put his arm around Lee Mo-bai, led him to a well-laid banquet, and sat next to Master Lieu. Lee Mo-bai asked everyone present to help him to find Mon Zhi-an.

A shifty-looking man Ca leo (six), bowed to Lee Mo-bai. "Master Lee, you have my immense gratitude. You saved and then buried Uncle Yu and escorted my sister Yu Ceo-lian to Da-ton. The carriage driver told us all about your kindness and bravery. Brother Su and I sincerely thank you." He told the details. Everyone praised Lee Mo-bai.

"I did what a decent man will do under the circumstances. I hope we can find Mon Zhi-an soon," Lee Mo-bai said. For the next few days, Lee Mo-bai thoroughly enjoyed his earned friendship and popularity among the guards and warriors. He liked their candid manners and the openhanded comradeship. When Master Lieu asked him to escort three months' wages for military forces and administration fund to Xi'an, he accepted.

Thin Buddha Hwang paid Lee Mo-bai another visit and apologized for his ridiculous behaviors earlier. "Master Lee, it was foolish of me to use a faked name. I did it because I knew that you would win. Why should I feel ashamed of my defeat? Even Saber King had met defeat at your hand. Please accept my apology and be my friend."

Lee Mo-bai replied, "Thank you for overlooking my silly behavior." They parted as friends. He suspected that Hwang's unexpected change of attitude might be a scheme in disguise. He told Fat Shih about it. Shih was worried.

Two days later, Lee Mo-bai was arrested and jailed. The charge was that someone reported him as a highly skilled burglar.

The arresting officers thanked Lee for his non-resistance, "Master Lee, we thank you for letting us do our job. You could kill all of us at will."

"Sergeant, I'm innocent. I do not hold any grudge against you." He wondered who the instigator was. They had extra strong manacles put on his feet and also a heavy chain on his neck. Huge Bo paid the captain well to have extra guards posted around Lee Mo-bai's cell.

In his favorite concubine's place, Huge Bo told the opium-addicted Vice Minister Hsu of the arrest. "Now the troublemaker Lee Mo-bai is out of the way. Violet will be yours. Congratulations."

Violet understood why the official arrested Lee Mo-bai. She put on her most charming smile and pleaded, "Lord Hsu, I'm so grateful for your patronage. That young upstart Lee Mo-bai is rude and crude. His boorish ways tired me." She rubbed Vice Minister Hsu's back and continued, "But, My Lord, I don't think Lee Mo-bai is a thief."

Huge Bo said, "Tell me then where did he get the silver? Come on! It does not come free for him to visit you so often. He does not have a job. He steals."

"Master Dae Wu gives him silver," Violet argued.

"Violet, I would be cautious. I heard that Lee Mo-bai jumped nearly three feet high when he kicked Saber King. No walls can stop him, and he is a wanted thief, and soon he will be beheaded. They considered anyone associated with him as his accomplice. They will search your parlor and confiscate your belongings if they consider you his accomplice. Do you and your mother want to be arrested on his account? Only Lord Hsu can shelter you," Huge Bo threatened Violet.

Her mother knelt and begged, "My lord, please help us. I told Violet again and again that Lee Mo-bai is a bad lot."

"Madam, please get up. You'll soon be Lord Hsu's mother-in-law," Huge Bo pulled the old woman up gently.

"Brother Bo, I advise caution. Just give that insolent Lee Mo-bai a good beating. You can't keep him jailed too long. You know this kind of criminal has friends who can scale the wall. They can kill us during the night, too.

You have to release him; give him silver and ask him to leave Beijing," Vice Minister Hsu said.

"My Lord. No need to worry. Dae Wu is away, and only Saber King and a couple of guards are on friendly terms with Lee Mo-bai. Feng Five and the others either hate him or are jealous of him. Master Hwang hates him, too. We should kill him as soon as possible."

Huge Bo coerced, threatened, and bribed Violet into agreeing to be Hsu's concubine. Violet and her mother were to move in with another concubine of Hugo Bo's on an auspicious day. Violet wept all the way home.

A very fat, well-dressed Fat Shih awaited them. "I'm Lee Mo-bai's friend, and you know in your heart that someone framed Lee Mo-bai. Huge Bo and Vice Minister Hsu schemed to get him jailed, and they wanted to kill him, too. We will get him out soon. Lee Mo-bai loves you, and I am here to warn you not to let them buy you out with their filthy silver. Otherwise..." Fat Shih said.

"Otherwise, what? No one can force me to marry or not to marry. Get out, get out my house," Violet said angrily.

"You should not have loved that Lee Mo-bai in the first place. Your father's soul will not forgive you if you marry a thief or anyone who knows martial arts. You forget how they had beaten your father to death. 'They beat you too. I always worry that the cruel Dart Mew will come and catch us. Only the rich and powerful Vice Minister Hsu can protect us. I want to live comfortably in my old age. You could have married Lord Hsu earlier if that rascal Lee Mo-bai had not won your heart," her mother scolded Violet.

Her father was good at martial arts, and also an outstanding artist. He wrote poems, too. He married a beautiful prostitute, and they had only one child, Violet, whom he taught well. Violet's parents bought a little place to retire close to the historical city of Kaifeng.

Kaifeng had been the capital of many dynasties and was famous for its rich collection of antiquities. Unfortunately, a vicious bandit leader, Dart Mew, lived not far away from them.

Dart Mew was a famous bandit. His throwing dart is deadly accurate. Many professional guards and martial arts masters were afraid of his darts. His nephew Jao nicknamed '*Golden Spear,*' married a fierce female fighter nicknamed '*She-Devil.*' Mew and the Jao terrorized the area around Kaifeng.

Dart Mew got many young concubines either by force or silver. The pretty Violet became Dart Mew's victim. In the beginning, the sadistic Dart Mew treated Violet well, but he started to torture her the same way he tortured the others after the novelty wore off. Violet's father plotted an escape, but

Dart Mew caught them, and had Violet's father beaten to death. She and her mother were also beaten and then heavily guarded. Violet charmed Dart Mew, and gradually the surveillance on her and her mother relaxed, and they managed to escape to Beijing. Once her father told them that Beijing, being the Manchu's capital, would protect them from Dart Mew. He also suggested that Violet should marry a powerful, rich man to shield them.

Violet cared for the scholarly Lee Mo-bai very much before his superior martial arts skills became known. He promised that he would fight off her enemies. She was certain that Lee Mo-bai could defeat Dart Mew, but now Lee was in jail. She and her mother might be compromised too. She also begrudged that Lee Mo-bai had sent the fat man here to threaten her. She decided to be Vice Minister Hsu's concubine.

5

Lee Mo-bai's arrest soon spread, and conflicting rumors circulated. His enemies wanted him dead or jailed for life. His friends tried to save him. Fat Shih brought him daily meals, rumors, and news. Master Lieu and other guards came to visit him in jail. The soldiers dared not abuse him. Saber King was halfway to Ba-tin. He doubled back, and visited Lee Mo-bai and reassured Lee that he would help Lee Mo-bai without any reservation. Lee Mo-bai was touched.

"I will have someone safeguard your personal belongings."

"Please take temporary custody of my books and my sword. Most of them are my late father's."

Saber King's sworn brother Chin was a boxing instructor at Prince Te's palace. Saber King asked Chin to tell Prince Te that Lee Mo-bai was no thief and the official should not jail him. Prince Te had returned from a half-year administration duty in Manchuria. All the Manchu princes must learn both literary arts and martial arts. Each prince would gather talented and capable men, Manchu and Han, around him to teach him, to be his counsel. Prince Te encouraged anyone to go to him with suggestions and opinions.

"Your Highness, Lee Mo-bai is a scholar, and he is waiting to write the civil services examination. He is Master Dea-ti's friend, and a highly trained martial arts master. When Saber King fought him, he could have sliced off Saber King's shoulder and arms, but he controlled his sword so well that he only ripped the sleeve. He is no thief." Chin requested an audience and told Prince Te.

"Master Chin, thanks for the information. I will look into it. I cannot believe Dae Wu would be a friend to a thief. I will not allow anyone to jail an innocent man."

Prince Te always respected Dae Wu's broad-minded way of being friends with the Han. When many of his men told Prince Te that Dae Wu and Lee

Mo-bai were good friends, they convinced him that the righteous and sensible Dae Wu would never befriend a lowly thief. He also thought a man good at both the literary arts and martial arts would not need to be a thief. Prince Te ordered his staff to investigate the case.

Fat Shih brought Lee Mo-bai a meal and whispered, "There is a file. Use it to break the chain. I will have a horse ready outside of East Gate for you. There is no moon tonight. Be ready." Lee Mo-bai also whispered, "I'm no criminal. If I escape, it would be my admission of the guilt. I'm grateful for your help. They cannot hold me long. Saber King told me that one of his friends told Prince Te of my innocence. Besides, If I want to escape, no chain could keep me."

Two days later, a uniformed Imperial guard came and got Lee Mo-bai out of jail. Fat Shih congratulated Lee, "Great! Nobody dares to touch you in Beijing anymore. But you still have to be cautious." Fat Shih told Lee that Violet became a concubine, "Mo-bai, forget her. She is a prostitute."

Saber King invited Lee Mo-bai and his sworn brother Chin to have a drink. Lee Mo-bai thanked Master Chin. "It's nothing. Master Gi Kon-jii, your late teacher, saved my brother and friends years ago. I'm glad to have a chance to help you. I know of your father and Master Chiang, too." He then told Lee some anecdotes of the three of them. Master Chin also advised Lee Mo-bai to study hard to become an administrator. He said, "You're a scholar, and now you have a powerful patron. You could become a high-ranking administer or a general in time, and you can do something good for us, the Hans. Mo-bai, don't waste your talent and time on fighting and senseless revenge. I'm older than you, and I hope you don't mind my boring comments." Lee Mo-bai bowed low, "Thank you. Uncle Kao and Dae Wu advised me to do the same."

Two days later, Prince Te sent summoned Lee Mo-bai.

"Mo-bai, study hard, pass the examination and be an administrator, or follow your father's step to be a military attaché for a general. Emperor needs talents." Prince Te advised him. They talked about the different sword fighting styles. Prince Te insisted that they should have a friendly duel. Lee Mo-bai hesitated and said, "It does not fit for me to have a duel with Your Highness. The sword is sharp and..."

Prince Te laughed, "You wanted to say that you may wound me. Is that right? We will wrap the swords with silk." They went to the training field, and a big crowd gathered there to watch the duel. Prince Te put on a black suit. He ordered to have two swords wrapped with silk and coated with lime.

"The white spots on my black suit will tell me where you hit me. Mo-bai, I don't want you to have any reservations. Don't hold back. you hear?" Lee Mo-bai made the duel last a long time. When he saw that Prince Te showed signs of weariness, he delivered the winning thrust. Someone called out, 'Watch out! The left shoulder." just before Lee Mo-bai's sword, flat, hit Prince Te's left shoulder. '*Ahe. He saw through my move. This person is an expert.*' Lee Mo-bai glanced in the direction where the voice came. He saw three young men there.

Prince Te said, "You're very good. There are only eleven white spots on my suit. *Ha. Ha.*" He then handed the sword he was using to Lee Mo-bai, "I'd like you to have it. It's a historically well-known piece."

"Your Highness, it's too valuable. I don't deserve it."

"If you don't deserve it, who does? Keep it. Mo-bai."

They had supper together. Prince Te said, "I have spare rooms here. Why don't you have one?"

Lee Mo-bai said, "Thanks. I don't want to impose on you."

"You want freedom. *Ha Ha.*" Prince Te ordered his valet, "Get a carriage ready to take him home." On his way out, Lee Mo-bai asked the valet, "Do you know who called out the warning at the end of the duel?"

"It must be Yu Er (two). He works in the stable. We will reprimand him for this insolence."

Lee Mo-bai walked around Violet's new home, but he did not see her coming out. Every day he drank heavily and ignored Fat Shih's advice of restraining. One night a noise woke the drunken Lee Mo-bai. He took his sword, staggered out of the room and found no one. A man rushed out of his room, holding the sword that Prince Te had given him.

Lee Mo-bai shouted, "You came to steal the sword. I know who you are! Yu Er (two)."

They fought, and Lee Mo-bai met his first worthy opponent. Yu Er (two) was an experienced fighter, and he had a better sword. He also was more agile and in better shape. Yu Er (two) forced Lee Mo-bai back and jumped up on the roof, and escaped. The bare-footed Lee Mo-bai chased after him but could not catch him.

The next day Lee Mo-bai went to Prince Te's and asked the guards about Yu Er (two). No one knew too much about him. One of them said, "A while ago, a Tibetan Monk brought him here and said he could tame horses. The manager let him work at the stable. Indeed he knows horses. Even the most difficult ones are docile at his hand." Lee Mo-bai could not go to the stable to seek Yu Er (two). He went to ask Master Lieu about him.

Lieu said, "'Yu' is not a common surname like 'Lee' and 'Lieu.' I wonder whether he is related to the late Brother Yu." Lieu also told him that a general had canceled the convoy to the west. Lee Mo-bai could leave Beijing now, but he was too proud to let Yu Er (two) walk away with stealing the sword right under his nose. *'He will come to fight me again. One of the days, his hand will get itchy. I'll wait...'*

It rained that night. Lee went to Violet's new home and wanted to know whether she is happy or not. *'If she is not happy, I'll take her with me and leave Beijing without that sword. Yu Er (two) can have it.'* He waited on the roof in the rain and heard Violet laughing and joking with another young woman. When he saw the other young woman come out of Violet's room, he slipped into Violet' room. She said, "Get out. How dare you have your friend threaten me! I'm happy, and I feel safe here, and I don't want to see you anymore."

"Who had threatened you? I know nothing."

"A fat man, and he said he is your friend. Mo-bai, we've been good together. Let's keep the good memory of the time we were together. Please forget me," Violet sobbed. When Lee left, he saw the curtain of the other girl's room drew close. *'Ahe! The other girl saw me. I hope that I didn't cause Violet any trouble.'*

Fat Shih came and found Lee Mo-bai very sick when he did not show up at Fat Shih's eatery. Shih said, "I'll be right back with some herbal medicine for your fever." Lee Mo-bai dropped into another feverish sleep. He woke up suddenly and found Yu Er (two) standing beside the bed. He came to return the sword. Lee Mo-bai said weakly, "I know it's you. Brother Yu. You should keep it, and you're a better swordsman."

"You're sick, and you should not be alone. Your enemies may come to kill you. I'll stay with you." Lee nodded. Yu suddenly turned around when Fat Shih came. Lee said, "Brother Yu, he is a friend. Master Shih, this is the accomplished young warrior. He is Yu Er (two)." Fat Shih brought medicine and a kettle of hot tea, a pot of porridge.

"Brother Yu, thank god you're here. I cannot fight his enemies off if they come to harm him." Shih said.

Yu Er (two) curled up in a corner on the *kon* (bed). During the night, Yu Er (two) helped Lee to drink some tea twice. The following day Yu Er (two), Prince Te's valet, and a doctor came. Lee Mo-bai had pneumonia. Yu Er (two) brought a charcoal burner, a pot to brew the herbs, and also to cook rice porridge. Fat Shih brought them both meals every day and extra bedding and warm clothes for the cooler autumn. Some professional guards came to visit Lee Mo-bai often. When Lee asked where Yu Er (two) learned martial arts so well, Yu Er (two) told him that a Tibetan monk had brought him to Master Hsu's place in Szechwan. Hawk Hsu's wife taught him. Chiang Nan-ho and his mute brother had stayed at Master Hsu's home for eight months before Master Hsu passed away. Both of them taught Yu Er (two) and the Mute mainly. The Mute liked Yu Er (two) very much. Lee Mo-bai said, "Ahe! That explains that some of our fighting styles are very similar. We're truly brothers. Chiang Nan-ho is my father's sworn brother. The last time I saw him, I was eight years old. He took me to my uncle's after my parents died. I often wished that Uncle Chiang had adopted me and take me places." Lee wanted to ask about Yu Er (two)'s past but did not want to probe. Yu Er (two) was reticent. He only told Lee Mo-bai that he had killed an evil man and he is in hiding.

A sergeant walked in, the same one who had arrested Lee Mo-bai earlier.
"Sergeant, I'm sick. Is this a follow-up check on me?"
"Master Lee, I came to see how you are. How long have you been sick?"
"Many days. I got sick shortly after I got out of jail. I'm going nowhere."
"I can see that. Someone killed Vice Minister Hsu and Master Bo last night."
"Really? I'm glad." Lee Mo-bai said.
"It was not a burglary. We're holding both concubines for questioning. Master Bo's concubine implicated you."
"Did the woman say that I was the killer?"
"No. She said you were there one night. She said the killer is short and fat. Two servants saw the killer and reported that the killer wrapped his fat legs and arms with strips of black cloth."
"Great, I'm tall and thin. Why do you come to me then, Sergeant?"
"I have to follow up on the inquiries. I'm only doing my job."
"I know nothing. Huge Bo got me jailed, but I would not murder him at night. It's not my style."
"Master Lee, you are not a suspect."
"I'm glad to hear you say that. We all know that Hsu and Bo, with their filthy money and power, abused and ruined many people. Their victims might have done it. Just between you and me, they deserved to be killed, sooner or later."
"I think I know who the killer is. I better leave Beijing as soon as I'm well. Brother Yu, will you go to Yin-kin, Shanxi with me? We may meet my friend Dae Wu there. Then we'll go to Da-ton." Lee Mo-bai said to Yu Er.
"Sorry, I cannot go to either city. Someone might recognize me there."

"We can ask Prince Te to clear your name. He will understand that you've killed an evil man."

"It would not be that easy. Brother Lee, I'd like to go down South to seek the Mute if he is still alive."

"Good idea, we'll go together. Uncle Chiang probably does not know that Teacher Gi had passed away. You know they were enemies first and then friends later. Master Chin told me that Uncle Chiang and Teacher Gi had fought over the same woman when they were young." Lee Mo-bai sighed and continued, "After Teacher Gi passed away, I've been very lonely. My aunt cares for me very much, but my uncle, a miser, only wants me to be an administrator to bring him wealth and status. I think of you as my true brother, Brother Yu."

"I'm honored. You did not judge me by my shabby appearance. You're the first true praiseworthy contender I have met. Here is your medicine." He handed Lee the medicine and continued, "Get well soon. I want to duel with you again. We can learn from each other."

"It is a deal." Lee Mo-bai laughed and coughed a little before he slept.

Close to midnight, Fat Shih came. There were strips of black cloth wrapped around his thick thighs. Lee Mo-bai laughed, "Master Shih, you finally show us your true identity."

"I never thought I could pull a fog over both of you. I came to say farewell."

"Did you know the sergeant came to question me this morning for the crime you've committed?"

"How can you say it is a crime? I consider it a heroic deed. Mo-bai, you're sick, and you are under the future Emperor's protection. I know they cannot touch you." Fat Shih sat on the edge of the bed and continued, "My nickname is '*Mountain Lizard.*' My enemies forced me to flee here to hide. Huge Bo and Master Hsu robbed you of a pretty woman, had you jailed, and made you sick. On behalf of YOU and other countless victims suffering at their hands, I killed them. Violet is a widow now, and you can marry her and live happily ever after. *Ha Ha.* Too bad we don't have wine to celebrate."

"Master Shih, I don't want to, and I cannot afford to marry Violet. Thanks to you, she lost her powerful protector. I hope that the law treated her and her mother not too rough. She definitely will lose her income, and somehow I have to help her." Lee Mo-bai complained.

"Fine. I knew you would not appreciate my effort. Here is some silver for Violet. I have to leave Beijing tonight. I want to warn you, Mo-bai, Thin Buddha Hwang pulled many strings to have you jailed. He is evil. I heard he sent someone to fetch Dart Mew, Golden Spear Jao, and others from

Kaifeng here to fight you. Be prepared. Bye." Fat Shih jumped upon the roof and left.

"I knew that they arrested and jailed you because of a pretty prostitute. Is Violet her name? Sorry, I shouldn't pry."

"I fell in love with Violet, and I believe she loves me, too. But… I don't want to marry her, because there is another woman who has haunted me ever since last spring. I went to Violet with the hope that I may forget the other woman."

"May I ask you a very personal question?"

"I would not hide anything from you. You are a true brother."

"When you were delirious, you called out two names; Violet and Ceo-lian. You called out Ceo-lian more. Is she the woman of your dreams?"

Lee Mo-bai sighed, "She is. I can't have her, and I can't forget her. Because of her, for months, I haven't had a good night's sleep, and no food tastes good to me. I'm agonizing over her." Lee Mo-bai sobbed, "Let me tell you from the beginning. You're the second person I've poured my heart out to. Talking it out would give me some relief, too." Between sobbing and coughing, Lee told Yu Er (two) everything.

Yu Er (two) laughed hard at the ridiculous duel that Lee had wishfully thought he could win a wife with his sword. He laughed so hard that his tears came. He suddenly stood up and said, "I need to go to the market." Lee Mo-bai did not see Yu Er (two)'s tears and sudden paleness in the semi-darkness.

Yu Er (two) stood at a corner, gulped air, and tried to keep his emotions in check. *'Ahe! It's her. I wondered about it. Now I know it, and I'm poor, and I have to hide all my life. What should I do?'* He thought about telling Lee the truth about himself. Another thought came to him, and he decided to keep quiet. Lee Mo-bai thought, *'Dart Mew will be here soon. Dart Mew uses poisonous darts. It's good that I have taught Ceo-lian how to catch and to throw a dart. I hope she will keep up the exercise. I wonder how they are. Is the Mon family treating her mother and her well?'* His thoughts darted from Yu Ceo-lian to Violet, back and forth.

Yu Er (two) told Lee, "I'm grateful that you consider me your brother. I truly think you should marry Yu Ceo-lian whether they could find the missing fiancé or not. You've done so much for her family. You're a scholar. Yu Ceo-lian could be the first-rank lady if you pass the examination and become an administrator. Your calligraphy is superb, and I know you can pass the exam if you want to. That fugitive Mon Zhi-an is the son of a guard. He would not have your polished looks, and he definitely could not make Yu Ceo-lian a lady and provide her a fine living even if he is not a wanted criminal."

"Thanks. Mon Zhi-an is a true hero; he dared to take justice into his own hands. He is her betrothal, and he is good at martial arts. He could change his name and be a guard. They are of the same background. Yu Ceo-lian will be happy with him. I have to find him for her. If you don't mind, I'd rather not talk about this anymore." Lee Mo-bai said. He closed his eyes and thought, *'I should not have been so open with him. He treats me with genuine concern, but he won't tell me anything about himself, not even his full name. 'Er' means he is a second son. I wonder what else he is hiding from me.'* He was worried about Violet and her mother, too. He asked Yu Er (two) to take some silver to them, but Yu Er (two) could not find them. The only consolation that Lee Mo-bai had is that a pretty woman would soon find another rich man.

Yu Er (two) soon moved back to Prince Te's stable.

It began getting colder each day. Lee Mo-bai put on his padded jackets and still felt the piercing cold wind when he went to visit Prince Te.

"Mo-bai, you have lost a lot of weight, and you're still pale. Let me find you a good wife to look after you," Prince Te said.

"Your Highness, thank you for everything, and thank you for letting Yu Er (two) take care of me. He is great."

"Oh! That's nothing. It was good of him to tell us that you were sick. I'll reward him."

"Brother Yu, I miss your company. And I can't thank you enough for what you've done for me." Lee Mo-Bai said.

"You will do the same for me. I'll soon leave Beijing. Before I leave, I'd like to have a duel with you in the daytime, not at night." Both of them laughed.

"I'd like that. Where are you going? Do you need help with travel funds?"

"I can manage." Yu Er (two) did not tell Lee where he was going and why he wanted to leave.

"You're a true brother. I often think you're hiding your worry from me. Please open up to me as I did to you. Maybe I can help."

"No. You can't." They drank in silence. "Brother Lee, one day, you will know that I'm not a sly person. It's just I can't tell you everything now. I have my reasons. I truly want your friendship. Someday you'll know that I have your best interests in mind."

"Do you mind accepting some warm winter clothes?"

"Thank you. I need some warm clothes. I'd better get back to work. See you in the evening."

Lee Mo-bai went to see Master Lieu at Grand Security and thanked all the friendly guards. He asked them again whether they have heard a young warrior named Yu Er (two). Master Lieu said, "The only 'Yu' good at martial arts I know of was the late Master Yu. By the way, Mo-bai, my man delivered your letter to Mrs. Yu. They came back with the news that Mrs. Yu is very ill and there is no information of the missing Mon Zhi-an."

"Ahe! That's bad. I wish I were free to go to Da-ton to see Aunt Yu. But I have to wait for the imminent fight with Dart Mew and the others from Kaifeng."

"Mo-bai, take care of yourself when they come. We'll be on your side."

Lee Mo-bai went to the market and bought some warm clothes, fur hats, and boots for Yu Er (two) and himself. He met Violet's mother. "Master Lee, Please come with me," the old woman begged in tears. Violet and her mother lived with some other poor prostitutes in a shabby house. Vice Minister Hsu's wife confiscated all of their savings and kicked them out. The law officers were not kind to Violet either. She was sick.

"Master Lee, we have you to thank for all of our troubles," Violet said bitterly.

"I am truly sorry. I was sick for a long time, and I did not kill Bo and Hsu."

"I know that you are sick. Can you say you're completely in the clear? Your fat friend killed them for you. Suppose I had told the law that he's your friend. Master Lee, you would not be free of blame either."

"Fat Shih did not kill Bo and Hsu for you and me only. He killed them for all the other victims they had ruined."

"I said it before, and I'll repeat it. You men who know martial arts are all conceited and inconsiderate. You and your kind only understand fighting and killing. That fat friend of yours did not care whether my mother and I could survive without a powerful protector."

"Violet, I couldn't foretell and control what Fat Shih would do. He left me some silver for you," Lee Mo-bai put the silver which Fat Shih had left with him and three silver certificates worth fifty ounces each on a table and then continued, "Farewell, Violet. I'm in no shape for a quarrel. I'm leaving Beijing after I kill Jao and Dart Mew from Kaifeng. They killed Uncle Yu."

"Who? Did you say Dart Mew from Kaifeng would be here soon?" Her eyes were full of terror. Lee Mo-bai had a coughing spell, so he did not notice it.

"Just as you said, all the ones who know martial arts like nothing better than fighting and revenge for something insignificant. They are coming from afar to challenge me, and I have to kill them even if they did not kill Uncle Yu, Yu Ceo-lian's father, themselves. I wish you all the best. Farewell." Lee Mo bai coughed and then left with remorse. He wondered again about Violet's hidden daggers and why do they need powerful protectors. He wanted to ask her, but he knew that she would not tell him. '*It's time to end the affair.*' He decided.

Yu Er (two) and Lee Mo-bai practiced and compared their fighting skills at dawn and dusk. Yu Er (two) had more real combat experience. His jumping skills were better, and his sword thrusts were more powerful and deadly. Lee Mo-bai knew more advanced breathing exercises and *Tai Chi* boxing and swords fighting techniques, which the Mute could not make Yu Er (two) fully understand.

"The Mute showed me a two-volume martial arts manual full of pictures and explanations in simple words. Chiang Nan-ho compiled them. He showed me some, but I did not absorb it well. Someone who has a mind as sharp as yours could learn well from studying the manuals. I hope they will not fall into evil hands." Yu Er said.

"Manuals? I know nothing about it. We have to find it. The last time I saw Uncle Chiang, I was eight years old. You and I have to find Uncle Chiang and the Mute to learn more. Uncle Chiang is older than Teacher Gi. I don't know whether they are still around or not." Their skills improved. Their friendship and the vigorous exercise cured Lee Mo-bai's insomnia and also stimulated his appetite. He got stronger.

One late afternoon, Dae Wu's servant came, "Master Lee, my master will be back soon. He sent someone ahead with this letter to you." It read, '*Mo-bai, we have been apart more than three months already. I still have some official business to do. I'll tell you in detail when we meet. I heard that you're out of jail, but something else must keep you from coming to meet me. Master Yan-ti heard so much about you, and he is coming to Beijing to meet you. He wants you to work for him if you want to be a guard. I have marvelous news. The lovely Yu Ceo-lian whom you cannot forget and for whom you have so many sleepless nights is here at Yin kin. Her mother passed away, and she is here to ask Master Yang about Mon Zhi-an. I told her that I'm your friend and she agrees to come to Beijing with us. So, my dear Mo-bai, your dream, and wish will be fulfilled soon. Be prepared. I'll have a grand wedding for you. Your humble brother Dae Wu.*'

He reread the letter and thought, '*Dae Wu is goodhearted but preposterous. Poor Ceo-lian, her mother passed away. From this letter, it seemed that Yu Ceo-lian might not object to marrying me. Am I dreaming again?*' He hit his thigh hard to see whether it was a dream and continued his musing, '*but, it's absurd. What if Mon Zhi-an shows up one day? I can't marry her until we know for sure Mon Zhi-an is dead. But how long should I wait? How long should Yu Ceo-lian and I suffer the uncertainty and loneliness? And how about my relationship with Violet? I know Violet still wants me, and I cannot forget her either.'*

He paced around, holding the wrinkled letter, laughed, and sighed. The sweat covered his thin face.

"Brother Lee, what's the matter? Are you sick again?" Yu Er (two) came.

"I..I," Lee Mo-bai shook his head and handed Yu Er (two) the letter, "Yu Ceo-lian will be here soon. Dae Wu wants us to get married. How can I? Mon Zhi-an is her fiancé," Lee Mo-bai moaned. His eyes flashed, and his face changed from pale to purple and back to a deathly white. Yu Er (two) took a long time to read the letter. He also paled, and his hand shook when he put the letter on the table.

"It's great. Of course, you should marry Yu Ceo-lian. Compared to you, Mon Zhi-an did nothing for her family. He probably is poor and destitute and can't provide Yu Ceo-lian a decent living. Maybe he does not want to be found. You should marry Yu Ceo-lian." Yu Er (two) said very loud. He shouted.

Lee Mo bai stared at the usually sedate Yu Er (two) who was shouting now. He Suddenly noticed Yu Er (two)'s abrupt bloodless face and his trembling shoulders. He grabbed Yu Er (two)'s arm and shouted, "You… You are Mon Zhi-an. I think I always knew…"

Yu Er (two) wrenched free and fled. Two streets later, the breathless Lee Mo-bai gave up the chase. He knew that even when he was at his best, he would have a hard time catching Yu Er (two). *'In my mind, I think I always knew that he is Mon Zhi-an. When I told him about Yu Ceo-lian, didn't he laugh hysterically and pale suddenly. He found an excuse to leave the room and said that he had to go to the market. He must want to hide his emotional turmoil. He must love Yu Ceo-lian, too, since he uses her last name 'Yu' and 'Er,' which means he is a second son. He guarded me and took care of me when I was sick, and now I rob him of his betrothed. What kind of evil man am I? My indecision has caused Violet and her mother to be miserable and poor. Now, if Mon Zhi-an does not want to be found, it's also my fault a young couple separated. Mon Zhi-an misunderstands me and thinks that there is an infatuation between Yu Ceo-lian and me. Where can I find him?'*

Lee Mo-bai rushed to Prince Te's palace in a wild hope that Mon Zhi-an would pick up his belongings. He asked the guards at the gate to allow him to go to the stable directly, but Prince Te was getting off a carriage and saw him. Prince Te said, "Mo-bai, Congratulations. Dae Wu wrote that you're going to be married soon. Oh! What's the matter? Are you ill again?"

"Your Highness, I'll explain later. I have to find Yu Er (two). I must see him before he leaves." Lee Mo-bai said with apparent urgency.

"What's wrong? I'll send someone to fetch him." Lee Mo-bai could not find Yu Er (two) in the stable, and neither could Prince Te's valet. Lee Mo-bai gushed out everything from the beginning to Mon Zhi-an's disappearance.

"Je, pass my order. Close all the gates out of Beijing now, apprehend Yu Er, and bring him to me," Prince Te barked his order halfway through the narrative.

"Mo-bai, I really feel for you. Now I can see why a conscientious young man could get mixed up with a prostitute. You were looking for a diversion then," Prince Te. said after he had heard all.

"Your Highness, I am ashamed, and I'm responsible for Violet's misfortune even though I did not kill Vice Minister Hsu myself. Now I'm responsible for breaking up a couple."

"Mo-bai, I'm ashamed, too. I did not recognize Yu Er (two) as a talented warrior while I paid much for mediocre ones. When he comes back, I'll clear his name, and I'll offer him an instructor's post. He can marry Yu Ceo-lian then. I'm curious to know how good he is."

"He is better than me. Your Highness, I'm afraid that Mon Zhi-an won't be back. He insisted that I could provide Yu Ceo-lian a better life than he could."

"Mo-bai, there is some truth to it. If she marries you, Yu Ceo-lian could be a lady. If she marries Mon Zhi-an, she would be a wife of a guard and nothing more. Besides Mo-bai, you have done so much for her family, and you're so good-looking. I won't doubt that the girl admires you."

"Your Highness, I behave properly around her, and I tried very hard to hide my feelings. I think Yu Ceo-lian only thinks of me as her older brother."

"Mo-bai, you tried to hide your feelings, and she probably did, too. I don't see why you cannot marry her. They have never met each other, and now Mon Zhi-an relinquishes his marital rights to let you marry her." *'Someday, you'll know that I have your best interests in mind.'* Mon Zhi-an, Yu Ear's words came back. Lee Mo-bai knew that Mon Zhi-an did not want to be found.

"You Highness, if I had never met Mon Zhi-an, or if Mon Zhi-an did not take care of me, I think I could marry Yu Ceo-lian after a certain length of time. Now, I can't, and I won't marry her. I have to find Mon Zhi-an."

"Mo-bai, you can stay here tonight. Tomorrow, I will get more men to catch him."

"Thanks, Your Highness. I better go back to my place. Maybe he is waiting for me."

"Tell me immediately of any new development."

Back at his room at the temple, a letter was waiting for Lee Mo-bai. It read, '*Brother Lee, please accept my blessings and marry Yu Ceo-lian. I have nothing to offer her, whereas you have plenty to offer and what great services you have already done for the family. I wish you two the best. Don't look for me. You can't find me. Farewell. PS. I took the sword Prince Te had given you again.*' Lee Mo-bai wept.

Prince Te often slept alone in his study. Sometime after midnight, sounds of soft footsteps woke up Prince Te. "Is that you, Je? Bring me a cup of tea!" No answer.

Prince Te unsheathed his sword. It was Yu Er (two). "It's you! Lee Mo-bai waited for you all day. Now I know your real name and your problem. I can clear your name. Zhi-an." Price Te said warmly.

"Thank you, Your Highness. I must leave at once. I will borrow one of your horses."

"You can have a dozen horses. I want to talk to you, Zhi-an."

"Sorry, I know what you want to tell me. I must leave. Farewell." Mon Zhi-an left as soundlessly as a breeze over the roofs.

"Je, wake up. Go to the stable and see which horse is missing. Be quiet about it," Prince Te ordered his valet.

"Your Highness, who would ride at this hour?" Je grumbled and left. He came back shortly and reported, "Your Highness. Yu Er (two) is not back yet. Your favorite black mare is missing, and the stable gate was unlocked and left open. Should I order a thorough search?"

"Yu Er (two) left with the horse. No need to make a fuss. Bring me tea and go back to sleep." Prince Te thought, '*There are nine inner gates and fifteen outer gates in Beijing. No way to tell which gate he will take.*'

He sent for Lee Mo-bai at dawn and told him that Mon Zhi-an had taken the horse.

"He came to me at midnight. I tried to talk some sense into him. He left without giving me a chance to say anything,"

Lee Mo-bai said, "Your Highness, if I can't find him, how could I face Yu Ceo-lian?"

Prince Te thought a moment and then said, "Mo-bai, if you make up your mind that you can't and don't want to marry her, no one can force the issue. Just tell her the truth. You did not force him away. He left on his own. I have resources and manpower to help you finding him."

"Thanks, Your Highness. I'm sorry I am not a pleasant company today."

"Mo-bai, you may leave. Prepare your mind and body for the impending fight with Dart Mew and his gang. Yu Er (two), Mon Zhi-an, is not here to help you. You're on your own."

6

Yu Ceo-lian and her mother suffered from indifference to downright abuse at their in-law's home. Mrs. Yu's stomach ulcer got worse. She constantly wept for her husband's death and her daughter's bleak future. Yu Ceo-lian had to work non-stop. She took care of her sick mother, and she had to serve her demanding future mother-in-law. She also had to do the housework under her sister-in-law's critical eyes. Sometimes she was too busy to think about her misfortune and to cry.

Mrs. Mon was a demanding and bitter woman. It was her father's money and fame that established the Mon Security Company. She had never forgiven her husband for taking a concubine. She resented that her son must share the family wealth with Mon Zhi-an, the concubine's son. As expected, she did not like Yu Ceo-lian. She and her own son's wife ordered Yu Ceo-lian around like a servant. She would not let any chance gone by without insinuating that she had to mercifully take in the now destitute Mrs. Yu and Yu Ceo-lian.

Mon Zhi-chi, the elder son, was in charge of the family business. Yu Ceo-lian soon realized that the Mon Senior was afraid of his wife and his elder son. Short Hsu and his wife were the only ones who were kind to Ceo-lian and her mother. Short Hsu found a doctor and brought the medical herbs for Yu Ceo-lian to brew for her mother. When Short Hsu's wife realized that Ceo-lian sure had mixed feelings for Lee Mo-bai, she talked to Mrs. Yu and suggested that it will be all right for Ceo-lian to marry Lee Mo-bai if no one could find Mon Zhi-an soon. They encouraged Yu Ceo-lian to learn how to read and write. Short Hsu did not know his words well, but he taught Yu Ceo-lian whatever he knew.

Mrs. Mon and Yu Ceo-lian's sister-in-law verbally abused Ceo-lian and her mother often.

Soon Yu Ceo-lian's mother died. Mon Zhi-chi, Ceo-lian's brother-in-law, sought every opportunity to ogle the pretty Yu Ceo-lian. His jealous wife treated Yu Ceo-lian worse.

Short Hsu's advised, "Ceo-lian, I know your difficulties very well and you want to leave. I need my job here, and I can't go with you. Do you want to go back to Lu Town?"

His wife said, "How can she travel alone? She is so young."

"I know martial arts well. I can travel by myself. My sworn brother Lee Mo-bai is in Beijing. He wrote to us that he did not find Mon Zhi-an yet, but he is still trying. I'm going there. He will help me. I know it's not very proper, but I have no one else."

Short Hsu said, "In this area, there are many young Mongolian and Manchu girls. They rode and wore their hairs in two braids. We'll get her a pair of boots, and she could look like a Manchu girl traveling alone. Master Lee is indeed a very decent man, and he sure will help you. Before you go to Beijing, I suggest you visit the famous Master Yang at Yin-kin Town. You have to pass there anyway. He knows the Mons, father, and sons. He may have some information."

"Do you know how to handle a horse, Ceo-lian?"

"Yes, I do. Brother Lee Mo-bai taught me everything: brushing the horse, riding, and saddling a horse. I'm taller now. I can manage any horse," she said proudly, and she thought about her father and the first time Lee Mo-bai helped her to mount her father's horse. Her tears came, and she also blushed when she tried to recall the sensation of Lee Mo-bai's strong hands pushing her up the tall horse. That was the first time a man had touched her.

Short Hsu saddled a good horse for her. Yu Ceo-lian wore a dark blue cotton short set with a silver comb in her hair, and strips of white cloth tied her braids. She also wore a white armband. She was in mourning. She took two pairs of sabers, her own and her father's, and had a small package with some silver and silver certificates tied around her waist under her tunic. Short Hsu's wife helped her sew a small pocket for the extra silver certificates, and stored it between the linings of her undershirt. *'Aunt, you and Ceo-lian should have some silver.'* Lee Mo-bai's words came clear to her. He had said it after he sold her father's horse. *'Ahe! He is honest, and he truly cares for us. He could have kept my father's good horse for himself. I remembered that his horse is old and thin. He could have sold that old horse instead or not care to sell the horse at all. He wanted us to have some silver.'* She remembered that Lee Mo-bai washed and brushed the horse before selling it. *'We can get more silver for a clean horse.'* He had explained.

Her clothes and other necessities were in the saddlebag. Wrapped tightly inside her spare clothes were a pair of gold hair combs and a sealed letter. The combs were the marriage keepsakes Master Mon gave her father six years ago when they arranged the marriage between her and Mon Zhi-an. When she finds Mon Zhi-an, this pair of gold combs will identify her as his bride. Short Hsu handed her a sealed letter and said that she should hand it to Lee Mo-bai in person. "Sister, give it to him, not his friend," Short Hsu told her, "Probably something about your late father's unfinished business that he wanted Lee Mo-bai to handle for him."

She had diligently practiced the deep breathing technique Lee Mo-bai had taught her. She felt strong and her senses became sharper. When she found a quiet place along the road, she practiced the throwing darts technique, which Lee Mo-bai taught her. *'Sister, try not to catch any dart your enemy throws at you. Just dodge it or push it away with your saber. The dart might be poisonous. If you want to catch it, wear something that covers your hand.'* Everything she did brought Lee Mo-bai's words and image vividly to her mind. At night she slept with her clothes and shoes on and with her sabers beside her. She remembered that Lee Mo-bai had told her to be alert all the time.

When she stopped at the first inn, the clerk looked at her in awe as she carried two pairs of sabers under one arm and her saddlebag with one hand. The owner's wife came to her room with her meal and asked, "Miss, where are your folks? You cannot be traveling alone?" Ceo-lian replied, "Thank you for your concern. I can take care of myself." She ate her bowl of noodle soup mixed with her tears and thought, *'I have nobody'*. The owner found her a long bag for her sabers and helped her tie the bag along the horse's flank. He said, "We don't want others to see your sabers."

She was very disappointed when Master Yang told her nothing about Mon Zhi-an's death or whereabouts.

"I will go to Beijing. My sworn brother Lee Mo-bai is in Beijing. Here is the address of his relative. If you ever have any information, please send a letter to this address."

"I will. I have heard about Lee Mo-bai. He fights well," Master Yang said.

Dae Wu was visiting Master Yang. He introduced himself to Ceo-lian, "Miss Yu, I overheard your conversation with Master Yang. Lee Mo-bai is my good friend. He told me about you. My name is Dae Wu. Master Yang and I are going to Beijing soon. We can travel together." Yu Ceo-lian wanted to hear more about Lee Mo-bai and agreed to travel with them.

Master Yang and Yu Ceo-lian road alongside Dae Wu's carriage. They followed the convoy of merchants and their goods that Yang was escorting to Beijing. Dae Wu told Yu Ceo-lian that Lee Mo-bai made himself quite a name in Beijing. Lee Mo-bai knew many professional guards and made inquiries about Mon Zhi-an's whereabouts. He did not mention that the officers arrested and jailed Lee Mo-bai because of a prostitute.

Two days later, they entered the Gu-bai Pass. Master Yang's assistant told them how Lee Mo-bai had chased away a group of bandits without drawing his sword. Dae Wu also mentioned how swiftly Lee Mo-bai defeated the bandit chieftain.

They chatted with each other and also became absorbed in their own thoughts.

Master Yang thought, *'This young man, Lee Mo-bai, must be very good. How can I get him to work for me? Dae Wu said he is a scholar and he may not want to be a guard. It seems that Dae Wu wants Lee Mo-bai to marry Yu Ceo-lian. They both could work for me. I wonder whether Lee Mo-bai's family would allow him to marry a poor living widow with not properly bounded feet.'*

Dae Wu thought, *'Yu Ceo-lian is sure pretty. No wonder Lee Mo-bai lost his heart over her. If we can't find Mon Zhi-an, I'll help them get married.'*

Yu Ceo-lian thought, *'It's too bad that I have an arranged marriage to marry the missing Mon Zhi-an. If no one can find him, I won't mind marrying Brother Lee if he still likes me.'* She had wishful ideas, but she was sure that Lee Mo-bai loves her. *'The way he had looked at me! He could not hide his feelings. What if he has found a wife already?'* She felt a sudden chill.

Dae Wu stole a glance at Yu Ceo-lian's pinkish glow and thought, *'Mo-bai, no more sadness.'* He had sent two letters to Lee Mo-bai and Prince Te to tell them about Ceo-lian.

Dae Wu took Yu Ceo-lian home to meet his wife and his mother. They all liked her right away. They let Yu Ceo-lian have her room and tried to make her feel at home. When Dae Wu whispered to his wife the hopeful marriage between Yu Ceo-lian and Lee Mo-bai, his wife got excited and said, "They are indeed a pair. Mo-bai is handsome, and Yu Ceo-lian is very pretty. I'm going to congratulate her."

"Hold it. First, we have to be sure that no one could find Mon Zhi-an. Second, I have to get Lee Mo-bai's agreement."

"Why shouldn't he agree? Didn't you tell me that Yu Ceo-lian is the very girl of his dreams? I'm certain of the marriage like I know tomorrow will be coming after today."

"Let's be cautious. Lee Mo-bai is a bit stiff-necked. He rigidly upholds the codes of ethics and honor. We'll know soon enough."

Dae Wu went to Prince Te's palace to report and found Lee Mo-bai there.

"Brother, I can't and I won't marry Yu Ceo-lian. She has a fiancé," Lee Mo-bai sighed and continued, "I know you're very kind, and you do have my best interests in mind. But you don't know that I found Mon Zhi-an, and I lost him again."

"What? Where did you find him, and how did you lose him again?"

Prince Te said, "Dae Wu, it is awkward for Mo-bai now. Mon Zhi-an called himself Yu Er (two), and he is Mo-bai's best friend and took good care of him when he was sick. Unfortunately, Mo-bai told him his longing for Yu Ceo-lian. He did not know Mon Zhi-an gave himself an alias, Yu Er (two), and worked for me incognito. We have to find him, and that's that."

"It's unbelievable. Mo-bai. Please tell me everything."

Lee Mo-bai explained in detail, and Dae Wu was dumbfounded.

"Your Highness and Brother Dea Wu, the worst is that I told Mon Zhi-an that the only way I could marry Yu Ceo-lian is if her missing fiancé is either missing forever or dead."

"Mo-bai, how could you be so gullible and stupid again?" Dae Wu was angry.

Prince Te said, "Dae Wu, don't blame him. Mo-bai is sick and lonely, and he needs to have someone to talk to."

"I called out her name and... 'Violet' when I was delirious. He was very reticent. He probably guessed it, but he kept it to himself. He knew about Violet. He asked me who Ceo-lian is, and...and I told him everything. I'm very grateful for his help, and I did not want to hide anything when he asked me. And...and I need to talk about it." Lee Mo-bai moaned.

"Dae Wu, where is Yu Ceo-lian now? At your home?" Prince Te asked,

"Yes. My mother and my wife like her very much. She wants to see Mo-bai as soon as possible. What should I tell her, Mo-bai."

"Please don't tell her where I live. It's a temple, and it's not proper for her to visit me there. Tell her I will come to your home to meet her. But, what do I tell her if she asks me about Mon Zhi-an?"

"Tell her the truth. The law wants Mon Zhi-an, he is on the run, and he used a faked name." Lee Mo-bai thought, *'How can I tell her the truth? When I was sick, I called out her name.'* Dae Wu's carriage dropped him off at the corner close to the temple.

Fat Shih's assistant waited for Lee Mo-bai at the temple. He told Lee Mo-bai urgently, "Master Lee, my master is awaiting you at the South Gate. Come quickly. My master sent me here to tell you…"

Lee Mo-bai said, "Please inform Master Dae Wu that I have to leave town to find Master Mon in a hurry. DON'T tell him where I'm going."

"Brother Dea, when can I meet with Brother Lee? Will he come to visit you tomorrow?" Yu Ceo-lian asked him. She was with Mrs. Dae Wu.

"I met Mo-bai at Prince Te's a short while ago. He said he would be here tomorrow. But, just now he sent someone to tell me that he has to leave Beijing in a hurry. He did not tell me where he is going, and he probably will be back soon."

"Ceo-lian, you know all men are alike. They don't tell us a lot," Mrs. Dae Wu said.

The following day, Mrs. Dae Wu circumspectly told Yu Ceo-lian that Lee Mo-bai had found Mon Zhi-an and then Mon Zhi-an left town suddenly. Lee Mo-bai tried to find him again. Yu Ceo-lian wondered why and hoped that Lee would be back with Mon Zhi-an or at least bring back some factual information about the man she's supposed to marry.

Fat Shih had two horses ready and they wanted to rush to Kao-yon Town, south of Ba-tin Town, but they could not ride fast on the busy highway out of Beijing. They talked.

"I met Yu Er (two), and he told me that you are his only true friend. He will die for you." Fat Shih said.

"His real name is Mon Zhi-an. He is the second son of Master Mon of Da-ton, Shanxi Province. He killed someone, and he is on the run," Lee Mo-bai told Fat Shih.

"I see. I know that Mon Zhi-an hid something. He told me that he wanted to intercept your enemies and fight them off for you. He said that he hopes to scare them away or at least curtail some of their arrogance. I admired his bravery and decided to accompany him."

"Mon Zhi-an fights better than me. I can't believe they could wound him."

"Mo-bai. He did fight very well. That evil Dart Mew's poisonous dart did him in. We met Golden Spear Jao and Dart Mew's gang just south of Kao-yon Town. Yu Er (two), Mon Zhi-an, stopped them first and wanted to reason with them. They ganged upon us. Mon Zhi-an's fast sword thrusts slightly pierced eight or nine of them in a flash…"

"Ahe! He is good. Wu-ton School of Martial Arts forbids us from killing unnecessarily," Lee Mo-bai praised.

"Dart Mew threw two darts at Mon Zhi-an. Mon caught one and threw one back at Mew. It scraped Mew's shoulder. Dart Mew pretended to be wounded badly and fell facedown to feign a faint. Mon Zhi-an was busy fighting Golden Spear Jao and more than seven gang members. Dart Mew threw a poisonous dart at Mon Zhi-an, Mon Zhi-an dodged, and the dart just barely scraped his ear. It must have been a fast poison, and Mon started to stagger. They ganged up on him and cut him up. The soldiers came, and I dragged him to safety. A doctor purged him of the poison, but the multiple wounds are fatal. Mon Zhi-an is holding his last breath to talk to you."

"If he dies, I can't live with my conscience. I'm his killer and poor Yu Ceo-lian…" Lee Mo-bai's chest tightened, and he nearly fell off the horse.

"Mo-bai, take it easy. Who is Yu Ceo-lian? A pretty woman?" Lee Mo-bai told Fat Shih the entanglement among the three of them.

"Ahe! I wish that I could say something to ease your pain. I thought the root of your sadness is losing Violet. I did not know you had lost your heart to this Yu Ceo-lian before you met Violet. You're tight-mouthed."

"No, not tight enough. When Mon Zhi-an asked me about Violet, I told him that Violet is only a diversion for me. I told him the impossible love I had for Yu Ceo-lian. I had thought that Yu Er (two) might not be his real name. He lied and told me he had killed someone in Szechwan. I believed him, and I never thought that he is Mon Zhi-an."

"Mo-bai, you were very sick then. You needed sympathy, and you trusted him. Your guard was down." Fat Shih sighed.

Mon Zhi-an had a deep cut on his chest, two cuts on his left thigh, and another wound on his right shoulder. He had lost a lot of blood. The doctor shook his head and said that he had done all he could. For two long days, Mon Zhi-an was not fully conscious. On the third day, Mon Zhi-an was momentarily clear, and he told them, little by little, "My mother is a concubine. My brother is the chief wife's only son. They hated my mother and me because I'm entitled to half of the family estate. She abused my mother. My mother became deaf. When I was eight years old, Someone kidnapped me, and now I believe that was a setup to get rid of me. The kidnappers took me to Szechwan. An old Tibetan monk saved me and started to teach me martial arts. Before his death, he took me to Master Hsu's place. They took me in and they treated me well and taught me martial arts. Six years ago, I went back home for my mother, but she died soon afterward. Brother Lee, you know the rest. I do sincerely think you will be a better husband for Yu Ceo-lian than I ever could be. I don't have many breaths left in me, and I beg you to marry her. Please don't argue with a dying man, and please pity her. If you don't marry her, she will be a living widow all her life. The superstitious folks will not have such an unlucky woman for a daughter-in-law. I'm certain that she loves you too. I beg you… go to Szechwan…Dirty trick, Dart Mew…You evil…" Mon Zhi-an yelled and died. Lee Mo-bai understood the unfinished request to go to Szechwan to check on Master Hsu's family and kill Dart Mew.

They buried Mon Zhi-an and the sword at a nearby hillside. Lee Mo-bai wrote Mon Zhi-an's name and ordered a tombstone to be carved and erected later. His immensurable guilt and remorse tore him apart. Fat Shih had to drag him away from the tomb.

"Mo-bai, there's no time to lament. You better hurry back to Beijing to fight them and avenge Brother Mon's death. I hope we are not too late, and I'm afraid this pack of jackals may have harassed Dae Wu already."

"Yes, I will ride Prince Te's black horse back to Beijing. I think Yu Ceo-lian and that famous Master Yang will have no trouble fighting them off for a while." The black mare seemed to know that her beloved master was buried there. She neighed and turned her head to look at the grave again and again.

In Beijing, Yu Ceo-lian killed Dart Mew with one of his poisonous darts.

Sixty-five years old Dart Mew did not want to leave Kaifeng at first. He had a new young concubine. Ca leo (six), the man Thin Buddha Hwang sent to invite him, told him that his runaway concubine, Chi Mi-neon, lives in Beijing with Lee Mo-bai. "Master Mew, your runaway concubine calls herself 'Violet' now. She is a prostitute. Lee Mo-bai visits her often, and they practically live together. She says that Lee Mo-bai will kill you for her." Dart Mew was furious. His nephew Golden Spear Jao, Jao's wife nicknamed '*She-Devil*' and thirty-some roughnecks left Kaifeng for Beijing. At Kao-yon Town, a young man fought them, and Dart Mew's poisonous dart killed the young man.

Thin Buddha Hwang welcomed them warmly. Dart Mew told him, "That young man I might have killed was very good. Is he Lee Mo-bai?"

"How many days ago?"

"About a half-month ago."

"It cannot be Lee Mo-bai. My man spotted him and Dae Wu coming out of Prince Te's palace about ten days ago." Thin Buddha had his spies kept surveillance on Lee Mo-bai. When he heard the report that Lee Mo-bai was sick, he had sent someone to kill Lee. But he was told a young man was staying with Lee. He thought that young man was Lee's classmate.

"Master Mew, did you say this young man fights well. He might be Lee Mo-bai's classmate or a friend. They are close. I knew that Lee Mo-bai left Beijing in a hurry."

"What does this Lee Mo-bai look like?"

"He is tall and thin with a pretty face. He is pretty as a woman. Dae Wu likes him very much *Ha Ha*."

"That young man was neither tall nor pretty. Master Hwang, find me some young girls. The younger, the better. Does this Lee Mo-bai live with a prostitute called 'Violet?'"

"Lee Mo-bai indeed visited Violet often. I heard she is sick and destitute now. Master Mew, I will find you young girls."

"Master Hwang, send your man to find Violet. She was my concubine."

"Not too long ago, Lee Mo-bai killed her protector. She is poor now."

Violet was scared after Lee Mo-bai had mentioned that Dart Mew would be in Beijing soon. Now someone told her that some famous martial arts experts from Kaifeng had come to Beijing to fight Lee Mo-bai, and she knew that Dart Mew must be in Beijing now, and she must have Lee Mo-bai's protection. Violet's mother did not find Lee Mo-bai at the temple, and so she went to Dae Wu's house. Dae Wu was not in, a servant told Mrs. Dae Wu. Yu Ceo-lian came out. The old woman told her that Dart Mew wanted to kill her and her daughter.

"Is this Dart Mew from Kaifeng?" Ceo-lian asked.

"Yes, he forced my daughter to be his concubine, he killed my husband. We escaped and hide here in Beijing. Lee Mo-bai knows how to fight. Now *She Devil* and the Ho brothers are here also to help Dart Mew to kill us. Master Lee loves my daughter; please tell him to help us. .. ..." She sobbed and told Ceo-lian everything.

Ahe, the Ho brothers are my father's murderers and now they are here in Beijing! I will kill them! Yu Ceo-lian was also curious and wanted to meet the woman Lee Mo-bai loves. She knew that she had no right to be jealous but she was.

"Aunty, I will help you. Lee Mo-bai is my sworn brother and the Ho brothers are my enemies, too." She helped the old woman get in the carriage. Violet's mother looked at Ceo-lian with doubt. *'She is a young girl. How can she help us?'*

Dart Mew and a few roughnecks had broken into the shabby house where Violet and her mother lived. Dart Mew slapped Violet hard, and she slashed Dart Mew's face with the dagger hidden under her pillow. Dart Mew wanted to kill her right there but Ca leo (six) stopped him, "Master Mew. We are in Beijing, the capital. You cannot kill her." Mew told Violet that he would come to get them the next day. He told Ca leo (six) and three men, "Stay here. Don't let them escape."

Ca leo (six) recognized Yu Ceo-lian and ran. The other three men ganged up on Ceo-lian and shouted obscenities. Yu Ceo-lian seized a staff and chased them away. She wanted to go after Dart Mew right away at first, and then

Two Swordmasters & Two Women

she thought, '*I can't get Dae Wu involved. Besides, I need to protect my hand because I may try to catch the darts automatically. Lee Mo-bai told me the darts might be poisonous.*' She looked at Violet's swollen face and found her a beauty. She thought, '*Where is Lee Mo-bai? He should protect her!*'

She told Violet, "Lee Mo-bai is my sworn brother. Your neighbors called the soldiers, and they are here now. I'm going back to talk with Master Dae Wu and see if we can find a way to keep you safe." Violet knew that Yu Ceo-lian was the young girl Lee Mo-bai had dreamed about. She noticed that Yu Ceo-lian still wore her hair in braids, the customary hairstyle for a maiden. Violet had to let go of her dream of marrying Lee Mo-bai. Violet wanted to show Ceo-lian the bloody dagger and tell her she also dared to fight. Before Violet could do so, Ceo-lian left.

Yu Ceo-lian told Dae Wu what had happened, "Violet and her mother are in danger. Is there any way we can help them?"

"I'll ask my friend Captain Wong to have some soldiers there to guard their home for a short while. We will have to move them to somewhere safe until this Dart Mew and his like leave Beijing. We cannot have them here. She is a prostitute, and I may lose my job." Dae Wu said.

Mrs. Dea Wu suggested, "The soldiers could not be there all the time. We can send them to the Peace Convent. The abbess there came to see mother often, and we always donate silver."

"That's a good idea. Violet and her mother will be safe in the convent. Someone told me that the abbess knows martial arts." Dae Wu sent his servants to move Violet and her mother to the convent.

Yu Ceo-lian and a maid sewed something like a glove for her right hand. Early next morning, she rode to the hotel where Dart Mew was. She shouted a challenge and dashed out of the city gate. Ca leo (six) had told Dart Mew how beautiful and how tough Ceo-lian is. Dart Mew wanted to have her. He rode after her. Ceo-lian led him a long way out of the city, and then she slowed and deliberately let Dart Mew get closer. Dart Mew tried to capture her at first, and he did not use a poisonous dart. But Ceo-lian dodged his dart quickly. Dart Mew then threw a poisonous one at her. Ceo-lian caught it and threw it back at him, aiming at his chest, but she missed. The dart slid off the side of Dart Mew's head. Yu Ceo-lian was scared, and she dashed for her life. When she found no horse behind, she carefully doubled back and saw Dart Mew lying on the ground, his face black, and he died. The poisonous dart scratched where Violet's dagger had pierced Dart Mew's face, and the poison worked fast. Yu Ceo-lian shook and vomited at the sight of his body.

Dae Wu was afraid that Golden Spear Jao would now come to kill Yu Ceo-lian and him.

He sent a servant to ask Yang to come over to help.

Meanwhile, Golden Spear Jao challenged Viscount Chiu. The Ho brothers ganged up on Viscount Chiu and wounded the count. Now a whole regiment of soldiers tried to catch Jao and his men. They hid at Hwang's place and then left Beijing with Dart Mew's coffin.

Nothing happened for a couple of days. Yu Ceo-lian recalled Lee Mo-bai's word of the importance of being alert. '*Miss Yu, your enemies are bandits. We have to be alert at all hours.*' She thought that this evil group might come in at the dead of the night. She slept with her tight-fitting combat suit and shoes on.

She-Devil and her two brothers came to kill her and Dae Wu one night. Yu Ceo-lian fought them off and chased after them. She came back and told Dea Wu.

"Brother, they are not that good. I chased them a few streets down. Someone woke up and called the law. I don't want the soldiers to spot me. they got away."

Dae Wu and his wife praised her for her readiness. Yu Ceo-lian said, "Brother Lee taught me a lot."

Dae Wu said, "Mo-bai told me that Mon Zhi-an is more experienced and fights better than him. Let's hope that Mo-bai will find him soon. Prince Te said he would pardon Mon Zhi-an, and then he will be a free man. We will have a nice wedding."

When Yu Ceo-lian was alone with Mrs. Dae Wu, she asked, "I'm a country girl, and we don't hear much talk about prostitutes. Violet is beautiful. Do you know anything about the prostitutes and…her?"

"I presume that there are prostitutes in the country, too. In the big cities, they lived in a special area, called the *'flower or red lantern'* district. Most of them are young and pretty. During a flood or drought, the poor and the refugees would sell their girls to be prostitutes. I'm lucky that my husband does not patron them. Sometimes he goes there to meet friends. You should hear the ridiculous tales he told me about them and their clients. He told me that Violet is an exceptional one. She is very artistic; she paints, and she writes poems. Her clients enjoy her company, and they can talk about poetry with her. She… but I remembered that Dae Wu said she is not young." Mrs. Dae Wu did not want to tell her that Lee Mo-bai visited Violet often, and they read and wrote poems together.

Yu Ceo-lian thought, '*My father is right. Lee Mo-bai is too sophisticated for me.*'

That night, Dae Wu told his wife, "Thin Buddha Hwang will be our foe forever. We better teach our sons martial arts."

"You can teach them yourself."

"No. I'm not good enough. I wish Mo-bai would marry Yu Ceo-lian and both of them teach our sons. But, the waiting has gotten on my nerves."

"The other day, Yu Ceo-lian showed me the 'gold combs,' the marriage token from the family of Mon. Ahe! Yu Ceo-lian is such a nice girl. It's not right these two young men…"

"Keep your voices down. Will you?" Dae Wu whispered.

Yu Ceo-lian's now sharpened hearing could only catch a segment of the conversation. Now she was sure that Mon Zhi-an's sudden disappearance had something to do with Lee Mo-bai. If Mon Zhi-an did not want to be found and Lee Mo-bai would not tell her the truth, she should not stay here and wait. She cried herself to sleep, and she decided to go back to Lu Town.

She told Mrs. Dae Wu the following day, "If Brother Lee does not come back soon, and I'll go back home and make arrangements to move my parents' caskets back to the family lot in Lu Town."

"Ceo-lian, it could snow any day now. The ground will soon be frozen, and you could not move the caskets. Please stay with us until next spring. If…if it's necessary, we'll find someone to accompany you home then." Mrs. Dae Wu said. Her unspoken word, *'If Lee Mo-bai can't find your missing fiancé and Lee does not want to marry you either,'* hang heavily in the air.

"Thank you. I don't think I should celebrate the New Year with you. I'm in mourning."

"Why not? It must be one of your Han customs. We would like to have you, and your parents would like to see you have a good time. There will be a lot of festival activities here in Beijing. You don't want to miss it. You know that I want you to stay with us as long as you want to. I feel safe to have you around." Mrs. Dae Wu said.

Lee Mo-bai came back two days later at night.

"Mon Zhi-an is dead. I'm responsible for his death." There were tears streaking Lee Mo-bai's weary and dusty thin faces. He told Dae Wu everything.

"Ahe! It's bad. Young Mon acted impulsively. You shouldn't blame yourself. How are we going to tell Yu Ceo-lian?"

"I'm damned. It's gods' way of punishing me for wanting another man's wife." Lee Mo-bai moaned.

"Take it easy. It's fate. You look awful. Have you eaten?" Dae Wu asked with concern.

"I don't know. I..." Lee Mo-bai murmured. A servant came in with a bowl of ginseng soup and then reported that a bath, a barber, and a masseur were ready.

Lee Mo-bai asked the servant, "How is the black mare? I rode her hard."

"Master Lee, the groom rubbed her down and said she is a champion, one in ten thousand."

"Mo-bai, you rode Prince-Te's favorite mare back."

"Yes. Mon Zhi-an groomed her every day. The mare did not want to leave his grave."

Over drinks and a light snack, Lee filled in the details and said, "Tomorrow, I'll kill Dart Mew. He killed Mon Zhi-an. That's the least I can do…"

Dae Wu said excitedly, "Yu Ceo-lian killed him with one of his own poisonous darts. The rest of the gang left Beijing with the casket. You see…" He explained.

"Ceo-lian must have improved her skills a great deal. Who said that Providence has no eyes? Ahe! she knows the dart is poisonous. Did she remember …"

"Yes. You are a good teacher. Yu Ceo-lian made some hand cover herself. She did not want to involve me and lured him out of the city gate. Isn't she smart? She thinks the world of you. Mo-bai."

"Yes, Ceo-lian is smart. Ahe! Violet is a runaway concubine. I know she knows martial arts, and that's why she had a dagger hidden. You're so kind to help her."

They talked about this and that for a while, avoiding the real issue. Finally, Dae Wu said, "Mo-bai, what are we going to do? We have to tell Yu Ceo-lian the truth."

"I cannot face her now. Please break the news to her."

"Mo-bai, of course, I'll tell her the news. How about her future? The only sensible answer is that you marry her. Isn't this Mon Zhi-an's dying wish, too?" He continued after he stopped Lee's protest. "I don't mean now or the immediate future. You can marry her a year, or even two years later. At least give her something to hope for, poor girl."

"I can't. I made a bargain with the gods to keep Mon Zhi-an alive. I vowed that I wouldn't covet his wife. Mon Zhi-an died for me. I can't marry Yu Ceo-lian. Don't you understand!"

"Mo-bai, you can't ignore his dying wish. He begged you to marry Yu Ceo-lian lest she would be a living widow forever."

"I understand, but I can't." Lee Mo-bai sobbed.

"Mo-bai, I know it's cruel, but I have to say it. You escorted Yu Ceo-lian for nearly a half month on the road. I know you behaved most honorably, but somehow her name was tarnished. Mon Zhi-an would naturally think there was infatuation between you two. I also think so. She blushed whenever someone mentioned your name. Now, she cannot stay with the Mon family, and she is alone. Of course, she can stay with us forever if she wants to. We all like her a lot, and she can protect us. But, a living widow at her tender age? Mo-bai, have mercy on her and yourself."

"I can't. Please pardon me." Lee Mo-bai knelt.

Dae Wu told his wife everything. She said, "Poor Ceo-lian and poor Mo-bai. I feel for both of them. I'll break the bad news to her gently, but how can I tell her that Mo-bai does not want to talk to her. She is entitled to ask Lee Mo-bai the details."

"It's a dilemma. You tell Ceo-lian that Lee is exhausted and he needs a couple of days to recuperate first. and.. tell her that Lee's uncle wants to see him immediately."

Lee Mo-bai woke up shortly before Dae Wu came home at noon. They reported to Prince Te together.

"Mo-bai, be strong and don't allow yourself to hide behind self-pity and self-loathing. Take the pain in stride and then face the future." Prince Te advised Lee.

"Thank you. Your Highness." Lee Mo-bai said.

"Your Highness," Dae Wu pleaded, "can you talk some common sense into his stubborn head and let him marry Yu Ceo-lian? Mo-bai looks up to you, and he will listen to you."

Lee Mo-bai said in a hurry, "Your Highness, I can't, and I won't marry her. Please don't order me. I'd rather die." He knelt.

"Up! Mo-bai, I'm not going to force you," Turning to Dae Wu, Prince Te said, "I think I understand Mo-bai better. You are happily married and never have to suffer from the torture of an impossible love."

"But, Your Highness. Mo-bai loves Yu Ceo-lian, and how can he bear to see that Ceo-lian be a living widow?"

"Mo-bai can't marry Yu Ceo-lian at the present just because he loves and respects her deeply. In a way, it's his fault that Mo-Zhi-an chose to die. I hope time will heal everything, and hopefully, Mo-bai will change his mind later. I doubt it will happen. I mean, I can see no marriage between them. Besides, we have to consider Yu Ceo-lian's feelings. She might want to be a faithful living widow."

"Thank you, Your Highness. You truly understand me."

"I'd like to share a part of myself with both of you. Do you ever wonder why I, having a beautiful wife and two royal consorts, spend most of the time alone in my study? I fell in desperate love with a maiden from a rival tribe, but I can't marry her. My marriage is a political one. True love never dies and never changes—woe for the pitiful ones who are under its spell. Mon Zhi-an died for Mo-bai. Mo-bai respects Yu Ceo-lian too much to covet her, his best friend's wife-to-be. But, Mo-bai, you have to be married to fulfill your duty to produce 'sons' as I did." Three of them sat in silence in a shared melancholy.

Prince Te sighed, "Mo-bai, My great grandfather Manchu Emperor Shoe Je, fell in love with a woman he was forbidden to love. With his noble position as an emperor, he could not make her the empress, not even a formal royal consort. After her death, he died soon and left the throne to an eight years old boy, Emperor Kangxi."

Lee Mo-bai dared not to ask or to mention an emperor's name. Somehow, Prince Te sensed it and explained, "Emperor Shue Je died of a broken heart. The Han resistance forces spread rumors to discredit the Manchu and said he became a monk. You see, Mo-bai, you're not the first man and not the last one either to suffer the torture of an impossible love. You have to be strong and look forward to the future."

Dae Wu said, "Mo-bai is a victim of a rigid custom. When Mo-bai first found out that Mon Zhi-an was missing, he could have asked Yu Ceo-lian's hand in marriage if the social custom does not bind him. I think the Mon Senior would not say no."

Prince Te recited a well-known verse, *'After experiencing the mighty ocean. One can hardly settle with any smaller body of water,'* and said, "Mo-bai, I don't think you will find another love easily."

"I'm always interested in '*Taoism*,' and I want to be a Taoist priest."

Dae Wu said, "Mo-bai, you can't take the easy way out. You have your earthly duties. You should strive for a better future. Don't let us down now."

Prince Te said, "Mo-bai, you can keep the mare. She was an average-looking horse. Mon Zhi-an was the one who recognized her rare quality from obscurity. It's too bad that I did not have the wisdom to recognize Mon Zhi-an's superiority."

7

"Mo-bai, your uncle and aunt are sick. You should go home right away." Uncle Kao continued with a somewhat sarcastic tone, "Now you're the number one martial arts master in Beijing and Prince Te's favorite. You do not need, or more clearly, that no one dares to offer you a minor clerk position anymore. I don't think you ever need to find a job. By the way, I should have you to thank for my promotion."

Aunt Kao said, "Look at you, you're so thin. You really should have a wife to look after you, and your uncle should let you have enough silver to live comfortably. Ahe! It's not for us to say that your uncle should relinquish his tight control on your inheritance a long time ago. Now, he is sick, and he needs you home to collect the year-end rental income from the tenants. I presume that he would have no choice but to let you manage your estate from now on."

Uncle Kao noticed Lee Mo-bai's puzzled look. He chuckled, and "It fits. Your uncle did not tell you that you're a substantial landowner. I've been wondering why your uncle wants you to find a minor position. You don't need to work for silver. Your uncle likes to live frugally, and he does not let you spend your silver either. Mo-bai, I presume that your uncle did not tell you that it was your father's reward and salaries that bought all the choice farmland."

Lee Mo-bai told Dae Wu of his own uncle's fraud and sighed, "He made me live like a pauper. I've always thought my uncle was a grump but a generous man when he arranged an average funeral for Teacher Gi. He was spending my inheritance."

Dae Wu counseled, "Bitterness does not suit you. Think of your bright future. Now you have the means and time to travel and to do what you want to do."

"Brother, you're right. My aunt cares for me. I'll go home. I want to say goodbye to Prince Te and…Violet. And it gives me a reason for not seeing Ceo-lian now. I'll leave as soon as possible."

Lee Mo-bai did not want to call unwanted attention by riding a champion mare around and neither to have someone spotted Dae Wu's carriage at the Convent. He hired a carriage. He thought, *'Now I can afford to provide Violet and her mother a better life. But I don't think I should marry her. I cannot marry Ceo-lian now, and I don't want to hurt her either.'*

The abbess told him that Violet wanted to be a nun, and she did not want to see anyone. Lee Mo-bai felt sad and relieved at the same time. The abbess's posture and gait told him that she is a highly-skilled martial arts master and modest. Lee Mo-bai now realized that his lack of modesty caused all his trouble. It started when he had provoked a fight with the bandit leader before he came to Beijing. After he defeated Feng Five, he should not have told him that he would fight his brother Saber King. The biggest mistake he had was to have a relationship with a prostitute, which cause him to beat Huge Bo. He thought, *'If I'm not in jail, I will not meet Mon Zhi-an. Ahe! It's predestined.'*

Lee Mo-bai told Prince Te of his plans to go home and Violet's intention of becoming a nun.

"Mo-bai, I was going to suggest that you go home for a while. You have been through a lot. I'll miss your company until you come back next spring." He continued after a short silence. "It's a good thing for Violet to enter the convent. There she can fully develop her artistry. I understand she is getting old for her trade. Mo-bai, you know the Japanese have a more sensible way. Shogun Toranaga established a particular class of '*Geisha*', a different kind of prostitute. The word '*Geisha*' means artists or entertainers. A *Geisha* entertains the clients only with her arts, and then age is not a problem anymore."

"Yes, Your Highness. Violet, indeed, is very talented. She composed refined verses and her paintings of flowers are exquisite, too."

"She is beautiful and talented. The late Vice Minister Hsu was a renowned scholar. He would not fall for mere beauty. Mo-bai, how about your sister Ceo-lian? Have you thought about an answer? I know you don't want to marry her yet."

"Your Highness, I thought a lot about it, but I can't find any solution until now. Uncle Kao told me that I have some inheritance. I have the means to help her now. Brother Su and Ceo-lian will have means to re-establish her father's security company," Lee Mo-bai chuckled mirthlessly, "And I will be a top-rank guard for her company then." He told in detail the conversation he had with Uncle Kao.

"Good. Mo-bai, I'm glad you're not poor anymore. I'm afraid that you would sell my black mare when you need silver. Now I feel better knowing you don't have to sell your horse like the famous General Chyn of the Tang Dynasty."

Lee Mo-bai laughed, "Your Highness, I did have to sell a horse when I first got here."

"Mo-bai, if Ceo-lian agrees, Dae Wu's mother can adopt her, and she will have a nice home, and she can protect them. Later, only if she agrees, a Manchu officer can marry her. I did not tell Dae Wu my idea yet. I want to discuss it with you first. You're her sworn brother. Of course, we will handle everything with sensitivity and subtlety." Lee Mo-bai agreed and thanked the Prince; he knelt and formerly bid his farewell.

It was early evening; Lee Mo-bai decided to leave Beijing immediately.

Dae Wu said, "It's getting dark, and it looks like it will snow soon. Wait and leave tomorrow morning."

"No, I want to leave now. I need a fast run to clear my head."

"Mo-bai, I think that you're afraid of facing Ceo-lian. I'll see you off at South Gate." Lee Mo-bai rode, and Dae Wu followed in his carriage. On his way back, Fat Shih's assistant Chen stopped Dae Wu's carriage and informed him that Golden Spear Jao and his gang did not go back to Kaifeng. They stayed at Ba-tin, and Thin Buddha Hwang kept in communication with them. "Master Dae Wu, they might be plotting to harm you."

"Oh! I see. Here is some silver for your trouble. If you have any information, please come to see me." Dae Wu decided to be extra cautious.

"Brother Dae, when will Brother Lee come to tell me the details of my...Mon Zhi-an's death and where he was buried?" Ceo-lian asked him.

"Mo-bai had to rush home today. His uncle and aunt are sick. He told me that he probably would meet with Brother Su soon. Ceo-lian, please stay with us. Lee Mo-bai will be back in the spring."

Ceo-lian was disappointed. It snowed after supper. When she was alone in her room, she absentmindedly poked at the charcoal in the small burner. She reviewed in her mind in detail the events of the last eight months. She seemed to see again Lee Mo-bai's laughing eyes full of admiration when he picked her scarf off the first time they met. She also saw again his sad eyes full of concern the night before he left Da-ton for Beijing. It just did not make any sense. A caring Lee Mo-bai patiently taught her martial arts skills and anticipated her mother's and her needs when he escorted them to Da-ton. How could he turn suddenly so cold toward her? She thought, *'He just deliberately avoids me and he must know why and how Mon Zhi-an died. I don't care whether it's proper or not for me to talk to him alone. I must demand that he tells me the truth.'* Snow or blizzard, she decided to leave at early dawn to go after Lee Mo-bai.

Before dawn, Ceo-lian saddled her horse the way Lee Mo-bai had taught her. *'Why did he ignore me? Because I knew that he had visited a prostitute?'* Ceo-lian rode fast out of Beijing through light snow. The snowflakes melted on her cheeks and tasted salty. She had been crying.

She was the lone rider on the road. On both sides of the road, graying fields with snow patches stretched ahead, touching the low overcast sky. The road was icy and slippery, Ceo-lian rode on carefully and she felt so alone. She sobbed aloud and murmured, *'Who cares whether I fall and die? Who cares whether I wail my head off? What if I catch up with Lee Mo-bai and he does not want to talk to me. I don't have any family and I'm going back to an empty house.'*

A rider came from behind passed her and shouted something like, "Let me pass! Lee Mo-bai, Brother Lee, wait for me." Ceo-lian thought, *'Is he trying to go after Lee Mo-bai? Is he one of Lee's friends, or enemies? Is he going to report to the enemies to waylay Lee Mo-bai? Dae Wu mentioned that Lee Mo-bai is not well. I can help him to fight the enemies off.'*

She carried her two pairs of sabers and her luggage with ease when she checked into a hotel. The innkeeper lit an oil lamp in a small room for her. The innkeeper told his servant to be polite and see to it that Ceo-lian is comfortable. "She carried four heavy sabers and luggage effortlessly. Nowadays, some women fight better than men."

Ceo-lian rested on the warm *'Kon'* (bed) and thought; *'Mrs. Dae Wu must be worrying about me now. I know that they wanted very much for Lee Mo-bai and me to get married. But, I'm not sure now that Lee Mo-bai wants to marry me.'* She forced back her tears and asked the clerk who brought her water and her supper.

"Do you think it will be clear tomorrow?"

"No, it's snowing heavily now. It may snow for a couple of days. Besides, the bandits are out. Stay with us and we'll make sure you're comfortable. When it's clear, you would be safe to travel with other travelers."

"Thanks, I'm not afraid of bandits," Ceo-lian replied somewhat proudly. The clerk looked puzzlingly at the sabers on the *kon* (bed) and her young face.

Early next morning, someone yelled in the courtyard, "Brother Lee, Lee Mo-bai."

"Please don't shout. A tall young man did not check in last night." the hotel clerk complained. Some travelers cursed.

"I checked the only other hotel in town and he is not there. He must have ridden through the night. Sorry. Everyone." Ceo-lian looked through a slit of the paper-paneled window and saw it was the same fat man who had passed her earlier.

She had a hasty breakfast and insisted on leaving. The innkeeper said, "Miss, the road is icy and slippery. At least wait until it warms up a bit."

It was treacherous to ride against the wind but Ceo-lian pushed on and thought that Lee Mo-bai might be not too far ahead. Another lone rider ahead of her, she pushed hard and saw it was Lee Mo-bai. She called, "Brother Lee, Lee Mo-bai. Wait! I'm Ceo-lian." The wind muffled her shouts and the preoccupied Lee Mo-bai did not hear her. Another rider coming from the opposite direction shouted, "Ahe, someone fell. Ahe! A woman!" Lee Mo-bai doubled back and saw her, "It's you. Ceo-Lian, are you all right?"

She had on a pair of fur boots that Mrs. Dae Wu said was the smallest one. It was made for Manchu women's natural-sized feet and it's too big for Ceo-lian's bound feet. She struggled and got up herself and evaded Lee Mo-bai's outreached hands, "Go away, I hate you. You pretended that you did not hear me. I know you ignored my call deliberately."

Lee said, "Oh! I didn't know that you're behind me. Honestly, I did not hear you. Did you sprain your ankles?"

"Go away! I don't want your help now. You are a hypocrite." Ceo-lian cried.

A man caught Ceo-lian's horse and brought it back to her. He chuckled, "Friend, don't quarrel with your little wife now. It is too cold. I better leave you young couple to sort it out yourself."

"Don't go now. I did not hear you. I'm sorry. I want to talk to you. Give me a chance and I will explain everything." Lee Mo-bai chased after the now ashamed and infuriated Ceo-lian.

A few travelers looked at them. Lee Mo-bai did not want to call more attention and he was also afraid that his chase might make the tense Ceo-lian ride fast and fall again. He gave up the chase.

Ceo-lian sobbed and she was disappointed when she heard no more calls from Lee Mo-bai and no more sounds of hooves behind her. Now she blamed herself. *'I should have asked him the why and how of Mon Zhi-an's death. Isn't that why I came after him in the snow? Instead, I called him a hypocrite, he probably would be too proud to talk to me again. Ahe! He is very thin and looks ill. I wonder what had happened between him and Mon Zhi-an? It must be awful. It left one dead, one sick, and me, a widow. What will I do with the letter, the one my mother gave me and I was supposed to hand Lee Mo-bai in person?'* She could not wipe the frozen tears away and her feet hurt. *'It is no use to cry. I have to be strong and I only have myself to look after me. I'm going home to reopen my father's security company and I'll be a woman guard.'*

She checked into a hotel before noon. The innkeeper bought some hot medicine patches for her swollen ankles. She practiced the deep breathing technique and meditated the way Lee Mo-bai taught her to relieve the pain. Everything led her mind back to him. She opened the sealed letter to Lee Mo-bai that her mother wanted her to give to Lee Mo-bai in person.

There was a note and another smaller, sealed envelope. The note was from Short Hsu. It said that her mother had asked a letter writer wrote this enclosed letter to Lee Mo-bai. Ceo-lian tore the sealed envelope open. She could not fully understand the words but she thought that her mother thanked Lee Mo-bai first and then agreed that Lee Mo-bai could marry her if Mon Zhi-an could not be found or is dead. Ceo-lian cried again. She wanted to tear the letters into pieces at first but she decided to keep the letter. *'Oh! How can I tell anyone about it?'* she sighed.

It snowed on and off. She stayed two more days. Late afternoon on the third day, she had a visitor, the fat rider she had met before.

Fat Shih introduced himself and told Ceo-lian that he was Lee Mo-bai's friend. He did not tell her that he had met Lee Mo-bai the day before and upon Lee's request, to meet with Ceo-lian and then escort her home.

But, against Lee Mo-bai's specific instruction of not telling Ceo-lian the details of Mon Zhi-an's death, he told her everything. From the beginning of how the two men met, how Mon Zhi-an guarded and nursed the very sick Lee Mo-bai back to health, and the details of Mon Zhi-an's death.

"Miss Yu, he did not want me to tell you this. But, I think you're entitled to know. Even acute grief is better than fogged suspicion and uncertainty."

"Thank you very much. Brother Shih, now I know why Master Dae Wu could not look at me straight in the eye when he told me about Mon Zhi-an's death. Thank you and now everything is clear to me. Please call me Ceo-lian," she said sincerely.

"Mon Zhi-an begged Lee Mo-bai to marry you with his last breath. I was there. That stiff-necked Lee Mo-bai said he couldn't marry you. I hope Dae Wu and Prince Ie could talk some sense into his stubborn head, and so you and he can get married later. Ceo-lian, you can't be alone as a…"

"Living widow? Under these circumstances, I could not and I don't want to marry Brother Lee either. I'm not a widow of a man I had never met. Let's talk more tomorrow. I'd like to be alone now." Ceo-lian wept and wept for herself, for Lee Mo-bai and the dead Mon Zhi-an. She believed that the impossible three-sided involvement among them must be predestinated. After her mother's death, she hoped that she could find her fiancé, or she could marry Lee Mo-bai if no one can find Mon Zhi-an. Now she lost both. In her destitute state, she unsheathed a saber and wanted to kill herself. The cold, frosty, shining blade reminded her once more of her duty to avenge her parents' murderers. During the long night, Ceo-lian gradually hardened her will as firm as the steel blade of her sabers. She had no more tears and she resolved to restore her father's honor and the fame of '*Iron Wings*' with her sabers.

The next morning, Fat Shih found Ceo-lian a hard, determined woman.

"Thank you, Brother Shih, now I know everything. I'm going home first. Next spring when the earth is unfrozen, I will arrange to have my parents reburied at my family cemetery lots. Could you send word to Master Mon at Da-ton and tell him where Mon Zhi-an is buried so they can take him home." Regardless of her resolutions, her voice choked but no tears.

Fat Shih suggested, "Ceo-lian, we're not far from Brother Mon's grave at Kao-yon Town. Would you like to go there to say goodbye?" Ceo-lian agreed.

Mon Zhi-an's tombstone was an expensive one with Lee Mo-bai's elegant calligraphy on it. Ceo-lian did not know the words enough but she recognized the name and the artistic quality of the writing. She bowed low and silently told Mon Zhi-an that there was no infatuation between Lee Mo-bai and her.

Ceo-lian touched the tombstone and asked, "Brother Shih, this is an expensive tombstone. Brother Lee is not rich, how could he pay for it?"

"It did not cost a thing. When we went to buy a tombstone, a member of another grieving family saw Lee's good writings and asked him to write their father's name and an epitaph on a tombstone. Lee wrote the name and composed a poem. They praised his work and paid for Mon Zhi-an's tombstone and the lot. Ceo-lian, Mo-bai is righteous, talented, and considerate. He adores you so much and that's why he has called out your name when he was delirious. I hope you two will get married later. I hope that time will heal the pain."

Ceo-lian said nothing.

Fat Shih said, "Ceo-lian, may I accompany you home?" He did not say that he thinks Ceo-lian should not be traveling alone at that moment.

"Thank you."

When they reached the town where her father was jailed after Lee Mo-bai helped them to repel *She-Devil* and the others. Ceo-lian told Fat Shih the details, "We knew our enemies were after us and we were forced to leave home last summer. We met Lee Mo-bai two days before the enemies ganged upon us. Now I regret that I did not want my father to ask for Lee Mo-bai's help when we met him. If Lee had been with us, my father would not have been jailed and died."

"It's fate. None of us can avoid it." Shih sighed. Ceo-lian relived the past and said, "Lee Mo-bai met a kind and just Manchu officer and got my father released. After his release, my father refused Brother Lee's good intention to travel with us but he followed us anyway. He saved my father from dying by the roadside. I owed him a lot."

"Ceo-lian, Mo-bai is conceited but a good man."

Two days short of reaching her home, Ceo-lian thanked Fat Shih again and said she will be all right to go home alone now.

Shih said, "It's not far from here to Nan-kon Village, I'll go to see Lee Mo-bai." Ceo-lian said, "If you hear anyone in Beijing dare harass Master Dae Wu, please come to fetch me, I'll defend him and his family."

"Ceo-lian, you're Dae Wu's worthy friend. Bye."

Ceo-lian cried as soon as Brother Han opened the gate for her. She told him that her mother had passed away, too. Han and his wife tried to make her comfortable first and then told her that Brother Su left for Da-ton to bring her mother and her home twenty days ago.

"Ceo-lian, Sam, the carriage driver, came back and told us everything; how Master Yu died and how the young Master Lee saved him, buried him, and escorted you and your mother to Da-ton. He also told us that your fiancé is missing. We were all worried. We sold most of the weapons and vehicles to get enough silver for Brother Su to go to Da-ton. He wanted to take your aunt and you back home in case you were not happy there. We did not know that Aunt Yu also passed away."

Ceo-lian sighed, "My mother had been sick ever since we left home. We paid a lot for the doctor and the medical herbs. You know that my father sold the small lot we rented out to a farmer. Now I only have enough silver to move my parents' caskets back and bury them at the family cemetery. We don't have any rental income and now we don't have weapons and vehicles to reopen the security company. What are we going to live on now? What am I going to do with the rest of my life? Why do all the gods abandon me?"

No one answered and she did not expect one either. Han hired himself out to do odd jobs. With his earnings to supplement the scant savings Ceo-lian had, they managed. Ceo-lian and Han's wife wanted to take home some sewing to make the ends meet. She did not have any close male relative to help her to claim her share of the Mons' estate. The cold winter was here and the New Year would be here soon.

Ten days later, a cart full of bags of wheat, rice, produce and a cage of live chickens came from Lee Mo-bai with a letter. Han and Ceo-lian could not fully understand the letter; they took the letter to the local letter writer.

"Miss Yu, we've been neighbors for a long time. I didn't know you have a brother." The letter writer said.

"Master Lee is my sworn brother."

The letter said, "Sister, greetings. Fat Shih told me that you're home. I'm sending you some of the crops I collected from the tenants. I would like to come to see you soon to discuss some important matters with you. Your brother, Lee Mo-bai."

Ceo-lian paid the letter writer. On her way home, she wondered what the 'important matters' would be. She thought, '*He changes his mind and wants to marry me, but why should he sign the letter as my real brother?*' Han and his wife secretly harbored the same hope. They were all grateful for the food.

Lee Mo-bai was very busy managing the huge family holdings. For many years, his uncle completely depended on Ma, the overseer, to collect the year-end rent from the tenants who farmed the land rented from the Lees. Ma became greedy and give or withhold his favor from the tenants. He also pilfered the rental income. Short of using his fists, Lee Mo-bai put the bully Ma in his place. He applied justice; he curbed the rowdy ones and helped the ones in need. The year-end rental income nearly doubled. He was thinking of finding a trusted new overseer. At home, he helped his widowed sister-in-law care for his uncle and aunt. His uncle recovered but not his aunt. His widowed sister-in-law was only four years older than Ceo-lian. She was depressed. It painted Lee Mo-bai very much to see her being changed from a robust and stout young girl to a dispirited and thin young widow. Lee Mo-bai realized sharply what a miserable life Ceo-lian would face. '*It's all my fault.*' His guilt feelings doubled when he came to a sad realization that he loved Violet more when he leafed through the poems they composed together.

Lee Mo-bai blamed himself, '*I should not look down on Violet because she is a lowly prostitute. The fact that she is a prostitute made me not knowing my true feelings toward her. If I knew my true feelings that I loved her, she would willingly be mine. Didn't she often remind me that she is only a poor substitute of Ceo-lian, and she even said that she would be willing to be a concubine. If I married her after Fat Shih killed her protector, Mon Zhi-an would still be alive and he and Ceo-lian could be married. My indecision and ambiguity had caused the tragedy. I don't deserve to live.'*

So many 'ifs' and 'consequences' went through his mind over and over. Days and nights he lived through his misery. Finally, he thought of ways of remedy. Lee Mo-bai went to see Ceo-lian. It was a painful and awkward moment for both of them.

"Sister, I came to ask for your forgiveness. It's my fault that Brother Mon died." Lee Mo-bai addressed Ceo-lian as a true brother should. He hoped to establish that he would think of her as a younger sister and nothing more.

Ceo-lian caught on immediately. She addressed him accordingly, "Brother, it's fate. Fat Shih told me everything."

Lee Mo-bai managed a mirthless chuckle, "I bet he did not tell you that I'm no longer a poor man," he continued seriously, "My uncle finally relinquished his control and gave me back my right to my inheritance of more than ten lots of profitable farmlands. I only kept four lots and yield to him the rest providing my widowed sister-in-law would adopt a son. I'm giving you the two pieces closest to your hometown and I would appreciate it if Brother Han would manage my two pieces for me."

"I'm grateful but I can't accept your generosity."

"Sister, you cannot refuse. I swore to look after you. I'm your brother and you're supposed to obey me. It's also for the deceased Brother Mon Zhi-an. You can say that it's my atonement. Next spring, I will go to Da-ton to demand your share of the estate. I'm not hesitating to use my sword if it's necessary." Ceo-lian thought, *'He does not want to marry me. We both know that the only way I can claim my share of the estate from the Mons is that I have to be a widow.'* She tried to force her tears back.

"Brother, thank you." Ceo-lian sobbed. Lee Mo-bai tried to cover the sob with a cough.

After a painful stretch of silence, Lee Mo-bai said with forced gaiety, "Sister, let's finish the transactions quickly. Don't you want me to teach you more martial arts skills before I leave? I'm an anxious teacher."

"I'm an eager student. I need to learn more. I must be good enough to kill my parents' murderers."

"We're in it together. Later, we'll get the security company in business again. You'll be a famous woman guard."

"We can't. The weapons and vehicles were sold." Ceo-lian sighed.

"We don't need weapons and vehicles. We have enough manpower. We can get your Short Brother back here to help us. We will specialize in escorting rich families and jewels," Lee Mo-bai assured Ceo-lian.

Before Lee Mo-bai left, he exchanged horses with Ceo-lian.

"This black beauty is Prince Te's champion horse. Brother Mon Zhi-an groomed her daily and cared for her very much. Sister, you should have her."

8

It was a mild winter, but Lee Mo-bai thought that it was the worst and coldest. His aunt was dying. He sat beside her bed and seriously considered whether he would become a Taoist priest.

His widowed sister-in-law adopted a baby boy of a poor distant cousin. She loved the baby. Her face now shone with joy and her gait became springy. Lee Mo-bai thought, '*Now, the continuation of the bloodline is secured and I'm free to do what I want to do. I'm now free to travel, to look for Uncle Chiang.*'

His aunt passed away shortly after the New Year. The customary mourning period called for seven sections of seven days, a total of forty-nine days. Lee Mo-bai could not attend the final interment of Ceo-lian's parents. Fat Shih helped Ceo-lian with the transportation of the caskets and the final funeral. He came to visit Lee Mo-bai and kowtowed to the casket of Lee's aunt to show his respect.

He told Lee Mo-bai, "Ceo-lian is very grateful that you gave her two lots of farmland."

"That's the least I can do for her and Mon Zhi-an." Lee Mo-bai sighed.

"You know you can do better. You can carry out Mon Zhi-an's dying wish and marry Ceo-lian later." Lee Mo-bai only sighed.

"Mo-bai, if I fight better than you, I would beat the stubbornness out of you. You know Mon Zhi-an's dying wish overrules the customary rule against marrying another man's wife. Besides, they never met each other. It's no use to argue with you anymore. I'm going back to Beijing to see whether Dae Wu and Master Lieu of Grand Security could convince you. By the way, Dart Mew's nephew Golden Spear Jao and his gang did not return to Kaifeng. They stayed at Ba-tin, and they are cooking some evil plot to harm you and Dae Wu".

"When I passed Ba-tin last winter, they did not harass me."

"You left Beijing rather suddenly. They dare not fight you in the open. They might have thought that you and Ceo-lian were traveling together. The rumor is that Ceo-lian is your woman."

"Please tell me if any harm comes to Dae Wu. I'll go to Beijing as soon as I can. I'm a free man with means now. Later we can go to Szechwan to check on the late Master Hsu's family. It's Mon Zhi-an's dying wish."

"It's a deal. On our way west, you can beat up some of my enemies."

The funeral and other family business finished, and Lee Mo-bai was ready to leave for Beijing. Fat Shih rushed in one late rainy night.

"Mo-bai, it's really bad. Dae Wu is in jail. Let me catch my breath."

"Someone stole forty-some big precious pearls and other art pieces from the Royal Palace before the New Year. Early this spring some of the missing goods were found in the stock of one of Master Yong's pawnshops. Master Yong is Dae Wu's friend, and Dae Wu tried to save him. Thin Buddha Hwang and a powerful eunuch implicated Dea Wu and other personages. Dae Wu was jailed and the soldiers searched Dae Wu's house twice. Some villains, obviously on Thin Buddha's payroll, harassed Dae Wu's family."

"Ahe! I remember meeting a fat man named Yong. I will go to Beijing immediately to help, at least to protect Dae Wu's family." Lee Mo-bai said.

"Great! We can leave at dawn."

"I'll leave right now. My indecisiveness and hesitation had caused enough misfortune already. Please go and get Ceo-lian. I want her in Beijing soon. She can protect the women."

Lee Mo-bai rushed. He checked into a hotel to rest every two days. He soon rode right up to the tightly closed gate of Dae Wu's mansion and knocked.

"My master is not home. We only open the gate to…"

"I'm Lee Mo-bai, your master's…"

The gate opened immediately, "Master Lee, my master is in jail. Please help us."

"I heard it so I rushed here. Please announce me to your mistress."

Mrs. Dae Wu received Lee Mo-bai in the inner court. She told him the details and the serious situation of the case.

"Mo-bai, the soldiers had thoroughly searched the whole house twice. We'll find some precious artifices and antiques missing after each search. We bribed the soldiers not to search Grandma's room. She thought that Dae Wu is on another business trip out of town. Some of the servants turned rowdy and I let them go. I only keep a few trusted ones. Some rough-looking men had been here twice to collect some supposed loans. We never had to borrow any silver. Prince Te sent his valet here to see us a few days earlier, I told him the harassment. Prince Te sent some soldiers here for a couple of days. But I don't think the soldiers will be here all the time. Mo-bai. I want you to stay at the study."

"Thanks. I'll see to things and let no one come to bother you again. I've sent word to Ceo-lian, she probably will be here in a couple of days."

"Oh! Very good. I can sleep again without fear if she is here. Mo-bai, you look tired. Take a rest first."

"I'm fine. It's early, I'll go to see Brother Dae Wu."

Dae Wu was on friendly terms with Prince Te and Viscount Chiu. His cell was airy and clean and had a comfortable bed. He was not chained either.

"Brother, Mo-bai is here."

"When did you get in?"

"This morning. Fat Shih told me everything and I rushed here. Ceo-lian is on the way here, too."

"Great! I'm grateful that I have good friends. Mo-bai, please be careful. They will try all means to provoke you to a fight, so they will have a reason to jail you. They already spread rumors that only you, since you have excellent night jumping skills, could steal the pearls."

"I see. I'll be careful. I'll go to visit Prince Te and see what else I can do to help."

"Mo-bai, don't come to see me every day. The jailers don't like it."

"Yes, I know." Le Mo-bai recalled that he had to bribe the jailer when the late Master Yu was jailed. His thoughts turned to Ceo-lian and he felt awful.

Prince Te and Viscount Chiu were discussing Dae Wu's case.

"Mo-bai, I want you to be extremely careful. Thin Buddha must have spent a fortune to get the eunuch Chang to implicate Dae Wu. Chang is the chief eunuch of Emperor's most favorite consort. My hands are tied. Don't give them an opportunity to jail you with some ridiculous cause."

"Your Highness, Viscount Chiu, I'll be careful. Yu Ceo-lian will be here soon and I'll warn her to be cautious."

"Oh! No! Mo-bai, don't let Ceo-lian ride through Beijing again. She and her horse will draw too much attention and we have enough trouble already," Prince Te said.

Lee Mo-bai could not help laughing, "She sure will draw attention. Your Highness, she has your favorite mare. I'll convince her that she should stay home."

"You gave her the horse," after a short silence, Prince Te continued, "I see your point. Mon Zhi-an loved that horse. She should have it."

Viscount Chiu asked, "Brother Lee, may I call you Mo-bai? Please drop the title when you address me."

"Thanks, Brother Chiu."

"Mo-bai, I'll tell you with confidence that Dae Wu will not be sentenced to beheading. The worst for him is a two-year exile. I was going to send my wife to tell Mrs. Dae Wu. Now you can tell her and ask her not to worry. The countess's visit her may call for unwanted attention. Also, my teacher Yang will come soon."

"Mo-bai, you look tired and I won't keep you to have supper with us," Prince Te noticed Lee's white armband and continued, "I see you're in mourning. Please have my belated condolence."

"Thanks. Your Highness, my aunt passed away. She raised me since I was eight. My cousin died a few years ago. I wear white as her son."

"Another death! You've gone through a lot. Take care," Prince Te sighed with compassion.

On his way back, Lee Mo-bai did not close the curtain of the carriage. He wanted all the hooligans working for Thin Buddha Hwang to know that he is back. He then thought about the three deceased that he buried In less than a year. He buried Ceo-lian's father last summer. He buried Mon Zhi-an last autumn and he buried his aunt recently. He also thought about the deaths of Huge Bo and Vice Minister Hsu. Fat Shih killed them because they took Violet away from him. Lee Mo-bai did not do the real killing himself. Nevertheless, he was responsible for their deaths and the incident that forced Violet to be a nun. He thought about the suffering and the transience of life. He wanted to end it all or enter the priesthood.

"Master Lee, look! They are coming to demand loan payment again." Fu, the coachman called. Lee recognized the shifty-eyed Ca leo (six), Feng Five and two clerks. He jumped out of the carriage when he heard Ca leo (six) say, "Today we'll chase them out of the house if they can't pay. Master Hwang will back us up."

"Stop!" Everyone froze when they saw Lee Mo-bai.

"Show me the promissory note at once," Lee Mo-bai demanded. Ca leo (six) and Feng Five ran away.

"Here it is. Master Lee, we are only doing our jobs." One of the clerks handed over a piece of folded paper. The note simply wrote that Dae Wu owed the Bo Loan Company twenty thousand ounces of silver. Witnessed and signed by Ca leo (six) and Feng Five.

Lee Mo-bai said, "If they want silver, come to me to collect it. Tell them to come with genuine notes, not these fakes." He let the two clerks go.

He told Mrs. Dae Wu that there would be no death penalty for Dae Wu. It might be a two-year exile. Mrs. Dae Wu was relieved.

A frightened butler came to the study and told Lee that there was a tall, fierce-looking man demanding to see him.

"Is he armed?"

"No. But he is very demanding." It was Brother Su, the late Master Yu's student.

"Brother Lee, thank you for everything you have done for us," the tall husky Brother Su wanted to kneel. Lee Mo-bai stopped him effortlessly. Su was surprised by the skinny Lee Mo-bai's strength.

"Brother Su, please call me Mo-bai."

"I came to Beijing ten days ago. Ca leo (six) is my sworn brother. He found me a guard position at Universal Security Company. He told me that you had harassed Master Hwang and he asked me to come here to beat you up. Of course, I come as your friend. I could not beat you up even if I want to. You're super."

"Ca leo (six) is a bad lot."

"Yes, I have known it for quite a while, but I need a job. Thin Buddha Hwang treated me royally and gave me silver twice already. Somehow I felt uneasy when they told me that Dae Wu and you persecuted them. They asked me to come here to fight you. I know better. Please tell me, why you and they are enemies?" Lee Mo bai told him.

"I'll beat Ca leo (six) to a pulp." The impatient Brother Su wanted to rush back to hit Ca leo (six). He tried and could not get away from Lee Mo-bai's restraining hand.

"Wait. Brother Su, I need your help. Please don't break up with them just now. Instead, you should pretend that you're on their side and then you can forewarn me of their plot. Uncle Yu made me Ceo-lian's sworn brother, so you are my brother. I need your help. I'm alone and they are so many. Ceo-lian will be here soon. Dae Wu opened his home to her last year."

"Sure, Mo-bai, just tell me what to do."

"Please don't come here unless I sent for you. One of Master Shih's men, named Little Snake, will contact you."

"But, Mo-bai, I told them that I admire you."

"Then tell them I'm conceited and I befriend rich Manchu. They will believe you."

Twice during the night, Lee Mo-bai scrutinized the mansion from the rooftops and found no danger. He chuckled when he recalled that Dae Wu had said that all the hooligans were afraid of him as mice to a cat.

He went to visit Uncle Lieu at Grand Security and told him the death of Mon Zhi-an and recommended Brother Su to Lieu. "Sure I'll hire him. *'Iron Wing*'s student must be good. Mo-bai, we are all willing to help Master Dae Wu."

"Thank you, Uncle Lieu. If you hear anything, rumors... talks... Anything concerning Dae Wu, please let me know."

"Sure, be careful Mo-bai. I heard that Thin Buddha Hwang practiced his martial arts skills and networked all his spies to prepare for pulling you down. Yesterday, he declared that you, not Dae Wu, are now his primary target. He was heard saying, '*Getting rid of that damned Lee Mo-bai and Dae Wu is nothing.*' Watch every step."

"I'll be cautious but I'm not afraid."

"Of course you're not afraid of any fight in the open. Please beware of their secret plots and false rumors to discredit you. Someone said you stole all the pearls."

"I also heard about it. I wonder who the thief is. He must be very good. Did you hear about any new highly skilled martial arts masters around?"

"No. If that person does not want to be known, no one can detect him. Mon Zhi-an is a good example. Up to today, I never knew about his existence. Beijing is worse than a jungle, who knows what's lurking around? The present Manchu emperor is kind and just. It's rumored that his father, the preceding Emperor, harbored a horde of highly-skilled martial arts masters. With their help, he got the throne. It's said that a nun murdered him in his heavily guarded bed-chamber." Lieu whispered.

"Ahe! A nun?" Lee Mo-bai thought, '*Isn't the abbess of the convent where Violet stays a martial arts master, and a super one too?*'

"Yes, someone said she was the last Ming Emperor's daughter."

That night, Lee Mo-bai leafed through one of the anthologies and then thought about Violet. He wanted to visit her at the convent. '*Just a visit to see how she is,*' he tried to convince himself but he continued his thought, '*to be honest, what if I find she did not want to shave her head and commit the last vow, I could not possibly ask her to marry me now. Mon Zhi-an died for me and I've caused Ceo-lian enough grief. My marrying Violet will push her further and deeper into her bottomless misery. I'm not blind to see that she wishes that I might eventually marry her. Could I marry Ceo-lian knowing Mon Zhi-an's death will be a perpetual shadow in my heart? I have dug my grave and I have to bear it as long as I live.*' He tossed around all night long.

He went to the convent to look for Violet the next day. He was disappointed and at the same time had a sense of reprieve when he was told that Violet and her mother went to Japan. Her past caused several villains to keep pestering the convent, so the Abbess made the arrangements for her to teach the Japanese novices Chinese arts. Lee Mo-bai thought, '*Providence sure has dealt me a hard hand. When the exquisite Violet was for my asking, I dreamed about the untouchable Ceo-lian. Now Ceo-lian is available, and I could not get Violet out of my mind. What kind of man am I, evil or stupid? Maybe both.*'

Ceo-lian's arrival four days later relieved some of Lee Mo-bai's distress. He told her the situation and then warned Ceo-lian to be cautious. "Sister, Prince Te suggested that you stay in and protect the family."

"No need to worry. I have grown and I'm not childish anymore. I won't go out. I'll guard the inner court. It's inconvenient for you to do."

"Ceo-lian, Mo-bai, I 'm grateful to have you, two good friends. Ceo-lian is here. I can sleep better," Mrs. Dae Wu said.

At midnight, Lee Mo-bai deliberately stepped a bit heavy on the roof. To his delight, Ceo-lian was out and on the roof immediately, fully clothed.

"It's me. Your hearing has improved. I hardly made any noise. And you're fast," Lee Mo-bai whispered happily.

"I have a good teacher," Ceo-lian whispered with her pleasant bell-like voice.

They sat companion-like on the roof. Lee Mo-bai told her the possibility that a highly-skilled, anonymous martial arts master stole the pearls. "I want you to be alert. Leave the fighting and chasing to me. Be assured that if anyone causes your suspicion that he's already under my surveillance. You have to protect the family. I heard some of the dark secrets of the ruling Manchu. Who knows if Dae Wu is a victim of a political scheme?"

"Oh! Do you know for sure?"

"No, I don't. I'll tell you the minute I know. Don't be scared."

"Do you remember that you said the same thing last year when we were traveling to Da-ton," Ceo-lian sobbed and continued, "I'm sad about the past but at least there are no barriers between us now, you're a true caring brother."

"We've been through a lot." He changed the subject and said, "I've thought about how to blend some of the quick sword thrusts into your saber fighting technique. Let's try it out sometime. Good night or good morning for now."

Another night when they met on the roof, Lee Mo-bai told Ceo-lian, "Thank you for helping Violet last year. You killed Dart Mew and set her free. She is a nun. Now, she and her mother are in a convent in Japan."

"I always wondered what had happened to them. Mrs. Dae Wu told me that she is not only beautiful, she also is very artistic and talented. I know she is also very brave; she threw a dagger at Dart Mew and slashed his face. The cut she inflicted on Mew's face had caused the poison on his own dart to kill him. I missed when I threw his dart back at him. I was so scared." She told Lee Mo-bai what happened that day when she killed Dart Mew.

"I know she had a dagger and she knows martial arts. She never talked about her past."

Many rumors discrediting Lee Mo-bai circulated in Beijing. Lee Mo-bai tried very hard to hold his temper in check. That's Thin Buddha's way to provoke him to fight and then they could arrest him for disturbing the peace. The pressure and the increasingly hot weather weakened Lee Mo-bai and he kept on losing weight.

Ceo-lian jumped up on the roof every night, secretly wanting to meet and talk to Lee Mo-bai. But Lee Mo-bai usually read and wrote in the study. Ceo-lian saw his silhouette through the window and she knew that he must have heard her. She was sad.

Mrs. Dae Wu worried about Lee Mo-bai's health and also his seemingly warm but also distant attitude toward Ceo-lian. Behind the façade of brotherly affection, there could be deeper feelings that he tried to conceal and control. *'It's not quite like love, more like the feelings of remorse and deep sorrow,'* Mrs. Dae Wu thought. Ceo-lian had told her that Violet had gone to Japan. That was good. No more third person. She harbored the hope that time will heal everything and eventually they will be married. Ceo-lian's feeling was transparent for everyone to see that she loved Lee, even though she tried her best to show that she thought of Lee like a true brother. Mrs. Dae Wu tried to bring them together and asked Lee to come in to dine with them often. Lee Mo-bai taught Ceo-lian martial arts. Mrs. Dae Wu taught Ceo-lian how to read and write.

Prince Te summoned Lee Mo-bai and told him that the sentencing would be very swift under the Manchu Law. Mrs. Dae Wu started to prepare extra clothes, common herbal preparations for Dae Wu's long trip and his two-year exile in the far west Xikang Province. It was about four thousand *Li* (mile) to the west of Beijing. Mrs. Dae Wu had to sell a parcel of land for silver.

Viscount Chiu invited all of Dae Wu's concerned friends to dinner. Master Yang, Viscount Chiu's teacher, offered to escort Dae Wu to Xikang. He will not have any major escorting business during the summer. He would go with Dae Wu and be back in the fall. There were bandits everywhere and he wanted to make sure Dae Wu would get there safely.

Lee Mo-bai said, "I'd like to go, too. But my uncle is not well and he needs me at home." He wanted to stay behind and kill Thin Buddha Hwang.

Viscount Chiu said, "For the long trip, Teacher Yang is more experienced. My concern is that *Golden Spear* Jao and the late Dart Mew's gang might ambush Dae Wu at Ba-tin. I heard the bandit leader Wu, the one whom Mo-bai wounded last year is now in league with them. The two-faced Thin Buddha paid them to kill Dae Wu and Mo-bai."

Lee Mo-bai said, "That's easy. I'll follow the convoy to Ba-tin to fight them off. Brother Su (brother) could follow the convoy discreetly to Xikang. He has no family and he can stay there and escort Dae Wu back to Beijing two years later."

Viscount Chiu said, "And Yu Ceo-lian will stay and guard the family. My wife will visit them once in a while to keep them informed."

The final sentencing came. Two men would be beheaded in the fall and Dae Wu and someone else was sentenced to two years of exile. The Manchu law was swift. The prisoners and a company of soldiers would leave right after the sentence and only permit the prisoners to have a short farewell. Lee Mo-bai told Dae Wu the arrangements. Dae Wu could have two servants with him. One would be Ton, his valet, and the other one would be Master Yang who carried silver and silver certificates. Brother Su would follow the convoy disguised as a merchant. The group of two carriages for the prisoners and a company of soldiers on horses left at noon.

Prince Te summoned Lee Mo-bai in the evening. He said, "Mo-bai, I know you have laboriously held back your anger at all the spiteful insults from Thin Buddha Hwang and his men for almost a month now, and you want to retaliate soon. That's why you did not escort Dae Wu yourself. I don't want you to do something drastic. It's not worth sacrificing your bright future for fighting the likes of them. You cannot fight them all unless you kill Thin Buddha. I won't allow it."

"Your Highness, I'll be cautious. But unless the evil Thin Buddha Hwang is eliminated, someone else in Beijing will suffer. And I bet he will find a way to harm Dae Wu two years later."

"So, you want to kill him. A killer will be hanged and even I can't protect you. Mo-bai, leave it to me. I promise that I will find a subtle way to get rid of him and his bad influence. Don't do anything irrational. Mo-bai."

"Yes. Your Highness."

"Mo-bai, don't kill anyone who might waylay Dae Wu at Ba-tin. I permit you to wound them if you have to. Thin Buddha Hwang manipulated them and they are only puppets. I suggest you go home or travel to Szechwan, or the South directly from Ba-tin. It's not good for you to come back to Beijing right away. You know the pearls are still missing. While the real thief is at large, you're the prime suspect. Have a safe trip and a good fight. Mo-bai."

Halfway home Fu yelled in pain, an arrow pierced his leg. A volley of arrows, aimed at the carriage, rained on them. Lee Mo-bai swiftly pulled out the seat pad and covered Fu with it. Ten or more men armed with long spears ganged up on Lee Mo-bai. He seized a spear, and with it, he pierced three attackers quickly and the rest fled. Then shouts and soldiers with lanterns approached fast. This was a planned trap. Lee Mo-bai threw the spear away, got back on the carriage, and ordered Fu to drive fast. He rearranged the seat pad and pulled the curtain of the carriage down.

"Hold!" The soldiers stopped them and accused Lee Mo-bai of piercing three men with a spear.

"Sergeant, I don't have the spear. There is no room in the carriage for a long spear. I also heard some commotion back there but I did not pay any attention."

"Lee Mo-bai, we know you. Who could have the skills to wound three and scared the rest away but you? Come with us for questioning."

"I just left Prince Te's palace. You know no one can bring any weapon to the palace. You should try to catch the hooligans. If I want to wound them, do you think anyone can get away alive?"

"Let's go," Lee Mo-bai ordered Fu.

His pounding heart told him that Thin Buddha Hwang had arranged the two-step ambush. First, Thin Buddha tried to kill him with arrows and gangs. If it failed, the soldiers would arrest him. Only his fighting skills and quick thinking of throwing the spear away saved him. '*How the soldiers can decide the wounds had been from no other weapons but a spear so quickly in the dark? They know.*' He renewed his oath to kill Thin Buddha Hwang regardless of Prince Te's admonition. He decided, '*Mon Zhi-an died for me. It's my fault that Ceo-lian is a living widow; I can't live in peace with the guilt. I'll kill Thin Buddha Hwang for all his victims in Beijing and let my best friend Dae Wu come back to live in peace. I'll be hanged. I wanted to die anyway and my death is worthwhile.*'

Lee Mo-bai sent a servant to ask Ceo-lian to come to the study.

"Sister, will you promise me something? I have a request, not for now, but for two years later. Dae Wu would be back then."

"Sure I will."

"Please go to Szechwan to look for Master Hsu's family. Help them if they need help. Mrs. Hsu gave Mon Zhi-an a home when he was a boy. It's one of his dying requests. I'd like you to carry it out if I can't. Please promise me."

"I promise. You will win the fight against Jao and the others at Ba-tin. Jao is not that good, but they all will gang up on you. I'll go with you."

"No, it's vital that you stay and protect the family. I better be on my way, the gate will soon be closed for the night. Bye."

Lee Mo-bai handed Ceo-lian Master Hsu's address in Szechwan, took a small bag and left.

"Ceo-lian, what did Lee Mo-bai tell you?" Mrs. Dae Wu sensed Ceo-lian's apprehension and asked.

"He asked me to go to Szechwan for him two years later. He should not have asked me so early. He was very strange and it almost sounded like a final goodbye. I'm worried."

"Did he take his books, Ceo-lian?"

"I don't think so. He took a small bag."

"Ceo-lian, he'll be back. He would not leave his books and writings behind."

Fat Shih waited for Lee Mo-bai a short way out of the South Gate. "Mo-bai, I knew sooner or later you would pass through."

"I don't want them spotting me traveling with the convoy. If I'm recognized, they might change their plan and attack Dae Wu further on the road. I want to finish this business soon." Shih interrupted, "And then come back to kill Thin Buddha Hwang. Ha Ha! Mo-bai, I read you like an open book. Mo-bai, don't do it. I'll do it for you. You should not sacrifice your bright future for killing a viper. I know you'll get away with it but you will be a wanted man your entire life. Not worth it."

"Maybe I'll just scare him a bit." Lee Mo-bai did not want to say that he wanted to die anyway. After the killing, he will confess and hand himself in. The only way to completely assure a clear way for Dae Wu later got to be the killer be found and hanged. If Fat Shih could kill Thin Buddha Hwang and escape, Dae Wu and Lee Mo-bai would still be under suspicion for being the instigators. Also, Fat Shih might not be able to kill the highly skilled Thin Buddha Hwang. Then Dae Wu and him could never be clear of suspicion. He knew some of the authorities still suspected him of being Huge Bo and Vice Minister Hsu's murderer even he was very sick when they were killed.

"Mo-bai, Saber King refused to join them. He denounced his two brothers: Feng Three and Feng Five. He also forbids his students to participate in the ambush."

"Saber King is righteous and a worthy friend to know. I will visit him sometime."

She-Devil and a group of men circled the carriages first. Yang and Brother Su fought on each side of the carriage. Lee Mo-bai moved in fast, he pierced Jao on the chest and sliced off the bandit leader Wu's left shoulder and arm. The others tried to flee at first and then sank to their knees begging for mercy. The accompanying soldiers knelt and told Lee Mo-bai, "Please spare us. Thin Buddha Hwang paid us to stay out of the fight. We know we're in the wrong. We beg for mercy."

Dae Wu said, "Mo-bai, they dare not disobey their boss. I'm sure they will treat me well now."

Lee Mo-bai said, "Have a good trip. Brother Dae, farewell." His tears came.

"Mo-bai, take care of yourself. Remember the saying; '*think twice before you take one step.*' I wish you a happy future. Come to visit me in Xikang. Ceo-lian will guard my family. You should not stay in Beijing. Bye."

9

Lee Mo-bai stood there and watched Dae Wu's carriage resume the long journey to the west. '*Farewell, my true friend and brother, we'll meet in the next life if there will be one. I'll buy you a peaceful future with my death.*' The next day he led his horse to the stable to be fed. and to have new shoes. There was a big, strong white horse at the stable. A long, heavy sheathed sword was strapped at the horse's flank. He thought, '*Whoever could ride that horse and wield that sword would sure be a tough opponent. Is he the real thief? I hope whoever he is, is not one of my enemies.*' Ever since he noticed the abbess of the convent where Violet had stayed is a highly trained martial arts master, he realized that there must be other superior masters around.

Two days later at sunset, Lee Mo-bai was the lone rider on the last stretch to Beijing. A tall old man, on the tall white horse, the one he had seen two days before, came fast from behind. The old man laughed and whipped at Lee Mo-bai slightly at the shoulder when he rode past. Lee Mo-bai was annoyed, he pushed his mount ahead hard to pursue but the white horse and laughter faded fast. '*He is super. The old man looked familiar. He's no enemy and he only teased me. He seemed to know me and I wonder who he is. I wish I had time to find out who he is. It's close to Beijing now; I need to concentrate on how and where I could kill Thin Buddha.*'

He thought about the saying, '*hidden dragons and crouching tigers*' and he thought, '*Nothing is as it seems in Beijing. Violet, an exquisite artistic prostitute, knew martial arts and dared to wound a sadistic bandit leader. Fat Shih, the owner of an eatery, killed the rich loan shark for the poor. Mon Zhi-an, an obscure groom, turned out to be a highly skilled warrior. An aged abbess is a superb martial arts master. Thin Buddha Hwang, a known philanthropist, is a vicious snake in disguise while scheming for more power ruthlessly. That old man I just met is another highly skilled one; he or his student might be the real thief who stole the pearl. I wish I had time to find out. If I want to clear my name and*

Dae Wu's, I have to kill Thin Buddha Hwang. I had to use a different name and try to be inconspicuous, too. For a few days, I will be one of the crouching tigers.'

Lee Mo-bai entered the city gate, boarded his horse at a stable with the instruction that the horse should be delivered to Master Lieu's security company four days later. *'I hope I can get it done in less than four days.'*

It took Lee Mo-bai two days to find Thin Buddha Hwang's hiding place and to corner him. Thin Buddha Hwang asked for mercy and offered him twenty thousand ounces of silver with a promise that he would do no more evil. Lee Mo-bai refused and killed him. He held the blood-dripping sword, and went to the nearby magistrate's office and told the guard, "My name is Lee Mo-bai. I killed the evil Thin Buddha Hwang." They jailed him.

Beijing was in turmoil. Viscount Chiu sent his whole regiment of soldiers out to break out the crowds everywhere. The vendors ran back home and the stores also hastily closed. Dae Wu's coachman Fu rushed into the inner court to tell Ceo-lian the news. Ceo-lian told Fu to gather all the men servants. She told them to keep quiet and forbade any of them, except Fu, from leaving the house. Fu said, "Miss Yu, we'll be cautious, and we will keep it from the maids. Master Lee told us to obey your orders completely. A few of us have been working for this family for two or more generations. You can trust us."

No one dared to treat Lee Mo-bai as a common thief and put him in a clean, airy cell in the innermost court. The captain put long heavy chains on Lee's ankles, and he was not handcuffed. They thanked Lee Mo-bai for his nonresistance. Viscount Chiu and Prince Te's servants brought Lee Mo-bai meals every day, and he told them to take the meals back. He said, "Please tell your masters that I had committed a horrible crime and I'm prepared to die for it." He refused to eat the jail food. He wanted to die soon, not wait for a lengthen trial and the death sentencing.

Prince Te told Viscount Chiu, "Lee Mo-bai wants to die and there is nothing we can do. His death will clear Dae Wu's name and ensure Dae Wu a peaceful life when he returns two years later. You know the Emperor wants to complete a set of encyclopedias of Chinese literature, and he called for scholars to work on the project. I could recommend Lee Mo-bai for the project and I could get him a pardon. I sent Lee Mo-bai a letter telling him my plan to help him. He refused. It's bad. He is such a talented young man."

Without eating and drinking, Lee Mo-bai knew and felt he would die soon. He was dizzy and lethargic and his senses dulled. On the third night, he woke up and heard a whisper, "Mo-bai, we come to get you out of here." It was Fat Shih who was working to loosen the chains on Lee Mo-bai's feet.

"Brother Shih, if I want to escape, no chains can hold me. Let me die to end my troubled and guilt-ridden miserable life. Please leave."

"Mo-bai, Ceo-lian is here, too."

"Please come with us. We will carry you out," Ceo-lian begged.

"Ceo-Lian, this is not a place for you. Leave quickly. You have to guard Dae Wu's family for me. Knowing you're there to guard them, I can die in peace. Please leave quickly."

Ceo-lian sobbed, "I won't go. You know that I can't live without you. If you don't want to leave, I'll stay and let us die together. There was nothing for me to live for anymore." She embraced him.

"Mon Zhi-an died for me. I wanted to die the day we buried him. I am to blame for your misfortune. I can't live with my conscience. Obey me and leave. I ruined both your and Violet's chance to be happy. I want to die. Only death could redeem my guilt. Leave! Ceo-lian, I want you to get married someday, don't let the unreasonable custom bind you. You had never met Mon Zhi-an."

Ceo-lian sobbed even harder, she threw herself on Lee Mo-bai's shoulder.

The sound of the night patrol's footsteps got closer. Fat Shih pulled Ceo-lian off Lee Mo-bai and they left.

The authority found the locks and chain to Lee Mo-bay's cell had been tampered with and increased surveillance. For the next two nights, Fat Shih and Ceo-lian could not get close to the cell.

On the night of the sixth day, Fat Shih sent his assistant to warn Ceo-lian, "Too dangerous, don't go tonight." Ceo-lian could not stop herself from going. She couldn't bear to think that her beloved Lee Mo-bai might have died or are dying in the cell. She wanted to go to see him one last time and to tell him that she would love him forever and she won't marry another man. She even thought about holding him and dying together. Her life would be meaningless without him, and there was nothing for her to live for anymore.

There were more soldiers on patrol. She could not even get close to the court where the cell is. She walked through the narrow lanes surrounding the prison, trying to find a way to slip in. Someone patted her shoulder. She turned around with her dagger ready and asked the tall old man who stood behind her, "Hi, old man, who are you? How dare you…!" The old man with a long white beard said urgently with a Southerner's accent, "Go home quickly! Go home!" and disappeared as suddenly as he had come.

'Ahe! A ghost! Was that my father's spirit coming to warn me? But my father was not that tall. I did not hear any sound of his coming and going. Anyway, ghost or man, he means me no harm. He could have killed me.' The hair on her arms stood up. She did not want to give up and keep walking around. Finally, she got to Lee Mo-bai's cell and found the door ajar. She went in and groped around the bed and the floor in the dark and found nothing. She went home scared. '*Did that old man kill Lee Mo-bai? But where is the body? If he killed Lee, why did he take the body out and to where? He must be super given how he moved around soundlessly. Who is he?*' Many questions came to her mind but no answers.

Early next morning, a maid told her that a man wanted to see her immediately. Fat Shih's assistant said urgently, "Master Lee Mo-bai escaped last night. Someone got him out. There are soldiers everywhere. Master Shih escaped. Could you give me some silver?"

"Sure, can you ride?"

"I better escape on foot." Ceo-lian gave him some silver and she asked a servant to get a package of food for him. She said, "Come back when it's safe."

Ceo-lian ordered Fu, "Keep everyone at home. You're the only one who can go out to do some marketing. I want you to go out shortly before noon and find out whatever you can for me. We don't want Mrs. Dae Wu and the maids to know anything."

She went back to her room and waited until the time she usually gets up. She chatted and joked with Mrs. Dae Wu, sat with grandma, and tried to act as if it was just another normal day. Her mind kept going back to Lee's escape and that strange old man she met. She thought, '*If he killed him why did he not leave his body in the cell? Besides, he would kill me, too. Is the old man Lee Mo-bai's Teacher? But Lee Mo-bai told me that his Teacher had passed away five years ago. He must have saved Lee Mo-bai and took him away. Lee Mo-bai is alive. Of course, he is alive, the old man wouldn't carry a corpse out!*' Her hope soared.

She could not concentrate when Mrs. Dae Wu taught her reading and writing in the afternoon. She said she had a headache. Indeed her head was aching from speculations. A maid told her that Fu was back.

Fu said, "Miss Yu the authority said that a short, fat man helped Master Lee to escape last night. Some soldiers reported that they saw this short man and another one lingered about the areas surrounding the prison. They started the door-to-door search."

"Will they come here and search us?" Ceo-lian asked.

"No, they are only searching the districts where the Han live. They won't search us." Fu continued, "There are all kinds of rumors. Someone said the late Thin Buddha Hwang's men killed Master Lee and used some kind of powder to turn the body into the water. Someone said Master Lee knew magic and turned into a big bird and flew away. Someone said a fat man helped him to escape. Most of the folks are happy that Master Lee escaped. They said killing the two-faced Thin Buddha Hwang is a heroic deed."

Ceo-lian sent Fu out every day to gather news. There were no new developments. Everything started to be normal again.

On the hot night of the sixth day after Lee Mo-bai's dramatic escape, Ceo-lian had a troubled sleep and she dreamed of being with her parents and she also dreamed that Lee Mo-bai hugged her. She woke up and turned over trying to sleep again when her bare arm touched something long and cold like a snake. She was scared and started to yell, 'Ahe!' But she immediately stopped herself. She lit the oil lamp and she almost yelled again. There was an unsheathed sword on top of a piece of paper with words on it beside her pillow. She grabbed one of her sabers, went out and jumped up on the roof and saw no one, and heard nothing. She trembled from fear and came back to check the window and found no sign of breaking in. Now she felt hairs standing on her arm. Her hand shook when she picked up the paper to read. It wrote, '*He is now with Chiang Nan-ho. His sword is for you to keep.*' Ceo-lian recognized Lee Mo-bai's sword immediately. She had learned enough to understand the words. Chiang Nan-ho must be the name of that strange old man she met the night Lee Mo-bai escaped. The old man saved Lee Mo-bai. She wanted to shout, '*He is alive*!' She was so happy, she cried.

The sword was a plain and heavy one. Lee Mo-bai once told her that it was his father's sword. '*Ahe! The old man wants me to keep it as a marriage token. Where did he get the sword? They must have confiscated it when they jailed him. At least the note told me that Lee Mo-bai is alive. Oh! I don't know what to think anymore.*' Ceo-lian carefully put the sword and note away. She could not and would not tell anyone about the whole bizarre affair.

Ceo-lian spent her days teaching Dae Wu's two sons martial arts and also learning reading and writing. Every morning and every night she practiced martial arts. Whenever she practiced the skills that Lee Mo-bai had taught her, her mind wondered about the sword, the note, the strange old man, and Lee Mo-bai. Once in a while when she was alone, Ceo-lian would take out the 'gold combs' and look at them. They were her marriage token to Mon Zhi-an, the husband-to-be whom she had never met. '*Fat Shih told me that Lee Mo-bai thought very highly of him. Lee Mo-bai is usually conceited but he had told Fat Shih and Dae Wu that Mon-Zhi-an was a better fighter than him. Mon-Zhi-an must be a hero and was very courageous when he killed the evil rich man. He also must be a very caring person when he guarded and took care of the very ill Lee Mo-bai. Oh! He must have loved me deeply in his heart when he called himself 'Yu Er (two)' He was using my surname. and ..and ..'* She started to understand the guilt Lee Mo-bai felt. She could have married Mon-Zhi. If Lee Mo-bai did not tell Mon Zhi-an his longing for her. She also kept speculating about the writing *'His sword is for you to keep.'* The old man Chiang Nan-ho wanted Lee Mo-bai and her to get married later.

Once Mrs. Dae Wu asked why Lee Mo-bai did not come to see them anymore. Ceo-lian told her that Lee Mo-bai probably went to Xikang to be with Dae Wu. Three months later, Master Yang came back from Xikang and said that Dae Wu was well. Her Brother Su would stay there for the next two years and then he would escort Dae Wu back home. Ceo-lian was content. There were maids to see to her needs and Mrs. Dae Wu was a good teacher and company. Mrs. Dae Wu would take her to visit Countess Chiu and the Countess would come to visit them. Both of them were refined and educated ladies. Ceo-lian was no longer the ignorant country girl. Ceo-lian was glad that Countess Chiu had never talked about Lee Mo-bai's escape. She presumed that Viscount Chiu had told his wife not to talk about it.

Time went fast as a throwing dart. Seasons changed from winter to summer and soon the third summer came. Dae Wu and Brother Su came home from Xikang. The two-year exile ended. Dae Wu was happy to be home again. Mrs. Dae Wu cried and laughed happily that her husband was home again. Both of them thanked Ceo-lian for keeping the family safe. Then Ceo-lian told them both everything; Lee Mo-bai killed Thin Buddha Hwang and he had disappeared from the jail. There was no news about Lee Mo-bai for two years. She showed them the sword, the note and told them about the strange old man whom she had met the night Lee Mo-bai escaped.

Dae Wu laughed happily and said, "No need to worry anymore. Chiang Nan-ho is his father's sworn brother. He rescued Lee Mo-bai from the jail and took him away. Now my dear Brother Lee must have learned more advanced martial arts. I'm home again, I think he will soon sneak back to Beijing and come to visit us. *Ha Ha.*" He handed back the sword and note to her, "Ceo-lian, keep them safe."

"Please tell me more about this Chiang Nan-ho," Ceo-lian asked.

"Chiang Nan-ho, Gi Kon-jii, and Lee Mo-bai's father Lee Feng-jii were about the same age. Gi was Lee Mo-bai's Teacher. When they were young, they fought with each other, and later they became close friends. Chiang Nan-ho is Lee Feng-jii's sworn brother and that made him Mo-bai's uncle. Mo-bai's parents died when Lee Mo-bai was eight years old. Chiang Nan-ho took him to Nan-ko Village to live with his uncle. Chiang Nan-ho must have arranged for Gi Kon-jii to teach Mo-bai martial arts and literature. I always wondered about that. Gi Kon-jii's home was in Szechwan." He did not tell Ceo-lian that it was obvious that Chiang Nan-ho gave her the sword as a marriage token for his nephew. '*She knows.*' Dae Wu smiled at his wife and she smiled back. They were happy for Ceo-lian.

Dae Wu told Prince Te about the note and the sword. Prince Te said, "I knew that someone with super skills took Lee Mo-bai out of the jail. They said it was an owner of a restaurant who did it. I never believed it. To take a nearly dying Mo-bai out of a heavily guarded jail surely was not an easy task. It required strength and skills. I'm happy to know that Lee Mo-bai is alive somewhere. I miss him."

"So do I, Your Highness."

"Chiang Nan-ho took the sword from my study. The sword was on that desk." Prince Te pointed to the desk in a corner. "After Mo-bai escaped, I asked for Mo-bai's sword as a memento, and I put it on that desk. One day it was gone. I did not want to make a big issue of it. How did he know it was Mo-bai's sword? And how did he know it was here?"

"Your Highness, Chiang Nan-ho knew the sword because Mo-bai was using his late father's sword. He must have watched you when you put the sword there."

"Thank all the gods that he is no assassin. It must be it. I remembered telling Je to find a sheath for it. I must have mentioned that it was Mo-bai's sword. Chiang Nan-ho must be a super expert, you know that I have the security increased after the night Mo-Zhi-an visited me."

"Your Highness, you know Mo-bai had made quite a name for himself in Beijing. Chiang Nan-ho must have heard about it and came to meet his nephew. He came just in time to save Mo-bai. It is another divine intervention."

"He took the sword and gave it to Ceo-lian as a marriage token. I hope Mo-bai will obey him and marry Ceo-lian later. Dae Wu, you have to find a way to keep Ceo-lian here. She knows martial arts. If she gets restless and wanders all over China, even Chiang Nan-ho will not find her easily."

"Your Highness, I plan to buy a small house close to mine for her to live. My wife gets along with her very well and my mother also likes her. My wife is teaching her reading and writing. Her Brother Su came back with me and now he is a guard at Grand Security where Ceo-lian's father used to be a guard. I think she will stay; she does not have any other family."

"Poor girl, I feel for her. I'm glad that you give her a home. Dae Wu, I want you to be careful. The case of the stolen pearls is not closed yet. When Lee Mo-bai was jailed, two of the pearls showed up at a jewel store at Ba-tin Town. Someone still thinks Lee Mo-bai's the thief even though he was in jail."

Dae Wu bought a small house not far from his house for Ceo-lian to live. Her Brother Su came to visit her often. Ceo-lian was content to stay. *'Lee Mo-bai definitely would come back to visit Dae Wu.'* Sometimes she would look at the two marriage tokens; the gold combs from Mon Zhi-an, the sword from Lee Mo-bai, she would shed a few tears.

She had never met Mon Zhi-an. Lee Mo-bai said, "Mon Zhi-an died for me. I am to be blamed for your being a widow." on that last night, she went into his jail. Sometimes Ceo-lian thought that she would be happy if Mon Zhi-an married her. Her parents had never met each other until their wedding night. So did a lot of others. Some parents even arranged their children's marriage before they were born. One father would tell another father, "My wife is with child. She told me that your wife is with child, too. My child will marry yours or they will be sworn, brothers or sisters." Now Mon Zhi-an was dead, and she would be considered his widow even though they did not have a wedding. That is the tradition. Unless another man who is brave enough and not superstitious and has his parents' approval wants to marry her. Not many parents would approve their son to marry such an unlucky woman.

She loves Lee Mo-bai very much but she does not understand him. She learned to be quiet when she sensed Lee Mo-bai was deep in thoughts on their journey to Da-ton. She also knew Lee Mo-bai still has some feelings for her even though he tried to hide it. But reading books and writing would take him to a faraway place she could never reach or understand. She wanted to learn the words and be prepared. She hoped and she waited. Sometimes she wondered whether she would be happy if Lee Mo-bai would marry her. She would have a chance to be happy with Lee Mo-bai if he met any other prostitute but the artistic Violet. *'I want Ceo-lian to be happy. Marriage between a man and a woman of the same class with similar backgrounds somehow could make a good marriage. Lee Mo-bai is too well educated for my Ceo-lian.'* She once overheard that her father said it when her mother suggested a marriage between Lee Mo-bai and her.

Once Mrs. Dae Wu and Countess Chiu were talking about how well-written Lee Mo-bai's poems were. Countess Chiu mentioned that Prince Te had commented that Lee Mo-bai's talent in writing poems might be even better than his swordsmanship. Ceo-lian felt that she was somewhat inadequate then.

The moon should be perfectly round and extra bright on the fifteenth day of the eighth month of the Lunar calendar. It's the Mid-Autumn Festival, the Moon Festival. It is an event to celebrate the union of the family and the good harvest. Dae Wu would have the first family gathering in three years. Dae Wu invited Brother Su, of course, Ceo-lian to the traditional family dinner and to eat the round-shaped moon cakes. Mrs. Dae Wu sighed and voiced out for everyone, "I wish Mo-bai is here with us."

To lighten the mood, Dae Wu opened a moon cake and chuckled, "There's no slip of paper with the message to call for killing the Manchu. *Ha Ha*! Hans and Manchu are sitting together at my table. Let's drink to it." Everyone joined in.

His elder son asked, "Daddy, why do Hans want to kill us?"

"I hope not. Our Emperor is just; he treats Han and Manchu equally. Many ministers and generals are capable Hans. I'm talking about something that happened more than three hundred years ago. Genghis Khan led the Mongols to breach the Great Wall and conquered China and establish the Yuan (Mongol) Dynasty. The Hans resisted them. One year, the Han resistance distributed thousands of 'moon cakes' to the Hans only in Beijing and asked them to eat the cakes at a specific divine hour on the night of the moon festival. They put slips of paper in the 'cakes' with the words asking them to kill Mongols. One night the Han regained control of Beijing and then overthrew the Mongol Dynasty. The Mongols ruled China for about one hundred years."

Brother Su chuckled. "Don't worry. We are friends aren't we?"

Mrs. Dae Wu said, "Sure we are friends. The Emperor encourages the Manchu to learn everything from the superiorly cultured Han. The other day, Countess Chiu told me that the Emperor hired many Han scholars to work on editing the history books. If Lee Mo-bai was here, he would be pardoned and given a very good position for sure."

Brother Su said, "One day, Brother Lee will show up and surprise us."

It was an enjoyable evening. Ceo-lian felt so alone afterward, she cried herself to sleep.

It's getting chilly. One morning Dae Wu's two sons came to her earlier than usual for their martial arts lessons. The older boy told her, "Aunt Yu, my father sent us here. He was upset and he did not want to teach us this morning."

Ceo-lian asked, "Why? Did something unpleasant happen?"

"I don't know. My father sighed and wrote Uncle Lee's name again and again. He paced around the study and sighed." Ceo-lian felt uneasy.

Halfway through the workout, Brother Su walked in and said, "That wicked Ca leo (six) scattered rumors all over saying that Lee Mo-bai drowned in the Yangtze River. Steady! Ceo-lian. It's only a rumor." Ceo-lian turned white and faltered.

"Tell me more. Please"

"Feng Five's friends came from the South. The younger Tan Brother said Lee Mo-bai is his Teacher. Lee Mo-bai stayed at his home for a few months two years ago. An old monk and six students fought a lone Lee Mo-bai on a boat because Lee Mo-bai stole a manual of *'Tien Hsueh'*. Lee Mo-bai fell off the boat into the mighty Yangtze River and drowned. That's all I have heard."

Ceo-lian told the boys, "Go and tell your father, we are coming to see him."

Dae Wu said, "Ceo-lian, I heard the rumor, too. But, I have doubts. Chiang Nan-ho knows *'Tien Hsueh'*. There is no need for Lee Mo-bai to steal and to fight the monks over the manual."

"What is *'Tien Hsueh'*? My father mentioned it once," Ceo-lian asked.

"I don't know too much about it either. It is one of the elite secret skills. From what I have heard, one who knows it can kill or cripple a man, or make him mute instantly with two fingers. Master Lieu of Grand Security may know something about it."

Dae Wu continued, "Mo-bai came to the North when he was eight years old. I don't know if he can swim or not. Let's hope he knows how to swim." Ceo-Lian thought, *'Could Lee Mo-bai swim so well that he can survive the huge Yangtze River?'*

A few days later, Mrs. Dae Wu and Ceo-lian came back late. A man and a sobbing girl waited for Ceo-lian at the gate at her house adjacent to Dae Wu's mansion. A servant said, "Miss Yu, they came here to see you. You were not home so we let them wait here. We gave them some water to drink."

The girl knelt and cried, "Aunt Yu please help me. Uncle Lee Mo-bai told me to come to you if I need any help. They killed grandpa and kidnapped my sister…"

The man said, "I'm a neighbor. We live just outside of the South Gate. Before dawn, some men came to rob them. They killed her grandpa. Her elder sister was gone. I found her hiding under a bed. She told me that they kidnapped her sister and wanted me to take her here to ask you to help her. We walked all the way here and we got lost before someone told us how to get here. Poor girl. Please help her."

Ceo-lian's maid asked, "Have you had any supper yet?"

The man said, "No."

Ceo-lian put her arm around the girl and said, "You must be hungry and cold. Both of you come with me and have something to eat. Then you tell me everything." She turned to the man and said, "You're a good neighbor. After you finish eating, you will stay here tonight. The city gate must have closed."

Ceo-lian sent someone to ask Dae Wu to come. Mrs. Dew Wu came also.

"My name is Yan Li-fon. My sister's name is Yan Li-in. My brother is Yan Bo (leopard). We are orphans. Someone murdered our parents. My mother was a concubine. After she died, the chief wife abused us. The old man we call Grandpa has the same last name but we're not related. He saved us and raised us. Some bad men crippled Grandpa and Grandpa Chiang came. He saved us and helped us move up here. We grow and sell flowers for a living. Grandpa and my brother sold the flowers in Beijing. Early this morning we were still sleeping when four bad men came. They killed Grandpa and took my sister away. I hid under the bed. I heard one of them say they will sell my sister." Between sobs, Yan Li-fon told them.

"Why did they kill your grandpa?"

"I don't know."

"Where is your brother?"

"Grandpa called him a thief and chased him away."

"A thief? When was that? Do you remember?"

"Two years ago, about the same time that Grandpa Chiang carried Uncle Lee Mo-bai on his back to our home."

"How long did Uncle Lee stay with you?"

"Almost two months. He was very sick for a long time. Grandpa knew medicine and Grandpa Chiang treated him with '*Tien Hsueh*', too. They said that Uncle Lee's lung was not good."

Mrs. Dae Wu pulled the girl close to her, tenderly wiped her tears, and said, "I've always wanted to have a daughter and I have one now. Ceo-lian, you have a niece." Yan Li-fon sobbed even harder. Ceo-lian shed a few tears too.

Ceo-lian's maid altered some of Ceo-lian's old clothes for Yan Li-fon.

The next day, Ceo-lian, Yan Li-fon, and a servant went with the neighbor to the girl's home. They reported the break-in and murder to the authority and buried the crippled old grandpa. Ceo-lian asked the neighbor to look after the house and told the neighbor to send the girl's brother to Dae Wu's place if he comes home.

Mrs. Dew Wu ordered new warmer clothes for Yan Li-fon.

Dae Wu asked, "Li-fon, did Grandpa Chiang visit you often?"

"No. I only remembered that he came twice. When I was five, Grandpa Chiang came with a Mute. They stayed with us for a long time. They taught my brother martial arts. Two years ago, he came again. He was out often and one night he carried Uncle Lee Mo-bai to our home. Uncle Lee told me that I could come to ask Aunt Yu for help anytime. He wrote down the address on a slip of paper."

Mrs. Dae Wu asked, "Li-fon, how old are you?"

"I'm thirteen, my sister is sixteen, and my brother is nineteen."

Dae Wu asked, "Tell me about the Mute, how old is he?"

"He is old but he is very nice. He gave us pieces of silver and he smiled a lot. Grandpa Chiang told us the mute is his classmate."

"Did you remember anything Grandpa Chiang and Uncle Lee were talking about two years ago?"

"Uncle Lee knelt and told Grandpa Chiang someone died. Grandpa Chiang scolded Uncle Lee and said Uncle Lee was not modest, and he should not show off his martial arts skills. My sister and I felt sorry for Uncle Lee then."

"Did Uncle Lee leave your home with Grandpa Chiang?"

"No, Grandpa Chiang left earlier. Uncle Lee stayed with us until he was well. I'm the one who brought him food. Grandpa said that my sister is older and it is not fitting for her to take care of Uncle Lee."

"Why did your Grandpa make your brother leave? Is he a thief?" Dae Wu asked.

"Grandpa did not want my brother to learn martial arts. Another friend of my parents took him to a Master Chen to learn martial arts somewhere near Kaifeng. He learned well and came back three years ago. He wanted to avenge my parent's murders. But we had no silver and Grandpa did not want him to go. My brother and grandpa sold flowers everywhere in Beijing. He knew where the rich people live. He must have stolen something. My grandpa called him a thief and chased him out. Uncle Lee was still sick in bed. When Uncle Lee left us, I begged him to find my brother and to look after him."

Brother Su came. Ceo-lian told him about the killing and the kidnapping. He said immediately, "Feng Five and the Tan brothers did this. Yesterday, I went to them to ask about Lee Mo-bai's supposed drowning, I was told they left Beijing in a hurry with a carriage. The Tan brothers told someone that they came to seek revenge. Yan Bo killed their father."

Ceo-lian said, "Li-fon heard one of them said that they wanted to sell her sister to a rich man. Where would they go?"

Dae Wu said, "They might go to Ba-tin, Feng Five's hometown. You remember that the dead Dart Mew and his nephew Jao had friends there. Mo-bai wounded Jao, *Golden Spear*, when they waylaid me on my way to Xikang. I bet the remaining gang is still there."

"We have to find Li-fon's sister before they sell her." Ceo-lian and Brother Su would leave immediately.

Yan Li-fon begged Ceo-lian, "Aunt Yu, please find my brother, too. He is almost as tall as Uncle Su." She sobbed again. Mrs. Dae Wu held her. Ceo-lian put her arms around the girl and said, "Li-fon, I hope that we can bring your sister back and both of you will stay with me. I am your big sister."

10

Dae Wu told Ceo-lian, "Yan Bo might have something to do with the stolen pearls. If so, he might be in danger. Greedy people may want to rob him, and he won't be able to fight off everyone. Sooner or later he will be killed. If you find him, ask him to hand them to Prince Te. Prince Te could help him."

"He was only seventeen two years ago. He wouldn't have enough experience to steal the pearls from the heavily guarded royal palace inside the Forbidden City."

"He didn't. Prince Te told me that the pearls were stolen from a secret chamber for the storage of rare treasures. A eunuch or a minister stole the pearls and hid them in his home. Someone very good at night jumping skills stole them from his home. Mo-bai was a suspect until someone sold two pearls at Ba-tin at the time Mo-bai was dying in jail. They said a tall young man sold the pearls at Ba-tin." Dae Wu explained.

"Yan Bo fits the description and the timing is right. It won't be difficult to find him if so many want to rob him. We'll keep our eyes open."

Dae Wu suggested, "When you stop at an inn, let Brother Su sleep in the mass sleeping room for single travelers. He could hear things and save some silver, too."

It worked. Brother Su heard a lot.

--*'Yan Bo is indeed formidable. He had three classmates with him. They unscrupulously killed whoever wanted to rob them of the pearls. Now the officials are searching in every province for him and he is probably hiding somewhere near Kaifeng.'*

-- *'Lee Mo-bai changed his name to Yan Bo. Who else could be that good?'*

--*'That's not true. Yan Bo is husky and very tall; Lee Mo-bai is pale and thin and looks like a scholar. Besides, Lee Mo-bai drowned. More than six monks fought him on a boat, he fell into the Yangtze River.'*

--'*Lee Mo-bai is not dead. I heard that the monks are still looking for him.*'

--'*I heard that the Tan brothers killed Yan Bo's grandfather and kidnapped his sister. Yan Bo killed their father.*'

--'*The elder Tan gathered more than thirty fighters to rob Yan Bo. Yan Bo and his three classmates killed half of Tan's men. The Tan brothers are cowards, they dare not fight Yan Bo and they killed the crippled old man instead.*'

--'*The Tan family owns a shipping fleet along the Yangtze River. They're rich and they don't need to rob.*'

--'*They are greedy. The Tan brothers don't have long to live. Yan Bo will kill them.*'

--'*Golden Spear Jao of Kaifeng gathered more friends. He declares that he will fight Yu Ceo-lian to the death to avenge his uncle Dart Mew's death.*'

Brother Su said, "That Yan Bo must be really good. But he is doomed. He won't be able to run forever from both the law and the greedy ones."

"You're right. No one talked about where Feng Five and the Tan brothers are. Maybe everyone is afraid of Saber King Feng Four. We'll go to see him, he should know where his brother is." Ceo-lian said.

"Feng Four is a good man. Lee Mo-bai defeated him, but he held no grudge against Mo-bai. It was his friend who told Prince Te about Mo-bai's innocence. Prince Te got Mo-bai out of jail."

Ceo-lian said, "I can see we'll have a lot of trouble. Everyone knows that Lee Mo-bai is not here to help us. But, I'm confident that I can beat them." She did not tell Brother Su that she had a bad feeling that a young man might be tailing them.

Brother Su said hesitantly, "Sister I almost beat someone when he called you names."

Ceo-lian sighed, "It cannot be helped. The enemies will discredit us any way they can. I'm glad that you held your temper. If Feng Five hears we're after him, he may hide Yan Li-in or even kill her."

They were noticed. For the next two nights, whenever Brother Su checked into the communal room of an inn, most travelers only joked about inconsequential things. At Ba-tin, Ceo-lian whispered, "I understand that the Feng brothers are well-known and powerful here. We better find out more about them first."

Ceo-lian asked the hotel clerk about the Feng Five.

The clerk said with obvious contempt, "Feng Five dares not come home. No one around here has seen him for three years now. Feng Five is notoriously wicked; his brother 'Saber King' disowned him and forbade him to come home. Feng Four is not home either; he and his wife are visiting their in-laws. But Feng One, Feng Three are home."

Brother Su told Ceo-lian, "Sister, we should check the Feng Villa out. Feng Five knew that his brother's away, he may hide the young girl there."

Ceo-lian agreed, "We may find out where Feng Five might have taken the girl to. Brother Su, please remember that we could only apprehend Feng Five, not his brothers."

Feng One, a retired guard, rudely exchanged words with the impatient Brother Su and called Ceo-lian 'a wanton woman'. Ceo-lian used the back of her saber to disable Feng One.

Someone told Ceo-lian that Feng Five probably escaped to Kaifeng to seek *Golden Spear* Jao's help. A beggar told Ceo-lian that he saw Feng Five. He said, "I saw Feng Five ride to Master Lin's villa yesterday. Master Lin is rich and always pays well for a pretty girl. Give me some silver, I'll take you there."

Ceo-lian asked, "Did you see him come with a carriage?"

"No, he was alone."

Master Lin lived in a fortified villa with tall and thick surrounding walls. The moat was dry. One drawbridge led to a heavy iron-coated gate. Master Lin invited Ceo-lian and Brother Su to his study cordially but denied seeing Feng Five lately.

The beggar yelled outside the window, "Feng Five rides away. Feng Five is escaping to the South and on a white horse."

Brother Su whipped Master Lin hard. Although Ceo-lian's champion horse was swift, Five had a good start so they did not catch him. When they came back to Master Lin's villa, the drawbridge was up and the gate was closed.

Ceo-lian told the angry Brother Su, "We'll be back tonight, although I don't think the girl is here."

"Sister, the thick stone wall is too high. We can't scale it, and I don't think you have the skills to jump so high."

"No, but we can..." Ceo-lian remembered a story that her father told her.

Ceo-lian asked Brother Su to buy a length of strong cord, and a heavy hook. In the dark, Brother Su threw the hook attached to the cord up a low section of the wall and hooked it on a post securely. He held the cord and climbed up the wall and then pulled Ceo-lian up. The night watch sounded the second night call and shouted 'beware of fire' and the whole village was dark, only a few rooms with lights on.

"The rich stay up late. *Sister*, let's go where the light is." Brother Su said.

"Wait! Let's plan our retreat route first... Did you hear that? They sounded the alarm. Must be another intruder."

By now, the whole villa was up with torches and loud shouting. A few came upon the wall. Ceo-lian quickly whipped a guard hard and told Brother Su to throw him down from the wall. They found the lowest part of the wall and jumped down to the debris-filled moat.

Their captive, who survived the fall, told them that Feng Five was here yesterday but he did not have a young woman with him. Tonight, a young man with a sword killed Master Lin.

"Ahe! The killer was a young man with a sword, who was he?"

"Is Lee Mo-bai?" Brother Su asked.

"No, I don't think so. Brother Lee does not kill unnecessarily."

They sat in Ceo-lian's room and speculated without any conclusion, and someone outside her window sneered, "A single man and a single woman in one room! Shame on you!" the man sounded like a Southerner.

Ceo-lian scanned the rooftops and the surrounding areas. She did not see anyone. *'This man must have followed us to the Lin Villa, and then killed Master Lin. His jumping skills must be better than mine. He shadowed us from Beijing and he knew what we're doing.'* Ceo-lian felt uneasy. On their way to Kaifeng the next day, Ceo-lian was subdued. Feng Four, *Saber King*, caught up with them and challenged them.

"Miss Yu, I know my brother Feng Five is bad and I will punish him. But you should not have wounded my elder brother."

Ceo-lian said, "Master Feng, your brother insulted me first."

Brother Su and Feng Four locked in a fierce fight. Two men were equally powerful and the three heavy sabers, Feng Four had two, and Brother Su had one, clashed and clanged loudly. When Ceo-lian noticed that her Brother Su could no longer keep up, she called, "Brother Su, let me fight him."

She was very skilled in avoiding Feng Four's powerful saber strikes and surprised the heavy-set man with the quick thrusts that Lee Mo-bai had taught her. But Ceo-lian was soon exhausted. Suddenly, a young man with a sword rushed in and started fighting Feng Four. "Three to one! I will fight all of you." Feng Four yelled.

Ceo-lian jumped away and shouted, "Stop! All of you, let's straighten out who's fighting who."

"Miss Yu, I helped you last night and I come to help you again. I'm Chen from Nanjing. I want to marry you."

"Brother Feng, I don't know this man. You have to believe me. He might be one of the men who killed Brother Lee Mo-bai." Ceo-lian said and she started fighting the young man.

"Lee Mo-bai is my friend. Miss Yu, Brother Su, let's forget our differences and join hands to fight him."

Chen fought them bravely and sneered, "The three of you fight me. You Northerners sure know how to win a fight."

Ceo-lian retorted, "You Southerners are no better. Seven monks fought a lone Lee Mo-bai and forced him to fall into the river."

"Lee Mo-bai is a thief. He stole something from my Teacher. If I were there, I would have killed him." *Saber King* yelled, "Braggart!"

Chen's arms numbed and hurt from the impact of the two powerful men's heavy sabers, and Ceo-lian's surprising quick thrusts were also hard to fend off. With agility and ferocity, Chen forced the three of them back momentarily and jumped on his horse, and galloped away.

Ceo-lian's champion mare almost caught up with him but bolted when the cunning Chen threw back a piece of red cloth. Brother Su threw the hook with the long cord and hooked onto a leg of Chen's horse. Chen managed to jump free and ran away through the narrow lanes between the fields.

Feng Four said, "We cannot tramp on the crops to chase him. Is it true that Brother Lee is dead?"

"Brother Feng, I know nothing more than the rumors," Ceo-lian told Feng Four that his brother Feng Five kidnapped a young woman from Beijing and she saw Feng Five escape from Master Lin's villa yesterday.

"I will punish my brother if I catch him. He probably ran to Kaifeng to ask Jao, Golden Spear, to help him."

Brother Su led Chen's white horse to Ceo-lian and said, "The horse is all right."

Ceo-lian said, "Let's search his saddlebag, we may find out something about him and why he came to the North."

"What is this heavy whip for?" Brother Su found a heavy whip of twined steel and cords among some clothes, a bag of silver, and a letter.

"I don't know. Let's see what the letter could tell us."

The letter was from Monk Pure to his student Chen. It said, "After you left the South, the rumor that the enemy is still alive and is on his way North was confirmed. If you meet him, don't fight him alone, but ask him to return our valuables. He had them for almost two years now and probably learned well how to use them. Be careful. Signed, Monk Pure."

Her hands shook, and she whispered, "Brother Su, This letter said that Lee Mo-bai is alive and is on his way North too."

"Ah! That's great. Are you sure?"

"I can read, but I would like to find a scribe to read it again. It is only a three-day ride home. Let's go home first to visit my parents' graves. I also want to keep my mare at home lest it gets hurt when I have to fight someone." Twice she sensed that the Southerner Chen was tailing them. She was happy. *'He wants us to lead him to Lee Mo-bai. Lee Mo-bai must be alive.'*

Brother Han told them, "If you two came back yesterday, you could have met Brother Wei. He came to ask you to help him."

"What's wrong?" Brother Su asked.

"Poor Brother Wei is a cripple now. Someone wounded him and seized his security company. He lost two fingers on his left hand and a half of his right foot."

"Tell us more," Ceo-lian asked.

"Jade Town is not far from Kaifeng. *Golden Spear* Jao vowed to eliminate his archenemies, Lee Mo-bai and you. He considered Brother Wei an enemy and tried to ruin Wei's business. Brother Wei had to pay a huge indemnity last year when the bandits robbed the merchant who bought his protection. The bandits were Jao's men. Jao wounded him and seized his business, house, vehicles, furniture, and weapons."

"I did not forget that it was this Golden Spear Jao who had forced my parents to flee and die. We'll go to Jade Town first and then Kaifeng." Ceo-lian said.

They visited her parent's graves and also found a scribe to read the letter they found in Chen's saddlebag. It confirmed that Lee Mo-bai is alive. She happily wrote Dae Wu the good news herself.

Ceo-lian and Brother Su stopped to eat at a small town two day's ride to Jade Town. There were horses and carriages parked there. When Ceo-lian unhooked her pair of sabers from the saddle, she heard someone call out her name. She saw a man look at her, and wondered, *'That's odd, I don't know this man and how can he know my name? He does not look hostile.'*

"Sister, you're well known with your sabers. I wouldn't worry."

Brother Wei lost his own home and now he lived with his aging father-in-law. He told them, "Tiger Jao is related to Golden Spear Jao of Kaifeng. They wanted to monopolize the security business in Henan Province. My company is not the only one they seized by force. Tiger Jao wounded me. A friend of his named Pai came. This Pai is a top-notch fighter. They threatened that they will kill my family and me if I dare go to the authority. They boasted that they will give me back my business if I or my friends could defeat them."

"Let's go to fight them now." Brother Su shouted.

Ceo-lian agreed, "It's early. Let's finish this business soon. We have to find the kidnapped girl." Briefly, she told Brother Wei their mission on the way to Brother Wei's security station.

As to be expected, Brother Su challenged Tiger Jao first. After thirty rounds, he chopped Tiger Jao heavily on the thigh. Ceo-lian stopped him in time to hold back the killing strike. The wounded Tiger Jao yelled, "Brother Pai, help me. Are you not my friend?"

A tall, robust and very good-looking young man came out and locked in a fight with the equally tall Brother Su. Both of them fought with a single heavy saber. After two rounds, Brother Su could hardly defend himself, and Ceo-lian immediately relieved him. She and Pai fought more than ten rounds and no one could gain an inch.

Pai forced Ceo-lian back a few steps and called with a genuine Beijing tongue, "Miss, we don't have enough room here in the yard to fight properly. Can we have a duel tomorrow afternoon at the Su Shiae Tomb out of town? I'm Pai. Please tell me your name."

Before Ceo-lian could answer, Brother Su shouted, "My sister is the famous Yu Ceo-lian. She killed Dart Mew three years ago in Beijing. You better surrender now and hand us back the property."

Pai ignored the remarks and said politely to Ceo-lian, "Miss Yu, your good name is far-reaching. I'm only a guest here, but I cannot let my friend be injured. Let's have the duel tomorrow to decide who will get the station."

Ceo-lian replied, "I agree."

Brother Su said, "This Pai fights better than Feng Four. I wonder why no one knows him in Beijing."

Ceo-lian said, "He fights even better than that conceited Chen from the South. But, I think he is in hiding. He won't tell us his first name. Brother Wei, do you know anything about him?"

"No, I only know he has been around a couple of months. He seldom leaves his room."

"Lee Mo-bai once mentioned that many Hans secretly resists the Manchu is constantly in hiding. But, this Pai is too young to know of the Manchu's atrocities when they invaded China." Ceo-lian said.

"Sister, it's no use to speculate, we'll know tomorrow."

After supper, Ceo-lian mentally reviewed the winning techniques Lee Mo-bai taught her. She seemed to hear him say, '*To confuse your opponent, use your right saber to defend and your left saber to attack. You're a woman so your strength is limited but you can move fast, I will teach you how to blend some of the swift sword thrusts into your accustomed saber techniques.'*

Pai bowed to Ceo-lian and said, "We don't have enormous animosity between us and we should not fight to the death. Since you're a woman, it won't be proper of us to have a fistfight. But, we will be careful with the sabers."

Brother Wei applauds, "It's very decent of you."

Ceo-lian said, "We will know defeat without drawing blood. Let's get on with it."

The duel began. Two persons moved closer or parted swiftly and their three sabers clashed and clanked continuously. They fought more than fifty rounds with no one winning but Ceo-lian started to show signs of weariness, and she knew that Pai had been fighting in defense for a while.

When Brother Su was just about to join the fight, a rider came and shouted, "Stop! Stop! Brother Pai, I have got an urgent message."

Pai jumped free. "Excuse me, we'll continue in a moment."

Ceo-lian took the chance to catch her breath. She noticed the newcomer was the same man who called her name two days earlier.

Pai listened to the messenger's urgent tone intently. Then he stamped heavily and cried. He handed his saber to his friend and walked to Ceo-lian and Brother Wei empty-handed.

With tears in his eyes, he bowed low first and then said, "Miss Yu, your martial arts skills are superior to mine. Tiger Jao will return the property to Brother Wei in three days. Now, I have a family emergency and I have to leave immediately. If you insist on resuming the duel, I admit I'm beaten."

Ceo-lian asked, "Why? You suggest that we duel today, and you know you're going to win."

"I was wrong to offend you. The property will be returned in three days."

"Original furniture and fittings must be left intact. Agreed?" Ceo-lian overrode Brother Su's loud interruptions.

"Sure, Miss Yu, you have my word. Bye." He and the newcomer galloped away.

Ceo-lian said, "Brother Wei, what's going on? He would have won for sure. I met the other one, the messenger, two days earlier."

"I think the authorities caught wind of his hiding and are on the way here to arrest him. His friend rushed here to warn him to escape."

"That might be it. We will wait three days before leaving for Kaifeng to seek Feng five and to find the missing Yan Li-in. Wait, this young man came from Beijing and he is almost as tall as Brother Su ... I wonder..." Ceo-lian said.

Ceo-lian's intuition proved to be true when the same man she met two days before visited them that evening. He requested that the front gate be closed and he whispered, "I'm Lu Na-an. Yan Li-fon called me brother. The young man you dueled today is Yan Bo, the two girls' brother. I told him about the tragedy of his family and that you are his benefactor. He is hurrying back to Beijing to take revenge. Now, I have more to tell Miss Yu in private."

"They are my Brothers. I don't keep anything from them." Ceo-lian said.

Lu Na-an looked out of the window first and then took out a cloth bundle. Opening it, he showed them four big pearls. He whispered, "Yan Bo's father was poisonous and his beautiful mother committed suicide lest the corrupt magistrate would make her his concubine. Their grandpa had the same surname but was not related to them. He saved the children, raised them but refused to let Yan Bo take revenge. My Teacher also knows the family and taught Yan Bo martial arts. Yan Bo learned well. Three years ago, we heard that the evil magistrate was in Nanjing. Yan Bo asked his grandpa to give him some traveling funds, but the old man refused. Yan Bo sold flowers in Beijing every day; he knew where a rich and wicked man lives. One night he stole a package and found forty-four precious pearls and some silver certificates. These pearls are the very ones that caused three officials' beheading, Dae Wu, and another man's exile. Yan Bo dared not use the silver certificates or sell the pearls. Somehow his grandpa sensed that he had stolen and chased him out of the house when your boyfriend Lee Mo-bai was hiding in their home."

Ceo-lian protested, "Lee Mo-bai is my sworn brother."

"After Yan Bo left home, he sold four pearls at Ba-tin and found me and two brothers to help him. But, the news of his pearls spread and many wanted to rob him. He killed and wounded all of them. Yan Bo killed the Tan brother's father when he tried to rob him. The Tan brothers killed Grandpa Yan and kidnapped Yan Li-in for revenge. Monk Pure's best student waylaid us and killed two of my companions, and wounded me. Yan Bo fought him three times and finally wounded him. Two months ago, the authorities recovered four pearls and are all out to catch him. Now he wants me to give you, Miss Yu, these four pearls."

"How dare you try to get my Sister in trouble. Ceo-Lian, don't accept them." Brother Su said angrily.

Brother Wei also said, "The pearls are royal property, coveting them will bring big disaster. Because of the pearls, Yan Bo killed the father Tan and

Tan's sons killed his grandpa and ruined his family. Who said Providence has no eyes?"

Lu Na-an solicited, "Yan Bo keeps the rest with him and won't give even one to anyone else. He wants to thank you." To Brother Su and Brother Wei's dismay, Ceo-lian accepted the pearls.

She told Lu, "Please tell Yan Bo not to sell any one of the pearls. Tell him I want to see him and talk to him. Brother Su and I are trying to rescue his sister. We heard the kidnapper, Feng Five might be in Kaifeng. We're going there soon. It's no use for Yan Bo to rush back to Beijing. Would you please go after him and bring him back here? He might not have gone far. Then we'll rescue his sister together. I repeat it's vital that I talk to him soon. Tell Yan Bo that his sister is at my house, not far from Dae Wu's place." She told Lu Na-na her address in Beijing.

Brother Wei complained, "Ceo-lian, you should not take the pearls. If the news leaks, everyone will want to rob you and the authorities will want to apprehend you. You may get Dae Wu in trouble again. Please keep them well hidden."

"Sister, what do you want the pearls for? You don't even have a husband. When and where will you wear them? Brother Wei is right. If anyone knows that you have the pearls, we'll have a catastrophe. You can never be in Beijing again." Brother Su echoed.

"Because I want to…," Ceo-lian hesitated and continued, "When Lu Na-an brings Yan Bo back, I'll ask him to give me the rest of them. I want…"

Brother Su interrupted her with open contempt, "Sister, you go after the pearls and I will go to Kaifeng to rescue the girl. Good night."

Ceo-lian wanted to tell them that she wanted to have all of the pearls Yan Bo had stolen and then return them to the palace. She wanted to clear Dae Wu's name permanently. She counted in her head. '*Yan Bo stole forty-four, he sold four at Ba-tin and now. He gave me four. Yan Bo should have thirty-six pearls. Dae Wu said there were forty-eight pearls stolen from the palace. He was jailed and exiled because someone, probably the original thief, sold four of them at Dae Wu's best friend's pawn shop. No ordinary thief could get into the heavily guarded Royal Palace. Dae Wu had said the first thief must be someone working in the palace, a eunuch.*'

Brother Wei sighed, "After we get back the property, I want to quit the security business and open a hotel instead. I'm crippled now and you cannot be here every day to protect me."

Ceo-lian nodded, "It's not a bad idea. It's better than competing with other conceited fighters. I learned my lesson on this trip. I cannot win every fight. No one can win every fight."

On the third day, Brother Su shouted angrily. "These turtle eggs stole everything. They only left empty walls."

Brother Wei asked, "What? What did you say?"

"I said 'Tiger Jao' and his gang stole every piece of furniture, every piece of hardware and gave you back an empty building."

The yard and rooms were empty. All the furniture, pictures on the wall, even the wooden frames of windows and doors, vehicles in the yard, and horses in the stable were gone. Worse, the thieves defecated everywhere in the yard.

On a section of the whitewashed wall, a crude message challenged Brother Su and Ceo-lian to go to Ta-hon Mountain. It read, *'Su the Bully, Yu Ceo-lian the Wanton Woman, dare you meet me at Ta-hon Mountain. Choose to be heroes and come, or to be chickens and stay home. Tiger Jao'.* Brother Su scrubbed the words off with his saber and said, "Sister, I'll leave immediately."

"Ah! The bandit leader, Nin, gathered more than a hundred desperadoes." Wei said.

Brother Su galloped to the west toward the Ta-hon Mountain alone. He left the package of silver Dae Wu handed him when they left Beijing and also the silver they found in Chen's saddlebag. Ceo-lian gave Brother Wei one hundred and fifty ounces of silver. She said, "I should not have trusted Yan Bo's word completely. Hope this silver will help you fix the building and start a hotel business. I'll leave for Ta-hon Mountain tomorrow."

"*Sister*, I heard that 'Tiger Jao' left some of his henchmen behind to harm me. I hope you can stay a couple of days, but I'm worried about Brother Su, too."

"If they have planned anything, it will be for tonight." Ceo-lian said.

Ceo-lian carefully sewed the pearls inside the lining of her undershirt. Then, she cleaned the blades of her saber with a piece of silk. She felt uneasy and restless and Lee Mo-bai's voice flashed through her mind. '*We have to be on our guard at all hours.*' Her tears came and she thought, '*Where are you? Lee Mo-bai, I miss you. I'm not hoping that you may marry me anymore. I'll be happy with just knowing you care and are around.*'

Loud dog barks sounded and there came four men. Ceo-lian wounded two and said, "We won't kill you, Take the wounded ones with you. Tell Tiger Jao that I'm the one who wounded you. He's no hero if he dares not challenge me directly. Get out."

Ceo-lian was ready to go, Brother Wei said, "It's overcast and it looks like it will rain. But, you better leave soon. I'm worried about Brother Su."

"I may go directly to Kaifeng and then Beijing from there. Send word to my home in Lu Town or Dae Wu's in Beijing if you need anything."

A few pedestrians walked with their heads lowered against the cold wind and drizzle. Ceo-lian rode with cheerfully mood, *'Lee Mo-bai is alive. Yan Bo is no evil. A hope of recovering all the missing pearlsand return them to the palace, and Dae Wu's name would be cleared.'*

"Did you see a tall, dark-complexioned, and robust man of his thirties pass by the last few days?" Ceo-lian asked a waiter.

"A lot of men who fit your description passed through."

Ceo-lian finished eating and left. She did not notice two men leaving immediately after her. The cold wind whistled with sand and dirt flying. Ta-ho Mountain Range lay ahead like a dirty yellow dragon. Turning a corner, she saw another lone rider ahead of her. She pushed her mount but soon she lost sight of the rider and she regretted that she was not riding her black champion mare.

The drizzle turned into heavy rain and the wind turned colder. Ceo-lian stopped at a dilapidated house. A man opened the gate and let Ceo-lian in. He said, "Come in, Miss, stay with us and share our poor food." He stared at her horse and weapons.

Ceo-lian cautioned herself that this man might be a thief. The house is very close to the mountain. On her second thought that she might find a clue. It rained even harder, the man said, "Miss, stay here tonight and leave tomorrow when it's clear. Where are you going in this foul weather?"

Ceo-lian replied, "I come to find someone."

The wife said, "Miss, it's not safe to travel alone."

"I'm not afraid. I have sabers and I know how to kill." Ceo-lian said.

The husband said, "You must know martial arts. Last month a woman wearing a red outfit and riding a chestnut mare came into town. She carried a pair of swords. I heard she fights very well."

Ceo-lian never heard of a woman like this. She said, "With so many bandits around, no one is safe without carrying weapons. Someone told me that a tall, husky guard called Su passed through here had been robbed."

"Please don't listen to rumors. I saw the man you mentioned two days ago. He passed the mountain unharmed."

Ceo-lian slept fully clothed. Shortly before dawn, she woke to hushed voices. Poking a hole in the paper window panel with a moistened finger, she peeked. There were five or six armed bandits, with her host among them, were getting ready to attack her.

She chopped two of them down with lightning speed.

"Dare you to ambush me!" The other three ganged upon her. Ceo-lian wounded two more bandits. The last one escaped likes a scared hare.

One dead. Her host had a big gash on his thigh, moaned in pain.

Ceo-lian said, "I saw through you and showed you my sabers deliberately. I better kill you now lest you rob and murder other travelers."

"Miss Yu please spare me. You were spotted and followed after lunch yesterday. If I did not notify them, they would come anyway."

"Tell me what happened to Master Su?"

"Tiger Jao escaped from Jade Town. Master Su chased him here. Amster Su wounded and killed more than fifteen of us before we managed to capture him."

"Did you kill him?"

"No, our chief wants to kill you and him together. He knows that you would come. But, someone rescued Su two nights ago."

"You're lying." Ceo-lian flashed her saber and demanded, "The truth!"

"It's the truth. Someone saved him at night. Filed through the heavy chains we put on Master Su and saved him. Master Su's wounds were not fatal."

Ceo-lian knocked him out with the back of her saber and rode toward the mountain.

11

Yu Ceo-lian rode through the dissipating fog to the mountain. After the rain, the curving narrow mountain path was slippery. The sun broke through the clouds. She spotted a cloister of mud huts half-hidden in a ravine. Twenty-some bandits swamped out of their cave-like shelters and charged at her.

One bandit shouted, "You are a whore, and our leader is waiting to bed you."

Ceo-lian was angry. She rode downward quickly to meet them and fell into a trap. Her sabers, her legs, and the horse dropped in a deep hole with loose rubble. The wounded horse cried pitifully, and the bandits threw stones and dirt or tried to aim their sharp hooks down the deep hole to hit her. She jumped out from the horse's back, seized a staff, and fought with the bandits. Her ankles and legs pained her, so she turned and ran up the steep rocky slope. The bandits shouted, "Come down and fight us. We will give you two sabers. Don't be a coward."

Ceo-lian ignored them and limped painfully back to the house where she stayed last night, thinking that she could find a weapon to use. The yard and the house were empty, but a broken staff remained. Using it as a cane, Ceo-lian walked into the first inn in town. Her clothes dirt-covered, and no luggage. The hotel clerk said, "Miss, you've been robbed! I'll take you to a room."

Ceo-lian said breathlessly, "Thanks, no need to worry; my brother will come for me soon." She immediately sat on the raised warm *kon* (bed) and stretched out her legs.

The manager said, "Miss, You may stay with us as long as you need to rest up. Don't worry about silver. Buddha will bless us if we help our guests in need. We will bring you meals and hot water with soothing herbs to bathe your legs. I have some ointment too."

"You're very kind. Twenty bandits robbed me of my weapon, horse. I will ask your local security station to help me."

The hotel manager shook his head, went out to look around to make sure there was no one. He whispered, "Miss, rest well and leave town as soon as possible. We'll even help you with some silver. We have two security stations, and all the guards are in league with the bandits. The bandit leader calls himself a 'Lord,' and the villagers are all bandits. Even the authorities have their eyes closed."

The herbs and ointment helped her legs. The following day, she went out. It was a market day. There were some axes, sickles for sale. She could use an ax or a sickle to fight the bandits, but she had no silver besides the hidden pearls.

-- *"She's coming. Look, 'Red Hornet' is back."*
-- *"She shacks up with a guard called 'Yellow Tiger,' a close friend of 'Tiger Joe' pretty soon, we will have a tiger ranch here. Ha! Ha!"*
-- *"This woman is nothing but a whore. I heard she threw herself at Lee Mo-bai. She lied to her brother Master Lieu that Lee intended to rape her. Lee wounded her brother and seized his super sharp sword, the one that can cut through metals. The monks had to use heavy whips to fight Lee Mo-bai..."*
-- *"I also heard that she begged 'Sword Chen' to marry her, and he refused. She has no shame, that woman! No decent woman will dress the way she does."*

Buyers and sellers ridiculed a pretty young woman dressed in red on a chestnut mare. A pair of swords with red cords hung from the saddle.

Ceo-lian heard the babble and remembered that hateful 'Sword Chen' who had a heavy whip. She smiled and thought, '*The letter in his saddlebag confirmed that Lee Mo-bai is alive.*' She was angry that this woman in red marred Lee Mo-bai's reputation. She thought, '*Her man probably is a bandit anyway. I'll take her swords and horse.*'

Ceo-lian followed the woman in red until there were fewer pedestrians.

"Lee Mo-bai would not have looked at you twice." Ceo-lian taunted her.

"Who are you? You dare ridicule me!"

To Ceo-lian's delight, the woman in red jumped down from her horse, drew her swords, and charged at Ceo-lian. Ceo-lian swiftly overpowered her, seized the swords, and galloped away on the chestnut mare through the gathering crowd.

She reentered the mountain path. Three riders chased after her with threatening shouts. The bandits could not stop her, and she rode right up to the brim of the trap where she fell. She looked down and saw only rubble. The bandits had her sabers and luggage.

The three riders gained on her, and more bandits gathered. Ceo-lian fought them. The bandit leader holding a long, heavy steel rod stopped his men and shouted at Ceo-lian, "It's between you and me. Don't injure my men. They are not fighters."

The three riders also shouted, "Yu Ceo-lian. Give us back the swords and horse."

"Let's fight. The winner will get it all." Ceo-lian showed no fear.

She fought the bandit leader's heavy rod with the borrowed swords. The three guards joined the fight. Like a tigress, Ceo-lian brandished the two swords snakelike and pierced two of them.

"Stop! We admit defeat. Yu Ceo-lian, we will give you back your sabers and a horse, too!" the bandit leader shouted. He ordered one of his men to fetch her luggage and sabers.

"Where is Brother Su? Release him," Ceo-lian demanded.

"He killed ten of my men and then fell into the trap four days earlier. His legs were injured, but he escaped."

Ceo-lian said, "How convincing. I don't believe you."

"It's the truth. Tiger Jao wanted to kill Su, but I wanted to hold him hostage. An old friend of mine, Brother Shih, happened to visit us the next day. He volunteered to guard the prisoner for us. They escaped together. They stole two of my good horses and also some silver. I sent my lieutenants to go after them. If my best lieutenants were here, you wouldn't win."

"Unbelievable lies. What's this Shih's name?" Ceo-lian asked. She remembered Fat Shih and the failed attempt to free the jailed Lee Mo-bai in Beijing three years ago.

"Shih Nin, nicknamed *'Mountain Lizard.'* He is short and fat."

"We also admit defeat. Please give us back Sister Lieu's swords and horse. take care of You have wounded her. Her brother Master Lieu is a man of prominence," the three guards told Ceo-lian.

The bandit came back with her luggage, "Chief, Tiger Jao ran away with her sabers."

"I must have them back. My father specially ordered that pair of sabers for me. Where did Tiger Jao go?" No one answered her. Ceo-lian mounted the chestnut mare again.

"Wait, Miss Yu, give us back Sister Lieu's horse and swords," the three guards yelled.

"I will return them when I get back my own. No sooner."

Back at the inn, her legs and ankles pained her, so she decided to stay another night. The hotel manager bought her more medicated salve. He said "*Miss*, you better leave. They won't let you get away. Two of their best guards are away, and I heard they have sent for their friends to come here to fight you."

"I'm not afraid of them. I will leave tomorrow morning, but no one can scare me away," Ceo-lian replied.

Fat Shih came to visit her in the evening and told her that Brother Su was recuperating at one of his friends' home not far away. Ceo-lian thanked Fat Shih and asked him to tell Brother Su to go back to Beijing afterward. She decided she could function better without the jittery Brother Su. They reminisced and talked about Ceo-lian's present mission.

Fat Shih said, "I knew about Yan Bo and the stolen pearls, but I don't know they kidnapped his sister and killed the old man. I heard that Feng Five hid at Golden Spear Jao's security station at Kaifeng. Jao gathered all his cronies, and bandits to help him to eliminate Lee Mo-bai and you."

Ceo-lian said, "Brother Shih, I'm still here, so why didn't they kill me?"

Fat Shih laughed, "They sure tried, but you are better. Besides, two of their best fighters are away. Be careful, Ceo-lian. They will trail you."

"Thank you. I will be on guard. You're a true brother."

"Ceo-lian, I heard Lee Mo-bai is alive. Monk Pure sent his students out to find him."

Ceo-lian remembered that night Fat Shih, and she tried to free Lee Mo-bai from the jail. She told Fat Shih the letter she found in Chen's luggage confirming that Lee Mo-bai is not dead.

"I'm glad. Mo-bai's skills will be even more advanced. See you soon, Ceo-lian." Fat Shih vanished in the night. Ceo-lian's legs hurt even more the following day when she rode toward Kaifeng. The drizzle and the biting cold wind intensified her discomfort and her feelings of self-pity. Tears rolled down her cheeks. She did not bother to wipe the tears and rode slowly on the nearly empty road. A carriage with blue cloth skirting came from the opposite direction, and the passenger drew the curtain closed. Ceo-lian had a glimpse of the passenger wearing the habit of a Taoist Priest and a pointed hat. She wondered why a Taoist Priest would be shy. Then she assumed that the priest must disapprove of her wearing a short, tight combat suit and riding alone, and she wished again that she were a pampered, protected wife.

On the flat ferry, Ceo-lian stood beside her horse. She felt dizzy from watching the seemingly endless muddy-colored Yellow River. She doubted that Lee Mo-bai could survive after falling in the even mightier Yangtze River. She checked into the first inn after the crossing.

"Miss, you probably are not used to riding. I'll bring medicated hot water for you to soothe your legs with." She sat on the warm *kon* (bed) and rubbed her sore legs.

"Thank you. How far is Kaifeng from here?" Ceo-lian asked.

"Not far, a day's ride if you ride fast. We have noodle soup and fresh fish."

"Bring me some. Tomorrow, I'd like to have a simple breakfast early."

Ceo-lian thought about the kidnapped Yan Li-in, who has been with her captors for at least a month. If the girl has a strong character and resisted her fate, she probably was killed. If she were weak and submissive, she would undoubtedly lose her virginity by now.

The hotel clerk coughed outside her window first and knocked.

"Come in," Ceo-lian said.

"Miss, are you Miss Lieu?"

"No, I'm..." Ceo-lian did not want to say her real name, and for a moment she could not think of another name besides her dead fiancé's, "Mrs. Mon of Da-ton. Is this for the register?" Further away from Beijing, most inns did not follow the rule of having the guest register.

"Guard Ton said he recognized the chestnut mare and thought you are its owner, Miss Lieu. I'll tell him that he made a mistake."

Ceo-lian knew someone must recognize the horse. She waited for the impending fight, but everything was peaceful. She slept fully clothed. Suddenly something or someone heavy fell to the ground outside her window. She heard more than one person moan in pain, and another guest yelled, "Thief! Thieves!"

"Who goes there?" and "Who are you?"

Many guests and servants stood around two men on the ground right beneath Ceo-lian's window with their sabers beside them. Ceo-lian was scared stiff. She was not afraid of the two men who came to kill her. She was afraid of the person who helped her and disabled her enemies. This person trailed her without her knowing, and she wondered how long this person had her movements covered. She was also puzzled. The two men were obviously in pain, but no visible wounds and blood showed.

--"You thieves dare come with sabers. You mean to kill, don't you?"
--"Tie them up and hand them to the authorities."
--"Which one of us do you want to rob? To kill?"
--"No blood, but they cannot move. That's odd."

--*"It's 'Tien Hsueh' you don't say that Respectful old Monk Pure caught them! I heard that the old Monk Pure is around here looking for his student, the famous 'Sword Chen.' We better..."*

A hotel clerk said with surprise, "Master Ton, what are you doing here at this hour?"

He told the angry guests, "Honorable guests, they are not thieves. Master Ton is one of the respected guards in town. Please don't kick them anymore." The 'kicks' seemed to loosen the men's stiffness somewhat. Ton sat up and shouted, "I'm no thief. I've property in town. Tonight I came here to apprehend a female thief."

Now, everyone stared at the only woman there. Ceo-lian shouted, "I'm the only woman here. How dare you accuse me of being a thief?" She kicked Ton.

Another guest said, "Miss, they fell off the roof, and they are thieves."

Ton sneered, "Yu Ceo-lian, you stole a horse and two swords. You're a thief, and you're a murderer. You killed six men and wounded fifteen men. Two of the wounded are professional guards and my friends. Your friend disabled us tonight. We admit defeat this time, but sooner or later, we'll kill you."

Everyone stared at her. Ceo-lian replied, "Come after me anytime."

Ceo-lian was wondering who her protector was. She decided, *'It must be 'Sword Chen.' He hopes that I will lead him to Lee Mo-bai somehow. But, his skills are not much better than mine. How could I hear nothing? I must be deadly tired.'* Ceo-lian slept with a happy thought that if 'Sword Chen' wanted her to lead him to Lee Mo-bai, then Lee must be alive. She was afraid that her presence and the incident of the night would reach Kaifeng fast and scare Feng Five away, so she left before dawn.

Ceo-lian ate at a food stall and saw a carriage with blue cloth skirting parked outside another inn. At first, she thought that it was odd that the same carriage she saw yesterday on the other side of the Yellow River had followed her here. Then she blamed her vivid imagination and thought, *'I'm sure paranoid now. Most carriages around here all look alike. They all have the blue cloth skirting.'*

She ignored the dull pain of her legs and pushed on, and got to Kaifeng soon. Someone told her that Golden Spear Jao had two security stations in town. The one close to the East Gate was his residence, and all the guards stayed at the bigger one near the North Gate, just an arrow's away from the inn she is staying in.

A huge white silk banner with black trimming and 'Victorious Golden Spear Jao Un-jing' embroidered in red hanged across the gate of the security station. Two clerk-typed persons met Ceo-lian and giggled, "Miss Lieu, how come you're not wearing red today. Don't tell me 'Yellow Tiger' wore you out. *Ha! Ha!*"

"You have made a mistake. I'm here to see Master Feng Five from Beijing," Ceo-lian replied, but the clerks kept on looking at the chestnut mare and the swords with the red cord.

"Sorry, we thought you're Miss Lieu. I'll go in and ask," one said.

A moment later, Ho chi (seven) came out and rushed back in again. Ceo-lian recognized him and called, "Wait. Brother Ho, I'm not here to fight you. I'm here to catch Feng Five."

Ho chi (seven) came out again with his brother Ho sam (three). Ho sam (three) pleaded, "Miss Yu, please let go of our animosity. Your father killed my daddy but we did not kill your father. You already wounded my sister and killed Uncle Mew. Are you not satisfied? We know we're not your match, but we'll fight you anyway if we have to."

Ceo-lian sighed, "I agree that we better let the past sleep. I'm here to catch Feng Five. He killed a crippled old man and kidnapped a young woman in Beijing."

Ho sam (three) said with genuine sincerity, "Thank you for letting the past rest. We all know of Feng Five's criminal behavior. He came here to ask my brother-in-law to shield him from your pursuit. He and Jao left Kaifeng two days ago, and they probably will be back soon. We'll help you to catch him. I promise."

"I'll stay and wait. But, if I know you two help him to escape, I will not let you get away without a scratch," Ceo-lian said.

"We won't help them. To tell you the truth, we, my brother and me, would like to see Golden Spear's downfall. He has concubines, and he does not treat my sister well. He looks down upon us and belittles us often," Ho sam (three) said.

More travelers checked into the inn where Ceo-lian was staying the next day. A long-robed Taoist priest stood talking with a clerk in front of a room. On seeing Ceo-lian, the Taoist priest turned around and entered the room quickly. She did not have a good look at the Taoist Priest, but she wondered whether that's the same shy one she met before.

"Miss Yu, Feng five must have sold the girl," Ho Three told her, "He came here with silver, and my brother-in-law treated him royally and let him disparage us. He's indeed out of town, but he probably will be back tomorrow. Golden Spear Jao married my sister and used my family's wealth to run the security stations. He treats us shabbily. I tell you this because I want you to believe my sincerity. Beware of Golden Spear Jao! He plots to destroy you. He gathers many friends to help him kill you and Lee Mo-bai. He hates Lee Mo-bai the most, not only because Lee almost killed him three years ago. Jao slept with most of Dart Mew's concubines, but Violet despised him, and later she loved Lee Mo-bai." The outspoken Ho sam (three) did not consider Ceo-lian's sensibility.

At midnight, Ceo-lian went out of her room holding one sword. The whole hotel was dark but the Taoist priest's room. Ceo-lian saw the silhouette of a man writing through the paper window panels. She shook off her feeling of Déjà vu and went on to scrutinize Jao's security station from the rooftop and saw nothing suspicious. She recalled that four years ago when Lee Mo-bai escorted her to Da-ton, she had sneaked by Lee Mo-bai's hotel room while he was writing. Her tears blurred her vision and she wondered when she would see Lee Mo-bai again. A sound on the roof of her room jerked Ceo-lian awake from her reverie. She was on the roof and thrust a sword forward but stopped when she heard, "Hold it, Sister Ceo-lian, I'm Ho Su-an. My brother told me that you forgo the animosity between our families. I come here with good intentions."

"I am not your sister. Get lost," Ceo-lian said.

"Please help me kill Jao. I'll help you catch Feng five."

"What, you want your husband dead?" Ceo-lian shouted in surprise.

"Miss Yu, my husband has many women and treats me and my brothers like dirt. The other day he raped one of my maids in front of me. He, Feng Five, and others insult my brothers often. We need your help to get back my family's property. Our fathers were sworn brothers, so we are practically sisters. Please help us."

"I don't want to have any part in it. You better leave."

"I will. Yu Ceo-lian, my husband, hates you. I warn you that he plots to ruin you. When you fight my husband, my brothers and I will be on your side."

"I don't need your help. Leave now."

She thought about Lee Mo-bai as usual. Lee's image came to her more sharply that night. She also thought about the shy Taoist priest. His height and the way he stood looked familiar. She shook her head and told herself that it was impossible and she had imagined too much.

"I saw a Taoist priest in the other court yesterday. Why would a priest not stay at a temple? He must be rich." Ceo-lian asked the clerk casually the following day.

"Priest Cao has a horse and a tea plantation in the South. He left before dawn." The clerk smiled at Ceo-lian. He must have wondered why a young woman would show so much interest in a Taoist priest.

"You say his surname is Cao, not Yu. I thought he might be my distant cousin who entered the priesthood. My aunt is worried about him," Ceo-lian said in the way of explanation. She felt somewhat disappointed that the priest had left.

"Do you know whether that famous guard Golden Spear is in town?" Ceo-lian asked again when the same clerk brought her breakfast.

"He and a couple of our guests went to the rich Master Tu's birthday party, a yearly event around here."

"Thank you." Ceo-lian decided to rest her sore legs for a day.

At nightfall, just when Ceo-lian prepared to scrutinize the security station again, She-Devil came and told her nervously, "Sister Ceo-lian, they are back and hiding at another house of ours. They plan to attack you."

"Where is the other house?" Ceo-lian asked.

"I'm here to fetch you. They are drinking at their favorite prostitutes' place now. Take your weapons and come with me, and we'll wait and ambush them."

"Tell me where the house is. I'll find it." Ceo-lian did not trust her.

"The house is outside of East Gate, and it's quite far from here. I've got a carriage waiting. We better hurry. The East Gate will be closed soon," She-Devil urged Ceo-lian.

A banquet with only two seats in a spacious room. She-Devil invited Ceo-lian to have a drink, "They won't be back so soon. You know how men are with prostitutes. I'd like to celebrate our renewed friendship. I'm so glad that we're no longer enemies, Sister Ceo-lian."

"It's karma. We cannot change the past and bring the dead back to life," Ceo-lian sighed.

"Sister Ceo-lian, a toast to seal our friendship" She-Devil raised her cup.

Ceo-lian raised the cup and pretended to sip the wine, "Pardon me, I hardly drink." She looked around and thought she saw another room behind an elaborately carved wood screen.

"Is there another room behind the screen?" she asked.

"Yes, it's cooler to sleep there in the summer," *She-Devil* held the chopsticks a while before she answered.

They talked. Two huge candles burned nearly halfway and it was pitch dark outside. Ceo-lian said impatiently, "It's late, and they probably won't be back tonight. I better leave."

"You're not afraid of the dark, are you? Who knows when we will meet again? Stay a bit longer. Both of us are lonely," She-Devil said.

Suddenly the sounds of weapons clashing and wounded men's moaning came from the room behind the lattice. She-Devil turned pale and yelled, "What's happening?"

"You tricked me here and set up an ambush, didn't you? Move forward!" Ceo-lian thrust the point of her sword against She-Devil's back and ordered. She also took a candle.

Two men were on the floor amongst the toppled furniture and broken weapons. The cold night air blew in from the open window. One man died, and Ceo-lian thought the fatally wounded one must be Golden Spear Jao. She immediately killed him and shouted,

"You faked our friendship and set up a trap. Where can you run?" She pierced She-Devil on her shoulder. Before Ceo-lian could deliver the final thrust, someone called her from outside the window, "Get out of here fast."

Ceo-lian jumped out of the open window and got a glimpse of a shadow upon the opposite roof.

"Who are you? Why are you helping me?" Ceo-lian found no one. She scanned around and was at a loss at what direction she should take when she heard the shouts of soldiers. "Thief, a woman thief."

"Hurry, don't let the soldiers catch you." The voice came from three houses away.

Ceo-lian dashed in that direction and asked, "Who are you? Wait. Please help me again. Are you...?"

"Tomorrow at dawn, you will find Feng Five at White Temple, ten miles south of the South Gate." The slightly Southern Chinese accented voice trailed away and led her to a lower section of the city wall. She jumped down and nearly fell. The shadowy figure ahead turned around. It seemed that he was concerned. Ceo-lian stood up, and the man faded into the night again.

"Wait, Lee Mo-bai...Brother Lee...?" Ceo-lian shouted but no reply.

Her heart pounded loudly. Ceo-lian realized that she could be killed if she loses, or got caught for murder and buggery if she wins. She trudged back to her hotel room with a happy thought and murmured to her imaginary listener, *'You don't want to face me. Are you afraid that seeing me may cause you to weaken your resolution to be a Taoist priest? You shadowed me and protected me. If this is the game you want to play, I'll gladly oblige you,'* Ceo-lian was not quite sure of her assumption. She wished that she could know for sure.

Ceo-lian prayed to her deceased parents that she now successfully avenged their murderers. She killed Dart Mew three years ago, and she killed Golden Spear Jao and wounded She-Devil tonight.

She rushed to White Temple and saw nothing but tombs through the dense fog the following day. Then she heard, "Mercy! Help me!"

"Who are you?" Ceo-lian followed the voice and found a man lying by the roadside. The man kept quiet.

Ceo-lian caught on and asked, "You are Feng Five, aren't you? Tell me the truth!"

"You must be Yu Ceo-lian. Please spare me. I did not kill the old man in Beijing. The elder Tan brother did. Golden Spear Jao and his wife She-Devil plotted to trap you last night. I warned them and tried to stop them. They wouldn't listen, and I hid at a pimp's home. A man caught me, tied me up, and threw me here."

"Do you know the man who captured you?" Ceo-lian asked.

"No, he only asked for my name once. He sounded a little like a Southerner. Is he the Sword Chen? I heard he wants to marry you."

"Are you sure your captor is not Lee Mo-bai?" Holding her breath, Ceo-lian waited.

"I don't think so. My captor is huskier and definitely unlike the skinny and soft Lee Mo-bai. Tan brothers told me that Lee Mo-bai drowned."

"Is the Yan girl dead? The truth!"

"She's alive. I sold her to Master Kim, South of Ba-tin. You and Brother Su were hard on my tail. I had to sell her for less."

"Tell me exactly the location of her new home. NOW!"

"About forty *li* (miles) south of Ba-tin. It's a huge villa with tall trees around and besides a small creek. Please spare me."

"You have to be punished for your atrocity." Ceo-lian killed him

She decided to go back to make sure that Brother Wei's hotel business was fine and then visited the kidnapped Yan girl at her new master's home before returning to Beijing. Ceo-lian could not push her mount forward. Her legs and ankles hurt her less than her feelings of self-doubt, disappointment, and destitution. The cruel realization that she could neither kill her father's murderer Jao, Golden Spear, nor find out where Feng Five was without assistance from her mysterious protector. Besides, if her protector was Lee Mo-bai, why did he not talk to her? Of course, she understood that Lee Mo-bai was now a wanted criminal, but he had ample chances to communicate with her secretly. Thinking about the letter in which her dying mother requested Lee Mo-bai to marry her, she regretted again that she could not let go of her shyness, jealousy and show it to Dae Wu. Lee Mo-bai would marry her out of honor even though he might not wholeheartedly in love with her. Then he would not have killed Thin Buddha Hwang. He would not have to become a wanted criminal, and he would not be forced down the boat and drowned.

Brother Wei's hotel business was prosperous. A chiropractor treated her injured legs and ankles. Ceo-lian decided to have a good rest before returning to Beijing. Also, she even could not explain to herself whether she was waiting for someone or something to happen soon.

Two days later, a boisterous Fat Shih came with her ill-tempered Brother Su.

Brother Wei welcomed them and went out to order a banquet, but then he came back in a flash holding a pair of sabers, Ceo-lian's missing sabers.

"A Taoist priest stopped me and asked me to give them to you after he confirmed that I'm your Brother ... Wait, Ceo-lian, What's wrong?"

Ceo-lian rushed out, but she soon came back.

"What's wrong, Ceo-lian? He could not be an enemy, couldn't he?"

"What does the Taoist priest look like? Is he young? Is he tall?" Ceo-lian asked quickly.

"He's taller than me but shorter than Brother Su. Ceo-lian, *what's* wrong? He looks like a scholar, and he is very polite. He would not tell me his name and said that he wanted to return your missing sabers and then walked away swiftly. Ceo-lian, he knows you. Is he an official detective traveling incognito and has something to do with the pearls?"

"I... don't think so. I... never mind, I'm glad to have my sabers back," Ceo-lian said and sat in a stupor.

"Ceo-lian, how could you, a proper woman, befriend a Taoist priest?" Brother Su complained as usual.

Fat Shih and Brother Wei exchanged unsettled looks. Fat Shih left, a strange and purposeful look on his face. Fat Shih found two of his trusted men, and he also met by chance 'Little Snake', his long time trusted underling in Beijing who knows Lee Mo-bai by sight. They found out which hotel the Taoist priest is staying at and set a trap. Three of them made catcalls from the rooftop, got the Taoist priest away from his room. Fat Shih sneaked into the priest's room and found a package on the bed with some silver and books, secular clothes, and a Taoist priest's long robe.

Fat Shih chuckled, "I'm glad. Not a real priest. You can surely marry Ceo-lian now."

A shadow came into the room, punched Fat Shih on the bed, grabbed the luggage, and left. Fat Shih was satisfied. He did not tell anyone, even his trusted men, his discovery.

Ceo-lian wanted to go back to Beijing alone. Brother Wei advised that she should wait for the nearly recovered Brother Su to accompany her. Ceo-lian indicated that she preferred traveling alone. Fat Shih smiled and said, "No need to worry. A guardian will see to it that Ceo-lian meets no danger."

Brother Wei complained, "Brother Shih, be serious. Enemies are awaiting Ceo-lian everywhere."

Fat Shih only laughed louder.

12

Ceo-lian had on new warmer clothes and a hooded cape when she set out alone to Beijing. Somehow she felt lethargic, and a deep melancholy seized her. She felt so alone. Lee Mo-bai's sword and the note that Chiang Nan-ho had put beside her pillow had sustained her with expectation for two long years. Chiang Nan-ho had given her the sword as a marriage token from Lee Mo-bai. She hoped that one day Lee Mo-bai would obey Uncle Chiang's wish and marry her. Then the news of Lee Mo-bai's drowning shocked her into despair. Now she was sure that Lee Mo-bai's alive. But why didn't he come forward to see her and talk to her? She thought, '*Am I that ugly and ignorant that he does not want to marry me? I am certain that he loved me very much when he escorted my mother and me on the long trip to Da-ton. Mrs. Dae Wu thought that the prostitute Violet was a replacement for me, too. When and why did he change his mind? Does he not love me enough to marry me? He's avoiding me, and it hurts.*' The passing brownish empty fields and the leafless trees mirrored her desolation.

She crossed the Yellow River, passed Kaifeng, and rode to Master Kim's villa south of Ba-tin. A well-mannered servant took her to an elegantly furnished study where she met Master Kim and his mother. Ceo-lian told them that Yan Li-in was kidnapped. The dignified old woman said, "We bought her last month, and she is still intact, and we like her very much. But, you have the right to take her home with you."

Ceo-lian said, "You are very generous. Why did you buy her?"

Madam Kim looked at her son and said, "My son's wife is dying. My son has been married for nine years, and they don't have any children. Yan Li-in is a beautiful girl. We bought her to be my son's wife. My son will formerly marry her when …" She sighed and then continued, "My daughter-in-law likes the girl, too."

Kim looked like an older version of Lee Mo-bai. He has the same sad eyes and the same scholarly look. He said, "The doctor told us that my wife would die soon. I honor my wife, and I won't take a concubine. Later, I'll marry and cherish Yan Li-in. But, you do have the right to take her back to her home."

Ceo-lian said, "Actually, she has no home to go back to. Their parents were murdered. The kidnappers killed the old man who had raised them. Her brother left home. Her younger sister is staying with my friend in Beijing. I want to ask her whether she wants to stay with you or not. I do believe you'll treat her with decency if she wishes to stay. Can I have a moment alone with her?"

Madam Kim said, "Certainly. I have only one son, and I would like to have a daughter. I hope she'd like to be my son's wife. Should I call her here to meet you, or would you rather go to her room to see her?"

Ceo-lian wanted to see the way Yan Li-in lives. She replied, "Please take me to her room."

A maid took Ceo-lian to a nicely decorated room. Ceo-lian was surprised to see that Yan Li-in was a well-mannered, elegantly but not over a fancily dressed beautiful girl. She noticed the resemblance among the siblings and thought, '*Ahe! The three of them are all very good-looking. Their mother must be a beauty.*' She said, "I'm Yu Ceo-lian, your sister Li-fon calls me Aunt Yu. Lee Mo-bai is my sworn brother. I'll take you home if you don't want to stay here with Master Kim." The girl blushed and told Ceo-lian that they had treated her very well and she would like to stay with them. She said, "Master Kim teaches me how to read and write. Madame Kim thinks and treats me as her daughter. I'd like to stay," she sobbed, "Aunt Yu, they killed Grandpa, They tied me up, put me in a carriage, and some time put me in a locked room…" She sobbed, "Madame Kim's very kind to me. How is my sister? Li-fon is so little."

"Li-fon came to me and asked me to find you. She is staying with my good friend Master Dae Wu in Beijing. I also met your brother, but I did not have a chance to talk to him. Do you know where your brother stole…the…valuables from?"

"He told me that it was from a big house in Beijing where he often went to sell flowers to the maids. I don't know the location. Wait, he said that the maids there all have small feet."

"I'm glad that you have a good home. I'll bring Li-fon here to see you sometime. Take care." The girl sobbed.

Madam Kim said, "I'm glad she likes to stay with us. If her sister wants to live with us, we'll welcome her, and we'll see to it that she will have a good marriage, too."

Mrs. Dae Wu told her that she would like to have Li-fon be her first son's wife. Ceo-lian was happy that both of the Yan girls would have a good home. If she could find Yan Bo in time, they would have a brother. She sighed, '*I have no one, and Lee Mo-bai is avoiding me.*'

It was not too much out of her way for her to go home first and then to Beijing. She missed the black mare. In her mind, the horse provided her with the only tangible connection to the two men in her life: Mon Zhi-an and Lee Mo-bai. Mon Zhi-an passed away, and Lee Mo-bai was ever elusive. She could not get either of them out of her mind. She was tired of traveling and fighting, and she decided that she would stay home for a while to rest and sort out her confused feelings. Three years ago, she killed Dart Mew and then repelled the Ho brothers when they sneaked into Dae Wu's home at night. She was rather proud and thought her fighting skills were superior to a lot of others. But now, she realized that she would need to learn more. Since she left Beijing, she met Sword Chen, who was better than her, and then she and Brother Su together had a hard time fighting Saber King, Feng Four. Yan Bo could defeat her, and her secret protector possessed higher skills.

She and Mrs. Han sew new clothes and shoes for her during the day, and she practiced martial arts at night. She practiced 'dart-throwing.' Lee Mo-bai had taught her how to throw a handful of pebbles, and now she wanted to throw steel darts, which would supplement her lack of strength and increase her odds of winning. A blacksmith made some slender and sharp darts small enough to hold two of them in her palm. She also had a leather pouch, which she could hide under her top. With her sabers belted on her back, she practiced throwing two darts in quick succession at the targets on foot and horseback. In a few days, she became good at it.

One night, she had a visitor, an injured man fell off his horse at the gate of her home. It was Sword Chen, the Southern swordmaster she disliked. Chen lost his left arm and part of his left shoulder.

Chen told Ceo-lian, "I will die soon. I came to warn you that my Teacher and others are on their way here to capture you to draw Lee Mo-bai out in the open."

Ceo-lian asked, "Brother Chen, who did this to you?"

"Monk Ta, my classmate. I found out that he is the one who convinced my Teacher and everyone that Lee Mo-bai stole the manual. He is my Teacher's favorite student, but he is wicked behind my Teacher's back. My Teacher taught him and Monk Guo' *Tien Hsueh*'. Our Teacher ordered Monk Guo to safeguard the manual. Monk Ta coveted the manual, and he was killing Monk Guo with some slow-acting poison. Monk Guo knew it. Monk Guo gave Lee Mo-bai the manual because he did not want the wicked Monk Ta to learn it well and use the deadly skills to do evil. Monk Guo died ten days ago. He told me the truth before he died. I told my Teacher, but he did not want to believe it, and he insisted that Lee Mo-bai stole the manual. Monk Ta '*Tien Hsueh*' me and wounded me. My Teacher wants to capture you…" Chen died.

Ceo-lian told Brother Han, "They are after me. If I stay, you all will be in danger." She left for Beijing immediately. She was very afraid of the monks' '*Tien Hsueh*' techniques. She wanted to run to Ba-tin to ask Saber King to help her, or at least she could hide in Feng Four's big villa for a while. She hoped Lee Mo-bai would come to help her. She thought, '*Lee Mo-bai is not a thief. He had the manual for two years, and now he must know how to 'Tien Hsueh.' Maybe he is afraid of the monks, and that's why he did not want to talk to me.*' Somehow she felt better knowing her hero Lee Mo-bai was not a thief.

Before she could reach Ba-tin Town, the first snow turned into a blizzard. She was lost and stopped at a house. The old man kindly let her stay for the night. It snowed even harder the next day, and she had to stay longer. There were only two sleeping rooms, the old man and his son slept in one room, Ceo-lian, the old woman, and her daughter-in-law crowded into the smaller room. They were very kind to her. When Ceo-lian told them her identity and the old man seemed not surprised. Ceo-lian felt uneasy.

The old man told her, "Miss Yu, I know of you and Lee Mo-bai. You're heroes. When I was young, I used to work at a security company in Ba-tin Town, and now I still have some connection. I also know of your father, the famous '*Iron Wings.*' I heard that the monks are looking for you at Ba-tin. They said you killed one of Monk Pure's secular students, Sword Chen, and they want to kill you. You're safe here. Besides, no one can go out for a couple of days. My son has to stay home, too."

The son added, "They are waiting to rob Yan Bo, too."

Monk Ta is rapacious. He is Feng Five's friend. They said that you killed Feng Five. He told Feng Four, Saber King, and tried to get him to fight you. Feng Four refused.

Ceo-lian said, "Feng Four is a righteous man. I did not kill Chen. Monk Ta did. I'm afraid of Monk Pure's '*Tien Hsueh*', which he seems to use at liberty. But, I must find Yan Bo and save him." She then told them the tragedy of Yan Bo's family.

The old man said, "We know some of it. When it's clear, let my son go to Ba-tin first to get more information for you."

The snowstorm turned into icy rains. It was not safe to travel. Two days later, the son ventured into Ba-tin Town. He came back with the news that the old Monk Pure was sick and turned back to the South. Monk Ta and the other greedy roughnecks had waylaid Yan Bo. Yan Bo was severely wounded because Monk Ta had '*Tien Hsueh*' him, and the others knifed him. Two of Yan Bo's brothers died. A Taoist priest came, fought the gang off, and carried the wounded Yan Bo away. The monks are looking for them.

Ceo-lian thought, '*It's Lee Mo-bai, all right. Why did he have to hide his identity?*' She asked the old man, "How old is this Monk Pure? He sounds like a superb martial arts master."

"Indeed he is. Monk Pure is about seventy years old. He met Chiang Nan-ho when they were teenagers. They are friends. Monk Pure is famous for his unique '*Tien Hsueh*' techniques. He taught many students. Two of the good ones are not monks. I heard that Yan Bo impaired one, and the other one was Sword Chen. Old Monk Pure enjoys being flattered and cannot stand for anyone more famous than him." The old man added, "His favorite student Monk Ta gets his ear completely. Behind his Teacher's back, Monk Ta is an incarnation of greed and evil."

The son said, "You and Lee Mo-bai are their arch enemies. They want to kill you. I dare not ask too many questions lest I lead them to you. Someone also said that old Monk Pure might feign sickness to trick you. The majority believes that the old Monk was not here. They thought that the Taoist priest could not get away if the old Monk were here. I'll go back to Ba-tin and try to find more news."

Ceo-lian asked, "What does Monk Ta look like?"

"He is of average height, but he looks square in the shoulders and thick around the middle. His weapon is a thin foot-long steel rod with a spiky point. He uses it to '*Tien Hsueh*' instead of pointing two fingers at the opponents."

"Did you hear anything about Lee Mo-bai?" Ceo-lian asked again.

"Not really. The same old news said Lee Mo-bai and Yan Bo are the same person." Ceo-lian thought, '*I'll keep moving fast and I won't give my enemy a chance to be close to me. Of course, I'll try to block Monk Ta's steel rod.*'

She asked her host, "Uncle, have you heard of any ways to avoid '*Tien Hsueh*?"

"Someone said that if one were hit, or a near thing, one should roll away fast. The rolling movements can prevent or loosen the effect of the attack. The danger of it is that the person rolling on the ground is defenseless." He added,

"A man could do it easily. It is not proper and convenient for a woman to do so." Ceo-lian decided that she would keep moving fast to avoid being hit.

Ceo-lian was anxious to find Yan Bo and to recover the missing pearls. She wanted to visit Feng Four, Saber King, and tell him that Lee Mo-bai did not steal the manual. Feng Four might have some news about Lee Mo-bai. Something inside her pushed her hard to find Lee Mo-bai. It was a treacherous ride. She stopped at Ba-tin Town to eat. Besides the usual stares she received for being a lone woman with weapons, no one harassed her.

In late afternoon, Ceo-lian arrived at the outskirts of Feng Four's huge villa. There the monks waylaid her. Five monks attacked her. Ceo-lian rode fast and threw the steel darts quickly and hit two of them before her horse bolted. She jumped down from the horse and brandished her two sabers to block the attacks from all directions. She spotted Monk Ta holding a steel rod, and he tried to '*Tien Hsueh*' her. She moved swiftly and wounded two other monks. Monk Ta tried to attack her from behind, but Ceo-lian twirled around and chopped at Monk Ta's steel rod. An old, short monk silently came from nowhere and applied '*Tien Hsueh*' to her leg. She fell. Monk Ta hit her forehead. Feng Four's tenants and fighters came, "Stop! We'll call the law." The monks escaped before they could carry the inert Ceo-lian away.

When Ceo-lian came to, Lee Mo-bai was massaging her forehead. Feng Four was rotating her leg.

"Sister, don't talk. Close your eyes and try to relax. Breathe in slowly and hold it, then released it gradually." Ceo-lian felt his strong fingers, and she was so happy, and her tears came. Lee Mo-bai continued, "You have been out three days. Monk Pure could have killed you. I don't know why he changed his mind and did not attack your 'death cavity'. I rescued Yan Bo took him to a deserted temple. Yesterday I carried Yan Bo here to seek Feng Four's help."

Feng Four added, "Miss Yu, I heard about the Monk's scheme of robbing Yan Bo of the precious pearls. When my greedy brother, Feng Three, came to me and tried to talk me into robbing Yan Bo, I refused. Then I heard that Brother Lee did not die, and the monks wanted to kidnap you to draw Brother Lee out. I told my men to be on alert. We saved you in time. We also get your mare."

Ceo-lian managed to tell them that Yan Li-in will marry a very decent man, and Yan Li-fon will marry Dae Wu's son. Yan Bo could die any moment, and he should know that both his sisters would be with good families.

"Sister, I'm going to put you into a deep sleep. Don't worry. You'll be all right." Lee Mo-bai said. Ceo-lian slept with a smile on her face.

Lee Mo-bai looked at her and thought, '*She is still in love with me. Somehow I just do not want to marry her after the death of Mon Zhi-an. I love Violet. I cannot get Violet out of my mind. I am afraid that the shadows of Mon Zhi-an and Violet will stay between us if I ever marry Ceo-lian. The saying' time will cure everything' does not work for me here. I'm confused, and I cannot get rid of my guilt, remorse, and love for Violet... Oh! What can I do? How can I let her know that I care for her very much but don't want to marry her?*'

Feng Four said, "Brother Lee, a man should be strong enough to forget and forgive. I'd like to see you forget the past and forgive yourself for Brother Mon's untimely death. You and Miss Yu will make a nice couple. I'm your friend, and I'm outspoken."

"Brother Feng, you're a true friend. What you just said is right and true, but I'm sorry that I just cannot do it. I care for Yu Ceo-lian very much, but I think of her only as my sister now. You know about Violet. I still have strong feelings for Violet. Sometimes I'm confused, too. Please also forgive me for catching your brother Feng Five, and Ceo-lian killed him. It is the truth, and I'd like you to know."

Feng Four sighed, "My brother Feng Five is a bad lot. Our family is rich; one of our ancestors was a very successful silk and fabric merchant. We don't need to work for a living. But my brothers are greedy and wicked. They had never helped me manage the estate, and they harassed and terrorized the neighbors with the family wealth. I chased them out. You and Yu Ceo-lian have the right to kill Feng Five for his atrocity. I'm sad about his death, but I'm your friend."

"Thank you very much." Lee Mo-bai bowed very low.

They went to the secret room in the servants' quarter to see the fatally wounded Yan Bo. Two doctors, who had treated Ceo-lian and were Feng Four's trusted friends, shook their heads. One of them said, "It's no use. The wounds are too many and too deep; he had lost too much blood. He is hanging on. He must have some unfinished and important matters on his mind."

Lee Mo-bai bent down and said, "Yan Bo, Aunt Yu is here. She is sleeping off her serious injuries right now. She will come to see you soon. She said that your sister Yan Li-in would be a very nice man's wife, not a concubine. Li-fon will marry Dae Wu's on. Aunt Yu killed the kidnapper."

Yan Bo said weakly, "Great. I want to tell you," then he indicated that Lee Mo-bai should bend down closer to his mouth, and he whispered. "Li-fon has them. Hu (Tiger) a brother..." He died.

Ceo-lian slept a long time. After she heard Yan Bo's death, she sighed, "Poor Yan Bo. You know they are orphans. Their parents' murderers are still at large. At least the two girls all have good homes." She sighed and continued, "Yan Bo is dead because he needed silver for revenge. It's too bad. He learned martial arts so well." They buried Yan Bo quietly at a corner of Feng Four's property.

Lee Mo-bai took Feng Four into his confidence and told him and Ceo-lian where the missing pearls are.

Ceo-lian said, "Brother Dae Wu had been jailed and exiled for four pearls. The officials confiscated four of them from one of the pawnshops at Ba-tin. Yan_Bo's friend gave me four. There should be thirty-six pearls in Beijing at Dae Wu's home. Brother Lee, we better go back to Beijing right away. I'm fine now. We must return the pearls to the palace to clear Brother Dae Wu's name."

Feng Four said, "My men reported to me that the monks are still looking for both of you everywhere. They came to my house to ask about you. My men politely but firmly turned them away. I also think you two should go back to Beijing to finish the business of the pearls. I advise you to leave here soon. I know Brother Lee is not afraid of fighting them. But it will cause more delay. I'm honored that you have taken me into your confidence. I have so many servants, and the news of Yan Bo's death will eventually get out. Then everyone would rush here to find the missing pearls. I'm not afraid of fighting them off, but it sure causes_more delay and trouble for you."

Lee Mo-bai said, "Brother Feng, you're right. I think I'll go to Beijing first. Miss Yu should not travel so soon."

Feng Four said, "It will be conspicuous for a Taoist priest, and a young woman with weapons travel together. Sister Yu is welcome to stay here as long as she needs to. My wife will keep her company."

Lee Mo-bai said, "I'd like to tell both of you that I did not steal the '*Tien Hsueh*' manual."

Both Feng Four and Ceo-lian said at the same time, "I know."

"How did you know?"

Ceo-lian said first, "The Southerner Sword Chen came to warn me that they are after me. He told me before he died…" She told them Chen came to her home at Lu Town with blood all over him and told her everything.

"Yes. Monk Guo did not want the wicked Monk Ta to have the manual. He knew that he would die from the poison, and he gave me the manual," Lee Mo-bai said.

Feng Four said, "We know for a long time that Monk Ta is wicked. The rumor has it that he stole the manual and hid it, and then he accused Brother Lee of stealing."

"Another thing I want you to know that I'm not afraid of Monk Pure now that I learned '*Tien Hsueh*'. I have to disguise my true identity because I do not want to confront the monks. Sister, I did not talk to you because I'm afraid that they will hold you as a hostage to draw me out in the open. I have studied the manual thoroughly for two years now. I'm confident that Monk Pure cannot defeat me anymore." Lee Mo-bai knew that he had not been honest with her and with himself. He was avoiding Ceo-lian. He dreaded facing her after that night two and a half years ago when he was jailed and wanted to die. Ceo-lian told him that she loved him. She said something like this, "*If you die, I will die, too. Without you, I have no life, and I cannot live without you.*"

Feng Four asked, "If you're not afraid of them, why did you not fight them to clear your name? I would."

Lee sighed, "Many times, I wanted to do just that. But, I'm afraid of my Teacher Chiang Nan-ho."

"I thought you are Gi Kon-jii's student."

"He was my first Teacher. Now, Chiang Han-ho teaches me. It's a long story. I did not know any of this until Chiang Nan-ho saved me three years ago."

Ceo-lian asked, "Brother, tell us where you have been the last three years. Will you? I know about the Tan brothers. I know you stayed with Yan Bo's family for a while, and then you also stayed with the Tan brother's family. I had met '*Red Hornet*' the woman others said that she wanted to marry you."

Lee Mo-bai answered, "After I got the manual, I went up to my Teacher's tea farm on Joe-hua Peak to study '*tien hsueh*' from the manual. That's about it. Brother Feng and I would massage your vital points again after lunch. I'll tell you more." He did not want to scare Ceo-lian and tell her that Monk Pure intended to cripple her or even kill her. She may need more than one session of massage. The massage would drain energy from the persons who would do it. He explained to Feng Four clearly, and he was willing to help her. Lee Mo-bai thought, '*I may not be able to leave soon. The monks might be still around, and I have to rest well to fight all of them.*'

Lee Mo-bai sat on the bed and firmly but gently massaged Ceo-lian's forehead. Feng Four sat on a chair next to the bed and moved her legs. Lee Mo-bai said, "Chiang Nan-ho, his name was Chiang Shiao- (small)ho when he was young. He is not only my teacher, but he is also my uncle, too. He is my late father's sworn brother. The three of them, my late father, Master Gi Kon-jii, and Uncle Chiang were friends later. They were enemies when they were young. I did not know anything about the past until I met Brother Ma, who worked at the tea farm. His father raised the orphaned Chiang Nan-ho for a couple of years, and he knows a lot about the tragic love affairs, an eternal triangle, between Chiang Nan-ho, Gi Kon-jii, and the granddaughter of the man who killed Chiang Nan-ho's father."

Feng Four said, "Ah! Now I remember that I heard some elders talk about the legend of the three Wu-ton superior warriors. Was your father Lee Feng-jii?"

"Yes. I lost my parents when I was eight years old. We used to live in Nanjing. I remember that Uncle Chiang taught me how to swim in Yangtze River."

Ceo-lian said, "So you're a good swimmer. That's why you did not drown. Dae Wu was wondering whether you are a good swimmer."

Lee continued, "Uncle Chiang took me to my real uncle at Nan-Kon Village. My uncle did not want me to learn martial arts, and he was rude to Uncle Chiang. Later my uncle wanted my cousin and me to learn some martial arts for self-defense. One year Uncle Chiang met Master Gi Kon-jii, a scholar who knew both martial arts and literary arts well. So they arranged for Master Gi to set up a school close to my home and taught us. I passed the first level of civil examination when I was seventeen. You may have heard that my late father was a poet as well as a Wu-ton school swordmaster."

"Brother, your calligraphy is superb and Mrs. Dae Wu often mentioned that you wrote excellent poems. I wish that I can read well to understand them." Ceo-lian said.

A cloud of sadness washed over Lee Mo-bai when he recalled his time with Violet and the beautiful verses they had composed together. He sighed, "That's the trouble, and I was conceited. Chiang Nan-ho saved me from jail and scolded me for being mixed up with a prostitute, for being proud and showing off my martial arts skills. …anyway, he sent me to visit his good friend Tan first and then Monk Pure." Lee Mo-bai asked Ceo-lian to lie on her stomach and showed Feng Four how to massage the back of her calves. He started to rub the back of Ceo-lian's head.

Feng Four thought, *'Chiang Nan-ho is right to say that Lee Mo-bai is too proud. He defeated my brother and openly challenged me. He was indeed very proud at that time. But I think he has grown out of it now.'*

Lee Mo-bai continued, "Next to Tan's estate, lived a woman who wears red all the time. Everyone called her *'Red Hornet.'* Her brother Lieu Pa-ye wounded my host Tan's elder son. I pierced him and seized 'Green Destiny', a historical famous super sharp sword, which could cut through metal. I went to Nanjing to visit Monk Pure. Uncle Chiang told me to show Monk Pure the highest respect. He wanted me to compare my leanings with Monk

Pure's students. I met Monk Guo, and we became good friends. Monk Pure's father was very nice to uncle Chiang when he was a homeless orphan. Later, Monk Pure saved the only woman whom Uncle Chiang intended to marry. For that, Uncle Chiang is forever grateful. Now Monk Pure accused me of stealing his manual. I know that I'm innocent, but Uncle Chiang does not know that I was framed. He may very well believe that I had stolen it." He did not want to tell them that Uncle Chiang did not want to teach him *'Tien Hsueh.'* *"Mo-bai, you're too proud until you truly understand what it is to be modest. I would not teach you 'Tien Hsueh' and other unique skills of the Wu-ton school."* He did not tell Uncle Chiang that he had the manual, and he studied from it secretly. Also, Chiang Nan-ho wanted him to marry Ceo-lian. Uncle Chiang had said, "You cannot revive the dead anyway. You cannot let that poor young woman be a living widow. You should marry her." He did want to talk much about *'Red Hornet'* either. She looks like Violet with the same crescent-shaped eyebrows, the long dark eyelashes, and the delicate neck. The first time they met, Lee Mo-bai could not stop looking at her

"Mo-bai, Chiang Nan-ho must care for you a lot. Maybe I can intercede for you, and I could tell him that you did not steal the manual. You may want to consider telling Monk Pure the truth and then give him back the manual. I believe you have learned well enough."

Ceo-lian said, "I will tell Uncle Chiang the truth, too. You can lead us to him."

Lee Mo-bai said, "Thank you both. The truth is that I don't know where Uncle Chiang is. He is coming and going all the time, and he is looking for his missing manuals all over the country," He continued, "For two years, Monk Pure presumed that I drowned. Now he calls me a thief and threatens my friend. I won't give him back his manual so easily."

Ceo-lian asked, "Were you following me? How did you know where I was?"

"Sister, I did not even know you had left Beijing. I was following Yan Bo and tried to help him. Yan Li-fon asked me to. Every year, I come down from Joe-hua Peak to sell the tea, and I heard all about Yan Bo's predicament. I spotted you by chance."

Lee Mo-bai told Ceo-lian to turn over and to lie on her back. He told her that he was going to *'Tien Hsueh'* her to put her into a deep sleep. Both men left Ceo-lian's room in the women's court. They knew that it was improper to give a woman, especially an unmarried young woman, massages. But the difficult circumstance called for a compromise. They were treating her together, not alone.

A letter came from Monk Pure. It read, "*Greetings, Master Feng. We honor your position, and we do not want to search your villa for Lee Mo-bai and Yu Ceo-lian. Please inform them that I am holding a fat man. I would like to have a duel with Lee Mo-bai to settle the matter of the manual. I will wait for them at Peace Temple for three days. If Lee Mo-bai does not show up, I'll cripple the fat man. Signed, Monk Pure.*"

Feng Four said, "How presumptuous! I'll gather all my friends in Ba-tin to fight them. They have to behave themselves around here."

Lee Mo-bai said, "It's my problem, and I will face them alone. Fat Shih is a dear friend. Brother Feng, you have your family to consider. We want to keep it quiet. I'll go to Peace Temple to meet them alone tomorrow morning. We better leave Miss Yu out of it. She needs complete rest."

"Brother Lee, you're alone, and they are so many. Monk Pure's '*Tien Hsueh*' skills must be very tough to deal with. I will go with you. I promise that I'll not bring anyone with me. They may still call you a thief even after you win. I will be a witness."

"Only you and me then. I will talk to the Old Monk first. He is Uncle Chiang's friend; I really should not fight him. But he is truly ruthless, and he wants to kill Yu Ceo-lian. For that, I'll fight him with all my might. Even I know he is not an easy contender."

When Lee Mo-bai and Feng Four got there, seventeen people, fifteen monks, and two others were waiting. They tied Fat Shih to a post. Two monks guarded him.

Lee Mo-bai jumped down from his horse, '*Tien Hsueh*' and disabled the two monks on guard, twisted off the cord that tied Fat Shih to the post, held the heavy Fat Shih under his left arm, brandished the sword with his right hand and chopped the attacking Monk Ta's short steel rod in half, and forced another two monks back. He did all of that in quick succession.

Monk Pure shouted at his students, "Stop! I want to talk to him first." He thought, '*Ah! He is tough. We could not catch him two years ago, and we could only force him to fall into the rushing Yangtze River. It seems to me that he has learned 'Tien Hsueh' from the manual well; I may not be able to defeat him. I better try to talk to him first.*'

Monk Pure said, "Lee Mo-bai, hand me the manual! I won't punish you. I'll leave your friends alone. I knew your late father, your late Teacher Gi, and Uncle Chiang. I'll go easy on you".

Lee Mo-bai sneered, "I should respectfully call you 'Uncle,' but you don't deserve it. I have the manual, and I'll return it if you punish Monk Ta for spreading rumors that I stole it," Monk Ta tried to attack Lee again, but the old monk stopped him, "Let him talk. He won't get away!"

Lee Mo-bai laughed, "How could you detain me? Your student Monk Guo knew that Monk Ta had poisoned him. He did not want to let the evil one have it, and he gave it to me for safekeeping. Monk Ta also killed your secular student Chen. Chen told Yu Ceo-lian everything before he died. You are blind to the truth. If you punish Monk Ta, I'll give you back the manual. That's my final word." Lee Mo-bai's words came out loud and clear while he handed the inert Fat Shih to Feng Four.

Monk Pure shouted, "Rubbish! Yu Ceo-lian killed my student Chen, and I want revenge. You stole the manual, and I will get it back. No more talk. Let's fight."

Everyone ganged up on Lee Mo-bai. Lee Mo-bai whirled around and swung his super sharp sword. All the monks except Monk Pure could not even come close to him.

Monk Pure shouted, "Stop! all of you, I'll handle him myself."

Lee Mo-bai took this time to run up to where Fat Shih was and slapped a few places on Fat Shih's back, forehead and leg. Fat Shih moaned, "Mo-bai, that wicked old monk made me mute. Make him pay!"

Monk Pure rushed at Lee Mo-bai with a long heavy whip.

Lee Mo-bai jumped free and said, "Wait. If you win, I'll hand the manual back to you, and I will kowtow to you and ask for forgiveness. But, what will you do if I win? I want to know."

"If you win, you can keep the manual. I'll not harass you and your friends anymore."

"Sure. To honor your age, please have the first move."

Lee Mo-bai stood still and waited. Monk Pure attacked Lee immediately. They fought. Lee Mo-bai would not let the monk's heavy whip touch his light but super sharp sword, and meanwhile, he pierced at the monk in quick succession. Monk Pure was in a defensive position now. He shouted, "Stop! You are using a super sharp sword. You have the advantage of a better weapon." Lee Mo-bai replied, "Let's fight with fists then." He was thinking, *'He is old, and he cannot last long with the heavy whip. It's no honor if I win, and I don't want to hurt him or humiliate him. Uncle Chiang will sure punish me if I do.'* He handed Feng Four his sword and whispered, "Prepare to run. I am sure that I will win, and I don't want to humiliate him. Let him chase us, so he can say that I am the one who ran away."

Fat Shih said, "You do not have a horse."

"I can run fast."

He bowed low to Monk Pure and said, "You go first." They fought with fists for a while. Suddenly, Lee Mo-bai started to run, Feng Four and Fat Shih galloped alongside him. The monks began to pursue and soon failed.

Monk Pure caught his breath and sighed, "Let him go for now." Monk Pure knew that Lee Mo-bai had won. He and his students went back to Nanjing.

Lee Mo-bai and Feng Four treated both Ceo-lian and Fat Shih. Shih's wound was not severe. He decided to accompany Lee Mo-bai back to Beijing. The second night they were on the road, Lee Mo-bai woke up to the sound of someone on the roof. He presumed that one of the monks came to attack. His sword cut off the right arm of the attacker before he heard a woman's voice. It was *Red Hornet*. She told him before she died, "I came to warn you that my brother wants his powerful friend in Ba-tin and Beijing to arrest you as a criminal. They will provoke you to fight so the officials can arrest you. I always loved you." She died. Fat Shih blamed him, "Mo-bai, you're too hasty. She came to warn you."

"What have I done? I'm guilty." Lee Mo-bai sighed, "I never thought that she would show up here. How can I explain to anyone that I killed her by mistake? What should I do now?"

"It's done. Let's bury her."

Lee Mo-bai could not sleep after that for a long time. Before dawn, he must have slept. He dreamed that he was swimming in the Yangtze River and the water was ice cold. It was freezing. He woke up and found the cotton quilt was not on him. Someone had undone the buttons on his top. The pouch holding the 'manual' that he had tied around his waist was gone. A cold sweat washed over him. *'Whoever it was, he could have killed me.'* He knew it was no use, but he jumped up on the roof and looked. As expected, he saw no one. He went back to his room crestfallen. Fat Shih woke up and found Lee Mo-bai just sitting there, holding his head in his arms. He asked with concern, "Mo-bai, are you ill? I know it was bad, but life goes on. There is nothing you can do about it now."

"Brother Shih, I want you to go back to get Ceo-lian. She should be better now. You and she will go to Beijing, and she has to manage things herself or wait for me there. I have urgent personal business to attend. I may see you in Beijing soon." He talked and packed his simple bag, saddled his horse, and left. He left Fat Shih there dumbfounded.

At Feng Four's villa, they all worried about what happened to Lee Mo-bai. Fat Shih thought, '*A big part of Lee Mo-bai's trouble is that he is afraid of facing Ceo-lian. He sure knows that Ceo-lian wants to marry him. All of his close friends and probably his Uncle Chiang also wanted them to get married. He keeps on saying that he cannot marry her because Ceo-lian's fiancé Mon Zhi-an died for him. I'm not sure about that. Ahe! Red Hornet resembled Violet a little, and I think Lee Mo-bai is still in love with Violet. Didn't he mention that he might go to Japan? He wants to find Violet again. Poor Ceo-lian. Mo-bai was infatuated with her since she was the first pretty young girl he met who knows martial arts well. His true love is the sophisticated Violet.'*

In Beijing, Ceo-lian went to Dae Wu's home alone. Fat Shih was a wanted killer, and he could only move around at night. So did Lee Mo-bai. One night when Ceo-lian, Dae Wu, and Mrs. Dae Wu were sitting around and talking, Lee Mo-bai walked in. Dae Wu welcomed him warmly, "Mo-bai, how I missed you? Let me have a good look at you. You look stronger, and you must have improved your skills, and now you move soundlessly. Did you find what you have lost?"

Lee Mo-bai got up from the kneeling position and choked on his tears, "My Brother, You look well. I have so much to tell you. I did not find the missing article." He turned around and bowed low to Mrs. Dae Wu, "Sister-in-law greetings." He then greeted Ceo-lian.

Mrs. Dae Wu suggested, "Mo-bai, you're welcome to stay in the study. When you two stayed with us three years ago, I felt so safe. Dae Wu was in jail, and the town rascals harassed us until you came. That was a nightmare." She sighed.

"I'm a wanted criminal. I cannot stay with you. I even cannot come to visit during the day. I don't want to compromise you. Uncle Chiang told me that I could stay at a dilapidated Tao Temple close to the East Gate. The abbot is Uncle Chiang's friend. That's where he would stay. I hope I will meet him there."

He then asked Ceo-lian, "Sister, did you do anything about the pearls?"

Mrs. Dae Wu heard the way he addressed Ceo-lian and thought, '*Oh! He does not want to marry her. He calls her sister. Violet is out of the picture. Did he meet someone else? He looks well and fit, and he is very good-looking indeed. Poor Ceo-lian.*'

Dae Wu answered, "We have the pearls, all of them. Yan Bo brought them to Li-fon and told her to tell us that he wants us to return the pearls for him. It's too bad that I did not have a chance to talk to him. I could have asked Prince Te to help him. He could change his identity."

"Did he come to your house? The inner court? We need to have better security around." Lee Mo-bai asked.

"Mo-bai, you do not know that Ceo-lian is living in a house just behind us. Li-fon is staying at Ceo-lian's place, and Ceo-lian's cleaning woman is looking after her." Mrs. Dae Wu explained.

"I met Yan Bo's friend and told him where Li-fon is staying. Yan Bo knew where he could find his sister." Ceo-lian said.

Dae Wu said, "We talked about it, and we did not come up with a proper way to return the pearls to the palace. The Emperor is getting old, and the royal princes are all trying to be the heir apparent. We mustn't cause Prince Te any trouble. I did not tell Prince Te that we have the pearls."

"I see. Did Li-fon ever tell you where Yan Bo stole the pearls? Did Li-fon and Li-in mention that they have another brother? Before he died, Yan Bo said something about '*Hu*' and a brother. '*Bo*' means leopard. Maybe they have another brother called '*Hu*' (tiger)?"

Ceo-lian replied, "Really? Another brother named *Hu* (tiger), Sure I will ask them. Li-in told me that Yan Bo stole the pearls from a wealthy family, not a royal palace. He and his grandpa went there to sell flowers to the maids."

Dae Wu said, "We thought the first thief might be someone who worked in the palace. Yan Bo did not steal them from the palace."

"Did Yan Bo tell his sister whether the wealthy family is Manchu or Han?" Lee Mo-bai asked.

"No. Wait! It's probably a rich Han family. Li-in mentioned that her brother told her the maids who bought flowers from him to have tiny feet. You know the maids here are Manchu women with big feet."

Mrs. Dae Wu laughed, "Indeed, most of our maids are Manchu. My mother-in-law did not like to see the Han women working hard on their tiny feet. Ceo-lian, I'm amazed that you can fight and jump around on your small feet."

Ceo-lian said, "It's a way of life. Rich or poor, the Han women all have their feet bound, and they could do anything. Do you remember that night the Ho sister and brothers came here to attack us because I killed their Uncle Dart Mew? The woman has very tiny feet," She thought, '*The beautiful Violet must have tiny feet. Why should I think of her all the time? She is in Japan.*'

Dae Wu said, "A powerful Han official or a eunuch?

He stole them from the royal palace. I was framed, and some others were, too. We have to handle this matter with extra caution."

They decided to write an anonymous letter stating the truth and indicating the location where the pearls would be. The next night when the night call sounded three times, Lee Mo-bai and Ceo-lian went to the tallest tower adjacent to the palace. Ceo-lian kept watching while Lee Mo-bai, moving like a bobcat, climbed up the central peak of the highest tower. He placed the bag of pearls under the third tile down from the top. They put the letter at the middle of the highest step leading to the Emperor's study.

Dae Wu was waiting for them in his study. When Lee Mo-bai and Ceo-lian were just about to enter the study, Lee Mo-bai got a glimpse of a dark form moving swiftly on the opposite roof. Immediately, he was on the roof and gone.

Ceo-lian was also on the roof. She saw no one. She remembered that Lee Mo-bai had mentioned that he was staying at a Taoist temple adjacent to the East Gate, Ceo-lian ran there. The whole complex of the temple was dark, but one small shed at the corner was glowing faintly. She approached it very cautiously. She heard, "You should not have stolen it. You should not kill that woman…Miss Yu come in!" a man sounding like a Southerner ordered. Ceo-lian went in and saw Lee Mo-bai kneeling in front of a tall older man. A bundle of clothes with pictures and writings on it was on the ground besides Lee Mo-bai.

"I'm Chiang Nan-ho. I met your late father once." He then ordered, "Mo-bai, get up."

"Reverent Uncle, Brother Lee did not steal the manual. The Southerner Chen told me …" Ceo-lian explained.

"I also heard that Monk Ta is a bad lot. Mo-bai, return it as soon as possible. Ceo-lian, I'd like to have you as my daughter-in-law…"

Lee Mo-bai sank to his knees again, "Uncle Chiang, I can't. I can't obey you. I'm her sworn brother..." He repeated the tragic death of Ceo-lian's fiancé and his guilt over it. "It's not right that I marry her."

"Listen to me…"

Ceo-lian said in a hurry, "Reverend Uncle, my father made us sworn siblings when he died. I honor the marriage that my late father had arranged for me. I won't marry anyone." Ceo-lian also knelt.

"Up! Both of you. we all should eradicate the unreasonable traditions and customs a long time ago. I'm a victim of one of them, too." With a heavy sigh, he told them briefly that he could not marry the granddaughter of his father's murderer.

"Ceo-lian, you're my niece then. You have to learn the '*Tien Hsueh*' technique and other higher martial arts skills. Monk Pure, and his Teacher, Steel Rod Monk, would not have anyone fight better and be more famous. The monks are your enemies now. Mo-bai, take Ceo-lian with you up Jeo-hua peak. I'll teach both of you. I'm getting old. I'd like to have students."

Ceo-lian kowtowed, Chiang Nan-ho accepted and then said affectionately, "Ceo-lian, bring warm clothes. It's cold on the peak, and we don't have the warm *kon* (bed) in the South. The first winter will be hard for you. Brother Ma's young daughter-in-law will keep you company." He thought, *'I will try to find her a good husband. It's too cruel to let a young woman be a living widow. Maybe Mo-bai will change his mind. They will be together for some time.'*

Ceo-lian thought, *'At least I will be with him for a long while. I hope that he will change his mind. Besides hope, what else do I have?'* She tried hard not to cry.

-End-

www.ingramcontent.com/pod-product-compliance
Lightning Source LLC
LaVergne TN
LVHW091530060526
838200LV00036B/547